D1306830

A CELEBRATION OF GARDENS

A
CELEBRATION
OF
GARDENS

ROY STRONG

Decorated by

JULIA TREVELYAN OMAN

Sagapress / Timber Press
Portland, Oregon

First published 1991
by HarperCollins *Publishers*, London

Reprinted 1993
by
Sagapress, Inc. / Timber Press, Inc.
9999 S.W. Wilshire, Suite 124
Portland, Oregon 97225, USA

ISBN 0-88192-244-7

Printed in Singapore

For
CALISTA COGGESHALL
whose tree grows in our garden

Labyrinth

CONTENTS

PREFACE

When Ariane Goodman, then of Collins, asked me to undertake this anthology a friend said, 'It's something you just peck away at popping things in a drawer and, suddenly, it's there.' Well, nothing turned out to be further from the truth. Like any writing project in the end it demanded total concentration, all day and every day, scouring one's bookstacks for pieces and working the poor photocopier to virtual extinction. I have to acknowledge my indebtedness to many previous garden anthologies, although this I believe to be the largest since Sieveking's a century ago. What struck me most about many previous ones is that they were not always strictly speaking garden anthologies but often made heavy use of pieces which I would classify simply as Nature.

From the outset I was determined that this should be a *gardener's* anthology, not one by an armchair practitioner or by someone whose knowledge was purely literary. I have tried to compile it as a person whose hands are deep in the earth day in and day out and at all seasons of the year. That accounts for the structure of the book with its emphasis on things all working gardeners contend with from the curse of pests to the joys of spring flowers. Something I have benefited from also which, on the whole, was absent from previous anthologies, is garden history, a subject which has only grown to maturity in the last ten to twenty years. That has provided a rich quarry.

Any anthology is personal and this represents what my own library has thrown up plus inroads into the treasure house of the London Library. I need hardly say that my greatest debt is to whoever invented the photocopier. However did anyone compile such a thing before? Friends have also contributed, although I have to confess that it is one thing to be told that there's a marvellous description of a rose garden in *The Moonstone* and quite another to find it! But I would like to thank John Morley for Cleland, Lady Antonia Fraser for the only reference I know to what people actually did in a wilderness. Stephen Orgel for flowers in masques, Beatrix Miller for Addison on tulips, George Clive for Nancy Mitford's non-U garden and David Hutt for, amongst other things, a rare publication of poetry on garden themes. Alan Titchmarsh exceeded the bounds of duty and wrote me delectable pages of quotes, including the inimitable Joyce Grenfell's response to Tennyson's *Maud*. Lastly a trip to Atlanta introduced me, thanks to the guidance of Tom Woodham and Phil Colson, to the rich heritage of American garden writing.

Celia Brown typed no less than 853 pages of the original manuscript impeccably, struggling bravely with my handwriting and with the idiosyncrasies of old English. My thanks also go to my editor at HarperCollins, Stuart Proffitt, who has always bravely maintained that I was the person to do this volume and I hope that he is proved right. My wife, Julia Trevelyan Oman, has not only put up with me through its compilation and fed me too with quotes but above all decorated the text in a way which we hope will give any reader a visual delight to match the literary content.

ROY STRONG
The Laskett, Much Birch, Herefordshire
7 January 1991

INTRODUCTION

A Gardener's Album! Ready to your hand,
For friends at home, or in some distant land;
Carrying a message, scented and aglow,
Of all the joys a garden can bestow.
Go, happy book, to capture and retain
These garden joys till summer comes again.

REGINALD ARKELL. *Flowers by the*
Fire (1954)

We owe it to Pliny the Younger, I suppose, that writing and gardening go
hand in hand for it is his descriptions of his two villas, one close to the sea at
Laurentum near Rome and the other in the Tuscan hills, that were to inspire
the villa gardens of renaissance humanism. Two thousand years later these
two gardens still exert their charm, bearing testimony to the fact that a
garden can live on and have influence through the power of words alone
when all trace of its physical reality has long since vanished. They are
gardens which I know that I would have liked, with their plane trees linked
by ivy trained into garlands, box shrubs cut into a 'thousand shapes', shady
laurel groves with dark cypresses piercing the Mediterranean sky, vine-clad
pergolas and walks, marble baths, fountains and everywhere an interplay
between house and garden and the landscape beyond. The plant range was
pathetically limited by our standards but there were pink, white and red
roses, sweet smelling violets, bold acanthus and pungent rosemary with its
lavender blue flowers. We can still stroll, two thousand years later, through
those gardens with pleasure because of the power of descriptive language.
How amazed Pliny would have been.

It is above all to Pliny that we owe the tradition, which the humanists of
the renaissance revived, that a man of letters should also be a gardener. I only
trust a writer on garden things if I know he had a garden or, if he didn't,
his writings betray that he was a man who could not only savour to the
full its beauties and delights but who also had a keen eye for structure and
practicalities. Into that category falls Geoffrey Chaucer who conveys to
perfection the atmosphere of the late medieval garden, for he moved in the
sympathetic ambience of the court of Richard II, the king who appointed the
first royal Professor of Botany. Chaucer's entrancing evocation of these late
medieval pleasaunces is a direct reflection of the sophistication and elegance
of the royal gardens. We step out with him into these magical enclosures of
flower bedecked turf with their raised seats, rose entwined fences and shady

arbours. It is difficult not to think, when he writes of a man entering his 'herber' in spring and going to sleep on a flower strewn turf bank, that he is not describing something which he has experienced himself. And for the English-speaking world the medieval garden lives on only through the works of Chaucer, for all reality has long since vanished. Chaucer achieved for the medieval garden what Pliny in his letters did for that of the Roman villa.

It is not, however, until the renaissance that our men of letters began to have gardens which we know about other than through the written word. Sir Thomas More had a famous garden at Chelsea. We can see it in the background of a miniature of the man and his descendants now in the Victoria and Albert Museum. We look through an archway out on to a vista to the Thames. There is a walled enclosure with a banqueting house at one corner with views riverwards and on to the clipped patterned knots below. Pleasure gardens were then something fairly new, reflecting the security of Tudor rule. By the Elizabethan age that security was an established fact and we are fortunate that our first golden age of garden-making coincided with our golden age of writing. Francis Bacon, whose essay *Of Gardens* remains the supreme masterpiece of garden writing in miniature, laid out a spectacular garden at Gorhambury with islands, a pavilion and statuary enclosed within gilded balustrading underplanted with strawberries. One of the islands had 'flowers and ascents' and another 'an arbor of Musk roses sett with double violetts for scent in the Autumn'. How pleasant it must have been to have taken a boat and drifted across those waters on a summer's evening.

Shakespeare we know had a garden, and we can see an attempt at re-creating it at New Place in Stratford-on-Avon today. But here, instead of 'Old English flowers' the knots are block planted in the Victorian manner with plants he would never have recognized. There is no reason to think that the playwright was ever a dedicated gardener, but his works are nonetheless the greatest single instance of the power of the pen over the gardener's spade. He bestowed a magic on the Elizabethan garden which its reality probably never had and ennobled its plants as purely English when many were in fact quite new to the country. We are all ensnared into Perdita's sheath of 'flowers o' the spring – daffodils that come before the swallow dares; violets dim . . . pale primroses . . . bold oxlips, the crown imperial, and lilies'. Four centuries on we are still busy planting knot gardens and filling them with what we believe to be old-fashioned flowers. Edmund Spenser, Richard Barnfield and Ben Jonson too have contributed to the timeless appeal of our early gardens (even E. F. Benson's notorious Lucia had a Shakespearean garden), although I sense that none of them ever wielded a spade or even gave orders to a gardener. It is their language and not the reality that has awoken us to a romantic yearning for knots and mazes, arbours and mounts – and for all those flowers whose very names evoke their fragile fragrance, "daffadowndillies', sops-in-wine, bears breeches, cuckoo flowers, gillyflowers, herb-o-grace or lady's mantle.

With the baroque age we move from a golden to a silver age of writing. None of these writers make us long to plant a late seventeenth-century garden with its stately *allées*, clipped topiary, formal *parterres* in swirling box, stately classical statuary and soaring *jets d'eau*. And yet they were certainly practical gardeners, these authors, and their gardens were gorgeous; but somehow they make them seem short on mystery and romance. Abraham Cowley certainly ached for his small house, large garden, books and friends – but did he ever get them? And if he did, what did they look like? Now I fancy that Andrew Marvell was a hands on gardener. His pretty house at Highgate, demolished in the last century, certainly had a garden and he writes of escaping there 'to enjoy the spring and my privacy'. I like to think of him at night watching the glowworms. Two others, who belonged to the well-heeled gentry class, undoubtedly did have marvellous gardens. The first is John Evelyn, whose diaries are crammed with garden material and Sayes Court at Deptford was a major garden of its age, with its walled garden of rare flowers and simples, its glass beehives and the vast holly hedge of which he was so proud until it was ruined by Peter the Great when he rented the house. But I always find Evelyn a cold fish and feel if only Pepys had been a gardener we should have a very different perception of Stuart gardening. The second is Sir William Temple whose huge garden at Moor Park in Surrey included an anticipation of the landscape style with its use of the serpentine line, 'sharawadgi', inspired by Chinese gardening. But its chief fame was its elaborately trained fruit trees and orangery, which Evelyn judged the 'most exquisite', and certainly a contemporary bird's eye drawing of the domain makes one keen to sample its pleasures, its enticing vistas and maze-like hedged enclosures.

In later life Jonathan Swift was Temple's amanuensis, something which takes us leaping on into the next century, and certainly he took his master's 'sharawadgi' to Ireland, for he was an early advocate of the 'winding and meandering' whose chief protagonist was his friend, Alexander Pope. With the emergence of the landscape style, in itself an artificial landscape of memory which was not only pictorial but literary in its allusions, garden writing takes a decided upturn again. Never were a writer and his garden to be so inextricably meshed together in the public mind as Pope, the subject in this century of a minor academic industry which would have appealed to his vanity. But I am not sure that I would have enjoyed Pope's garden, place of pilgrimage though it became. It has always seemed to me a somewhat joyless place with its gloomy obelisk to his mother's memory closing a vista of funereal cypresses; its seeming absence of a single flower; its dripping grotto and trees and shrubs massed in dramatic chiaroscuro. I can never think of it in terms of sunshine but of heavy, rain laden clouds adding an oppressive ceiling to the grim experience, and the even more menacing thought of bumping into the waspish poet lurking behind one of the smart urns Mr Kent designed for him.

But the garden of another poet, William Shenstone's The Leasowes, is one I would love to have visited. Nothing like it has survived, the equivalent in today's terms of arranging garden walks and tableaux through a working farm. Today it would be eccentric to view a combine harvester from a shell seat or to position a cascade and grotto in the corner of a field of rape. But then Shenstone was seen as placing the toil of the agricultural year into a framework of classical allusion, and the visitor could dwell in arcady while viewing the labour of the peasantry. I like the idea of the idyllic and the working landscape being locked into one composition, something which we give too little thought to in our own time.

William Mason is another poet-gardener whose own rectory garden at

Aston in Yorkshire was to be the scene for trials of the effects which were to reach their grandest fulfilment in the flower garden at Nuneham Courtney inspired by Rousseau's *Nouvelle Héloise*. And that, one certainly would have thoroughly enjoyed, for we know it well through Sandby's evocative, flower-filled watercolours. With those, and the proliferation of graphic records of gardens through the eighteenth century, we are touching upon something which in the long run was to curtail radically the role of the pen in respect of the spade. Gardens being essentially pictorial, any amplification in the ability of the visual media to convey them to the absent onlooker inevitably diminished the role of the writer.

Shenstone belongs to the middle years of the century; William Mason and William Cowper belong to its end, by which time greenhouses were becoming as common as conservatories are to us. How one sympathizes with Cowper's entreaty to Lady Hesketh not to come before the warm weather because then the greenhouse will be emptied of its tender plants enabling them to bask in its pleasures as a summer room. Mignonette, honeysuckle, roses and jasmine will scent the air and he promises her a daily bouquet of myrtle. I would have liked a visit to his greenhouse and would have left, I feel, with a cutting or two to remember him by, for with Cowper's correspondence we touch on an atmosphere which is close to our own age, one of small-scale gardening and a huge and unaffected delight in plants. Now we find ourselves rapidly moving into the era of sentiment shortly to culminate in the Victorian language of flowers. Women writers appear upon the scene and the path to Miss Jekyll is laid. The novelist Maria Edgeworth was more besotted with her garden the older she became, and it is a subject which never quite disappears from the correspondence of Mary Russell Mitford. If Shakespeare and his contemporaries were responsible for the perennial fixation with 'old-fashioned flowers' Miss Mitford must take a large part of the blame for the cult of the cottage garden. Both in her novel *Our Village* and in her letters a refined gentility marches hand-in-hand with her effusion over the super-abundance of bloom dripping everywhere that only just misses the excesses of the treacle tin. At times Miss Mitford seems like Beverley Nichols' Mrs M whose garden, on the approach of any visitor, opened its petals in a horticultural ecstasy.

From this point on garden makers and garden writers come thick and fast. Garden writing becomes a category of its own as the nineteenth century progresses, the direct result of the vast expansion of gardening activity by the middle classes. We have arrived in the age of the Loudons and the gardening monthly magazine. By the death of Queen Victoria there was an audience for books which charted the exploits of the plant hunters as well as the mutations of a vicarage garden throughout the year. Canon Ellacombe's garden at Bitton Vicarage near Bristol was a place of pilgrimage for all plant lovers; William Robinson's Gravetye was likewise one of the great gardens of the age as, later, was Miss Jekyll's Munstead Wood. Garden writing and garden creation henceforth seem to advance together. Sir George Sitwell's creation of Renishaw matches his advocacy of the Italian style as much as Vita Sackville-West's Sissinghurst is an accurate reflection of her gardening philosophy. But what has changed is that we can still see most of their gardens, if not in reality then at least by way of the camera's lens. So in that sense the importance of the pen has been eroded. No amount of ink spilt

across the page is an adequate substitute for a picture of a border planted by
Gertrude Jekyll.

We can follow that diminution of the writer's role in another perennial of
gardening reading, the garden description. That remains at its most potent
when we are devoid of visual evidence or when it is confined perhaps only to
a bird's eye view in a plate in Kip's *Nouvelle Théâtre de la Grande Bretagne*.
The English were slow to visit their own gardens and the earliest descriptions
are those by German Protestants come to view the England of their heroine,
Elizabeth I. To them we owe vivid glimpses of the Tudor palace gardens with
their extraordinary topiary and heraldic beasts scattered across the
flowerbeds. Theobalds, Lord Burghley's great house, is depicted with its
marble banqueting house, busts of Roman emperors, miniature windmills
and a toy galleon floating on its encompassing canal. These are respectful,
admiring accounts which I include, although without exception they were
written originally in either German or humanist Latin. The first long
description in English of a real garden is by Robert Laneham in his account
of the Earl of Leicester's 'Princely Pleasures' at Kenilworth Castle in 1575.
Although the orthography can only be described as agony and its purpose a
public relations exercise for the ambitious earl, I warm to his sensitivity as he
relates of the 'sweet shadoed wallk of Terres in heat of Soomer, too feel the
pleazaunt whysking winde aboove . . . Too smell such fragrancy of sweet
odoourz breathing from the plants earbs and floourz. . .'.

We have to wait until the reign of Charles I for another such account, this
time of the pre-Civil War garden at Wilton, one of the marvels of the age.
Here we are in a different world, for Wilton was the first great Italianate
garden in England and its wonders were very different from those of
Kenilworth. Here our visitor, Lieutenant Hammond, paints a picture which
is less concerned with 'Pots for Flowers of the best kind' than with the
fantastic water tricks which astonished him in which jets balanced golden
coronets or made the sound of nightingales. In his engaging naivety he is
close to our first great native garden visitor, Celia Fiennes, a lady of gentle
birth, of resolutely Protestant outlook who possessed an undimmed enthusiasm for all things new in the last decade of the seventeenth century. Through
her pen we experience the gardens of William and Mary more vividly than in
any other source and enter into their spirit with her keen appreciation of 'fine
gravel walks', the use of clipped 'greens' and her genuine wonder at
fountains, grottoes and cascades.

But the golden age of garden description surely only comes with the
landscape style, itself literary. By then the landed classes had developed a
passion for 'improvement' sweeping away their formal gardens and re-
sculpting the terrain into landscape parks in response to the successive
phases of the movement from William Kent to Humphry Repton. Travel was
easier and garden visiting became an established pastime not only for visitors
to this country such as Thomas Jefferson but for the landowners themselves
seeking inspiration and ideas from each other's estates. Such gardens were
designed to play upon the intellect and sensibilities, evoking a wide mental
and emotional response which is encapsulated in these descriptions. Patrio-
tism, arcady, freedom, fear, tranquillity, were only some of the effects
wrought upon the visitor as he wended his way past tableaux as decrepit as
the ruins of a Gothic castle, a dilapidated hermitage, a gorge with a rushing

torrent or a classical temple presiding over a calm meadow. Every winding walk, temple, grotto, statue and inscription warranted a detailed commentary, some, I must admit, in too wearisome detail. (They are offset by the waspish pens of Horace Walpole or John Wesley, who make a curious duo in debunking some of the more famous set pieces of eighteenth-century garden design as disaster areas.) Many of these country house elysiums are with us today, albeit overgrown or sunk beneath Edwardian plantations of rhododendrons, but I would encourage any reader to take a walk in them in his imagination with a companion from the century in which they were created. They give a wonderful insight into a totally different perception of gardens and make us query our own assumptions about how we perceive gardens in our own time.

The landscape style called for interpretative writing. Its successor in the Victorian age no longer did. Such writing was now a display of horticultural skill and an expression of wealth. In addition, with the arrival of photography, words were replaced by images. By 1909, when Avray Tipping's *Gardens Old and New* was published in three huge folio volumes, the text is largely about the history of the house and the family and the garden is allowed to tell its own story in the miraculous photographs of Charles Latham. It is ironic that no previous age was to produce so much garden literature but so little that was to be memorable. In our own age much garden writing has in fact become just a commentary on the plates in books.

But that is not quite the end of the story, for a word picture of a garden has a role in descriptive metaphor. So as descriptions of actual gardens go into eclipse we turn to the new art of the novel for some of the most telling portrayals of the garden, whether it is Jane Austen's use of a Regency shrubbery in *Mansfield Park* or Disraeli's depiction of an 'olde worlde' pleasaunce in *Lothair*. That metaphor has never lost its vitality as Nancy Mitford's wicked description of the garden of that 'horrible house' Planes in *Love in a Cold Climate* demonstrates.

I haven't touched much on poets yet and for a very good reason. So much poetry is in fact about nature and not about the garden, or the garden is only incidental. It is no good looking in this celebration, therefore, for those 'golden daffodils' which I have discarded as marginal to my garden quest, and which I found refreshingly filled by the work of poets of the last few decades. It has been to me a discovery and a great joy to find poets once again as firmly in the garden as ever Andrew Marvell was and even more so. The work of Robert Lowell, Sylvia Plath, Ted Hughes, Alan Brownjohn and Dom Moraes, to name only a few, have added a special lustre to the garden theme as it wends its way to the close of this century.

And what of my own commitment to gardens? Gardening came to me quite late in life and as a surprise. In childhood the garden had been my father's sacred province, not to be touched without rebuke or punishment by any other member of the family. It was attached to one of those 1920s terrace houses that swelled the suburbs of London between the wars with a front garden with a crazy paving path up to the front door and at the back a rectangular tongue of land about 40 by 120 feet, also delineated by a crazy paving path which this time marched straight down from the back door to the back gate. At the front there was a lawn and narrow beds which in summer were bedded out in the Victorian manner with borders of alyssum and lobelia backed by antirhinums. There was a yellow privet hedge along one side and a large green one along the other, cut into bastions and domes. The back garden was lawn, with espaliered pear trees set against the fence and a few climbing roses, including one splendid Paul's Scarlet which clambered over the garage and which I was once allowed to prune. A small rectangular pond held goldfish and gave on to a tiny rockery in which were bedded stones transported from Cornwall in the boot of the car on my parents' honeymoon. In summer the beds were filled with annuals, cosmos, night scented stocks and asters but with no sense of design or colour control. Near the house there was a plum tree which seemed never to fruit while at the far end rose a mountain ash which was bright with scarlet berries until devoured by the birds each autumn. There was an occasion when a tiny patch of earth was vouchsafed to me: I transferred to it flowers in full bloom and arranged them lovingly like the picture on a packet of 'Rainbow Mix', but next morning they were sadly limp or dead.

But my main memory was of the impact of the war which broke out when I was four and seemingly lasted until the close of the 1950s, by which time I was twenty-five. Every square foot of the garden, for a great deal of that period, was put to vegetable growing. The bay window at the front of the house became a backcloth for elaborately staked and tied tomato plants in front of which stretched lines of cabbages, lettuces, curly kale and onions. The back garden seemed to be nothing but a forest of runner beans and potatoes. As the fifties gave place to the sixties little changed in that tiny garden, although all around it other gardens did begin to reawaken to the horticulture of peace. Whatever I left that house with towards the end of the 1960s it was not with green fingers. Indeed I departed rather associating gardening with someone I had come to to dislike.

The first person who ever seriously walked me round a garden was Cecil Beaton. I remember those weekends at Reddish House as a revelation in living expressed through creativity in both house and garden. After lunch he would put a broad-brimmed hat on his head and out we would go. First on to the terrace where pink roses jostled in profusion through the balustrading and up the rear facade of the house. The land rose steeply away from it towards Edwardian rope rose garlands looking as though they had been lifted from a stage set for Lily Elsie. Our route would not be there but away from the house to one side across a broad sweep of perfectly kept lawn, the pride of Smallpiece the gardener. The garden was held within a hollow, the high perimeters of which had handsome old trees curtaining the cultivated area within. Our walk would take us boldly across the greenward and up towards two huge herbaceous borders framing a stone path ending with a comfortable wooden seat. In summer those borders were magnificent with huge clumps of *crambe cordifolia* with its star-like white flowers waving in the background. We would then turn sharp right to admire roses trained flat over frames, and then on down through a small paved garden of lavender nestling at the foot of a sundial and back past a wide shrub border. In spring that border was full of purple lilac and one left the house with huge armfuls to sit embowered on the train back to London. But the horticultural experience didn't end with the garden, for a small greenhouse filled the main house with flowers, no meal table lacked its bouquet and the conservatory was a haven of climbing pelargoniums and geraniums. Cecil still lives on in

our own house in the exquisite pink geramiun of which he gave us a cutting, and at the Reddish sale I bought the lavender garden sundial which now acts as a focal point for memory in my own garden.

My first garden was at the back of a Gothick terrace house in Brighton which I bought in 1969. It was very small and contained within three whitewashed walls into the far one of which I inserted a dolphin mask which dribbled water into a minute pool. I had a terrace made at the back of the house with trellis cut into gothic arches up which grew a *vitis coignetiae* with which a more knowledgeable friend presented me. Within the walls the surface was paved and on it I arranged plants in containers, the result of scavenging in antique shops, and filled them with geraniums. Containers, I failed to realize, are labour intensive and too often I returned to find trophies of dead blooms. One friend presented me with a large rosemary and not long after I married her.

Julia had always gardened and it was through her that I came into contact with my second great garden inspiration, the decorator John Fowler. We used to stay with him at the Gothick Lodge at Odiham which now belongs to the National Trust. If Cecil had stirred in me the first awareness of what it was to create a garden, John made me conscious of perfection in the design of one. Everyone knows that garden through reproduction in a hundred books. It remains in my memory as the most perfectly articulated small space I have ever seen. History had already attuned my eye to formality but the Gothick Lodge was an example created in our own time, every detail exact, from the ariel hedge leading the eye one way to the tiny house and the other into the beyond, to the garden pavilions and the beds edged with clipped box housing white roses underplanted with frothy lime-green *alchemilla mollis*. I remember John explaining how to get mistletoe to grow on the branches of an old apple tree and prizing houseleeks off a gate pier, the only plants which survive virtually without watering and an effect we were to copy again and again.

In 1973 we moved into our present house in the country, an unpretentious red sandstone early nineteenth-century box on the Welsh borders with three and a half acres around it. I can date very precisely when garden fever seized me. Most of that land was a field let to a farmer for cattle. In the summer of 1974 he rang up and said that he no longer required it. We stood together looking at the rapidly growing grass in despair when Julia spotted that there had once been a grass tennis court there. Our garden help mowed that grass back to reveal a flat plateau on which, in the autumn of 1974, I planted the yew hedge which now makes up the mighty walls of our rose garden. It was only then that I realized that everything that Cecil and John had achieved was attainable in our own garden. But we had to begin with a plan. I still have those drawings which I made in the summer of 1975 and the main disposition of the garden has never changed. I was also aware that the key to making a garden was structure and we had none. So there followed the planting of the yew hedges and avenues, most of which still remain. But there was another motive in that gesture (mad though it seemed to every friend who saw it in its infancy for there was no permanent gardener), and one which expressed deep thoughts on England and its future. In 1974 the Heath government fell. The oil crisis signalled appalling inflation. A Socialist government threatened a wealth tax designed to expunge the making of such a garden ever again. At the Victoria and Albert Museum I staged an exhibition entitled *The Destruction of the Country House*, a lament for the tragic loss of not only buildings but gardens too. The planting of the garden was a deliberate pledge that that most quintessentially English of all art forms, the making of a great garden, would go on.

I couldn't foresee then that it would end up consisting of thirty-two different rooms, be described as the largest formal garden to be made in England since 1945, or be the gateway to a second period of life. It was to lead me first to garden history and then to garden design and writing. Above all it has led me to happiness, rejoicing in its beauties in every season, never walking through it without feeling held in by some mysterious affection. It has brought me new friends from the past, from William Lawson to Shirley Hibberd, and new friends in the present, whose plants cheerfully recall their presence in every corner of our garden. It has opened new avenues of thought for my mind and filled my eyes with a new perception for which I never cease to give thanks, for the garden crosses every field of human endeavour and unites all men with the world of nature. Above all it has restored a never-ceasing sense of wonder to my life. This celebration is a humble offering in gratitude for just that.

A Maze   910

PART
I

THE
GARDEN

One way of looking at a garden.

The story of mankind began in a garden and ended in revelations.

OSCAR WILDE

And another.

A Garden was the Habitation of our first Parents before the Fall. It is naturally apt to fill the Mind with Calmness and Tranquillity, and to lay all its turbulent Passions at Rest. It gives us a great Insight into the Contrivance and Wisdom of Providence, and suggests innumerable Subjects for Meditation. I cannot but think the very Complacency and Satisfaction which a Man takes in these Works of Nature, to be a laudable, if not a virtuous Habit of Mind.

JOSEPH ADDISON, The Spectator,
No. 477, 6 September 1712

Apparently the earliest English poem on a garden appears in Tottell's Miscellany *which was first published in 1557.*

Here pleasans wanteth not, to make a man full fayn:
Here marveilous the mixture is of solace, and of gain.
To water sundry seeds, the furrow by the waye
A ronning river, trilling down with liquor, can convey.
Beholde, with lively heew, fair flowers that shine so bright:
With riches, like the orient gems, they paynt the molde in sight.
Beez, humming with soft sound, (their murmur is so small)
Of blooms and blossoms suck the topps, on dewéd leaves they fall.
The creeping vine holds down her on bewedded elms:
And, wandering out with branches thick, reeds folded overwhelms:
Trees spred their coverts wide, with shadows fresh and gaye:
Full well their branchéd bowz defend the fervent sonne awaye.
Birds chatter, and some chirp, and some sweet tunes do yield:
All mirthfull, with their songs so blithe, they make both ayre and field.

From heavy hartes all doolfull dumps the garden chaseth quite.
Strength it restores to lims, draws, and fulfils the sight:
With chere revives the senses all, and maketh labour light
O, what delites to us the garden ground doth bring?
Seed, leaf, flowr, frute, herb, bee, and tree, and more, than I may sing.
The issue of great Jove, draw nere, you Muses nine:

Help us to praise the blissful plot of garden ground so fine.
The garden gives good food, and ayd for leaches cure:
The garden, full of great delite, his master doth allure.
Sweet sallet herbs be here, and herbs of every kind:
The ruddy grapes, the seemly frutes be here at hand to finde.

NICHOLAS GRIMALD, *The Garden*

Here is one of the masters of the art, Humphry Repton (1752–1818), defining a garden.

Let us, then, begin by defining what a garden is, and what it ought to be. It is a piece of ground fenced off from cattle, and appropriated to the use and pleasure of man: it is or ought to be, cultivated and enriched by art, with such products as are not natural to this country, and, consequently, it must be artificial in its treatment, and may, without impropriety, be so in its appearance; yet, there is so much of littleness in art, when compared with nature, that they cannot well be blended; it were, therefore, to be wished, that the exterior of a garden should be made to assimilate with park scenery, or the landscape of nature; the interior may then be laid out with all the variety, contrast, and even whim, that can produce pleasing objects to the eye.

HUMPHRY REPTON, *Observations on the Theory and Practice of Landscape Gardening* [1803]

WHAT is a garden?
Goodness knows!
You've got a garden,
I suppose:

To one it is a piece of ground
For which some gravel must be found.
To some, those seeds that must be sown,
To some a lawn that must be mown.
To some a ton of Cheddar rocks;
To some it means a window-box;
To some, who dare not pick a flower –
A man, at eighteen pence an hour.
To some, it is a silly jest
About the latest garden pest;
To some, a haven where they find
Forgetfulness and peace of mind . . .

What is a garden
Large or small
'Tis just a garden,
After all.

REGINALD ARKELL, *Green Fingers*
[1939]

No one can escape this justly famous poem by Andrew Marvell (1621–78), so here it is.

THE GARDEN

I

How vainly men themselves amaze
To win the Palm, the Oke, or Bayes;
And their uncessant Labours see
Crown'd from some single Herb or Tree,
Whose short and narrow verged Shade
Does prudently their Toyles upbraid;
While all Flow'rs and all Trees do close
To weave the Garlands of repose.

II

Fair Quiet, have I found thee here,
And Innocence, thy Sister dear!
Mistaken long, I sought you then
In busie Companies of Men.
Your sacred Plants, if here below,
Only among the Plants will grow;
Society is all but rude,
To this delicious Solitude.

III

No white nor red was ever seen
So am'rous as this lovely green.
Fond Lovers, cruel as their Flame,
Cut in these Trees their Mistress' name.
Little, Alas! they know, or heed,
How far these Beauties Hers exceed!
Fair Trees! wheres'e'er your barkes I wound,
No Name shall but your own be found.

IV

When we have run our Passion's heat,
Love hither makes his best retreat.
The *Gods*, that mortal Beauty chase,
Still in a Tree did end their race.
Apollo hunted *Daphne* so,
Only that she might Laurel grow.
And *Pan* did after *Syrinx* speed,
Not as a Nymph, but for a Reed.

V

What wond'rous Life is this I lead!
Ripe Apples drop about my head;
The Luscious Clusters of the Vine
Upon my Mouth do crush their Wine;
The Nectaren, and curious Peach,
Into my hands themselves do reach;
Stumbling on Melons, as I pass,
Insnar'd with Flow'rs, I fall on Grass.

VI

Meanwhile the Mind, from Pleasure less,
Withdraws into its happiness:
The Mind, that Ocean where each kind
Does straight its own resemblance find;
Yet it creates, transcending these,
Far other Worlds, and other Seas;
Annihilating all that's made
To a green Thought in a green Shade.

VII

Here at the Fountain's sliding foot,
Or at some Fruit-tree's mossy root,
Casting the Bodies vest aside,
My Soul into the boughs does glide:
There, like a Bird, it sits and sings,
Then whets and combs its silver Wings;
And, till prepar'd for longer flight,
Waves in its Plumes the various Light.

VIII

Such was that happy Garden-state
While Man there walk'd without a Mate:
After a Place so pure, and sweet,
What other Help could yet be meet!
But 'twas beyond a Mortal's share
To wander solitary there:
Two Paradises 'twere in one
To live in Paradise alone.

IX

How well the skilful Gardner drew
Of flow'rs and herbs this Dial new;
Where from above the milder Sun
Does through a fragrant Zodiac run;
And, as it works, th'industrious Bee
Computes its time as well as we.
How could such sweet and wholsome Hours
Be reckon'd but with herbs and flow'rs!

ANDREW MARVELL

And this is the view of the third President of the United States.

I have often thought that if heaven had given me choice of my position and calling, it should have been on a rich spot of earth, well watered, and near a good market for the productions of the garden. No occupation is so delightful to me as the culture of the earth, and no culture comparable to that of a garden.
THOMAS JEFFERSON TO CHARLES
WILLSON PEALE, 20 August 1811

The Reverend Samuel Reynolds Hole, Vicar of Caunton, Nottingham-shire from 1850 to 1887 and later Dean of Rochester viewed gardening as 'character reform'. He was a great rosarian.

I asked a schoolboy, in the sweet summertide, 'what he thought a garden was for?' and he said, *Strawberries*. His younger sister suggested *Croquet* and the elder *Garden-parties*. The brother from Oxford made a prompt declaration in favour of *Lawn Tennis and Cigarettes*, but he was rebuked by a solemn senior, who wore spectacles, and more back hair than is usual with males, and was told that 'a garden was designed for botanical research, and for the classification of plants'. He was about to demonstrate the differences between the *Acoty-* and the *Monocoty-ledonous* divisions when the collegian remembered an engagement elsewhere.

I repeated my question to a middle-aged nymph, who wore a feathered hat of noble proportions over a loose green tunic with a silver belt, and she replied, with a rapturous disdain of the ignorance which presumed to ask – 'What is a garden for? For the soul, sir, for the soul of the poet! For visions of the invisible, for grasping the intangible, for hearing the inaudible, for exaltations above the miserable dullness of common life into the splendid regions of imaginations and romance.' . . . A capacious gentleman informed me that nothing in horticulture touched him so sensibly as green peas and new potatoes, and he spoke with so much cheerful candour that I could not get angry; but my indignation was roused by a morose millionaire, when he declared that of all his expenses he grudged most the outlay on his confounded garden.
DEAN HOLE, *Our Gardens* [1899]

Doctor Hackwill in his Apology for the world's not decaying, tells a story of a German gentleman who lived fourteen yeares without receiving any nourishment downe his throat, but onely walked frequently in a spacious Garden full of Odoriferous Herbes and Flowers.
WILLIAM COLES, *The Art of*
Simpling [1656]

Take it from us, it is utterly forbidden to be half-hearted about Gardening. You have got to LOVE your garden, whether you like it or not.
W. C. SELLAR AND R. J. YEATMAN,
Garden Rubbish [1936]

Abraham Cowley (1618–67) sums up what I would most like in life and indeed am lucky enough to have.

> Ah, yet, ere I descend to the grave,
> May I a small house and large garden have;
> And a few friends, and many books, both true,
> Both wise, and both delightful too!
>   And since love ne'er will from me flee,
> A Mistress moderately fair,
> And good as guardian angels are,
>   Only beloved and loving me.
>
> O fountains! when in you shall I
> Myself eased of unpeaceful thoughts espy?
> O fields! O woods! when, when shall I be made
> The happy tenant of your shade?
>   Here's the spring-head of Pleasure's flood:
> Here's wealthy nature's treasury,
> Where all the riches lie that she
>   Has coin'd and stamp'd for good.
>
> Pride and ambition here
> Only in far-fetched metaphors appear;
> Here nought but winds can hurtful murmurs scatter,
> And nought but Echo flatter.
>   The gods, when they descended, hither
> From Heaven did always choose their way:
> And therefore we may boldly say
>   That 'tis the way too thither.
>
> ABRAHAM COWLEY, *The Wish*

I never see a great garden (even in my mind's eye, which is the best place to see great gardens around here) but I think of the calamities that have visited it, unsuspected by the delighted visitor who supposes it must be nice to garden here.

It is not nice to garden anywhere. Everywhere there are violent winds, startling once-per-five-centuries floods, unprecedented droughts, record-setting freezes, abusive and blasting heats never known before. There is no place, no garden, where these terrible things do not drive gardeners mad.

I smile when I hear the ignorant speak of lawns that take 300 years to get the velvet look (for so the ignorant think). It is far otherwise. A garden is very old (though not yet mature) at 40 years, and already, by that time, many things have had to be replaced, many treasures have died, many great schemes abandoned, many temporary triumphs have come to nothing and worse than nothing. If I see a garden that is very beautiful, I know it is a new garden. It may have an occasional surviving wonder – a triumphant old cedar – from the past, but I know the intensive care is of the present.

So there is no point dreading the next summer storm that, as I predict, so soon to come, in which the temperature will drop to ten below zero and the ground freezes forty inches deep and we all say there never was such a winter since the beginning of the world. There have been such winters; there will be more.

Now the gardener is the one who has seen everything ruined so many times that (even as his pain increases with each loss) he comprehends – truly knows – that where there was a garden once, it can be again, or where there never was, there yet can be a garden so that all who see it say, 'Well, you have favorable conditions here. Everything grows for you.' Everything grows for everybody. Everything dies for everybody, too.

There are no green thumbs or black thumbs. There are only gardeners and non-gardeners. Gardeners are the ones who ruin after ruin get on with the high defiance of nature herself, creating, in the very face of her chaos and tornado, the bower of roses and the pride of irises. It sounds very well to garden a 'natural way.' You may see the natural way in any desert, any swamp, any leech-filled laurel hell. Defiance, on the other hand, is what makes gardeners.
        HARRY MITCHELL, *The Essential Earthman* [1981]

A garden is like those pernicious machineries which catch a man's coat-skirt or his hand, and draw in his arm, his leg, and his whole body to irresistible destruction.

    RALPH WALDO EMERSON

The Excellency of a *Garden* is better manifested by Experience, which is the best Mistress, than indicated by an imperfect Pen, which can never sufficiently convince the Reader of those transcendent pleasures, that the Owner of a Complete *Garden* with its Magnificent *Ornaments*, its Stately *Groves*, and infinite variety of never dying *Objects of Delight* every day enjoys: Nor how all his Senses are satiated with the great variety of Objects it yields to every one of them: Nor what an influence they have upon the passions of the mind, reducing a discomposed fancy to a more sedate temper by contemplating on those miracles of Nature *Gardens* afford; deemed Miracles, because their admired and strange forms and effects proceed from occult causes . . .
      JOHN WORLIDGE, *Systema Horti-Culturae* [1677]

Brown (1830–97), a Manx clergyman, was responsible for this oft-quoted piece of doggerel.

   A garden is a lovesome thing, God wot!
   Rose plot,
   Fringed pool,
   Ferned grot –
   The veriest school
   Of peace; and yet the fool
   Contends that God is not –
   Not God! in gardens when the eve is cool?
   May, but I have a sign;
   'Tis very sure God walks in mine.
     T. E. BROWN, *My Garden* [1875]

The most moving account of the creation and loss of a garden that I know.

'What can we do with this place?' Aleksandr had asked Yenya, looking helplessly around him. She did not answer at first. Then, 'We shall have a garden,' she said with quiet determination. 'A garden the like of which Archangel has never had before. We shall enlarge the pond and raise the mound. It will be a small hill and on top we shall build a fine summer house. There,' she added, 'on this field will be lawns and flower beds, rare trees and bushes. I promise you,' she went on earnestly, 'if you will allow me, we and our future children shall have a beautiful garden. A rare garden that will be a great heritage which they will also pass on to their children.'

She kept her promise. At least part of it. It was not within her power to see too far into the future.

Helped by books, workmen, clever joiners and painters, there gradually appeared out of a wilderness a unique garden which was the true realization of her dream.

All walls were rebuilt. A leafy hedge, spangled with golden flowers, separated the courtyard from the garden. The pond was enlarged and stocked with carp which bred and multiplied. Irises, daffodils, bullrushes grouped themselves around the grassy edge. Two white piers complete with railings jutted out over the water. On the west bank behind one of them, was built a rustic summer house nestling against a clump of birches.

Dominating the whole garden, on top of what was now a small hill, stood a miniature replica of a fairy castle. Steps between flowering bushes led to a room furnished with table and chairs. The diamond-shaped multi-coloured panes of the Gothic-style windows were a great source of delight to us children when we gazed through them and saw the garden immediately transformed into a strange, mysterious place, dark and haunting, or in turn golden and bright.

From this room was a door to an outside stair leading to a flat roof, enclosed by low crenellated walls. In the corner was a tower through which a steep stair came out on to a small platform with a flagpole. From this high point one had a fine view of the surrounding district and the river.

Looking down on to the garden below were lawns, flower beds, unusual trees and bushes. They came from many parts. The blue spruce and stately dark-green pines from our own district, the balsam poplar with crimson, scented catkins from Siberia. Plants and bulbs from the steppes. The surrounding shores of the great Lake Baikal provided a source of many rare and beautiful flowers. Lilac bushes in all shades grew in great profusion, for they could stand up against the destructive frosts.

Throughout my childhood bundles wrapped in straw and sacking kept arriving to the house. From the north of Scotland came roses and, on one exciting day, an apple tree.

Perhaps nowadays apple trees can flourish in the distant north, but seventy years ago our apple tree was the only one in the whole of Archangel, if not in the district. In the early summer, groups of schoolchildren were often brought round to see this great rarity blossoming in our garden.

The garden was a living monument to a great achievement. She who created it could have stood alongside many of the greatest gardeners, for it

has to be remembered that everything had to be coaxed out of earth frozen for eight months in the year.

Many years later, after everything was destroyed, they came to her, to the small room where she and Dedushka were living some distance away from the plundered house and garden. In beguiling tones of flattery they asked her to rebuild the garden all over again. They would assist her in every way, they added grandly. My grandmother looked at them coldly. She was now an old woman whose life was drawing to a close. She walked over to a corner of the room where were kept her few remaining precious books. Placing them in their hands she said with fine irony: 'You have destroyed. You can rebuild.' The garden remained untouched.

EUGENIE FRASER, *The House by the Dvina. A Russian Childhood* [1984]

England is a garden.

(The Duke of York's garden. The Queen and Ladies hidden. Enter a gardener and two servants.)

GARDENER: Go, bind thou up yon dangling apricocks,
Which, like unruly children, make their sire
Stoop with oppression of their prodigal weight:
Give some supportance to the bending twigs.
Go thou, and like an executioner,
Cut off the heads of too fast growing sprays,
That look too lofty in our commonwealth:
All must be even employ'd I will go root away
The noisome weeds, that without profit suck
The soil's fertility from wholesome flowers.

FIRST SERVANT: Why should we in the compass of a pale
Keep law and form and due proportion,
Showing, as in a model, our firm estate,
When our sea-walled garden, the whole land,
Is full of weeds, her fairest flowers chok'd up,
Her fruit-trees all unprun'd, her hedges ruin'd,
Her knots disorder'd, and her wholesome herbs
Swarming with caterpillars?

GARDENER: Hold thy peace:
He that hath suffer'd this disorder'd spring
Hath now himself met with the fall of leaf;
The weeds that his broad-spreading leaves did shelter;
That seem'd in eating him to hold him up,
Are pluck'd up root and all by Bolingbroke.

SHAKESPEARE, *Richard II*, Act III, sc. iv

And a garden is the attribute of the true Englishman.

Tea finished, Mrs Martin rose with a sprightliness that surprised me, seized a stick, and commanded me to follow. I must see her garden. A few steps, and I was back in old England. The transformation was staggering. The lawn, the rockery, the sundial, the pergola, the rose arbours and a little tiled summer-house, they were all perfect in their fidelity to the English type. Here, in the middle of the Florida groves, fighting the tropical heat of summer, the un-English warmth of winter, the human will had triumphed over Nature. 'It is like an English garden, isn't it?' asked the old lady. Had it been like the Malay jungle I should have agreed. But my agreement and enthusiasm needed no hypocrisy.

'It must be nothing compared with yours,' said old Mrs Martin.

'I haven't a garden. You see I —'

She gave me a swift, keen look, sharp as an eagle.

'You haven't a garden!' she cried scornfully. 'Then why are you an Englishman?'

CECIL ROBERTS, *Gone Rustic* [1934]

Rudyard Kipling's (1865–1936) own house and garden, Bateman's, belongs to the National Trust. Next to Shakespeare it is he who uses the garden the most powerfully as metaphor for England, in his case with all the overtones of mission and empire.

THE GLORY OF THE GARDEN

Our England is a garden that is full of stately views,
Of borders, beds and shrubberies and lawns and avenues,
With statues on the terraces and peacocks strutting by;
But the Glory of the Garden lies in more than meets the eye.

For where the old thick laurels grow, along the thin red wall,
You find the tool- and potting-sheds which are the heart of all;
The cold-frames and the hot-houses, the dungpits and the tanks,
The rollers, carts and drain-pipes, with the barrows and the planks.

And there you'll see the gardeners, the men and 'prentice boys
Told off to do as they are bid and do it without noise:
For, except when seeds are planted and we shout to scare the birds,
The Glory of the Garden it abideth not in words.

And some can pot begonias and some can bud a rose,
And some are hardly fit to trust with anything that grows;
But they can roll and trim the lawns and sift the sand and loam,
For the Glory of the Garden occupieth all who come.

Our England is a garden, and such gardens are not made
By singing:– 'Oh, how beautiful!' and sitting in the shade,
While better men than we go out and start their working lives
At grubbing weeds from gravel-paths with broken dinner-knives.

There's not a pair of legs so thin, there's not a head so thick,
There's not a hand so weak and white, nor yet a heart so sick,
But it can find some needful job that's crying to be done,
For the Glory of the Garden glorifieth every one.

Then seek your job with thankfulness and work till further orders,
If it's only netting strawberries or killing slugs on borders;
And when your back stops aching and your hands begin to harden,
You will find yourself a partner in the Glory of the Garden.

Oh, Adam was a gardener, and God who made him sees
That half a proper gardener's work is done upon his knees,
So when your work is finished, you can wash your hands and pray
For the Glory of the Garden, that it may not pass away!
And the Glory of the Garden it shall never pass away!
RUDYARD KIPLING

Sir William Temple (1628–99), remembered above all for his correspondence with Dorothy Osborne, had a famous garden at Moor Park, Surrey.

In every Garden four things are necessary to be provided for, Flowers, Fruit, Shade, and Water; and whoever lays out a Garden without all these, must not pretend it in any Perfection. It ought to lie to the best Parts of the House, or to those of the Master's commonest use, so as to be but like one of the Rooms out of which you step into another. The part of your garden next your House (besides the Walks that go round it), should be a Parterre for Flowers, or Grass-plots bordered with Flowers; or if, according to the newest Mode, it be cast all into Grass-plots and Gravel Walks, the dryness of these should be relieved with fountains, and the plainness of those with Statues; otherwise, if large, they have an ill effect upon the Eye. However, the part next the House should be open, and no other Fruit but upon the Walls. If this take up one half of the Garden, the other should be Fruit-trees, unless some Grove for shade lie in the middle. If it take up a third part only, then the next third may be Dwarf-trees, and the last Standard-fruit; or else the second part Fruit-trees; and the third all sorts of Winter-Greens, which provide for all Seasons of the Year. . . .

The best Figure of a Garden is either a Square or an Oblong, and either upon a Flat or a Descent; they have all their Beauties, but the best I esteem an Oblong upon a Descent. The Beauty, the Air, the View makes amends for the Expense, which is very great in finishing and supporting the Terrace-walks, in levelling the Parterres, and in the Stone-stairs that are necessary from one to the other.
SIR WILLIAM TEMPLE, *Upon the Gardens of Epicurus: or Of Gardening, in the Year 1685* [1692]

And so you have a garden of your own, and you plant and transplant, and are dirty and amused! Are you not ashamed of yourself? Why, I have no such thing, you monster, nor ever shall be either dirty or amused as long as I live. My gardens are in the windows, like those of a lodger up three pair of stairs in Petticoat Lane, or Camomile Street, and they do go to bed regularly under the same roof that I do. Dear, how charming it must be to walk in one's own garding, and sit on a bench in the open air, with a fountain and a leaden statue, and a rolling stone, and an arbour: have a care of sore throats though, and the ague!
THOMAS GRAY TO NORTON NICHOLLS, 27 June 1769

A fine Garden being no less difficult to contrive and order well than a good Building.

A. J. Dézallier D'Argenville
The Theory and Practice of Gardening
translated by John James [1712]

Gardens, of course, change.

Every garden is subject to many changes; in each year trees and bushes grow, and call for more room; and then paths must be altered, and old beds, perhaps, destroyed, and new ones made. And I have always noticed that the more a man loves his garden, the more he delights in constantly changing the arrangements, which were, perhaps, good for a time, but which, as time goes on, must give way to others; and the most uninteresting garden is one that has been made on a fixed plan, rigidly adhered to through succeeding years, till what may have been good and beautiful at the beginning becomes dull, uninteresting, and ugly. Personally, I have little faith in fixed plans, perhaps because I have never had any plan in my own garden; such as it is, it has grown into its present shape and plan, and has almost formed itself; and I may say with certainty that though I have many trees, shrubs, and other plants which have been in their present places for many years – many over seventy years – yet there is not a single path or flower-bed that is the same now as it was thirty or even twenty years ago. And this adds much to the pleasure of a garden; this power of altering to suit the wants of growing trees and shrubs, or it may be only to suit one's own peculiar taste or fancy, gives a pleasant feeling of ownership which nothing else will give.

Canon Ellacombe, *In a Gloucestershire Garden* [1895]

Many, as they get older, would re-echo these sentiments.

I find the love of garden grows upon me as I grow older more and more. Shrubs and flowers and such small gay things, that bloom and please and fade and wither and are gone and we care not for them, are refreshing interests, in life, and if we cannot say never fading pleasures, we may say unreproved pleasures and never grieving losses.

Maria Edgeworth to Mrs Bushe [1832]

Sir Cecil Beaton (1904–80) adored the house he had at Ashcombe, Wiltshire, which he leased in 1930. In 1946 the lease was not renewed and he captures the feelings of all those who have had to leave a garden they loved. Dove was the gardener.

. . . I went out into the garden. Since the war everything wore a shabbier air: so much had been demolished or fallen into disrepair: Ashcombe had survived in pretty good trim. The former tennis court was now a jungle of tall stinging nettles; the grotto mouldered half-hidden by weeds; and most of the garden statuary lay smashed in the long grass. But I surveyed with pride the cultivation that had been effected here since my arrival. The orchard, once a refuse dump, had yielded its fruit, and the kitchen garden its untold bounty.

Now for the last time I walked around, visiting with the *sécateurs* my favourite spots and cutting the remnants of summer flowers. It was a sunny afternoon, and although there had been such inclement spells that only the sturdy blooms of autumn were flourishing, there were a few roses still in bloom. I snapped off the buds, trusting that perhaps they might open for me in London and remain, a few days longer, a link with my vanishing home. I walked down to the glass-houses: there were geraniums, maidenhair fern; under the wall some rather soggy dahlias. Then I came across a blaze of colour. Most gardeners admire a display of asters. Dove had provided me with a bank of them. They looked extraordinarily brilliant in the autumn sunlight. Like Japanese paper flowers, they were clustered tight together, a mass of puce pink, pastille mauve and poisonous purple; but what made them now appear suddenly so fantastic was the fact that hundreds of butterflies, red admirals and tortoiseshells, had come to visit them and with flapping wings were feeding on the pollen of the yellow centres. As I cut bundles of the asters the butterflies flew around my head like confetti.

The baskets were overflowing with flowers. I took them to the potting shed and thrust them into buckets of water.

I went out again. This was the last opportunity I had of collecting the flowers of Ashcombe. I would not do the job sparingly. I got out the long ladder-clippers and sawed off the highest branches of yellow roses growing on the sides of the house. I slashed at the bushes of rosemary and thyme. The baskets again filled, I rested on the balustrade of the terrace, and for the millionth time surveyed my favourite view across the blue distances of the valley.   CECIL BEATON, *Ashcombe. The Story of a Fifteen-Year Lease* [1949]

PART
II

GARDENERS
AND
GARDENING

Views as to the nature or nobility of the physical act of gardening have varied widely.

It is not graceful, and it makes one hot; but it is a blessed sort of work, and if Eve had had a spade in Paradise and known what to do with it, we should not have had all that sad business of the apple.

COUNTESS VON ARNIM, *Elizabeth and her German Garden* [1898]

Let no one think that real gardening is a bucolic and meditative occupation. It is an insatiable passion, like everything else to which a man gives his heart.

KAREL ČAPEK, *The Gardener's Year* [1929]

Gardening, as far as Gardening is an Art, or entitled to that appellation, is a deviation from nature; for if the true taste consists, as many hold, in banishing every appearance of Art, or any traces of the footsteps of man, it would then be no longer a Garden.   JOSHUA REYNOLDS, *Thirteenth Discourse* [1786]

I have a strong antipathy to everything connected with gardens, gardening and gardeners . . . Gardening seems to me a kind of admission of defeat . . . Man was made for better things than pruning his rose trees. The state of mind of the confirmed gardener seems to me as reprehensible as that of the confirmed alcoholic. Both have capitulated to the world. Both have become lotus eaters and drifters.   COLIN WILSON, *A Book of Gardens* [1963]

Gardeners as a breed always get a good press.

Come, my spade. There is no ancient gentlemen but gardeners, ditchers, and grave-makers; they hold up Adam's profession.

SHAKESPEARE, *Hamlet*, Act V, sc. i

Looked at through the eyes of a child the occupation seems just lack-lustre.

THE GARDENER

The gardener does not love to talk,
He makes me keep the gravel walk;
And when he puts his tools away,
He locks the door and takes the key.

Away behind the currant row
Where no one else but cook may go,
Far in the plots, I see him dig,
Old and serious, brown and big.

He digs the flowers, green, red, and blue,
Nor wishes to be spoken to.
He digs the flowers and cuts the hay,
And never seems to want to play.

Silly gardener summer goes,
And winter comes with pinching toes,
When in the garden bare and brown
You must lay your barrow down.

Well now, and while the summer stays,
To profit by these garden days,
O how much wiser you would be
To play at Indian wars with me!

ROBERT LOUIS STEVENSON,
A Child's Garden of Verses [1885]

The "Godiva" Lawn Mower.

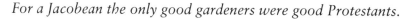

For a Jacobean the only good gardeners were good Protestants.

Your Gardiner had not need be an idle or lazie Lubber . . . but one that is religious, honest, skilfull in that facultie, and therewithall painfull: By religious, I mean (because many think religion but a fashion or custome to goe to Church) maintaining, and cherishing things religious; as Schooles of Learning, Churches, Tythes, Church-goods, and rights; and above all thinges, God's word, and the Preachers thereof, so much as hee is able, practising prayers, comfortable conference, mutuall instruction to edifie, almes, and other workes of Charity, and all out of a good conscience.

Honestie in a Gardner, will grace your Garden, and all your house, and help to stay unbrideled Servingemen, giving offence to none, not calling your name into question by dishonest acts, nor inflecting your family by evill counsell or example. For there is no plague so infectious as Popery and Knavery, hee will not purloin your profite, nor hinder your pleasures.

Such a gardner as will conscionably, quietly and patiently travell, God shall crowne the labors of his hands with joyfulnesse, and make the cloudes droppe fatnesse upon your Trees, hee will provoke your love, and earne his Wages, and fees belonging to his place: The house being served, fallen fruict, superfluity of hearbes, and floures, seeds, graffes, sets and besides other offall, that fruict which your bountifull hand shall award him withall will much augment his Wages, and the profite of your bees will paye you backe againe.

If you bee not able, nor willing to hyre a gardner, keepe your profites to your selfe, but then you must take all the paines.

WILLIAM LAWSON, *A New Orchard
and Garden* [1618]

John Hoskyns (1566–1638), Welsh judge and friend of Sir Walter Raleigh, had a garden at Morhampton in Herefordshire. Aubrey records . . .

In the Garden, the picture of the Gardiner, on the Wall of the Howse, with his Rake, Spade, and water-pott in his left hand. Under severall venerable and shady Oakes in the Parke, he had seates made; and where was a fine purling Spring, he did curbe it with stone.

JOHN AUBREY [1626–1697],
Brief Lives

The sibyl of Sissinghurst waxes lyrical, writing in a period which saw gardeners as a breed practically disappear.

Honour the gardener! that patient man
Who from his schooldays follows up his calling,
Starting so modestly, a little boy
Red-nosed, red-fingered, doing what he's told,
Not knowing what he does or why he does it,
Having no concept of the larger plan,
But gradually, (if the love be there,
Irrational as any passion, strong,)
Enlarging vision slowly turns the key
And swings the door wide open on the long
Vistas of true significance. No more
Is toil a vacant drudgery, when purport
Attends each small and conscientious task
– As the stone-mason setting yard by yard
Each stone in place, exalting not his gaze
To mesure growth of structure, or assess
That slow accomplishment, but in the end
Tops the last finial and, stepping back
To wipe the grit for the last time from eyes,
Sees that he built a temple, – so the true
Born gardener toils with love that is not toil
In detailed time of minutes, hours, and days,
Months, years, a life of doing each thing well;
The Life-line in his hand not rubbed away
As you might think, by constant scrape and rasp,
But deepened rather, as the line of Fate,
By earth imbedded in his wrinkled palm;
A golden ring worn thin upon his finger,
A signet ring, no ring of human marriage,
On that brown hand, dry as a crust of bread,
A ring that in its circle belts him close
To earthly seasons, and in its slow thinning
Wears out its life with his.
That hand, that broke with tenderness and strength
Clumps of the primrose and the primula.
Watched by a loving woman who desired
Such tenderness and strength to hold her close,

And take her passionate giving, as he held
His broken plants and set them in the ground,
New children; but he had no thought of her.
She only stood and watched his capable hand
Brown with the earth and golden with the ring,
And knew her part was small in his lone heart.

So comes he at the last to that long Paradise
Where grateful Pharaoh hews a mountain tomb
For the good gardener, the faithful slave,
(Slave not of royalty, but his own piety,)
Painting the vaulted roof of that deep cave
With fresco of imperishable fruit
Such as no earthly gardener ever grew,
Pale peaches and pale grapes, so healthy-heavy
Yet slung from tendrils of a filament
Too weak to bear a locust's weight. He sleeps,
No pest, no canker troubling that deep sleep
Under the pattern that he scarce divined.

VITA SACKVILLE-WEST,
The Garden [1946]

The feminist viewpoint.

At Woburn Abbey in the seventeenth century there was a famous lifelike statue of a woman weeding, and records of English estates show that from a very early period this chore was almost exclusively performed by females. It is, says my source (who is, naturally, a man), 'a task at which they have always been pre-eminent,' and this is an assessment with which male gardeners have long agreed. La Quintinie, who was in charge of Louis XIV's *potagers* and otherwise an adorable person, recommended the hiring of married men rather than bachelors (as was the usual custom), on the ground that wives would be available for weeding, as well as cleaning and scraping out pots. In the Orient, women weed the rice paddies in water up to their knees. In general, it is to be observed that men plow while women sow; prune fruit and nut-trees but leave the harvest to women; and most men like working with vegetables (all, that is, but the weeding). Other crops appear to be largely in the hands of women. In that part of Turkey where tobacco is grown, I saw them patting together the raised beds, setting out seedlings, and of course weeding, while the male population sat under pergolas playing tric-trac. But why pick on Turks? In other parts of the world women are thought to be pre-eminent at hauling brushwood on their backs. Russian grannies sweep leaves in parks and streets.

Altogether, it is pretty obvious that relative physical strength isn't the determining factor in most cases of divided labor but rather which tasks men prefer to do and which they have decided to leave to women. The man in charge of our Hungarian vineyard was the envy of the neighborhood on account of his ten terrific daughters, who could and did get through twice the work of any male, and he didn't hesitate to lay it on them. In peasant societies nobody worries very much about overtaxing women's strength. I

doubt if they do in any society. What men fear is competition and losing the services of women as drudges. Thus, La Quintinie must have known that women could be trained as well as men to perform a hundred more exacting and interesting horticultural tasks than scraping out pots.

This is all the more striking when you consider that it was women who invented horticulture in the first place, women who ventured into field and forest in search of wild plants, and women who domesticated them while men were still out chasing wild beasts. Women were the first gardeners; but when men retired from the hunting field and decided in favor of agriculture instead, women steadily lost control. No longer were they the ones to decide what was planted, how, or where; and accordingly the space allotted to them diminished too, until flowers and herbs were the only plants left under their direct management while their former power passed into myth. The inventor of agriculture became the goddess of agriculture, her daughter the bringer of spring, when plants come to life; and each of these had a flower or flowers assigned to her – almost certainly by men and as a form of propitiation. For make no mistake: Men were always half in terror of women's complicity with nature, and the power it had given them. The other face of the goddess belongs to the witch brewing her spells from plants, able to cure and also curse with her knowledge of their properties. In some societies this fear of women amounted to panic. It was believed that their mere presence could blight vegetation. Democritus wrote that a menstruating woman could kill young produce 'merely by looking at it.' On the one hand, the benign giver of life and fertility; on the other, the baneful caster of withering spells – it's a tall order and no wonder that men were inclined to confine such a dangerously two-faced influence to a safe place.

For that is how I have come to interpret the two-thousand-odd years of women's incarceration in the flower garden. The superstitious fear that women were in league with nature in some way that men were not was thus simultaneously catered to and kept in check. Flowers are of all plants the least menacing and the most useless. Their sole purpose is to be beautiful and to give pleasure – which is what one half of man wants from woman (the other, it is needless to say, asks for qualities more practical and down-to-earth) – and as such they are the perfect combination of tribute and demand. A gift of flowers to a woman implies that she is as deliciously desirable as the blossoms themselves; but there may be another and hidden message, contained in old-fashioned phrases like 'shy as a violet,' 'clinging vine,' not originally conceived as pejoratives, that tells more of the truth – which is that flowers are also emblems of feminine submission. In the western world, this is rarely explicit. In the Orient, where fewer bones are made about the position of women, two examples may be cited. The art of Japanese flower arrangement, *ikebana*, whose masters are male, was originally imparted to women as a means of silent communication with stern samurai husbands to whom words, and especially plaintive words, would have been an intolerable presumption; whereas an iris and a pussy willow and perhaps a convolvulus, arranged in the right order, conveyed a world of meaning. In China, we find another example, one that borders on the atrocious: the bound foot, to be encountered as late as the 1920s. My Chinese amah's feet were bound, and filled me with fascinated horror. What unspeakable distortion lay inside that delicate little slipper that caused her to sway

(seductively to men, that was the point) as she walked? She would never show me but I have seen photographs since, and learned that the hideously crushed mass of flesh and bone was compared by Chinese poets to a lotus bud.

With this in mind, one may feel that those paintings of Chinese gardens in which exquisitely clad ladies float about tending to potted peonies depict scenes less idyllic than they appear. What we are seeing is a sort of floral cage – one that in the Hindu and Moslem world was an actual prison. Purdah and the harem were mitigated for their captives by the presence of many beautiful flowers. The illiterate women in the Ottoman seraglio even devised a 'language of flowers' (described with some scorn by Lady Mary Wortley Montagu in her letters from Turkey and later all the rage among European females with nothing better to do) to take the place of the written langauge forbidden them. But there was no escape from the famous tulip gardens of the seraglio. Call them what you will – and as everybody knows the word 'paradise' derives from the Persian word for garden, an idea later expanded in Moslem usage to mean heaven where male wants were attended to by ravishing and submissive houris – one of the principal functions of the Oriental garden from Turkey to China was the incarceration of women.

To equate European gardens with any such purpose might seem to carry feminist interpretation too far, and obviously the differences are great. Garden plans nevertheless suggest a similar if less drastic impulse on the part of men. The Roman atrium was a flower-filled enclosure chiefly for women's use, and it is in marked contrast to the pleasure grounds laid out by a rich Roman gentleman and intellectual like Pliny, who makes it perfectly clear that his were entirely for male diversion. Those pavilions for reading and sunbathing, dining with friends, those philosopher's walks, were for himself and his male companions. Possibly there was somewhere an inner courtyard where the women of the household could spend their leisure time, and more than likely it was filled with flowers, if only those that would be picked for the house; but except for his violet beds, he doesn't speak of flowers – or of women.

Medieval gardens repeat the pattern of the *hortus conclusus*, with the difference that they are more elaborate and better adapted to feminine comfort. Trellised walks, turf seats, tiny flower beds, all mark a female presence that is borne out in the illuminations and tapestries where we almost invariably see a lady stooping to pluck a strawberry, a rose, or at her ease with embroidery and lute. So plainly were they designed for women that they even convey an illusion of female supremacy at last – and it wasn't entirely an illusion. The mass folly of the Crusades occupied European men for the better part of two hundred years, and with her lord away at the wars the chatelaine did often manage his estate at home, and not badly either. She lived behind fortified walls nevertheless, and it isn't hard to conjecture that her garden was in the nature of a chastity belt, locking her in until the return of her lord and master. 'A garden inclosed is my sister, my spouse; a spring shut up, a fountain sealed,' says the Song of Solomon – to all of course but him. That feminine purity is only to be preserved within four walls is another ancient idea, and in the late Middle Ages it found indirect expression in those curious paintings of so-called Mary gardens, which show the Virgin seated in a castellated enclosure surrounded by richly symbolic fruits, vines and flowers. But the fortified walls came down with the return of something like peace and leisure, and the Renaissance garden with its magical perspectives, its cascades and fountains, was another story altogether – a celebration of humanism – except that in Italy at least it always had an odd little appendix attached, as it were, to the grand design: the *giardino segreto*.

Garden histories don't try to account for the *giardini segreti* except to note that flowers, largely absent in the rest of the garden, grew in them. To me it is at least plausible that these fossilized remnants of the medieval garden were for women, intended to be so, and that in fact they kept alive the tradition of the flower-filled feminine ghetto.

'Know that it doesn't displease but rather pleases me that you should have roses to grow and violets to care for,' wrote a fifteenth-century French merchant to his wife, sounding the note to be heard again and again for the next three hundred years: from 1500 to 1800 was the great age of garden design: visions of what a garden should be shifted like scenery upon a stage, theories multiplied and books on the subject poured from the presses. But in England only two were in all that time specifically directed to women, and both assume her province to be flowers and herbs. Lawson's *Countrie Housewife* (1618) gives her a list of sixteen flowers for nosegays, five kinds of bulbs including 'Tulippos,' and twenty-six herbs. Charles Evelyn's *Lady's Recreation* (1707) discusses most of the same flowers while permitting a fountain and 'an excellent contriv'd statue.' He also allows her a wilderness where 'being no longer pleas'd with a solitary Amusement you come out into a large Road, where you have the Diversion of seeing Travellers pass by, to compleat your Variety.' Why she should be solitary and driven to watch travelers in the road he doesn't say. His whole tone, however, is one of a patronage that is echoed elsewhere. Sir William Temple (*Garden of Epicurus*, 1685): 'I will not enter upon any account of flowers, having only pleased myself with seeing or smelling them, and not troubled myself with the care, which is more the ladies' part than the men's . . .' John Lawrence (*New System . . . a Complete Body of Husbandry and Gardening*, 1726) adds to patronage something like a scolding; 'I flatter myself the Ladies would soon think that their vacant Hours in the Culture of the *Flower-Garden* would be more innocently spent and with greater Satisfaction than the common Talk over a Tea-Table where Envy and Detraction so commonly preside. Whereas when Opportunity and Weather invite them amongst their Flowers, there they may dress, and admire and cultivate Beauties like themselves without *envying* or *being envied*.' Here the argument for keeping women shut up with flowers is almost entirely trivialized. The Virgin's bower is now a school for decorum.

What amazes me is the way female scholars have failed to notice the implictions of statements like these. Elenour Sinclair Rohde (*The Story of the Garden*, 1932), to whom I am indebted for many of my quotations, gives no hint that she catches their drift. She takes no umbrage at her adored Parkinson (or perhaps doesn't choose to understand him) when she quotes a passage like this from the *Paradisus*: 'Gentlewomen, these pleasures are the delights of leasure (*sic*), which hath bred your love and liking to them, and although you are not herein predominant, yet cannot they be barred from your beloved, who I doubt not, will share with you in the delight as much as is fit.' Not the cleanest prose in the world, and Mrs Rhode construes it as a

Umbrella Rose Trainer

tribute to the central place of women in seventeenth-century gardening. I read it as the opposite: a warning to wives with ideas about garden layout to leave that area to their husbands, who know best but will, if not aggravated, allow a share in the result.

Whichever of us is right, history is on my side. Not until the twentieth century did any woman play a recognizable part in garden design. We know why, of course. The great gardens of the world have been reflections of men's intellectual and spiritual experience: visions of Arcadia, hymns to rationalism or the divine right of kings, Zen parables – and the well-known reasons for our failure to compose symphonies, paint masterpieces, conceive the Einstein theory, apply equally to our failure to produce a feminine incarnation of, say, Le Nôtre.

ELEANOR PERÉNYI, *Green Thoughts: A Writer in the Garden* [1981]

Every gardener's prayer.

O Lord, grant that in some way it may rain every day, say from about midnight until three o-clock in the morning, but, you see, it must be gentle and warm so that it can soak in; grant that at the same time it would not rain on campion, alyssum, helianthemum, lavender, and the others which you in your infinite wisdom know are drought-loving plants – I will write their names on a bit of paper if you like – and grant that the sun may shine the whole day long, but not everywhere (not, for instance, on spiraea, or on gentian, plantain lily, and rhododendron), and not too much; that there may be plenty of dew and little wind, enough worms, no plant-lice and snails, no mildew, and that once a week thin liquid manure and guano may fall from heaven. Amen.

KAREL ČAPEK, *The Gardener's Year* [1929]

MR GARDENER

The "Godiva" Lawn Mower

He always comes at crack of dawn
And always starts to mow the lawn
When you are only half awake
'Oh, stop that noise, for goodness' sake!'

You always pay him by the hour
And if you want to pick a flower
To make a nosegay or a wreath,
He snarls at you and shows his teeth.

There are some things he likes to do,
And some he likes to leave to you –
While *he* is putting in the seeds,
You will be pulling up the weeds.

REGINALD ARKELL,
Green Fingers [1934]

An encounter with a medieval gardener.

MAN: – How much have you earned?

GARDENER: ... I have grafted all the trees in my garden with the fairest grafts that I have seen for a long while, and they are beginning to put forth green; also I have dug another garden and I have carefully planted cabbages, porray, parsley and sage and other goodly herbs. And furthermore I have pulled up and cleared away from it all the nettles, brambles and wicked weeds, and I have sown it full with many good seeds; and in it I have likewise many fair trees bearing divers fruits, such as apples, pears, plums, cherries and nuts, and everywhere have I very well looked after them, yet all I have earned this week is 3d. and my expenses; but last week I earned as much again, and I was very quick about it.

MAN: Hé, my friend, never mind, for one must earn what one can today.

> *Dialogue between an Englishman and a gardener at Bury St Edmunds* [French, late fourteenth century]

To Miles Kington we owe the invention of franglais, a language which brings its own irresistible hilarity of encounter. Among them is one with today's part-time gardener.

Avec le Part-Time Gardener

MONSIEUR: Bonjour, Twining.

JARDINIER: Arrh.

MONSIEUR: Everything est lovely dans le jardin, then?

JARDINIER: Arrh.

MONSIEUR: Bon bon. Bon ... Pourquoi la magnolia a disparu?

JARDINIER: Pas disparu, monsieur. Je l'ai prunée un peu.

MONSIEUR: Vous l'avez beaucoup prunée. Drastiquement. C'est maintenant un stump.

JARDINIER: Elle aime le hard pruning. Elle adore ça.

MONSIEUR: Hmm ... Où sont mes dahlias?

JARDINIER: Ils sont finished.

MONSIEUR: La semaine passée, elles n'étaient pas started.

JARDINIER: C'est une saison désastreuse pour les dahlias.

MONSIEUR: Hmm ... Je ne vois pas le flowering cherry.

JARDINIER: Ce n'est pas flowering maintenant.

MONSIEUR: Je ne vois pas un non-flowering cherry.

JARDINIER: Ah. Well. Non. Le Cherry n'aimait pas sa position. Il détestait le soil. Donc, je l'ai transplanté.

MONSIEUR: Transplanté? Ou ça?

JARDINIER: Dans mon jardin.

MONSIEUR: Dans votre ... ?

JARDINIER: C'est dans vos meilleurs interêts.

MONSIEUR: Oh, well ... Où est le lawn?

JARDINIER: Lawn, squire? Oh, le patch d'herbe. Je l'ai excavé pour y planter les oignons et les spuds, comme vous avez dit.

MONSIEUR: Moi? J'ai dit ça?

JARDINIER: Absolument. Pas une ombre de doute. 'Ce damned lawn,' vous avez dit.

MONSIEUR: Et les chaises longues qui étaient sur le lawn? Et le croquet? Et le mower et la summer maison?

JARDINIER: Tous en shocking condition. J'en ai disposé.

MONSIEUR: Correctez-moi si ja'i tort, mais dans la semaine vous avez rémové les fleurs et les arbres, ruiné le lawn et auctionné ma furniture. Right?

JARDINIER: Je fais mon job. C'est tout.

MONSIEUR: Ha!

JARDINIER: Il est très difficile de trouver les jobbing gardeners, vous savez. *Très* difficile. Espéciellement pour peanuts. Si vous n'aimez pas mon travail . . .

MONSIEUR: OK, OK. Sorry si j'ai été hasty.

JARDINIER: J'accepte vos apologies.

MONSIEUR: Aujourd'hui, si vous faites seulement le tidying-up . . .

JARDINIER: Just laissez-moi à mes devices, OK, squire? C'est très difficile avec le criticisme constant.

MONSIEUR: Right. D'accord. Sorry. Maintenant il me faut aller au travail.

JARDINIER: Et moi aussi.

> MILES KINGTON, *Punch*,
> *19 August 1981*

Even in the early eighteenth century one had to be on the guard against gardeners who aspired to be garden designers.

. . . the very meanest Gardeners, who, laying aside the Rake and Spade, take upon them to give Designs of Gardens, when they understand nothing of the Matter. Unhappy are those that fall into the Hands of such Persons, who put them to a great Expence to plant a sorry Garden; when it costs no more to execute a good Design, than an ill one! The same Trees and Plants are constantly made use of, and produce an ill Effect only through their Bad Disposition.

> A. J. DÉZALLIER D'ARGENVILLE
> *The Theory and Practice of Gardening*
> translated by John James [1712]

If this was true in the eighteenth century, it is even truer in ours.

The *furor hortensis* has seized me, and my acre of ground here affords me more pleasure than kingdoms do to kings; for my object is not to extend, but to enrich it. My gardener calls me, and I must obey.

> PHILIP DORMER STANHOPE, EARL
> OF CHESTERFIELD, TO THE BISHOP
> OF WATERFORD [1751]

The Yorkes of Erddig, near Wrexham in North Wales, had a tradition of commissioning portraits of their servants. In 1830 Thomas Pritchard, then aged sixty-seven, was painted seated outside his house with this verse below the picture.

> Our Gardener, old, and run to seed,
> Was once a tall and slender reed,
> Though in this Hall become a Bencher,
> He often held the Pole for Hencher;
> Of Cock and Partridge rung the knell,
> And loudly call'd 'as dead as Hell.'

From Pond to Pool he was a Trotter,
And proved himself an arrant Otter,
When Fishing was the Squire's pleasure,
And Ale he drank above all measure.
We next record the Horticulture,
Wherein he seem'd a noble Vulture.

The Melons raised by Glass and Frame,
Wth Cucumbers of various Name,
The trees he pruned with stubby knife,
To bear their fruit for longer life.
He shone more bright in Marriage State,
And raised young plants for teaming Mate.

May he survive for many a year
And teach his Grandchildren to shear
Until old Time with scythe in Hand
Hath mowed his crop of Garden Land
For then the Best must leave them All
And sink to Earth at Nature's Call.

> Quoted by MERLIN WATERSON, *The
> Servants' Hall*   [1980]

Gardeners are good. Such vices as they have
Are. like the warts and bosses in the wood
Of an old oak. They're patient, stubborn folk,
As needs must be whose busyness it is
To tutor wildness, making war on weeds.
With slow sagacious words and knowing glance
They can scan the sky, do all that mortals may
To learn civility to pesty birds
Come after new green peas, cosset and prune
Roses, wash with lime the orchard trees,
Make sun-parlours for seedlings.
                              Patient, stubborn.
Add cunning next, unless you'd put it first;
For while to dig and delve is all their text
There's cunning in their fingers to persuade
Beauty to bloom and riot to run right,
Mattock and spade, trowel and rake and hoe
Being not tools to learn by learning rules
But extra limbs these husbands of the earth
Had from their birth. Of malice they've no more
Than snaring slugs and wireworms will appease,
Or may with ease be drowned in mugs of mild.
Wherefore I say again, whether or no
It is their occupation makes them so,
Gardeners are good, in grain.

> GERALD BULLETT   [1893–1958]

J. C. Loudon (1783–1843) describing a gardener's house on the Duke of Bedford's estate.

The gardener's house is altogether one of the best we have seen; it does honour to the feelings of the duke, who thus evinces a wish to see his upper servants not only comfortable and healthy, but living in a comparatively elegant and respectable style; and to Mr Atkinson, his architect, for so completely embodying the duke's wishes. We could name a duke, the whole of whose head-gardener's shed, chimney-top included, in which the gardener keeps a tall young wife, and one or two children, might be erected in the parlour referred to.

JOHN CLAUDIUS LOUDON, *Calls in Hertfordshire, Bedfordshire, Berkshire, Surrey, Sussex and Middlesex* July–August 1829

A gardener's work is never at an end; it begins with the year, and continues to the next: he prepares the ground, and then he sows it; after that he plants, and then he gathers the fruits . . .   JOHN EVELYN, *Kalendarium Hortense* [1706 ed.]

And he battles with the seasons.

The fair-weather gardener, who will do nothing except when wind and weather and everything else are favourable, is never a master of his craft. Gardening, above all crafts, is a matter of faith, grounded, however (if on nothing better), on his experience that somehow or other seasons go on in their right course, and bring their right results. No doubt bad seasons are a trial of his faith; it is grievous to lose the fruits of much labour by a frosty winter or a droughty summer, but, after all, frost and drought are necessities for which, in all his calculations, he must leave an ample margin; but even in the extreme cases, when the margin is past, the gardener's occupation is not gone.

CANON ELLACOMBE, *In a Gloucestershire Garden* [1895]

GARDENER

When they moved into the house it was winter.
In the garden a sycamore stood.
No other root nor shoot, but wild nettles
Good only for a bitter soup. He planned
Flowers around the sycamore for summer,
The great splayed rose, the military tulip,
All colours, smell of sun, himself with spade
Drinking cold beer with his wife. Spring came.
He rooted up the nettles with his hands.
He burnt them all, stamped on the clotted ash,
Tamping new seeds in, fingering stones aside.
This work he wanted, his hands came alive.
They wanted flowers to touch. But from his care
Only the tough nasturtiums came. They crawled
In sullen fire by the wall a week.
But the soil was sour, the roots went unfed.
Even they ceased to clutch, their heads fell forward.

All summer was the same. He fed the soil,
Flicking out stones, plucking the few sparse shoots.
The trapped flowers were trying to escape,
But died in their cells, and winter came.

Next year he planted early. Spring brought up
Over fussed tussocks, a green scanty surf.
Then it receded, but a tidewrack stayed
Of shrivelled leaves, shoots like dead dragonflies.
Then nettles crawled back. Now he didn't care.
His hands were useless, the earth was not his.
It did things to him, never he to it.
He watched the nettles with a little smile.

Then in the snowdrift of a summer bed
He planted himself, and a child came –
News that he knew early one winter day.
He came home dumbly from the hospital.
The garden gate was open. He went out,
Stood by the sycamore, watched the clouds moult,
Stood in the chilly and falling feathers
Under the sycamore, and not knowing why,
He felt his hands become alive, and touched
The tree's smooth body with a kind of joy,
Thinking next summer it would have new leaves.

DOM MORAES [1938–   ]

*Mr Pinnegar, known as Old Herbaceous, observes the Chelsea Flower
Show of 1913 and describes the pre-1914 head gardener.*

The exhibits were, of course, wonderful, but what took his eye was the way
owners of great estates and their head gardeners strolled through the big
marquees, chatting together, very much as he and George Honey might have
done at their own local flower show. It was difficult sometimes to tell them
apart, for what with the employers wearing rough country tweeds and their
gardeners being in Sunday best for the occasion, you were often left
wondering which was master and which was man.

   While Mrs Charteris was resting on a rustic seat, for which she had placed
an order, Mr Pinnegar followed such a couple in order to study this social
phenomenon. The head gardener, he noticed, always kept half a pace behind
his employer. When they stopped to consider an exhibit, the latter did all the
talking, but his head gardener was always at hand, with a metaphorical
boat-hook, to pull him ashore if he got into deep waters. Tact, decided Mr
Pinnegar, was the saving grace on such occasions. You had to let your
guv'nor think he was deciding what to order, while making sure that he
didn't waste *his* money and *your* time. No use in cluttering up the garden
with fancy things that would die on you in a week . . .

   They reached a stand on which every known variety of rhododendron was
displayed. A discreet salesman waited with an open order book to receive
instructions.

'Yes,' said the master. 'I think we'd better have some of those. What d'you think, Perkins? Make a fine show in that corner by the summer house — what?'

'Very fine; very fine indeed, Sir John. If you think they'd *do* in our soil. We're a bit on the wet side – as you reminded me, Sir John, when I wanted to plant that magnolia . . .'

Sir John rubbed his chin thoughtfully, as one pondering great decisions. 'Ah, yes, the soil! Ours is a bit tricky for rhododendrons, eh, Perkins?'

'And the lime; *that's* our trouble,' the head gardener confided to the salesman. 'You can't go against lime. Wonderful for irises but, as Sir John says, a bit tricky for rhododendrons.'

REGINALD ARKELL,
Old Herbaceous [1950]

As in the case of the Jacobean, William Lawson, anti-Catholicism appears as an attribute even if only this time of the gardener's wife.

MR NUTCH

Mr Nutch
Brown-bearded bear,
Chased the scamps of boys through fruit trees.
'Scamps', he called them,
But it was a serious affair,
Breaking down the palings
And Stealing Property.
    Clumsily he would grab and ramble,
    Angrily he would dart and grumble,
    Heavily he would sway and shamble
        After the nimble boys.
He would stumble among the trees,
Full-branchèd apples
That sagged beneath their rosy swags,
Or crabs that trailed their bitter-sweet rockets
Across the crisp autumn air.

Bombardments of apples
And impudent laughter
Met Mr Nutch
Where'er he might wander,
His crinkled boots crusted with crystals
Under the glittering cobweb-tangled autumn.
(Oh,
    If only Mrs Nutch
        Could have tidied up the season,
        What a different autumn it would have been,
        With its neatly piled pyramids of apples,
        Sorted accordingly to size and colour,
        Even the branches graded,
        Placed symmetrically

One above another,
The grass dry, well-aired
And of an even height!)
But, as it was,
There, heavily trudging,
Angry and out of breath
Mr Nutch must grab and ramble
From one walled garden to another.
At his approach
The birds would flutter in the fruit nets,
Bump and struggle in the fruit nets;
Each small bird that pecked the honeyed heart
Of golden or grape-blushing plum,
Was in reality a vulture
Feeding on Mr Nutch's entrails –
Mr Nutch,
That Ranetheus bound to an orchard.
But the birds would flutter and struggle,
For Mr Nutch
Was the natural enemy of every bird
However soft or gaudy-feathered,
Just as Mrs Nutch
Was the sworn foe
Of every cobweb,
        Mouse and
          Roman Catholic.

    SIR OSBERT SITWELL [1892–1969]

With behaviour of the kind recorded here it is hardly surprising that gardeners as a breed have virtually vanished.

I shall never forget a June evening when we went for a walk in the kitchen garden, which was immense and furnished with enough asparagus to feed battalions of orphans for months. Everything was immaculate; not a weed on the smooth surface of the cinder paths, not a trace of blight on the heavily laden broad beans. Suddenly Molly stopped in her tracks. There at her feet lay a small trowel which must have been left by one of the gardener's boys.

'Do you see,' said Molly in a strangled voice, 'what I see?'

I did indeed, and I bent down to pick it up.

'No!' she exclaimed. 'Do not touch it. Leave it alone!'

She might have been talking of a high explosive. But she was not looking at me, she was staring to the end of the path, down which Hawkins, the head gardener, was slowly approaching.

He came up to us and touched his cap.

'Good evening, Hawkins.'

'Good evening, m'lady.'

'This, Hawkins, is Mr Beverley Nichols.'

'Good evening, sir.'

'Mr Nichols is a very famous gardener.'

Hawkins made no comment on this assertion.

She pointed to the trowel. 'Is *this* the sort of thing we like Mr Nichols to see at Broadlands, Hawkins? Garden tools scattered all over the place?'

He bent down slowly and picked it up. When he straightened himself he was very red in the face. Again he touched his cap. 'Good evening, m'lady.'

Molly had given her little sting, and as with the bee, she had parted with something of herself in doing so. She was tired and dispirited when we walked back to the house, not with Hawkins but with herself. For she was, I repeat, a kindly woman at heart, and when she died she did something which must have made Hawkins forgive her for all her tiresomeness – she remembered him in her will.

How strange are the ways of some very rich people with their gardeners! How seldom they allow themselves to be guided! They obey their doctors' orders, they follow the advice of their lawyers, they do as their stockbrokers tell them, but in the garden they behave like ignorant and arrogant dictators. As a result, a relationship which should be a happy partnership is often soured and embittered.

BEVERLEY NICHOLS, *Garden Open Today* [1963]

Even before the disappearance of gardeners in this century, there had emerged a code of practice of what the owner could and could not do and still preserve class.

> . . . if the garden with its many cares,
> All well repaid, demand him, he attends
> The welcome call, conscious how much the hand
> Of lubbard labour needs his watchful eye,
> Oft loit'ring lazily if not o'erseen,
> Or misapplying his unskilful strength
> Nor does he govern only or direct,
> But much performs himself; no works indeed
> That ask robust, tough sinews, bred to toil,
> Servile employ – but such as may amuse,
> Not tire, demanding rather skill than force.
> Proud of his well-spread walls, he views his trees
> That meet (no barren interval between)
> With pleasure more than ev'n their fruits afford,
> Which, save himself who trains them, none can feel.
> These therefore are his own peculiar charge,
> No meaner hand may discipline the shoots,
> None but his steel approach them. What is weak,
> Distemper'd, or has lost prolific powers,
> Impair'd by age, his unrelenting hand
> Dooms to the knife. Nor does he spare the soft
> And succulent that feeds its giant growth,
> But barren, at th'expense of neighb'ring twigs
> Less ostentatious, and yet studded thick
> With hopeful gems. The rest, no portion left
> That may disgrace his art, or disappoint
> Large expectation, he disposes neat
> At measured distances, that air and sun

Admitted freely may afford their aid,
And ventilate and warm the swelling buds.

WILLIAM COWPER, *The Task*   [1785]

Charles Dickens catches the emergence of the suburban gardener.

There is another and a very different class of men, whose recreation is their
garden. An individual of this class, resides some short distance from town –
say in the Hampstead-road, or the Kilburn-road, or any other road where
the houses are small and neat, and have little slips of back garden. He and his
wife . . . have occupied the same house ever since he retired from business
twenty years ago . . .

   In fine weather the old gentleman is almost constantly in the garden; and
when it is too wet to go into it, he will look out of the window at it, by the
hour together. He has always something to do there, and you will see him
digging, and sweeping, and cutting, and planting, with manifest delight. In
spring-time there is no end to the sowing of seeds, and sticking little bits of
wood over them, with labels, which look like epitaphs to their memory; and
in the evening, when the sun has gone down, the perseverance with which he
lugs a great watering-pot about is perfectly astonishing . . . The old lady is
very fond of flowers, as the hyacinth-glasses in the parlour-window, and
geranium-pots in the little front court, testify. She takes great pride in the
garden too: and when one of the four fruit-trees produces rather a larger
gooseberry than usual, it is carefully preserved under a wine-glass on the
side-board, for the edification of visitors, who are duly informed that Mr So-
and-so planted the tree which produced it, with his own hands.

CHARLES DICKENS, *Sketches by Boz*
[1836]

And here is today's owner gardener.

Toward seven o'clock every morning, I leave my study and step
Out on the bright terrace; the sun already burns resplendent
Between the shadows of the fig tree, makes the low wall of coarse
Granite warm to the touch. Here my tools lie ready and waiting,
Each one an intimate, an ally: the round basket for weeds;
The *zappetta*, the small hoe with a short haft (taking the advice
Of a clever old man of Ticino, I've put a strip of
Shoe leather between the wood and the iron; and I keep the tool
In a damp place so the wood won't split; you need it all the time).
There's a rake here as well, and at times a mattock and spade,
Or two watering cans filled with water warmed by the sun.
With my basket and small hoe in hand, facing the sun, I
Go out for my morning walk . . .

HERMANN HESSE, *Hours in the
Garden. An Idyll*   [1952], translated
by Rika Lesser

Nowadays we're lucky if we can get anything approaching knowledge-able part-time help. To be honest what one gets is labour with all its attendant deficiencies.

Well-trained gardeners who like their work must live in America, but not around here and not in my price range. When I look back on the long procession of incompetents, dumbbells and eccentrics, young and old, foreign and domestic, who have worked for me, I wonder how I and the garden have survived their ministrations. I recall, for example, Mr R., a well-known figure in town because in spite of his shabby get-up he is said to be very rich, with large plantations in Brazil – or it may be the Cape Verde Islands. You see him moving at a rapid hobble along the street, on his way to some garden or other, usually belonging to a newcomer because we old-timers know that he brings death and destruction with him. Those he has worked for discuss him with tears in their eyes. The summer he gardened for me he killed two cherry trees, uprooted a plantation of Dutch iris and imparted crooked lines to the perennial beds from which they have never fully recovered. I worked in New York in those days, and when I came up for week-ends, my first wish was naturally to see the garden – a wish strongly opposed by the family, who offered me drinks, produced piles of mail, announced that we have to leave immediately for a dinner twenty miles away, anything to keep me from a tour of inspection. It was, they explained, Mr R.'s canny habit to get his job done between five and six A.M., long before anyone was around to stop him. By breakfast time, the little heaps of plants he had pulled up were already past saving, the cement already setting between the bricks laid in the wrong place. Nothing one could say or do made any impression. I fired him in a blazing passion, but when we meet, which is often, he beams upon me and invariably passes a pleasant remark about the weather.

He was followed by A., who was, as they say, right off the boat. He spoke only Portuguese. I addressed him in Spanish, which he seemed to understand. Or I thought he did until I found him mowing the grass strip in front of the house, the grasscatcher not on the mower, which was blasting a steady stream of damp cuttings onto the facade. When this was pointed out, he smiled dreamily and moved into the street, the mower still going. I watched him cover a half-block of naked asphalt before I led him gently to the back door and paid him off.

He, as I remember it, was followed by Mr H., of impeccable Yankee lineage – no language trouble there, and he was handy too, could make or mend anything; and the most remarkable painter I ever knew: Any object painted by him, including the house, stayed pristine for a decade. But Mr H. had two problems. He weighed close to four hundred pounds, and he was mad, certifiably so, poor man, for he had done time. It showed in his stream-of-consciousness talk – which flowed on and on without pause or relevance and was distracting until one learned to tune out – and in a tendency to paranoid outbursts, which one also learned to ignore. His weight caused him to adopt some peculiar methods as well. He weeded, for example, in the reclining position of those stout riverine gods on Roman fountains, and dug in the same attitude, using a small trowel. I remember him attacking in this manner three large, well-rooted shrubs I wanted removed. It took a week.

Mr H. stayed with me for five or six years, getting fatter and crazier every year, until he retired at his own request, fuming over some fancied slight.

It occurs to me that I attract the mentally unbalanced. Or perhaps their therapists have advised them to take up outdoor work? There was the beautiful young Italian, a veritable Donatello with black curly hair and a bronze torso we saw a lot of because he liked to bare it while he worked. He arrived in a Cadillac of immense size, did little work but talked a lot about trips he intended to make, businesses he meant to start, and often asked to use the telephone. He was eventually arrested for having tried to murder his mistress, and though he was given a suspended sentence it seemed better not to have him around.

Eleanor Perényi, *Green Thoughts* [1981]

A recollection of the death of Charles Darwin's gardener.

He passed quietly on one May morning. Old Lakeman died as he had lived – serenely, gently, calmly, entirely certain of himself. He had set himself to live after the fashion of a simple gentleman; it behoved him to die in the same resolve.

He had his cup of tea and sent down orders to the under-gardener. 'Tell him,' he said, 'to dig up the tulips to make room for the dianthus, and then' (with a wink) 'he can do what he likes pottering about with a hoe.' Then he lay back on his pillow, and soon his gardening days were ended – ended when his own little garden was so perfect and full of bloom. It was the first warm day of summer, after a long and inhospitable winter.

Old Lakeman was ninety-six when he died; he had started work as a garden boy at fourteen years of age. He was gardener to Charles Darwin, the famous English naturalist and biologist, for thirty years, but when the old professor retired, he had to leave and entered upon a well-earned rest. But he sought other triumphs in retirement, and threw himself whole-heartedly into the task of making his third garden on the outskirts of a little Sussex town. So for eight years, or more, he pursued his absorbing hobby and with limited opportunities produced over again an entrancing garden never so lovely as on that May morning when, at a ripe old age, the summons came to him to leave it.

After his passing many of his earthly treasures went to those who would value them most, and who had helped him make his last garden. They were mementoes of one of the sweetest and most intellectual gardeners who ever lived. And so the memory of his garden lives on.

M. Allwood, *English Countryside and Gardens* [1947]

DEATH OF A GARDENER

> He rested through the Winter, watched the rain
> On his cold garden, slept, awoke to snow
> Padding the window, thatching the roof again
> With silence. He was grateful for the slow
> Nights and undemanding days; the dark
> Protected him; the pause grew big with cold.

Mice in the shed scuffled like leaves; a spark
Hissed from his pipe as he dreamed beside the fire.
All at once light sharpened; earth drew breath,
Stirred; and he woke to strangeness that was Spring,
Stood on the grass, felt movement underneath
Like a child in the womb; hope troubled him to bring
Barrow and spade once more to the waiting soil.
Slower his lift and thrust; a blackbird filled
Long intervals with song; a worm could coil
To safety underneath the hesitant blade.
Hands tremulous as cherry branches kept
Faith with struggling seedlings till the earth
Kept faith with him, claimed him as he slept
Cold in the sun beside his guardian spade.

PHOEBE HESKETH, in *New
Poetry* [1965]

*Reginald Arkell's whimsical tale of the gardener, Old Herbaceous, and
his mistress, Mrs Charteris, ends with her, now in a retirement home,
recalling him.*

'You were very fond of Pinnegar, weren't you?' said the nurse.

'Not always,' replied the old lady. 'Sometimes, when he was being
difficult, I could have *smacked* him.'

'Oh dear,' smiled the nurse. 'I hope you never did.'

'Of course not. That was only my fun. But he *was* a little trying. One
minute he would *exasperate* you, because he *would* do things *his* way, and
then he would be so sweet you almost wanted to cry.'

'How very odd.'

'Odd? Not at all,' said Mrs Charteris. 'Pinnegar was a gardener . . . just a
gardener . . . and gardeners are all a little like that.'

REGINALD ARKELL, *Old Herbaceous*
[1950]

Miss Jekyll carries the good gardener heavenwards.

The good gardener knows with absolute certainty that if he does his part, if
he gives the labour, the love, and every aid that his knowledge of his craft,
experience of the conditions of his place, and exercise of his personal wit can
work together to suggest, that so surely will God give the increase. Then with
the honestly-earned success comes the consciousness of encouragement to
renewed effort, and, as it were, an echo of the gracious words, 'Well done,
good and faithful servant.'   GERTRUDE JEKYLL, *Wood and
Garden* [1899]

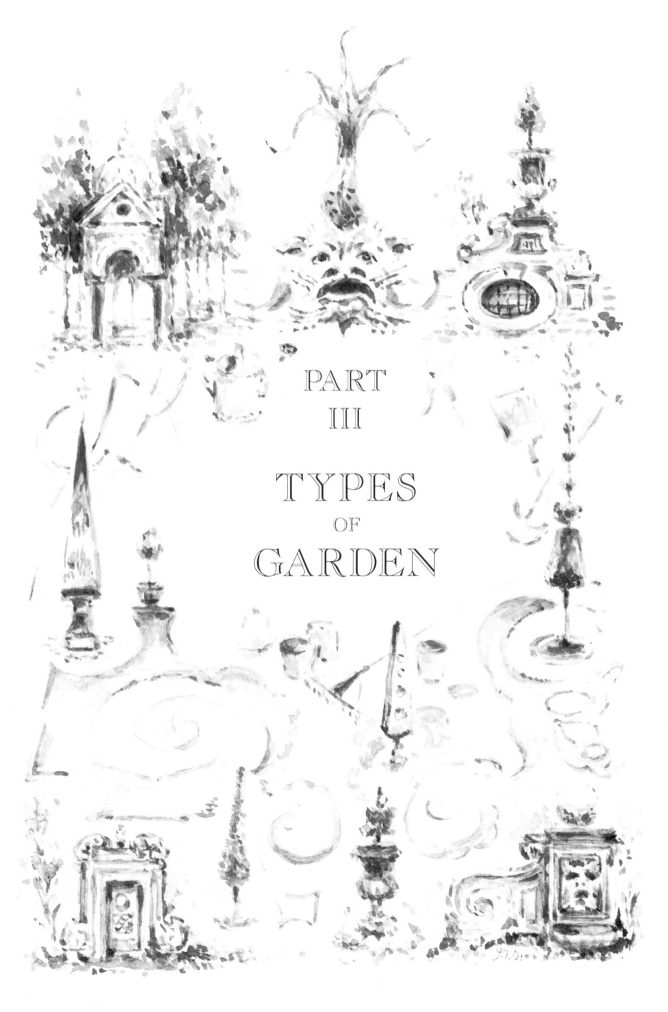

PART
III

TYPES
OF
GARDEN

A FORSAKEN GARDEN

In a coign of the cliff between lowland and highland,
    At the sea-down's edge between windward and lee,
Walled round with rocks as an inland island,
    The ghost of a garden fronts the sea.
A girdle of brushwood and thorn encloses
    The steep square slope of the blossomless bed
Where the weeds that grew green from the graves of its roses
        Now lie dead.

The fields fall southward, abrupt and broken,
    To the low last edge of the long lone land.
If a step should sound or a word be spoken
    Would a ghost not rise at the strange guest's hand?
So long have the grey bare walks lain guestless,
    Through branches and briers if a man make way,
He shall find no life but the sea-wind's, restless
        Night and day.

The dense hard passage is blind and stifled
    That crawls by a track none turn to climb
To the strait waste place that the years have rifled
    Of all but the thorns that are touched not of time.
The thorns he spares when the rose is taken;
    The rocks are left when he wastes the plain.
The wind that wanders, the weeds wind-shaken,
        These remain.

Not a flower to be pressed of the foot that falls not;
    As the heart of a dead man the seed-plots are dry;
From the thicket of thorns whence the nightingale calls not,
    Could she call, there were never a rose to reply.
Over the meadows that blossom and wither
    Rings but the note of a sea-bird's song;
Only the sun and the rain come hither
        All year long.

ALGERNON CHARLES
SWINBURNE [1878]

Coole was Lady Gregory's (1852–1932) country house and the setting for gatherings of the leaders of the Irish literary and dramatic renaissance. As in the case of so many other Irish houses in the aftermath of the Troubles, it was demolished in 1932. J. M. Synge (1871–1909) stayed there often and recalls its tragedy.

A stone's throw from an old house where I spent several summers in Co. Wicklow, there was a garden that had been left to itself for fifteen or twenty years. Just inside the gate, as one entered, two paths led up through a couple of strawberry beds, half choked with leaves, where a few white and narrow strawberries were still hidden away. Further on was nearly half an acre of tall raspberry canes and thistles five feet high, growing together in a dense mass, where one could still pick raspberries enough to last a household for the season. Then, in a waste of hemlock, there were some half-dozen apple trees covered with lichen and moss, and against the northern walls a few dying plum trees hanging from their nails. Beyond them there was a dead pear tree, and just inside the gate, as one came back to it, a large fuchsia filled with empty nests. A few lines of box here and there showed where the flower-beds had been laid out, and when anyone who had the knowledge looked carefully among them many remnants could be found of beautiful and rare plants.

All round this garden there was a wall seven or eight feet high, in which one could see three or four tracks with well-worn holes, like the paths down a cliff in Kerry, where boys and tramps came over to steal and take away any apples or other fruits that were in season. Above the wall on the three windy sides there were rows of finely-grown lime trees, the place of meeting in the summer for ten thousand bees. Under the east wall there was the roof of a greenhouse, where one could sit, when it was wet or dry, and watch the birds and butterflies, many of which were not common. The seasons were late in this place – it was high above the sea – and redpolls often used to nest not far off late in the summer; siskins did the same once or twice, and greenfinches, till the beginning of August, used to cackle endlessly in the lime trees.

Everyone is used in Ireland to the tragedy that is bound up with the lives of farmers and fishing people; but in this garden one seemed to feel the tragedy of the landlord class also, and of the innumerable old families that are quickly dwindling away. These owners of the land are not much pitied at the present day, or much deserving of pity; and yet one cannot quite forget that they are the descendants of what was at one time, in the eighteenth century, a high-spirited and highly-cultivated aristocracy. The broken greenhouses and mouse-eaten libraries, that were designed and collected by men who voted with Grattan, are perhaps as mournful in the end as the four mud walls that are so often left in Wicklow as the only remnants of a farmhouse.

J. M. SYNGE, *A Landlord's Garden in County Wicklow* written after 1903; published 1907

BOTANIC GARDENS

The Oxford Botanic Garden was founded in 1621 and is still there today. For Mr Bobart see also p. 265.

As to the Phisick Garden & its Rarityes of that nature, since it stands on ground lately purchased from Magdalen Collegge, it may now justly challenge a remembrance, & that you may haue a true charater of its work & beauty take here an account of't from him y.ᵉ now keeps it, the skilfull and Ingenious Gardener himselfe, my friend Mr Jacob Bobert.

Amongst y.ᵉ severall famous structures & curiosities wherewith y.ᵉ flourishing University of Oxford is enriched, that of y.ᵉ Publick Physick Garden deserues not y.ᵉ last place, being a matter of great use and ornament, prouving serviceable not only to all Physitians, Apothecaryes, and those who are more imediately concerned in the practise of Physick, but to persons of all qualities seruing to help y.ᵉ diseased and for y.ᵉ delight & pleasure of those of perfect health, containing therein 3000 seuerall sorts of plants for y.ᵉ honor of our nation and Universities & service of y.ᵉ Commonwealth. This noble thing was y.ᵉ Benefaction of y.ᵉ Right Honourable Henry, Earle of Danby, who then liued at his house at Cornebury, who, purchasing a most convenient plot of ground of 5 acres of Magdalen Colledge land thereto adjoyning, being aptly watered w.ᵗʰ y.ᵉ Riuer Charwell by it gliding, and built thereon a most stately wall of hewen stone 14 foot high with three very considerable Gates thereto, one whereof was to cost of at least 500 pounds, wᶜʰ worthy work was all finished in y.ᵉ yeare 1632. And endowed the same with the Parsonage impropriate of Kirkdale in the County of York, to remain for perpetuitie.

After the walls & gates of this famous garden were built, old Jacob Bobert father to this present Jacob may be said to be y.ᵉ man y.ᵗ first gave life & beauty to this famous place, who by his care and industry replenish'd the walls, w.ᵗʰ all manner of good fruits our clime would ripen, & bedeck the earth w.ᵗʰ great variety of trees plants & exotick flowers, dayly augmented by the Botanists, who bring them hither from y.ᵉ remote Quarters of y.ᵉ world, but to proceed.

This Garden Plot is not exactly square, for y.ᵉ walkes East and West are about 120 of my paces or strides wch are more than a yard. But North and South I trod out but 106 and 112 yards with y.ᵉ length of y.ᵉ North-Gate wᶜʰ is extended w.ᵗʰ out y.ᵉ square of y.ᵉ wall. Here is a door way lately broke through the middle of y.ᵉ South Wall, but the gates spoken of by Mr Bobert are in the East West & Northerne sides, that in the North wall wᶜʰ admits entrance from the City being fairest built, by this Old Jacob some years past got two yew trees wch being formed by his skill are now grown up to be Gigantick bulkey fellows, one holding a Bill th'other a Club on his shoulder which fancy made an Ingenious person strow this Copie of verses on them.

'Upon the most hopefull & ever-flourishing Sprouts of Valour,
The Indefatigable Centrys of the Physick-Garden.
Although no brandish'd Cherubins are here,
Yet sons of Adam venture not too near,
Nor pluck forbidden fruit, if with intent
To visit Paradise be innocent.
Here's your (nil ultra) else; in each of these
Is both a Pillar and an Hercules.
If you do not dread their looks, yet may you fear
The many strange fatalities they bear.
The Embleme of mortality the Yew

Does likewise now y.ᵉ armed Agent shew;
And if unwearie Mortals slight their guard
They doubly make the Garden a Church-yard.'

Seventeenth-century description quoted
in R. T. Gunther, *Oxford
Gardens* [1912]

And, in very different vein.

IN THE BOTANICAL GARDENS

They are such a subtle combination of the artificial and the natural – that is, partly, the secret of their charm.

From the entrance gate down the broad central walk, with the orthodox banality of carpet bedding on either side, stroll men and women and children – a great many children, who call to each other lustily, and jump up and down the green wooden seats. They seem as meaningless, as lacking in individuality, as the little figures in an impressionist landscape.

Above the carpet bedding, on one hand, there is a green hedge, and above the hedge a long row of cabbage trees. I stare up at them, and suddenly the green hedge is a stave, and the cabbage trees, now high, now low, have become an arrangement of notes – a curious, pattering, native melody.

In the enclosure the spring flowers are almost too beautiful – a great stretch of foam-like cowslips. As I bend over them, the air is heavy and sweet with their scent, like hay and new milk and the kisses of children, and, further on, a sunlit wonder of chiming daffodils.

Before me two great rhododendron bushes. Against the dark, broad leaves the blossoms rise, flame-like, tremulous in the still air, and the pearl rose loving-cup of a magnolia hangs delicately on the grey bough.

Everywhere there are clusters of china blue pansies, a mist of forget-me-nots, a tangle of anemones. Strange that these anemones – scarlet, and amethyst, and purple – vibrant with colour, always appear to me a trifle dangerous, sinister, seductive, but poisonous.

And, leaving the enclosure, I pass a little gully, filled with tree ferns, and lit with pale virgin lamps of arum lilies.

I turn from the smooth swept paths, and climb up a steep track, where the knotted tree roots have seared a rude pattern in the yellow clay. And suddenly, it disappears – all the pretty, carefully tended surface of gravel and sward and blossom, and there is bush, silent and splendid. On the green moss, on the brown earth, a wide splashing of yellow sunlight. And everywhere that strange indefinable scent. As I breathe it, it seems to absorb, to become part of me – and I am old with the age of centuries, strong with the strength of savagery.

Somewhere I hear the soft rhythmic flowing of water, and I follow the path down and down until I come to a little stream idly, dreamily floating past. I fling myself down and put my hands in the water. An inexplicable, persistent feeling seizes me that I must become one with it all. Remembrance has gone – this is the Lotus Land – the green trees stir languorously, sleepily – there is the silver sound of a bird's call. Bending down, I drink a little of the water, Oh! is it magic? Shall I, looking intently, see vague forms lurking in the shadow staring at me malevolently, wildly, the thief of their birthright? Shall

I, down the hillside, through the bush, ever in the shadow, see a great company moving towards me, their faces averted, wreathed with green garlands, passing, passing, following the little stream in silence until it is sucked into the wide sea . . .

There is a sudden, restless movement, a pressure of the trees – they sway against one another – it is like the sound of weeping . . .

I pass down the central walk towards the entrance gates. The men and women and children are crowding the pathway, looking reverently, admiringly, at the carpet bedding, spelling aloud the Latin names of the flowers.

Here is laughter and movement and bright sunlight – but behind me – is it near, or miles and miles away? – the bush lies hidden in the shadow.

KATHERINE MANSFIELD [1907]

GARDEN CEMETERIES

Below are some of the exhortations of the Victorian promoters of this means of coping with the urban deceased.

A garden cemetery, and monumental decoration afford the most convincing token of a nation's progress in civilization and the arts, which are its result.

A garden cemetery is the sworn foe to preternatural fear and superstition.

A garden cemetery and monumental decoration, are not only beneficial to public morals, to the improvement of manners, but are likewise calculated to extend virtuous and generous feelings.

JOHN STRANG, *Necropolis Glasguensis: with Osbervations* (sic) *on Ancient and Modern Tombs and Sepulture* [1831]

Churchyards and cemeteries are scenes not only calculated to improve the morals and the taste, and by their botanical riches to cultivate the intellect, but they serve as *historical records*.

JOHN CLAUDIUS LOUDON, 'Principles of Landscape-Gardening applied to Public Cemeteries', *The Gardener's Magazine* [1843]

CHILDREN'S GARDENS

John Clare catches the wonder.

> The stonecrop that on ruins comes
>   And hangs like golden balls –
> How oft to reach its shining blooms
>   We scaled the mossy walls!
> And weeds – we gathered weeds as well,
>   Of all that bore a flower,
> And tied our little posies up
>   Beneath the eldern bower.
>
> Our little gardens there we made
>   Of blossoms all arow,
> And though they had no roots at all
>   We hoped to see them grow;

> And in the cart ruts after showers
> Of sudden summer rain
> We filled our tiny waterpots,
> And cherished them in vain.

JOHN CLARE, *Childhood* [1819–20]

Enemies to horticulture all of them but . . .

The garden had to be put in order, and each sister had a quarter of the little plot to do what she liked with . . . for the girls' tastes differed as much as their characters. Meg had roses and heliotrope, myrtle and a little orange tree in it. Jo's bed was never alike two seasons, for she was always trying experiments. This year it was to be a plantation of sunflowers . . . Beth had old-fashioned, fragrant flowers in her garden – sweet peas and mignonette, larkspur, pinks, pansies, and southern-wood, with chickweed for the birds and catnip for the pussies. Amy had a bower in hers, rather small and earwiggy, but very pretty to look at, with honeysuckles and morning glories hanging their coloured horns and bells in graceful wreaths all over it; tall white lilies, delicate ferns and as many brilliant, picturesque plants as would consent to blossom there.   LOUISA M. ALCOTT,
Little Women [1868]

CHINESE GARDENS

The architect Sir William Chambers (1723–96), the designer of the pagoda at Kew, wrote an influential account of Chinese gardens. Here the garden is used to evoke in the mind of the visitor scenes of horror akin to those in a Gothick novel. Such accounts had a huge impact on the development of the landscape garden in its Picturesque and Romantic phase. The result is as though Hammer Films ran the Chelsea Flower Show.

The scenes which I have hitherto described, are chiefly of the pleasing kind: but the Chinese Gardeners have many sorts, which they employ as circumstances vary . . .

Their scenes of terror are composed of gloomy woods, deep vallies inaccessible to the sun, impending barren rocks, dark caverns, and impetuous cataracts rushing down the mountains from all parts. The trees are ill formed, forced out of their natural directions, and seemingly torn to pieces by the violence of tempests: some are thrown down, and intercept the course of the torrents; others look as if blasted and shattered by the power of lightening: the buildings are in ruins; or half consumed by fire, or swept away by the fury of the waters: nothing remaining entire but a few miserable huts dispersed in the mountains, which serve at once to indicate the existence and wretchedness of the inhabitants. Bats, owls, vultures, and every bird of prey flutter in the groves; wolves, tigers and jackalls howl in the forests; half-famished animals wander upon the plains; gibbets, crosses, wheels, and the whole apparatus of torture, are seen from the roads; and in the most dismal recesses of the woods, where the ways are rugged and overgrown with weeds, and where every object bears the marks of depopulation, are temples dedicated to the king of vengeance, deep caverns in the rocks, and descents to subterraneous habitations, overgrown with brushwood and brambles; near which are placed pillars of stone, with pathetic descriptions of tragical events, and many horrid acts of cruelty, perpetrated there by outlaws and robbers of former times: and to add both to the horror and sublimity of these scenes, they sometimes conceal in cavities, on the summits of the highest mountains, founderies, lime-kilns, and glass-works; which send forth large volumes of flame, and continued columns of thick smoke, that give to these mountains the appearance of volcanoes.

Their surprizing, or supernatural scenes, are of the romantic kind, and abound in the marvellous; being calculated to excite in the minds of the spectators, quick successions of opposite and violent sensations. Sometimes the passenger is hurried by steep descending paths to subterraneous vaults, divided into departments, where lamps which yield a faint glimmering light, discover the pale images of ancient kings and heroes, reclining on beds of state; their heads are crowned with garlands of stars, and in their hands are tablets of moral sentences: flutes, and soft harmonious organs, impelled by subterraneous waters, interrupt, at stated intervals, the silence of the place, and fill the air with solemn melody.

Sometimes the traveller, after having wandered in the dusk of the forest, finds himself on the edge of precipices, in the glare of day-light, with cataracts falling from the mountains around, and torrents raging in the depths beneath him; or at the foot of impending rocks, in gloomy vallies, overhung with woods, on the banks of dull moving rivers, whose shores are covered with sepulchral monuments, under the shade of willows, laurels, and other plants, sacred to Manchew, the genius of sorrow.

His way now lies through dark passages cut in the rocks, on the side of which are recesses, filled with colossal figures of dragons, infernal fiends, and other horrid forms, which hold in their monstrous talons, mysterious, cabalistical sentences, inscribed on tables of brass; with preparations that yield a constant flame; serving at once to guide and to astonish the passenger: from time to time he is surprized with repeated shocks of electrical impulse, with showers of artificial rain, or sudden violent gusts of wind, and instantaneous explosions of fire: the earth trembles under him, by the power of confined air; and his ears are successively struck with many different sounds, produced by the same means; some resembling the cries of men in torment; others the roaring of bulls, and howl of ferocious animals, with the yell of hounds, and the voices of hunters; others are like the mixed croaking of ravenous birds; and others imitate thunder, of the raging of the sea, the explosion of cannon, the sound of trumpets, and all the noise of war.

His road then lies through lofty woods, where serpents and lizards of many beautiful sorts crawl upon the ground, and where innumerable monkies, cats and parrots, clamber upon the trees, and intimidate him as he passes; or through flowery thickets, where he is delighted with the singing of birds, the harmony of flutes, and all kinds of soft instrumental music: sometimes, in this romantic excursion, the passenger finds himself in extensive recesses, surrounded with arbors of jessamine, vine and roses, where beauteous Tartarean damsels, in loose transparent robes, that flutter in the air, present him with rich wines, mangostans, ananas, and fruits of Quangsi; crown him with garlands of flowers, and invite him to taste the sweets of retirement, on Persian carpets, and beds of camusath skin down . . .

WILLIAM CHAMBERS AND WILLIAM MASON, *A Dissertation on Oriental Gardening* [1772]

Chinese gardens, of course, have their own special aesthetic beauty, one only understood properly in the West in our century. Their greatest work on garden design, Yvan Ye *or* The Craft of Gardens, *was written by one Ji Cheng between 1631–4 simultaneously with Lord Pembroke's creation of the great garden at Wilton (see pp. 324–5).*

Generally, in the construction of gardens, whether in the countryside or on the outskirts of a city, a secluded location is the best. In clearing woodland one should select and prune the tangled undergrowth; where a fine piece of natural scenery occurs one should make the most of it. Where there is a mountain torrent one may cultivate orchids and angelica together. Paths should be lined with the 'three auspicious things' whose property it is to symbolize eternity. The surrounding wall should be concealed under creepers, and rooftops should emerge here and there above the tops of the trees. If you climb a tower on a hill-top to gaze into the distance, nothing but beauty will meet your eye; if you seek a secluded spot among banks of bamboo, intoxication will flood your heart. The pillars of your verandah should be tall and widely spaced; your windows and doors should give an unimpeded view.

The view should include a watery expanse of many acres and contain the changing brilliance of the four seasons. The shadow of phoenix trees should cover the ground, the shade of pagoda trees pattern the walls. Willows should be set along the embankments, plum trees around the buildings; reeds should be planted among the bamboos. A long channel should be dug out for the stream. With hillsides as tapestries and mountains as screens, set up a thousand feet of emerald slopes; though man-made, they will look like something naturally created. Shadowy temples should appear through round windows, like a painting by the Younger Li. Lofty summits should be heaped up from rocks cut to look as if they were painted with slash strokes, uneven like the half-cliffs of Dachi. If you can have a Buddhist monastery as your neighbour, the chanting of Sanskrit will come to your ears; if distant mountain ranges can be included in the view, their fresh beauty is there for you to absorb. With the grey-violet of vaporous morning or pale evening mist, the cry of cranes will drift to your pillow. Among the white duckweed and red polygonum, flocks of gulls will gather beside your jetty. To see the mountains, ride on a bamboo litter; to visit the river, lean on an oaken staff. Slantwise soar the parapets, crosswise strides the long rainbow bridge. You need not envy Wang Wei's Wangchuan; Jilun's Golden Valley will count for nothing. Is Xiaoxia the only bay worthy of the name? There are more open spaces here than Cangchun.

If you raise deer they can roam freely about; if you breed fish they can be caught. In cool summer pavilions you can play drinking-games, mix ice with your drinks, and feel the breeze rising among the bamboos and trees. In warm winter apartments you can gather round the stove, and melt snow to make your tea while the water bubbles in the wine-warmer. Your troubles will be quenched along with your thirst. The night-rain patters on the plantain leaves like a mermaid's tears. The dawn breeze soughs through the willows, as if caressing Xiaoman's slender waist. Transplant some bamboos in front of your window, and set aside some pear trees to form a courtyard. The scene is bathed in moonlight, the wind whispers. The moonlight plays

quietly over lute and books, the wind ruffles a half-circle of autumn water.
We feel a pure atmosphere around our table and seats; the common dust of
the world is far from our souls.   Ji CHENG, *The Craft of Gardens*
[1631–4]; translated by Alison Hardie,
1988

COLLEGE GARDENS

Henry James recalling the security of late Victorian Oxford.

We repaired in turn to a series of gardens and spent long hours sitting in their
greenest places. They struck us as the fairest things in England and the ripest
and sweetest fruit of the English system. Locked in their antique verdure,
guarded, as in the case of New College, by gentle battlements of silver-grey,
outshouldering the matted leafage of undisseverable plants, filled with
nightingales and memories, a sort of chorus of tradition; with vaguely-
generous youth sprawling bookishly on the turf as if to spare it the injury of
their boot-heels, and with the great conservative college countenance appealing gravely from the restless outer world, they seem places to lie down on
the grass in for ever, in the happy faith that life is all a vast old English
garden, and time an endless summer afternoon.

HENRY JAMES, *A Passionate Pilgrim*
[1875]

SNOWFALL ON A COLLEGE GARDEN

While we slept, these formal gardens
Worked into their disguise. The Warden's
Judas and tulip trees awake
In ermine. Here and there a flake
Of white falls from the painted scene,
Or a dark scowl of evergreen
Glares through the shroud, or a leaf dumps
Its load and the soft burden slumps
Earthward like a fainting girl.
No movement else. The blizzard's whirl
Froze to this cataleptic trance
Where nature sleeps and sleep commands
A transformation. See this bush
Furred and fluffed out like a thrush
Against the cold: snow which could snap
A robust veteran branch, piled up
On the razor edge of a weak spray,
Plumping it out in mimicry
Of white buddleia. Like the Elect
Ghosts of summer resurrect
In snowy robes. Only the twangling
Noise of unseen sparrows wrangling
Tells me that my window-view
Holds the garden I once knew.

CECIL DAY LEWIS [1904–72]

A Maze   970.

CONSERVATORY GARDENS

I love a still conservatory
    That's full of giant, breathless palms,
Azaleas, clematis and vines
    Whose quietness great Trees becalms
Filling the air with foliage,
    A curved and dreamy statuary . . .

I love the mossy quietness
    That grows upon the great stone flags,
The dark tree-ferns, the staghorn ferns,
    The prehistoric, antlered stags
That carven stand and stare among
    The silent, ferny wilderness . . .

I like to hear a cold, pure rill
    Of water trickling low, afar
With sudden littler jerks and purls
    Into a tank or stoneware jar,
The song of a tiny sleeping bird
    Held like a shadow in its trill.

I watch a white Nyanza float
    Upon a green, untroubled pool,
A fairyland Ophelia, she
    Has cast herself in water cool,
And lies while fairy cymbals ring
    Drowned in her fairy castle moat.

Still as a great jewel is the air
    With boughs and leaves smooth-carved in it,
And rocks and trees and giant ferns,
    And blooms with inner radiance lit,
And naked water like a nymph
    That dances tireless, slim and bare.

Silent the Cattleyas blaze
    And thin red orchid shapes of Death
Peer savagely with twisted lips
    Sucking an eerie, phantom breath
With that bright, spotted, fever'd lust
    That watches lonely travellers craze.

Gigantic, mauve and hairy leaves
    Hang like obliterated faces
Full of dim unattained expression
    Such as haunts virgin forest places
When Silence leaps among the trees
    And the echoing heart deceives.

W. J. TURNER [1889–1946]

IN A CONVENT GARDEN

In the convent vegetable garden the nuns
Have erected a scarecrow in front of the runner beans,
And it has an old wimple on its head.

In the spring the beans will climb and climb
But the crows are coming:
The wimple will chase them away.

In the convent vegetable garden the nuns
Have erected a scarecrow alongside the cauliflowers,
And it has an old wimple on its head.

In the spring the cauliflowers will rise will rise
But the daws are deadly:
The wimple will drive them away.

In the convent vegetable garden the nuns
Have erected a scarecrow behind the marrow plants,
And it has an old wimple on its head.

In the spring the marrows will expand will expand
But the tits are terrible:
The wimple will turn them away.

In the summer the marrows will fructify completely,
And will be scrubbed under rubber-nozzled taps and peeled
And sliced and cored and stuffed with mutton,

And the scarecrow will be taken apart
And at the long tables in the cool refectory
The Mother Superior and the nuns and the novice nuns
    and the symbolists will sit and
        stuff themselves for a considerable
           length of time.

                ALAN BROWNJOHN [1965]

Few pictures of the cottage garden are as vivid as those of Mary Russell COTTAGE
Mitford (1787–1855). GARDENS

To Miss BARRETT, Wimpole Street

Three Mile Cross, 20 June 1842

MY DEAR LOVE,
It is now half-past one, and my father has only this very moment gone into
his room to bed. He sleeps all the afternoon in the garden, and then would sit
up all night to be read to. I have now several letters to answer before going to
bed. At present, I write to say that on Saturday next (the very day on which
you will receive this) we shall send you some flowers. Oh, how I wish we
could transport you into the garden where they grow! You would like it – the

'*entourage*', as Mrs Mackie calls it, is so pretty: one side (it is nearly an acre of show flowers) a high hedge of hawthorn, with giant trees rising above it beyond the hedge, whilst all down within the garden are clumps of matchless hollyhocks and splendid dahlias; the top of the garden being shut in by the old irregular cottage, with its dark brickwork covered with vines and roses, and its picturesque chimneys mingling with the bay tree, again rising into its bright and shining cone, and two old pear trees festooned with honeysuckle; the bottom of the garden and the remaining side consisting of lower hedgerows melting into wooded uplands, dotted with white cottages and patches of common. Nothing can well be imagined more beautiful than this little bit of ground is now. Huge masses of lupines (say fifty or sixty spiral spikes), some white, some lilac; immense clumps of the enamelled Siberian larkspur, glittering like some enormous Chinese jar; the white and azure blossoms of the variegated monkshood; flags of all colours; roses of every shade, some covering the house and stables and overtopping the roofs, others mingling with tall apple trees, others again (especially the beautiful double Scotch rose) low but broad, standing in bright relief to the blues and purples; and the oriental poppy, like an orange lamp (for it really seems to have light within it) shining amidst the deeper greens; above all, the pyramid of geraniums, beautiful beyond all beauty, rising in front of our garden room, whilst each corner is filled with the same beautiful flower, and the whole air perfumed by the delicious honeysuckle. Nothing can be more lovely.

MARY RUSSELL MITFORD to
ELIZABETH BARRETT BROWNING,
20 June 1842

A century on the picture seems little changed in Flora Thompson's description of the postmistress' garden at Candleford.

Narrow paths between high, built-up banks supporting flower borders, crowded with jonquils, auriculas, forget-me-nots and other spring flowers, led from one part of the garden to another. One winding path led to the earth closet in its bower of nut-trees halfway down the garden, another to the vegetable garden and on to the rough grass plot before the beehives. Between each section were thick groves of bushes with ferns and capers and Solomon's seal, so closed in that the long, rough grass there was always damp. Wasted ground, a good gardener might have said, but delightful in its cool, green shadiness.

Nearer the house was a portion given up entirely to flowers, not growing in beds or borders, but crammed together in an irregular square, where they bloomed in half-wild profusion. There were rose bushes there and lavender and rosemary and a bush apple-tree which bore little red and yellow streaked apples in later summer, and Michaelmas daisies and red-hot pokers and old-fashioned pompom dahlias in autumn and peonies and pinks already budding.

An old man in the village came one day a week to till the vegetable garden, but the flower garden was no one's especial business. Miss Lane herself would occasionally pull on a pair of wash-leather gloves and transplant a few seedlings; Matthew would pull up a weed or stake a plant as he passed, and the smiths once a year, turned out of the shop to dig between the roots

and cut down dead canes. Betweenwhiles the flowers grew just as they would in crowded masses, perfect in their imperfection.

FLORA THOMPSON, *Lark Rise to Candleford* [1939]

Here Daphnis tempts the beautiful boy Ganymede with an idealized Elizabethan garden.

ELIZABETHAN GARDENS

> Nay more than this, I have a Garden-plot,
> Wherein there wants nor hearbs, nor roots, nor flowers
> (Flowers to smell, roots to eate, hearbs for the pot.)
> And dainty shelters when the Welkin lowers:
> Sweet-smelling beds of Lillies and of Roses,
> Which Rosemary banks and Lavender encloses.
>
> There growes the Gilliflowre, the Mynt, the Dayzie
> (Both red and white,) the blew-veynd-Violet:
> The purple Hyacinth, the Spyke to please thee,
> The scarlet dyde Carnation bleeding yet;
> The Sage, the Savery, and sweet Margerum,
> Isop, Tyme, and Eye-Bright, good for blinde and dumbe.
>
> The Pink, the Primrose, Cowslip and Daffadilly,
> The Harebell blue, the crimson Columbine,
> Sage, Lettis, Parsley, and the milk-white Lilly,
> The Rose, and speckled flowre called Sops-in-Wine,
> Fine pretty King-cups, and the yellow Bootes,
> That growes by Rivers, and by shallow Brookes.
>
> And manie thousand moe (I cannot name)
> Of hearbs and flowers that in gardens grow,
> I have for thee . . . the highest trees
> For Apples, Cherries, Medlars, Peares or Plumbs,
> Nuts, Walnuts, Filbeards, Chest-nuts, Cervices,
> The hoary Peach, when snowy winter comes;
> . . . fine Orchards full of mellowed frute . . .

RICHARD BARNFIELD, *The Teares of an Affectionate Shepheard Sicke for Love* [1594]

Edmund Spenser (1522?–1599) evokes better than any of his contemporaries the beauty of the Elizabethan garden which, when he wrote this poem, still had all the elements of a novelty. The 'he' is a butterfly.

> To the gay gardins his unstaid desire
> Him wholly carried, to refresh his sprights;
> There lavish nature, in her best attire,
> Powres forth sweete odors and alluring sights;
> And arte, with her contending, doth aspire

T'excell the naturall with made delights;
And all, that faire or pleasant may be found,
In riotous excesse doth there abound.

There he arriving round about doth flie,
From bed to bed, from one to other border,
And takes survey, with curious busie eye,
Of every flowre and herbe there set in order:
Now this, now that he tasteth tenderly,
Yet none of them he rudely doth disorder;
Ne with his feete their silken leaves deface,
But pastures on the pleasures of each place.

And evermore, with most varietie
And change of sweetnesse, (for all change is sweete)
He casts his glutton sense to satisfie,
Now sucking of the sap of herbe most meete,
Or of the deaw which yet on them does lie,
Now in the same bathing his tender feete;
And then he pearcheth on some braunch thereby,
To weather him, and his moist wings to dry.

And then again he turneth to his play,
To spoyle the pleasures of that Paradise;
The wholesome Saulge, and Lavender still gray,
Rank-smelling Rue, and Cummin good for eyes,
The Roses raigning in the pride of May,
Sharpe Isope, good for greene wounds remedies,
Faire Marigoldes, and Bees alluring Thime,
Sweet Marjoram, and Daysies decking prime.

Coole violets, and Orpine growing still,
Embathed Balme, and chearfull Galingale,
Fresh Costmarie, and breathfull Camomill,
Dull Poppie, and drink-quickning Setuale,
Veyne-healing Verven, and hed-purging Dill,
Sound Savorie, and Bazil hartie-hale,
Fat Colworts, and comforting Perseline,
Colde Lettuce, and refreshing Rosmarine.

And whatso else of vertue good or ill
Grewe in this Gardin, fetcht from farre away,
Of everie one he takes, and tastes at will,
And on their pleasures greedily doth pray.
Then, when he hath both plaid and fed his fill,
In the warme sunne he doth himselfe embay,
And there him rests in riotous suffisaunce
Of all his gladfulness and kingly joyaunce.

EDMUND SPENSER, *Muiopotmos* in
Complaints [1591]

It is difficult to think of such gardens existing amidst the religious wars of late sixteenth-century France, but they evoke a tradition of country gardens both sides of the Channel. It is one which is not aristocratic but belonging to the yeoman class.

The most plesant and delectable thing for recreation belonging unto our farmes is our flower gardens . . . It is a commendable and seemely thing to behold out at a window many acres of ground well tilled and husbanded . . . But yet it is much more to behold faire and comely proportions, handsome and pleasant arboures and as it were closets, delightfull borders of lavender, rosemarie, boxe, and other such like: to heare the ravishing musicke of an infinite number of prettie small birdes, which continually day and night doe chatter and chant their proper and naturall branch songs upon the hedges and trees of the garden: and to smell so sweet a nosegaie so neere at hand: seeing that this so fragrant a smell cannot but refresh the Lord of the farme exceedingly, when going out of his bed-chamber in the morning after the sunne-rise, and whiles as yet the cleere and pearlelike dew doth pearch unto the grasse. He giveth himselfe to heare the melodious musicke of the Bees: which busying themselves in gathering of the same, do also fill the aire with a most acceptable, sweet and pleasant harmonie: besides the borders and continued rowes of soveraigne, thyme, balme, rosemarie, marierome, cypers, soothern-wood, and other fragrant herbes, the sight and view whereof cannot but give great contentment unto the beholder.

The garden of pleasure must be cast and contrived close to the one side of the kitchin garden, but yet so, as that they be sundred by the intercourse of a great large alleye, as also a hedge of quickset, having three doores . . . The kitchin garden is to be compassed and set about with lattise worke, and yoong common bordering stuffe to be made up afterward and contrived into arbours, or as it were into small chappels, or oratories and places to make a speech out of, that many standing about and below may heare. In like sort shall the garden of pleasure be set about and compassed in with arbours made of Jesamin, rosemarie, boxe, juniper, cyper-trees, savin, cedars, rose-trees, and other dainties first planted and pruned according as the nature of every one doth require, but after brought into some forme and order with willow or juniper poles, such as may serve for the making of arbours . . .

This garden shall be devided into two equall parts. The one shall containe the herbes and flowres used to make nosegaies and garlands of . . . and it may be called the nosegaie garden. The other part shall have all other sweet smelling herbes, . . . and this may be called the garden for herbs of a good smell.

Richard Surflet's translation (1600) of
CHARLES ESTIENNE, *Maison
Rustique* [1572]

John Parkinson (1567–1650) describes how to plant a flower garden four years into the reign of Charles I.

Your knot or beds being prepared fitly, as before is declared, you may place and order your rootes therein thus: Eyther many rootes of one kinde set together in a round or cluster, or longwise crosse a bed one by another, whereby the beauty of many flowers of one kinde being together, may make a faire shew well pleasing to many; Or else you may plant one or two in a place dispersedly ouer the whole knot, or in a proportion or diameter one place answering another of the knot, as your store will suffer you, or your knot permit: Or you may also mingle these rootes in their planting many diuers sorts together, that they may giue the more glorious shew when they are in flower; and that you may so doe, you must first obserue the seuerall kindes of them, which doe flower at one and the same time, and then to place them in such order and so neare one vnto another, that their flowers appearing together of severall colours, will cause the more admiration in the beholders: as thus, The Vernall Crocus of Saffron flowers of the Spring, white, purple, yellow, and stript, with some Vernall Colchicum or Medow Saffron among them, some Deus Caninus or Doggesteeth, and some of the small early Leucoium or Bulbous Violet, all planted in some proportion as neare one vnto another as is fit for them, will giue such a grace to the Garden, that the place will seeme like a peece of tapestry of many glorious colours, to encrease euery ones delight: Or else many of one sort together, as the blew, white and blush Grape flowers in the same manner intermingled, doe make a maruellous delectable shew, especially because all of them rise almost to an equall height, which causeth the greater grace, as well neare hand as farre of. The like order may be kept with many other things, as the Hepatica, white, blew, purple, and red set or sowne together, will make many to beleeue that one roote doth beare all those colours: But aboue and beyond all others, the Tulipas may be so matched, one colour answering and setting of another, that the place where they stand may resemble a peece of curious needle-worke, or peece of painting: and I haue knowne in a Garden, the Master as much commended for this artificiall forme in placing the colours of Tulipas, as for the goodnesse of his flowers, or any other thing. The diuers sorts and colours of Anemones or Winde-flowers may be so ordered likewise, which are oft very beautifull, to haue the seuerall varieties planted one neare vnto another, that their seuerall colours appearing in one place will be a very great grace in a Garden, or if they be dispersed among the other sorts of flowers, they will make a glorious shew. Another order in planting you may obserue: which is this, That those plants that grow low, as the Aconitum Hyemale or Winterwolues bane, the Vernall Crocus or Saffron-flowers of diuers sorts, the little early Leucoium or Bulbous Violet, and some such other as rise not vp high, as also some Anemones may be very well placed somewhat neare or about your Martagons, Lillies, or Crownes Imperiall, both because these little plants will flower earlier than they, and so will bee gone and past, before the other greater plants will rise vp to any height to hinder them; which is a way may well be admitted in those Gardens that are small, to saue roome, and to place things to the most aduantage.

JOHN PARKINSON, *Paradisi in sole paradisus terrestris* [1629]

James Thomson (1700–48) captures the early Georgian flower garden thus.

Along these blushing borders bright with dew,
And in yon mingled wilderness of flowers,
Fair-handed Spring unbosoms every grace —
Throws out the snowdrop and the crocus first,

The daisy, primrose, violet, darkly blue,
The polyanthus of unnumbered dyes;
The yellow wall-flower, stained with iron-brown,
And lavish stock, that scents the garden round:
From the soft wings of vernal breezes shed,
Anemones; auricula, enriched
With shining meal o'er all their velvet leaves:
. And full ranunculus of flowing red.
Then comes the tulip race, where beauty plays
Her idle freaks: from family diffused
To family, as flies the father dust,
The varied colours run; and while they break
On the charmed eye, the exulting florist marks
With secret pride the wonders of his hand.

No gradual bloom is wanting – from the bud
First-born of Spring to Summer's musky tribes;
Nor hyacinths, of purest Virgin white,
Low bent and blushing inward, nor jonquils,
Of potent fragrance; nor narcissus fair,
As o'er the fabled fountain hanging still;
Nor broad carnations, nor gay-spotted pinks;
Nor, showered from every bush, the damask-rose:
Infinite numbers, delicacies, smells,
With hues on hues expression cannot paint,
The breath of Nature and her endless bloom.

JAMES THOMSON, *The Seasons*
[1730]

FORMAL GARDENS

The word is unfortunate and seems not to have been used before being adopted by Sir Reginald Blomfield in his The Formal Garden in England *(1892). In our time the word has even more misleading connotations.*

I am frankly and absolutely for a formal garden. This may turn you away from me, but I hope not. Once and all I declare against the thing called 'landscape-gardening', and cleave to classic precedents. Note the high tone I take in this matter. With a house like mine there is really some excuse for seeking to ignore it, and developing a garden that shall be independent of architecture so dreadful; but no, I will be just; my garden shall shame my house by its correct proportions and proper adherence to what a garden ought to be. Not that this garden is classic – far from that; I wish it was. But it is a garden, no mere feeble deception. It is a small piece of ground enclosed by walls; and, concerning those walls, you are in no doubt for one moment. There is not the least attempt to imitate natural scenery. There are no winding walks, no boskages, no sylvan dells, no grottoes stuck with stones and stalactites. My garden is simply an artificial, but none the less beautiful, arrangement of all the best plants that I can contrive to collect.

Consider the word 'garden.' It develops by evolution from the Anglo-Saxon 'geard' and the Middle English 'garth'. It means 'a yard'. It has rather less than nothing to do with wild nature, or any other sort of nature. It is a highly artificial contrivance within hard and fast boundaries. We speak of a zoological garden, a garden of pleasure, a garden of vegetables. To talk of a 'natural' or a 'wild' garden, is a contradiction in terms. You might as well talk of a natural 'zoo,' and do away with the bars, and arrange bamboo brakes for the tigers, mountain-tops for the eagles and an iceberg for the polar bears.

EDEN PHILLPOTTS, *My Garden*
[1906]

IMAGINARY
GARDENS

One of the most famous of all garden descriptions.

Close to the Gates a spacious Garden lies,
From Storms defended and inclement Skies:
Four Acres was th'allotted Space of Ground,
Fenc'd with a green Enclosure all around.
Tall thriving Trees confest the fruitful Mold;
The red'ning Apple ripens here to Gold,
Here the blue Figg with luscious Juice o'erflows,
With deeper Red the full Pomegranate glows,
The Branch here bends beneath the weighty Pear,
And verdant Olives flourish round the Year.
The balmy Spirit of the Western Gale
Eternal breathes on Fruits untaught to fail:
Each dropping Pear a following Pear supplies,
On Apples Apples, Figs on Figs arise:
The same mild Season gives the Blooms to blow,
The Buds to harden, and the Fruits to grow.

Here order'd Vines in equal Ranks appear,
With all th'United Labours of the Year.
Some to unload the fertile Branches run,
Some dry the black'ning Clusters in the Sun,
Others to tread the liquid Harvest join,
The groaning Presses foam with Floods of Wine.
Here are the Vines in early Flow'r descry'd,
Here Grapes discolour'd on the Sunny Side,
And there in *Autumn's* richest Purple dy'd.

Beds of all various Herbs, for ever green,
In beauteous Order terminate the Scene.

Two plenteous Fountains the whole Prospect crown'd;
This thro' the Gardens leads its Streams around,
Visits each Plant, and waters all the Ground:
While that in Pipes beneath the Palace flows,
And thence its Current on the town bestows;
To various Use their various Streams they bring,
The People one, and one supplies the King.

HOMER, *Odyssey*, translated by
Alexander Pope [1725–6]

Sylvester (1563–1618) translated the French Huguenot poet Du Bartas's La Semaine *into English. The poem describes the seven days of the*

Creation story in which the Garden of Eden assumes the guise of a geometrical Northern Renaissance garden.

> Heer, unerneath a fragrant hedge reposes,
> Full of all kinds of sweet all-coloured Roses,
> Which (one would think) the angels daily dresse
> In true love-knots, tri-angles, lozenges.
>   Anon he walketh in a levell lane,
> On eyther side beset with shady Plane,
> Whose archèd boughs, for Frize and Cornich bear
> Thick groves, to change from future change of air:
> Then in a path impal'd, in pleasant wise,
> With sharp-sweet Orange, Limon, Citron trees;
> Whose leavie twigs, that intricately tangle,
> Seem painted walls, whereon true fruits do dangle.
>   Now in a plenteous orchard planted rare
> With un-graft trees, in checker, round and square:
> Whose goodly fruits so on his will do wait,
> That plucking one, another's ready straight:
> And having tasted all (with due satiety)
> Finds all one goodness, but in taste variety.
>
>   Du Bartas, *Divine Weekes and*
>   *Workes*, translated by Joshua
>   Sylvester [1606]

A Border of Beds

The description of a garden in this torrid love-poem embedded in the Old Testament was to be a fruitful source for gardenists over the centuries.

> A garden inclosed is my sister, my spouse; a spring
> shut up, a fountain sealed.
>   Thy plants are an orchard of pomegranates, with
> pleasant fruits; camphire, with spikenard,
>   Spikenard and saffron; calamus and cinnamon,
> with all trees of frankincense; myrrh and aloes, with
> all the chief spices:
>   A fountain of gardens, a well of living waters, and
> streams from Lebanon.
>   Awake, O north wind; and come, thou south; blow
> upon my garden, that the spices thereof may flow out.
> Let my beloved come into his garden, and eat his
> pleasant fruits.   The Song of Solomon

Milton's description of Eden became a prime text for the exponents of the landscape movement. No one would have been more surprised than the poet.

> Southward through *Eden* went a River large,
> Nor chang'd his course, but through the shaggie hill
> Pass'd underneath ingulft, for God had thrown
> That Mountain as his Garden mound high rais'd

Upon the rapid current, which through veins
Of porous Earth with Kindly thirst up drawn,
Rose a fresh fountain, and with many a rill
Water'd the Garden; thence united fell
Down the steep glade, and met the neather Flood,
Which from his darksom passage now appeers,
And now divided into four main Streams,
Runs divers, wandring many a famous Realme
And Country whereof here needs no account,
But rather to tell how, if Art could tell,
How from that Saphire Fount the crisped Brooks,
Rowling on orient Pearl and sands of Gold,
With mazie error under pendant shades
Ran Nectar, visiting each plant, and fed
Flours worthy of Paradise which not nice Art
In Beds and curious Knots, but Nature boon
Pow'r'd forth profuse on Hill and Dale and Plaine,
Both where the morning Sun first warmly smote
The open field, and where the unpierc't shade
Imbround the noontide Bowrs: Thus was this place,
A happy rural seat of various view;
Groves whose rich Trees wept odorous Gumms and Balme,
Others whose fruit burnisht with Golden Rinde
Hung amiable, *Hesperian* Fables true,
If true, here onely, and of delicious taste:
Betwixt them Lawns, or level Downs, and Flocks
Grasing the tender herb, were interpos'd,
Or palmie hilloc, or the flourie lap
Of som irriguous Valley spred her store,
Flours of all hue, and without Thorn the Rose:
Another side, unbrageous Grots and Caves
Of coole recess, ore which the mantling Vine
Layes forth her purple Grape, and gently creeps
Luxuriant; mean while murmuring waters fall
Down the slope hills, disperst, or in a Lake,
That go to the fringed Bank with Myrtle crown'd,
Her chrystall mirror holds, unite their streams.

JOHN MILTON, *Paradise Lost*,
Book IV [1667]

A minor industry now surrounds the inner meaning of The Wind in the Willows. *It remains, however, a delightful read as exemplified by this description of Mole's garden.*

The Mole struck a match, and by its light the Rat saw that they were standing in an open space, neatly swept and sanded underfoot, and directly facing them was Mole's little front door, with 'Mile End' painted, in gothic lettering, over the bell-pull at the side.

Mole reached down a lantern from a nail on the wall and lit it, and the Rat, looking round him, saw that they were in a sort of fore-court. A garden-seat

stood on one side of the door, and on the other, a roller; for the Mole, who
was a tidy animal when at home, could not stand having his ground kicked
up by other animals into little runs that ended in earth-heaps. On the walls
hung wire baskets with ferns in them, alternating with brackets carrying
plaster statuary – Garibaldi, and the infant Samuel, and Queen Victoria, and
other heroes of modern Italy. Down one side of the fore-court ran a skittle-
alley, with benches along it and little wooden tables marked with rings that
hinted at beer-mugs. In the middle was a small round pond containing
goldfish and surrounded by a cockle-shell border. Out of the centre of the
pond rose a fanciful erection clothed in more cockle-shells and topped by a
large silvered glass ball that reflected everything all wrong and had a very
pleasing effect.

> KENNETH GRAHAME, *The Wind in the Willows* [1908]

I'd like to have been around on any of these occasions!

INDOOR GARDENS

The arrangement of the plants in the rooms is various, and depends on the
kind of rout or entertainment. In common cases they are placed in recesses,
and on side-tables, and near glasses which may reflect them; and a few choice
specimens are scattered over the floor as single objects. But in more select
entertainments, a proportionate attention is paid to their arrangement.
During dinner a few pots of fruit-bearing shrubs, or trees with their fruit
ripe, are ranged along the centre of the table, from which, during the dessert,
the fruit is gathered by the company. Sometimes a row of orange trees, or
standard peach trees, or cherries, or all of them, in fruit, surround the table
of the guests; one plant being placed exactly behind each chair, leaving room
for the servants to approach between. Sometimes only one small handsome
tree is placed behind the master, and another behind the mistress; and
sometimes only a few pots of lesser articles are placed on the side-board, or
here and there round the room . . .

The drawing-room is sometimes laid out like an orange-grove by distributing tall orange trees all over it in regular quincunx, so that the heads of
the trees may be higher than those of the company: seats are also neatly made
over the pots and boxes, to conceal them, and serve the purpose of chairs.
One or two cages with nightingales and canary-birds are distributed among
the branches, and where there is a want of real fruit, that is supplied by art.
Sometimes also art supplies the entire tree, which during artificial illumination is hardly recognized as a work of art, and a very few real trees and
flowers interspersed with these made ones, will keep up the odour and the
illusion to nature.

Sometimes large picture galleries are laid out in imitation of parks in the
ancient or modern style, with avenues or with groups and scattered trees. At
masqued routs, caves and grottos are formed under conical stages, and
covered with moss and pots of trees, in imitation of wooded hills. In short,
there is no end to the arrangement of plants at routs: and the reader is not to
suppose that only real plants with roots are necessary for this purpose; for,
provided a few of these be judiciously introduced, all the rest can be effected
by branches of box, laurustinus, laurel, juniper, holly, &c., decorated with
artifical flowers and fruits, and fitted to stems or trunks to answer either as
trees or shrubs; and besides these, whole pine and fir trees, the spruce
especially, can be cut over, and thus admirable groves formed in a short time.

Artificial supplies of odour of the rose, the orange, or the jasmine, are readily supplied. Much romantic splendour may be produced in this way with little expense of green-house plants. JOHN CLAUDIUS LOUDON, *The Green-house Companion* [1824]

ITALIAN GARDENS

An Englishman looks at Italian gardens through the eyes of the landscape movement and finds them deficient. Smollett (1721–1771) records the radical shift in taste from Evelyn's eulogies a century before (see pp. 338–9)

I shall now hazard my thoughts upon the gardens of this country, which the inhabitants extol with all the hyperboles of admiration and applause . . . In a fine extensive garden or park, an Englishman expects to see a number of groves and glades intermixed with an agreeable negligence, which seems to be the effect of nature and accident. He looks for shady walks encrusted with gravel; for open lawns covered with verdure as smooth as velvet, but much more lively and agreeable: for ponds, canals, basins, cascades and running streams of water; for clumps of trees, woods and wildernesses, cut into delightful alleys, perfumed with honey-suckle and sweet briar, and resounding with the mingling melody of all the singing birds of heaven. He looks for plats of flowers in different parts to refresh the sense, and please the fancy; for arbours, grottoes, hermitages, temples, and alcoves, to shelter him from the sun, and afford him means of contemplation and repose; and he expects to find the hedges, groves, and walks, and lawns kept with the utmost order and propriety. He who loves the beauties of simple nature, and the charms of neatness, will seek for them in vain amidst the groves of Italy.

In the garden of the Villa Pinciana, there is a plantation of four hundred pines, which the Italians view with rapture and admiration. There is likewise a long walk of trees extending from the garden gate to the palace; and plenty of shade, with alleys and hedges in different parts of the ground. But the groves are neglected; the walks are laid with nothing but common mould or sand, black and dusty; the hedges are tall and shabby; the trees stunted; the open ground, brown and parched, has scarce any appearance of verdure. The flat regular alleys of evergreens are cut into fantastic figures; the flower-gardens embellished with their cypress and flourished figures in box, while the flowers grow in rows of earthen pots, and the ground appears as dusty as if it was covered with the cinders of a blacksmith's forge.

The water, of which there is great plenty, instead of being collected in large pieces, or conveyed in little rivulets and streams, to refresh the thirsty soil, or managed so as to form agreeable cascades, is squirted from fountains in different parts of the garden, through tubes little bigger than common glyster-pipes. It must be owned, indeed, that the fountains have their merit in the way of sculpture and architecture; and that here is a great number of statues which merit attention. But they serve only to encumber the ground, and destroy that effect of rural simplicity which our gardens are designed to produce. In a word, here we see a variety of walks, and groves, and fountains, a wood of four hundred pines, a paddock with a few meagre deer, a flower-garden, an aviary, a grotto, and a fish-pond and in spite of all these particulars, it is, in my opinion, a very contemptible garden, when compared to that of Stowe in Buckinghamshire, or even to those of Kensington and Richmond.

The Italians understand, because they study, the excellencies of art; but they have no idea of the beauties of nature.

TOBIAS SMOLLETT, *Travels in France
and Italy* [1766]

The American writer Edith Wharton (1862–1937) looks at Italian gardens through transatlantic eyes at the turn of the century. She was in fact wrong that Italian gardens were almost flowerless.

Though it is an exaggeration to say that there are no flowers in Italian gardens, yet to enjoy and appreciate the Italian garden-craft one must always bear in mind that it is independent of floriculture.

The Italian garden does not exist for flowers; its flowers exist for it: they are a late and infrequent adjunct to its beauties, a parenthetical grace counting only as one more touch in the general effect of enchantment. This is no doubt partly explained by the difficulty of cultivating any but spring flowers in so hot and dry a climate, and the result has been a wonderful development of the more permanent effects to be obtained from the three other factors in garden-composition – marble, water and perennial verdure – and the achievement, by their skillful blending, of a charm independent of the seasons.

It is hard to explain to the modern garden-lover, whose whole conception of the charm of gardens is formed of successive pictures of flower-loveliness, how this effect of enchantment can be produced by anything so dull and monotonous as a mere combination of clipped green and stone work.

The traveler returning from Italy, with his eyes and imagination full of the ineffable Italian garden-magic, knows vaguely that the enchantment exists; that he has been under its spell, and that it is more potent, more enduring, more intoxicating to every sense than the most elaborate and glowing effects of modern horticulture; but he may not have found the key to the mystery. Is it because the sky is bluer, because the vegetation is more luxuriant? Our midsummer skies are almost as deep, our foliage is as rich, and perhaps more varied; there are, indeed, not a few resemblances between the North American summer climate and that of Italy in spring and autumn.

Some of those who have fallen under the spell are inclined to ascribe the Italian garden-magic to the effect of time; but, wonder-working as this undoubtedly is, it leaves many beauties unaccounted for. To seek the answer one must go deeper: the garden must be studied in relation to the house, and both in relation to the landscape. The garden of the Middle Ages, the garden one sees in old missal illuminations and in early woodcuts, was a mere patch of ground within the castle precincts, where 'simples' were grown around a central well-head and fruit was espaliered against the walls. But in the rapid flowering of Italian civilization the castle walls were soon thrown down, and the garden expanded, taking in the fish pond, the bowling green, the rose arbor and the clipped walk. The Italian country house, especially in the center and the south of Italy, was almost always built on a hillside, and one day the architect looked forth from the terrace of his villa, and saw that, in his survey of the garden, the enclosing landscape was naturally included: the two formed a part of the same composition.

The recognition of this fact was the first step in the development of the great garden art of the Renaissance: the next was the architect's discovery of

the means by which nature and art might be fused in his picture. He had now three problems to deal with: his garden must be adapted to the architectural lines of the house it adjoined; it must be adapted to the requirements of the inmates of the house, in the sense of providing shady walks, sunny bowling greens, parterres and orchards, all conveniently accessible; and lastly it must be adapted to the landscape around it. At no time and in no country has this triple problem been so successfully dealt with as in the treatment of the Italian country house from the beginning of the sixteenth to the end of the eighteenth century; and in the blending of different elements, the subtle transition from the fixed and formal lines of art to the shifting and irregular lines of nature, and lastly in the essential convenience and livableness of the garden, lies the fundamental secret of the old garden-magic.

EDITH WHARTON, *Italian Villas and their Gardens* [1904]

IRREGULAR
GARDENS

Sir Henry Wootton (1568–1639) was our ambassador to Venice under James I and responsible for promoting most things Italian in England. He was an early apostle of the winding and meandering which was not to catch on until the following century.

First, I must note a certaine contrarietie betweene *building* and *gardening*: For as Fabriques should bee *regular*, so Gardens should bee *irregular*, or at least cast into a very wilde *Regularitie*. To exemplifie my conceit; I have seene a *Garden* (for the manner perchance incomparable) into which the first Accesse was a high walke like a *Tarrace*, from whence might bee taken a generall view of the whole *Plott* below but rather in a delightfull confusion, then with any plaine distinction of the pieces. From this the *Beholder* descending many steps, was afterwards conveyed againe, by severall *mountings* and *valings*, to various entertainments of his *sent*, and *sight*: which I shall not neede to describe for that were poeticall) let me onely note this, that every one of these diversities, was as if hee had beene *Magically* transported into a new Garden.

SIR HENRY WOOTTON, *The Elements of Architecture* [1624]

JACOBEAN
GARDENS

One of the best descriptions of a Jacobean garden I know occurs in a masque presented by the students of Gray's Inn at court in January 1614, on the occasion of the notorious marriage of the King's favourite, Somerset, to the divorced Frances Howard. Francis Bacon is said to have footed the bill for it.

The traverse being drawn, was seen a garden of a glorious and strange beauty, cast into four quarters, with a cross-walk and alleys, compassing each quarter. In the middle of the cross-walk stood a goodly fountain raised on four columnes of silver; on the tops whereof stood four statues of silver, which supported a bowl, in circuit containing four-and-twenty foot, and was raised from the ground nine foot in height; in the middle whereof, upon scrolls of silver and gold, was plac'd a globe, garnished with four golden mask-heads, out of the which issued water into the bowl; above stood a golden Neptune, in height three foot, holding in his hand a trident, and riding on a dolphin so cunningly framed that a river seemed to stream out of his mouth.

The garden-walls were of brick artificially painted in perspective, all along which were placed fruit-trees with artificial leaves and fruit. The garden within the wall was railed about with rails of three foot high, adorned with balusters of silver, between which were placed pedestals, beautified with transparent lights of variable colours; upon the pedestals stood silver columns, upon the tops whereof were personages of gold, lions of gold, and unicorns of silver; every personage and beast did hold a torchet burning, that gave light and lustre to the whole fabrique.

Every quarter of the garden was finely hedged about with a low hedge of cypress and juniper; the knots within set with artificial green herbs, embellished with all sorts of artificial flowers. In the two first quarters were two pyramids garnished with gold and silver, and glistering with transparent lights, resembling carbuncles, sapphires and rubies. In every corner of each quarter were great pots of gilly-flowers, which shadowed certain lights placed behind them, and made a resplendent and admirable lustre.

The two further quarters were beautified with tulips of divers colours, and in the corners of the said quarters were set great tufts of several kinds of flowers, receiving lustre from several lights placed behind them.

At the further end of the garden was a mount raised by degrees resembling banks of earth covered with grass; on the top of the mount stood a goodly arbour substantially made, and covered with artificial trees and with arbour-flowers, as eglantine, honeysuckles, and the like.

The arbour was in length three-and-thirty foot, in height one-and-twenty, supported with terms of gold and silver; it was divided into six double arches, and three doors answered to the three walks of the garden. In the middle part of the arbour rose a goodly large turret, and at either end a smaller.

Upon the top of the mount on the front thereof was a bank of flowers curiously painted, behind which, within the arches, the Masquers sat unseen. Behind the garden over the top of the arbour were set artificial trees, appearing like an orchard joining to the garden, and over all was drawn in perspective a firmament like the skies in a clear night.

> ANONYMOUS, *The Masque of Flowers* [1614]

KITCHEN GARDENS

Few garden achievements match those of the kitchen garden whose produce can be consumed. The eulogies fall thick and fast.

I have always thought a Kitchin-garden a more pleasant Sight, than the finest Orangerie, or artificial Green-house. I love to see every Thing in its Perfection, and am more pleased to survey my Rows of Colworts and Cabbages, with a thousand nameless Pot-herbs, springing up in their full Fragrancy and Verdure, than to see the tender Plants of foreign Countries kept alive by artificial Heats, or withering in an Air and Soil that are not adapted to them.

> JOSEPH ADDISON, *The Spectator*, No. 477, 6 September 1712

. . . can the Garden afford any thing more delightful to view than those forests of asparagus, artichokes, lettuce, pease, beans and other legumes and edulous plants so different in colour and of such various shapes, rising as it were from the dead and piercing the ground in so many thousand places as they do, courting the admiration or requiring the care of the diligent Gardiner.

STEPHEN SWITZER, *The Practical Gardiner* [1727]

If well managed, nothing is more beautiful than the kitchen garden: the earliest blossoms come there: we shall in vain seek for flowering shrubs in March, and early in April, to equal the peaches, nectarines, apricots, and plums; late in April, we shall find nothing to equal the pear and the cherry; and, in May, the dwarf, or espalier, apple-trees, are just so many immense garlands of carnations. The walks are unshaded: they are not greasy or covered with moss, in the spring of the year, like those in the shrubberies: to watch the progress of crops is by no means unentertaining to any rational creature; and the kitchen-garden gives you all this long before the ornamental part of the garden affords you any thing worth looking at.

WILLIAM COBBETT, *The English Gardener* [1829]

It is an enthusiasm shared across the Atlantic.

It was one of the most bewitching sights in the world to observe a hill of beans thrusting aside the soil, or a row of early peas just peeping forth sufficiently to trace a line of delicate green. Later in the season the humming-birds were attracted by the blossoms of a peculiar variety of bean; and they were a joy to me, those little spiritual visitants, for deigning to sip airy food out of my nectar-cups. Multitudes of bees used to bury themselves in the yellow blossoms of the summer-squashes. This, too, was a deep satisfaction; although, when they had laden themselves with sweets, they flew away to some unknown hive, which would give back nothing in requital of what my garden had contributed. But I was glad thus to fling a benefaction upon the passing breeze with the certainty that somebody must profit by it, and that there would be a little more honey in the world to allay the sourness and bitterness which mankind is always complaining of. Yes, indeed; my life was the sweeter for that honey. . . .

But not merely the squeamish love of the beautiful was gratified by my toil in the kitchen garden. There was a hearty enjoyment, likewise, in observing the growth of the crook-necked winter squashes, from the first little bulb, with the withered blossom adhering to it, until they lay strewn upon the soil, big, round fellows, hiding their heads beneath the leaves, but turning up their great, yellow rotundities to the noon-tide sun. Gazing at them, I felt that by my agency something worth living for had been done. A new substance had been born into the world. They were real and tangible existences, which the mind could seize hold of, and rejoice in. A cabbage, too, – especially the early Dutch cabbage, which swells to a monstrous circumference, until its ambitious heart often bursts asunder – is a matter to be proud of when we can claim a share with the earth and sky in producing it. But, after all, the highest pleasure is reserved until these vegetable children of ours are smoking on the table, and we, like Saturn, make a meal of them.

NATHANIEL HAWTHORNE, *Mosses from an Old Manse* [1845]

LANDSCAPE GARDENS

The advocates of the landscape style were adept at dipping their pens in venom and assassinating its predecessor. This anti-formal diatribe was dedicated to Charles Howard, 3rd Earl of Carlisle (1674–1738), creator of Castle Howard.

Before the House you view a large *Parterre*,
Not crouded with the Trifles brought from far:
No Borders, Alleys, Edgings spoil the Scene,
'Tis one unvary'd piece of Pleasing Green:
No starv'd Exoticks here lament their Fate,
Fetter'd and bound like Pris'ners of State:
Or as *Diogenes* in Tub confin'd,
Wishing like him th'enlivening Sun to find.
'Tis ornamented by the Sculpture's Hand,
Here Statues, Obilisks, and Vases stand.
Beyond 'tis circled by a pleasant Grove,
Rais'd from the Family of constant Love:
No boist'rous Storms, nor an inclement Sky,
Which tender Leaves, and springing Buds destroy,
Affect the Sombre Shade you here enjoy;
Perpetual Verdure all the Trees disclose,
Which like true Love no Change of Seasons knows . . .

ANONYMOUS, *Castle Howard* [c. 1733]

Those who attempted to squeeze what was a quart-sized garden style into a pint-pot plot were easily subject to ridicule.

But the triumph of his genius was seen in the disposition of his gardens, which contain every thing in less than two acres of ground. At your first entrance, the eye is saluted with a yellow serpentine river, stagnating through a beautiful valley, which extends near twenty yards in length. Over the river is thrown a bridge, *partly in the chinese manner*, and a little ship with sails spread and streamers flying, floats in the midst of it. When you have passed this bridge, you enter into a grove perplexed with errors and crooked walks; where having trod the same ground over and over again, through a labyrinth of horn-beam hedges, you are led into an old hermitage built with roots of trees, which the squire is pleased to call St Austin's cave. Here he desires you to repose yourself, and expects encomiums on his taste; after which a second ramble begins through another maze of walks, and the last error is much worse than the first. At length, when you almost despair of ever visiting daylight any more, you emerge on a sudden into an open and circular area, richly chequered with beds of flowers, and embellished with a little fountain playing in the centre of it. As every folly must have a name, the squire informs you, that *by way of whim* he has christened this place *little*

Mary bon; and the upper end of which you are conducted into a pompous, clumsy and gilded building, said to be a temple, and consecrated to Venus; for no other reason which I could learn, but because the squire riots here sometimes in vulgar love with a couple of orange-wenches, taken from the purlieus of the playhouse.
FRANCIS COVENTRY in *The World*, No. 15 [1753]

Whole villages were swept away to create these landscape parks, the inhabitants being re-housed to suit the scene. The result could be bleak . . .

No village dames and maidens now are seen,
But madams, and the misses of the green!
Farm-house, and farm too, are in deep disgrace,
'Tis now the lodge, the cottage, or the place!
Or if a farm, *ferme ornée* is the phrase
And if a cottage, of these modern days,
Expect no more to see the straw-built shed,
But a fantastic villa in its stead
Pride, thinly veil'd in mock humility;
The name of cot, without its poverty
By affectation, still with thatching crown'd;
By affectation, still with ivy bound;
By affectation, still the mantling vine
The door-way and the window-frames entwine;
The hawthorn bow'rs, and benches near the grove
Give place to temples, and the rich alcove:
A naked Venus here, a Bacchus there,
And mimic ruins, kept in good repair;
The real rustic's sweet and simple bounds,
Quick-set and garden, chang'd to pleasure-grounds,
And the fresh sod, that form'd the pathway green,
The strawberry bed, and currant-bush between
The honey-suckle hedge and lily tall,
Yield to the shrubbery and high-rais'd wall;
Then for exotics of botanic fame,
Of which the lady scarcely knows the name;
Yet, as with country friend she goes the round,
She christens them with words of learned sound.
The wall, in foreign fruits so rich and fine,
Forms the dessert, when farmer-gentry dine
And then for water geese and ducks no more
Have leave to puddle round a modern door;
Fair on the glassy lake they sail in state,
And seem to know a prouder change of fate;
From thence, on china serv'd, they grace the dish,
And vie in honours with the silver fish.
THE REVEREND SAMUEL JACKSON PRATT [c.1780]

The American Washington Irving (1783–1830) responds to the landscape tradition in its Regency phase.

Nothing can be more imposing than the magnificence of English park scenery. Vast lawns that extend like sheets of vivid green, with here and there clumps of gigantic trees, heaping up rich piles of foliage; the solemn pomp of groves and woodland glades, with the deer trooping in silent herds across them; the hare, bounding away to the covert; or the pheasant, suddenly bursting upon the wing: the brook, taught to wind in natural meanderings, or expand into a glassy lake: the sequestered pool, reflecting the quivering trees, with the yellow leaf sleeping on its bosom, and the trout roaming fearlessly about its limpid waters, while some rustic temple or sylvan statue, grown green and dank with age, gives an air of classic sanctity to the seclusion.

These are but a few of the features of park scenery; but what most delights me is the creative talent with which the English decorate the unostentatious abodes of middle life. The rudest habitation, the most unpromising and scanty portion of land, in the hands of an Englishman of taste, becomes a little paradise.

With a nicely discriminating eye, he seizes at once upon its capabilities, and pictures in his mind the future landscape. The sterile spot grows into loveliness under his hand; and yet the operations of art which produce the effect are scarcely to be perceived. The cherishing and training of some trees; the cautious pruning of other; the nice distribution of flowers and plants of tender and graceful foliage; the introduction of a green slope of velvet turf; the partial opening to a peep of blue distance, or silver gleam of water: all these are managed with a delicate tact, a pervading yet quiet assiduity, like the magic touchings with which a painter finishes up a favourite picture.

WASHINGTON IRVING, *Rural Life in England* in *The Sketch Book* [1820]

GARDENS OF LOVE

The garden to which John Donne (1573–1631) resorted for solace was that of Lucy Harington, Countess of Bedford (1582–1627), at Twickenham Park, planted early in the reign of James I.

> Blasted with sighs, and surrounded with teares,
>   Hither I come to seeke the spring,
>   And at mine eyes, and at mine eares,
>   Receive such balmes, as else cure every thing;
>   But O, selfe traytor, I do bring
> The spider love, which transubstantiates all,
>   And can convert Manna to gall,
> And that this place may thoroughly be thought
>   True Paradise, I have the serpent brought.
>
> 'Twere wholsomer for mee, that winter did
>   Benight the glory of this place,
>   And that a grave frost did forbid
> These trees to laugh, and mocke mee to my face;
>   But that I may not this disgrace

Indure, nor yet leave loving, Love let mee
    Some senslesse peece of this place bee;
Make me a mandrake, so I may groane here,
    Or a stone fountaine weeping out my yeare.

Hither with christall vyals, lovers come,
    And take my teares, which are loves wine,
    And try your mistresse Teares at home,
For all are false, that tast not just like mine;
    Alas, hearts do not in eyes shine,
Nor can you more judge womans thoughts by teares,
    Than by her shadow, what she weares.
O perverse sexe, where none is true but shee,
    Who's therefore true, because her truth kills me.

JOHN DONNE, *Twickenham Garden*

The Irish poet Thomas Moore (1779–1852) takes up the theme two centuries later.

I have a garden of my own,
    Shining with flowers of every hue;
I loved it dearly while alone,
    But I shall love it more with you:
And there the golden bees shall come,
    In summer time at break of morn,
And wake us with their busy hum
    Around the Siha's fragrant thorn.

I have a fawn from Aden's land,
    On leafy buds and berries nursed;
And you shall feed him from your hand,
    Though he may start with fear at first.
And I will lead you where he lies
    For shelter in the noon-tide heat;
And you may touch his sleeping eyes,
    And feel his little silvery feet.

THOMAS MOORE, *The Casket*
[1835]

MANOR GARDENS

THE MANOR GARDEN

The fountains are dry and the roses over.
Incense of death. Your day approaches.
The pears fatten like little buddhas.
A blue mist is dragging the lake.

You move through the era of fishes,
The smug centuries of the pig –
Head, toe and finger
Come clear of the shadow. History

Nourishes these broken flutings,
These crowns of acanthus,
And the crow settles her garments.
You inherit white heather, a bee's wing,

Two suicides, the family wolves,
Hours of blankness. Some hard stars
Already yellow the heavens.
The spider on its own string

Crosses the lake. The worms
Quit their usual habitations.
The small birds converge, converge
With their gifts to a difficult borning.

SYLVIA PLATH [1932–63]

MEDIEVAL GARDENS

Alexander of Neckham (born 1157) was the first Englishman to write about gardens.

. . . the garden should be adorned with roses and lilies, the turnsole (heliotrope), violets, and mandrake; there you should have parsley, cost, fennel, southern-wood, coriander, sage, savory, hyssop, mint, rue, dittany, smallage, pellitory, lettuces, garden-cress, and peonies.

There should also be beds planted with onions, leeks, garlic, pumpkins and shallots. The cucumber growing in its lap, the drowsy poppy, the daffodil and brank-ursine (acanthus) ennoble a garden. Nor are there wanting, if occasion further thee, pottage-herbs: beets, herb-mercury, orache, sorrel and mallows, anise, mustard, white pepper and wormwood (absinth) do good service to the gardener.

A noble garden will give thee also medlars, quinces, warden-trees, peaches, pears of St Riole, pomegranates, lemons (citron apples), oranges (golden apples), almonds, dates, which are the fruit of palms, and figs. I make no mention of ginger and gariofiliae, cinnamon . . . Virgae Sabae distilling incense, myrrh, aloe and lavender, resin, storax and balsaam, and Indian laburnam.

Saffron and sandyz will not be absent, if thou wilt follow our counsel. Who has not experienced the virtues of thyme and pennyroyal?

ALEXANDER OF NECKHAM,
Of the Nature of Things

Chaucer (1340?–1400), however, at the close of the fourteenth century gives us our most evocative glimpses. Here Criseyde goes out into the town garden of a great lord accompanied by her ladies-in-waiting.

Adoun the steyre anoon-right tho she went
Into the gardin, with her nices three,
And up and down ther madé amny a wente,
Flexippé she, Tharbe, and Antigone,
To pleyen, that it joyé was to see;

And othere of hir women, a great route,
Hir folwede in the gardin al about.

This yerd was large, and rayléd alle the aleyes,
And shadwed wel with blosmy bowés grene,
And benchéd newe, and sonded alle the weyes,
In which she walketh arm in arm betwene;
Til at the last Antigoné the shene
Gan on a trojan song to singé clere,
That it an heven was her voys to here . . .

The dayés honour, and the hevenes ye,
The nightés fo, al this clepe I the sonne,
Gan westren faste, and dounward for to wrye,
As he that hadde his dayés cours y-ronne;
And whyté thingés wexen dimme and donne
For lak of light, and sterres for to appere,
That she and al hir folk in wente y-fere.

GEOFFREY CHAUCER, *Troilvs and
Criseyde*, Book II: 117, 118, 130

*This is the first mention in English poetry of a man taking pleasure in his
garden.*

When passéd was almost the month of May,
And I had roméd al the someres day,
The grené medew, of which that I yow tolde,
Upon the fresshé daysy to beholde,
And that the sonne out of the south gan weste,
And closéd was the flour and goon to reste
For derkness of the night, of which she dredde,
Hoom to myn hous ful swiftly I me spedde;
And in the litel erber that I have,
Y-benchéd new with turvés fresshe y-grave,
I bad men shuldé me my couché make;
For deyntee of the newé someres sake,
I bad hem strowé flourés on my bed.
When I was layd, and had myn eyen hed,
I fel a-slepe within an houre or two.

GEOFFREY CHAUCER, *The Legend of
Good Women*, Text A (lines 89–103)

*And here Chaucer lists off the flowers in a medieval garden and registers
the appreciation of both their colour and scent.*

Ther sprang the violete al newe,
And fresshe pervinke riche of hewe,
And floures yelowe, whyte and rede:
Swich plentee grew ther never in mede.
Ful gay was al the ground, the queynt

And poudred, as men had it peynt,
With many a fresh and sondry flour,
That casten up a ful good savour.

GEOFFREY CHAUCER, *Romaunt de la
Rose* (line 1431)

Only Nancy Mitford (1904–1972) could do it.

NON-U GARDENS

Planes was a horrible house. It was an overgrown cottage, that is to say, the rooms were large, with all the disadvantages of a cottage, low ceilings, small windows with diamond panes, uneven floorboards, and a great deal of naked knotted wood. It was furnished neither in good nor in bad taste, but simply with no attempt at taste at all, and was not even very comfortable. The garden which lay around it would be a lady water-colourist's heaven, herbaceous borders, rockeries, and water-gardens were carried to a perfection of vulgarity, and flaunted a riot of huge and hideous flowers, each individual bloom appearing twice as large, three times as brilliant as it ought to have been and if possible of a different colour from that which nature intended. It would be hard to say whether it was more frightful, more like glorious Technicolor, in spring, in summer, or in autumn. Only in the depth of winter, covered by the kindly snow, did it melt into the landscape and become tolerable.

One April Saturday morning, in 1937, Linda, with whom I had been staying in London, took me down there for the night, as she sometimes did, I think she liked to have a buffer between herself and the Kroesigs, perhaps especially between herself and Moira. The old Kroesigs were by way of being very fond of me, and Sir Leicester sometimes took me for walks and hinted how much he wished that it had been me, so serious, so well educated, such a good wife and mother, whom Tony had married.

We motored down past acres of blossom.

'The great difference,' said Linda, 'between Surrey and proper, real country, is that in Surrey, when you see blossom, you know there will be no fruit. Think of the Vale of Evesham, and then look at all this pointless pink stuff – it gives you quite a different feeling. The garden at Planes will be a riot of sterility, just you wait.'

It was. You could hardly see any beautiful, pale, bright yellow-green of spring, every tree appeared to be entirely covered with a waving mass of pink or mauve tissue-paper. The daffodils were so thick on the ground that they too obscured the green, they were new varieties of a terrifying size, either dead white or dark yellow, thick and fleshy; they did not look at all like the fragile friends of one's childhood. The whole effect was of a scene for musical comedy, and it exactly suited Sir Leicester, who, in the country, gave surprisingly adequate performance of the old English squire. Picturesque. Delightful.

He was pottering in the garden as we drove up, in an old pair of corduroy trousers, so much designed as an old pair that it seemed improbable that they had ever been new, an old tweed coat on the same lines, secateurs in his hand, a depressed Corgi at his heels, and a mellow smile on his face.

'Here you are,' he said, heartily. (One could almost see, as in the strip advertisements, a bubble coming out of his head – thinks – 'You are a most unsatisfactory daughter-in-law, but nobody can say it's our fault, we always have a welcome and a kind smile for you.') 'Car going well, I hope? Tony and Moira have gone out riding, I thought you might have passed them. Isn't the garden looking grand just now, I can hardly bear to go to London and leave all this beauty with no one to see it. Come for a stroll before lunch – Foster will see to your gear – just ring the front-door bell, Fanny, he may not have heard the car.'

He led us off into Madam Butterfly-land.

NANCY MITFORD, *The Pursuit of Love* [1947]

NURSERY GARDENS
Nurseries in some form or other go back to the Elizabethan period and proliferated in the Victorian, coming under the critical gaze of those busybodies, the Loudons.

KNAPP HILL NURSERY; MR WATERER. AUGUST 6. – We had heard much in London, and from various gardeners in the country, of the splendid collection of new seedling azaleas which flowered here in June last, not one of which is yet given out to the trade; but, of course, at this season we could only see the foliage. Among other things we noted Andromeda arborea, 10 ft. high, and finely in flower; Vaccinium Arctostaphylos, the Madeira bilberry, 6 ft. high, and richly covered with fruit; another species, unknown, bearing very large fruit. Both species well deserve culture, where peat earth is not scarce, as fruits for tarts and for eating with cream, like other bilberries. Magnolia auriculata, very luxuriant; measured one of the leaves, and found it 22 in. long, and 11 in. wide. Lilium superbum, 10 ft. high, coming into flower. The great art in getting this species to flower well, as Mr Cameron of Bury Hill informed us, is to keep the bulbs single, by taking them up, separating, and replanting. It is evident that, by this practice, the greatest possible supply of nourishment will be obtained by each plant. Phlox Thomsoni, a new variety, in flower. Daphina collina, a variety with striped leaves. This nursery excells in the management of hedges, which are in some cases 8 or 10 ft. high, and not more than 8 or 10 in. thick: but, in general, it is not quite so neat and orderly as we could wish; and though we have never seen the weeds exceed the economic point, we would rather see weeding carried lower. We never yet knew a nursery or market-garden, where any money was made, that was not kept *orderly*, at all events, and most of them even *neatly*. We do not say that much is wanting at Knapp Hill; but still we should like to see both principles pushed farther; a good many of the old things grubbed up, the walks and compartments more correctly lined out, and no weeds ever suffered to grow above an inch high. We hint this with the more confidence, knowing that Mr Waterer will take it in good part, and that it will be in his favour with the hundreds of gardeners and gentlemen that will come from all quarters next June to see the bloom of new azaleas.

JOHN CLAUDIUS LOUDON, *Calls in Hertfordshire, Bedfordshire, Berkshire, Surrey, Sussex and Middlesex*, July– August 1829

OLD GARDENS
To these delights of a garden age may add a further interest which can hardly be distinguished from beauty, for the mind, at least with those who have the

historic instinct, is always longing to be connected with the past, and dreading for itself confinement upon the plane of time, delights in evidences of the long continuance of nations, families and institutions, in hale and vigorous old age, in long-settled peace beyond the turn of Fortune's wheel, the 'scornful dominion of Accident'. Restfulness is the prevailing note of an old garden; in this fairy world of echo and suggestion where the Present never comes but to commune with the Past, we feel the glamour of a Golden Age, of a state of society just and secure which has grown and blossomed as the rose. How few there are who are incapable of feeling the mysterious appeal of such a place – of the scenes which reflect upon us the passion and the happiness of bygone generations, the statues which gleam out under the deepening spell of the twilight like phantoms of old-world greatness, the still pools that slumber in the sunshine and call our spirits to their dreamland of abiding peace, the rippling music of the fountain, like trills of elfin laughter, and the hoarse water-voices that are hasting with passionate earnestness to the everlasting sea. But beyond all this there is a deeper mystery. In such scenes there is the same elusive suggestiveness that is found in the perfume of the flowers. That which is interesting is real, and the old garden is very real. It has the power of fixing attention, it grips you by the sleeve, it is instinct with a silent eloquence; you feel in the Spiritualist phrase that it is 'seeking to communicate', to open vistas into the past, that it has a secret to unfold, a message to deliver. What then is this secret of the old-world garden? This, – that it knows us well. We have come back to an earlier home, to scenes which are strangely familiar to us, to the life of former generations whose being was one with ours. Every living creature is adapted to its environment by changes in brain structure produced either by the natural selection of accidental variations or by multitudinous repetition of the same impressions and the same actions. It is this harmony with the surroundings which we feel upon entering an old house or garden; vague ancestral memories are faintly stirred and the sentiment which may attach to objects that have been habitual sources of enjoyment to generation after generation.

Sir George Sitwell, *On the Making of Gardens* [1909]

Chaucer's orchard includes a wonderful list of trees, flowers and spices: notémigges (nutmeg), alemandres (almond-trees), clow-gelofre (clove-pink), greyn de paradys (cardamom), canelle (cinnamon), setéwale (zedoary), coynes (quinces), chesteynés (chestnuts), notés (nuts) and aleys (semie-berries).

ORCHARD GARDENS

Ther were, and that I wot ful wel,
Of pomgarnettes a ful gret del;
That is a fruyt ful wel to lyke,
Namely to folk whan they ben syke.
And trees ther weré, greet foisoun,
That baren notes in hir sesoun,
Such as men notémigges calle,
That swote of savour been withalle.
And alemandres greet plentee,
Figés, and many a daté-tree

Ther weren, if men haddlé nede,
Through the yerd in length and brede.
There was eke wexing many a spyce,
As clow-gelofre, and licoryce,
Gingere, and greyn de paradys,
Canelle, and setéwale of prys,
And many a spycé delitable,
To eten whan men ryse fro table.
And many hoomly trees ther were,
That peches, coynes, and apples bere,
Medlers, ploumés, peres, chesteynés,
Cheryse, of whiché many on fayn is,
Notés, aleys, and bolas,
That for to seen it was solas.

GEOFFREY CHAUCER, *Romaunt de la
Rose* (lines 1349–98)

William Lawson (fl. 1618) waxes lyrical on the joys of an orchard.

The very works of, and in an Orchard and Garden, are better than the ease
and rest of and from other laboures. When God had made man after his
owne Image, in a perfect state, and would have him to represent himselfe in
authoritie, tranquilitie, and pleasure upon the Earth, He placed him in
Paradise. What was *Paradise?* But a Garden and Orchard of trees and
hearbs, full of all pleasure? and nothing there but delights. The gods of the
Earth, resembling the great God of heaven in authoritie, Majestie, and
abundance of all things, wherein is their most delight? And whether doe they
withdraw themselves from the troublesome affayres of their estate, being
tyred with the hearing and judging of litigious Controversies? choked (as it
were), with the close ayres of their sumptuous buildings, their stomacks
cloyed with varietie of Banquets, their eares filled and over-burthened with
tedious discoursings. Wither? but into their Orchards? made and prepared,
dressed and destinated for that purpose to renew and refresh their sences,
and to call home their over-wearied spirits. Nay, it is (no doubt) a comfort to
them, to set open their Cazements into a most delicate Garden and Orchard,
whereby they may not only see that, wherein they are so much delighted,
but also to give fresh, sweete, and pleasant ayre to their Galleries and
Chambers.

What can your eye desire to see, your eares to heare, your mouth to taste,
or your nose to smell, that is not to be had in an orchard?

WILLIAM LAWSON, *A New Orchard
and Garden* [1618]

PARSONAGE
GARDENS

*Canon Ellacombe (born 1822) paints a picture of a vanished
phenomenon, the rectory gardens of Victorian England.*

And a country parson without some knowledge of plants is surely as
incomplete as a country parsonage without a garden . . .

I need not describe the ideal English parsonage and its garden. It has been
described over and over again, and indeed it has passed into a proverb, so

that when a house is described as 'like an ordinary English parsonage', as Wordsworth's home is described, we know at once what it means. We picture to ourselves a building of moderate size – not pretentious – neither a mansion nor a suburban villa (*Parva sed apta domino* is the inscription on an old Wiltshire parsonage), and of an old foundation; yet with many additions and accretions of different dates, each bearing some impress of the successive owners; and the garden is of the same character, often standing (and always in the ideal parsonage garden) near the church and churchyard, so that the church forms the feature in the garden. The parsonage garden is not large, seldom exceeding two acres, and more often not exceeding one, with little glass, and no pretension to a high-class garden, but with a good spread of old lawn and many old trees and flowering shrubs, all suggestive of repose and quiet, pleasant shade, and freedom from the bustle of the outside world. The parsonage garden some years ago was a home for hundreds of good old-fashioned flowers, but I am afraid no gardens suffered more from the bedding craze, which swept them clear of all their old long-cherished beauties, and reduced them to the dull level of uniformity with their neighbour's gardens, or to miniature mockeries of Trentham or Cliveden. That craze has to a great extent passed away, and the parsonage gardens are gradually recovering their old features, and fortunately they are able to do so more easily than some other gardens, because in most of them the trees and shrubs were spared, and have been a valuable help in the restoration to a better and more healthy style of gardening, and one more in keeping with the character of the country parson's garden. There are hundreds of such good old gardens scattered throughout England, of which Charles Kingsley's garden at Eversley and White's garden at Selborne are well-known typical examples.

That such gardens are a real pleasure and refreshment to the owners we all know, and they are none the less so when the refreshment is taken in hard manual labour for many a country parson can bear witness that 'the very works of and in an orchard and garden are better than the ease and rest of and from other labores' (William Lawson, 1618). But I said also that parsonage gardens had their usefulness, by which I mean they may be made useful to the clergyman in his parochial work. How this may be done I need not say at any length, because the method that would be very useful in the hands of one would be perfectly useless in the hands of another. I would only say generally, that the love of flowers and gardening is so universal amongst the English peasantry that a country parson will often find a better introduction to a cottager through his garden than by any other means. And though the love of flowers is so universal, and the garden may be such a useful adjunct to the cottage, yet there is a very great ignorance of the right principles of gardening, and the parson may be of great use to his poorer neighbours, not only by teaching, but still more by showing them better ways in his own garden. For the parsonage garden gate should be always open, and every parishioner welcomed; there need to be no fear of any undue advantage being taken of the free permission to enter – the one difficulty will be to induce them to come in. And the parson may do much to brighten the gardens of his parish, and so to increse the interest in them by giving plants from his own garden. I have for many years been a cultivator of hardy plants, and have been able to gather together a large number of species; and I was long ago taught, and have always held, that it is impossible to get or keep a large collection except by constant liberality in giving. 'There is that scattereth, and yet increaseth,' was Solomon's experience, and it certainly is so with gardening; and the parson who is liberal with his plants will find the increase not only in the pleasant intercourse with his neighbours, but also in the enlargement of his own garden, which thus spreads beyond his own fences into the gardens of the cottages.

CANON ELLACOMBE, *In a Gloucestershire Garden* [1895]

And Rupert Brooke (1887–1915) remembers one before the holocaust of 1914 in a justly famous poem.

Just now the lilac is in bloom,
All before my little room;
And in my flower-beds, I think,
Smile the carnation and the pink;
And down the borders, well I know,
The poppy and the pansy blow . . .
Oh! there the chestnuts, summer through,
Beside the river make for you
A tunnel of green gloom, and sleep
Deeply above; and green and deep
The stream mysterious glides beneath,
Green as a dream and deep as death.

RUPERT BROOKE, *The Old Vicarage, Grantchester*, May 1912

PLEASURE GARDENS

Of these perhaps Vauxhall Gardens in Southwark were the most famous under the management of Jonathan Tyers in the eighteenth century with their music, supper boxes, pavilions and illuminations. From their beginning until their end, however, as both Pepys and Thackeray catch, there was always a seamy side not far below the surface.

. . . by water to Fox-hall and there walked in Spring garden; a great deal of company, and the weather and garden pleasant; that it is very pleasant and cheap going thither, for a man may go to spend what he will, or nothing, all as one – but to hear the nightingale and other birds, and here fiddles, and there a harp, and here a jews trump, and here laughing, and there fine people walking, is mighty divertising. Among others, there were two pretty women alone, that walked a great while: which [being] discovered by some idle gentlemen, they would needs take them up; but to see the poor ladies, how they were put to it to run from them, and they after them: and sometimes the ladies put themselves along with other company, then the others drew back; at last, the ladies did get off out of the house and took boat and away.

SAMUEL PEPYS, *Diary*, 28 May 1667

Although the gardens of Vauxhall have passed away as much as the gardens of Babylon, yet there is no need to describe what our young people saw on their visit to the first mentioned of these two places of splendid entertainment. Fond memory has not forgotten as yet all the delights and wonders of the Royal Gardens –

The hundred thousand extra lamps, which were always lighted; the fiddlers, in cocked-hats, who played ravishing melodies under the gilded cockleshell in the midst of the Gardens; the singers, both of comic and sentimental ballads, who charmed the ears there; the country dances, formed by bouncing cockneys and cockneyesses, and executed amidst jumping, thumping, and laughter; the signal which announced that Madame Saqui was about to mount skyward on a slack-rope ascending to the stars; the hermit that always sat in the illuminated hermitage; the dark walks, so favourable to the interviews of young lovers; the pots of stout handed about by the people in the shabby old liveries; and the twinkling boxes, in which the happy feasters made believe to eat slices of almost invisible ham . . .

WILLIAM MAKEPEACE THACKERAY,
Vanity Fair [1848]

Already twelve years before Dickens had recorded their squalid daylight reality.

We paid our shilling at the gate, and then we saw for the first time, that the entrance, if there had been any magic about it at all, was now decidedly disenchanted, being, in fact, nothing more nor less than a combination of very roughly-painted boards and sawdust. We glanced at the orchestra and supper-room as we hurried past . . . we just recognized them, and that was all.

We walked about, and met with a disappointment at every turn; our favourite views were mere patches of paint; the fountain that had sparkled so showily by lamp-light, presented very much the appearance of a water-pipe that had burst; all the ornaments were dingy, and all the walks gloomy. There was a spectral attempt at rope-dancing in the little open theatre; the sun shone upon the spangled dresses of the performers, and their evolutions were about as inspiriting and appropriate as a country-dance in a family vault.

CHARLES DICKENS, *Sketches by Boz* [1836]

Worse fates could befall the inmate of a Victorian gaol than becoming the governor's gardener.

PRISON GARDENS

The garden of the Reading Gaol well deserves notice in a work, the great object of which is to promote a taste for this art. It is, as may be supposed, small; but the governor had a taste not only for gardening, but for natural history. He has, on his lawn or grass plot, a beautiful piece of rockwork, composed of flints and fragments of rural antiquities. He has, also, a variety of plants of the choicest kinds, such as Wistaria, double furze, Ribes several species, Petunia phoenicea, and numerous pelargoniums, the whole mixed with fruit trees. Every advantage was taken of the high brick walls of the gaol for training vines and fruit trees. The governor had also a collection of fancy rabbits, a beautiful cockatoo, &c. The prisoners were watering the plants;

and we can only account for the neatness of the whole from the abundance of hands at the command of the master.

JOHN CLAUDIUS LOUDON, *Calls in Hertfordshire, Bedfordshire, Berkshire, Surrey, Sussex and Middlesex*, July–August 1829

PUBLIC GARDENS   *Municipal gardens were the invention of the Victorians, although this began its life as a royal one.*

LINES WRITTEN IN KENSINGTON GARDENS

In this lone, open glade I lie,
Screen'd by deep boughs on either hand;
And at its end, to stay the eye
Those black-crown'd, red-boled pine-trees stand!

Birds here make song, each bird has his,
Across the girdling city's hum.
How green under the boughs it is!
How thick the tremulous sheep-cries come!

Sometimes a child will cross the glade
To take his nurse his broken toy;
Sometimes a thrush flit overhead
Deep in her unknown day's employ.

Here at my feet what wonders pass,
What endless, active life is here!
What blowing daisies, fragrant grass!
An air-stirr'd forest, fresh and clear.

Scarce fresher is the mountain-sod
Where the tired angler lies, stretch'd out,
And, eased of basket and of rod,
Counts his day's spoil, the spotted trout.

In the huge world, which roars hard by,
Be others happy if they can!
But in my helpless cradle I
Was breathed on by the rural Pan.

I, on men's impious uproar hurl'd,
Think often, as I hear them rave,
That peace has left the upper world
And now keeps only the grave.

Yet here is peace for ever new!
When I who watch them am away,
Still all things in this glade go through
The changes of their quiet day.

Then to their happy rest they pass!
The flowers upclose, the birds are fed,
The night comes down upon the grass,
The child sleeps warmly in his bed.

Calm soul of all things! make it mine
To feel, amid the city's jar,
That there abides a peace of thine,
Man did not make, and cannot mar.

The will to neither strive nor cry,
The power to feel with others give!
Calm, calm me more! nor let me die
Before I have begun to live.

MATTHEW ARNOLD [1822–88]

A century later another poet encapsulates the mood.

THE PUBLIC GARDEN

Burnished, burned-out, still burning as the year
you lead me to our stamping ground
The city and its cruising cars surround
the Public Garden. All's alive –
the children crowding home from school at five,
punting a football in the bricky air,
the sailors and their pick-ups under trees
with Latin labels. And the jaded flock
of swanboats paddles to its dock.
The park is drying.
Dead leaves thicken to a ball
inside the basin of a fountain, where
the heads of four stone lions stare
and suck on empty fawcets. Night
deepens. From the arched bridge, we see
the shedding park-bound mallards, how they keep
circling and diving in the lanternlight,
searching for something hidden in the muck.
And now the moon, earth's friend, that cared so much
for us, and cared so little, comes again –
always a stranger! As we walk,
it lies like chalk
over the waters. Everything's aground.
Remember summer! Bubbles filled
the fountain, and we splashed. We drowned
in Eden, while Jehovah's grass-green lyre
was rustling all about us in the leaves
that gurgled by us, turning upside down . . .
The fountain's failing waters flash around
the garden. Nothing catches fire.

ROBERT LOWELL [1917–77]

ROCK GARDENS

Not one of my favourite garden types, I tend to share the views of those who regard rock gardens as bad taste.

Rustic work and rock work are, I consider, in the very worst taste, anywhere in front of a neat villa . . . you will see in front of fine establishments, where there is space for a grand style of promenade gardening, pyramids of brick planted with ferns and trailing plants, piles of stone and wild masses of shrub, even rustic arbours with thatched roofs, and sometimes a few garden seats . . . I could almost wish that ferns and rockeries had never become fashionable, when I see people pitch them down before the hall door, as if to intimate that they have built their house on the face of a cliff, to which they must look *down*, instead of *up*, and where the vegetation, which would prove delightful a few yards off, is an eyesore and an abortion.

SHIRLEY HIBBERD, *The Town Garden* [1859]

Reginald Farrer (1880–1920), the classic exponent of the rock garden, successfully kills them off in the following passage.

The ideal rock-garden must have a plan. But there are three prevailing plans, none of which are good. The first is what I may call the Almond-pudding scheme, and obtains generally, especially in the north of England. You take a round bed; you pile it up with soil; you then choose out the spikiest pinnacles of limestone you can find, and you insert them thickly with their points in the air, until the general effect is that of a tipsy-cake stuck with almonds. In this vast petrified porcupine nothing will grow except Welsh poppy, ferns and some of the uglier sedums. The second style is that of the Dog's Grave. It marks a higher stage of horticulture, and is affected by many good growers of alpines. The pudding-shape is more or less the same in both, but the stones are laid flat in the Dog's Grave ideal. Plants will grow on this, but its scheme is so stodgy and so abhorrent to Nature that it should be discarded. The third style is that of the Devil's Lapful, and prevailed very largely when alpines first began to be used out of doors. The finest specimens of this style are to be seen in such gardens as Glasnevin and Edinburgh. The plan is simplicity itself. You take a hundred or a thousand cartloads of bald square-faced boulders. You next drop them all about absolutely anyhow; and you then plant things amongst them. The chaotic hideousness of the result is something to be remembered with shudders ever after.

REGINALD FARRER, *My Rock Garden* [1907]

Added to which,

A CONCRETE EXAMPLE

My next-door neighbour, Mrs Jones,
Has got a garden full of stones:
A crazy path, a lily pond,
A rockery, and, just beyond,
A Sundial with a strange device,
Which Mrs Jones thinks rather nice.

My next-door neighbour, Mrs Jones,
Puts little plants between the stones.
They are so delicate and small
They don't mean anything at all.
I can't think how she gets them in,
Unless she plants them with a pin.

My next-door neighbour, Mrs Jones,
Once asked me in to see her stones.
We stood and talked about a flower
For quite a quarter of an hour.
'Where is this lovely thing?' I cried.
'You're standing on it,' she replied.

REGINALD ARKELL, *Green
Fingers* [1934]

*I'm not sure whether this poem is a send-up or not. On the whole, I regret
to think, the latter.*

At breakfast time on summer days
Our rockery is all ablaze
With mingled rose and mauve and white
To dazzle and enchant the sight;
It is not trimmed with tidy care
And little labels here and there
To point some almost hidden treasure
But heaped with overflowing measure
Of purple catmint, saxifrages,
Cerastrium in snowy stages,
While gorgeous in the sunlight glows
The colour of the Alpine rose,
The deepest, rarest pink that blesses
Only these flowers and silken dresses.
Then when the sun has mounted high
The rosy petals fall and die
Until the brilliant morning scene
In quiet mauve and white and green,
At eventide to fade away
Into a softly shaded grey.
But with the light of morning, lo!
Triumphant the rock roses glow:
New every day they tell their story
Of radiance and morning glory.

MARGARET LODGE, *Rock Roses*

*In this instance I have some sympathy with Beverley Nichols' arch enemy
Mrs M.*

Mrs M. stared at me with undisguised suspicion. 'Rock garden?' she cried.
'What do you mean . . . rock garden?'

'By a rock garden,' I replied, 'I mean a garden containing a quantity of rocks.'

'But you haven't any rocks.'

'Not yet . . . no.'

'Where are you going to get them?'

I had not the least idea where I was going to get them, so I said, in a sepulchral voice, 'They Are Coming,' rather as though the skies might open at any moment and deluge us with a cascade of boulders.

'Yes . . . but where from?'

'Yorkshire.' This was partly guess-work and partly memory, because I remembered reading in some book of a man who had a quarry of stone in Yorkshire which he used to export.

Mrs M. snorted again. 'That'll cost you a pretty penny,' she said. I could hear signs of fierce envy in her voice. She swung her string-bag backwards and forwards, and glared at my mountain. Then she said:

'But you're surely not just going to stuff a lot of rocks on all that mud?'

'Stuff them? No. I shan't stuff them.'

'Well . . . throw them, then. You've got to have some sort of design.'

'I have.'

'What is it?'

'It is being Done For Me,' I said.

'By whom?'

I could think of nobody but Sir Edwin Lutyens, who designed Delhi. So I said 'You will catch cold, Mrs M., if you stand in the wet grass.'

I am glad to be able to record that she did.

BEVERLEY NICHOLS, *Down the Garden Path* [1932]

ROOF GARDENS *A garden type to be pursued with caution, in case tons of earth and shattered containers descend through the bedroom ceiling.*

Many years ago, after I had given a lecture at the People's Palace, White-chapel, a rather shy, faltering individual came up to me and said: 'Would you like to see my garden?' I thought to myself: 'What kind of garden can he have right in the heart of the largest city in the world? How can anyone make anything which could be called a garden among all these great buildings?'

Presently he was leading me up and up flights and flights of stairs and through dark passage-ways to the top of a tenement building. There I saw a wonderful garden. The owner was a slight man with rather long grey hair thrust back in disorder almost like Beethoven. He had the fine, sensitive, serene face of the dreamer, one of those men who did unpractical things, the person people laugh at, but in the end, if they are fair-minded, learn to admire.

The whole flat roof of the building was a garden full of blooms and vegetables. Flowers of every kind seemed to be everywhere: plants growing on little shelves all over the place, cunningly constructed; many pots containing all sorts of plants, such as heliotropes, fuchsias, carnations, geraniums, and pinks, growing round the edges of boxes, with the flowers hanging down and filling the air with as rare a fragrance as ever one enjoyed in the country. All I could say was, 'How wonderful!' but he said apologetically: 'It is nothing. The air is not too good and the sun does not always shine, so that some plants are rather weak. It is not like the country.'

But there was evidence here of much loving care, infinite pains, and much patience. I watched how his hands touched his plants, how he fondled them with the sympathy of the enthusiast. He could not hide the touch of pride in his eyes. He told me with joy the history of every plant and its peculiarties, the abstinacy of this one, the thirst of that one, and the trickiness of yet another. There was not a square foot of space wasted. There was even a vegetable marrow which he showed me with great pride, growing in a box of earth close to the chimney wall and trained up trellis-work. As he said, 'There is plenty of room in the sky.'

This great amateur gardener told me how he had brought up each pail of earth, how he had required and gathered horse manure from the streets. He showed me the cunning device he had made for sprinkling his roof garden with a piece of hosepipe. He had his vegetable garden too; lettuces in boxes and radishes round the edges all seemed growing quite well, and in each corner of the boxes with mathematical precision he had a cabbage plant.

M. ALLWOOD, *The Nobodies* [1950]

ROSE GARDENS

Umbrella Rose Trainer

So, if it is to be a rose-garden, do not choose these stunted, unnatural, earth-loving strains, which have nothing of vigour and wilderness in them, nor banish other flowers which may do homage to the beauty of a rose as courtiers to a queen. Let climbing roses drop in a veil from the terrace and smother with flower-spangled embroidery the garden walls, run riot over vaulted arcades, clamber up lofty obelisks of leaf-tangled trellis, twine themselves round the pillars of a rose-roofed temple, where little avalanches of sweetness shall rustle down at a touch and the dusty gold of the sunshine shall mingle with the summer snow of the flying petals. Let them leap in a great bow or fall in a creamy cataract to a foaming pool of flowers. In the midst of the garden set a statue of Venus with a great bloom trained to her hand, or of Flora, her cornucopia overflowing with white rosettes, or a tiny basin where leaden *amorini* seated upon the margin are fishing with trailing buds. If the place be away from the house and surrounded by forest trees, let there be a rose balloon weighed down by struggling cupids, or the hollow ribs and bellying curves of an old-world ship with ruddy sail and cordage flecked with ivory blossom, or one of those rose-castles which the French romance gave to the garden for a mimic siege in May, low towers of carpenter's work with flanking turrets and iron-studded postern. Such a *Château d'Amour* is represented on many a mediaeval casket and mirror-case. Ponderous mangonels are bombarding the fortress with monstrous blossoms, while from the battlements fair ladies hurl down roses still heavy with morning dew full in the faces of the attacking knights.

SIR GEORGE SITWELL, *On the Making of Gardens* [1909]

SCENTED
GARDENS

Eleanour Sinclair Rohde was the apostle of both herb and scented gardens between-the-wars. Here she explains her discovery of scent in the garden of a great-aunt.

When I think of scented gardens I remember hers first and foremost, for though since those days I have seen many gardens, I do not think I have ever seen a pleasanter, homelier one. The house was Georgian, and the short drive to it was flanked on both sides by pollarded lime trees. (I have only to shut my eyes to hear the hum of the bees now.) The drive was never used by the household nor indeed by anyone who came on foot, for the shortest way from the village was through a gate leading from the road to a side door. The path was perfectly straight, and bordered on either side by very broad beds, and except in midwinter they were full of scent and colour. I can see the big bushes of the pale pink China roses and smell their delicate perfume; I see the tall old-fashioned delphiniums and the big red peonies and the clumps of borage, the sweet-williams, the Madonna and tiger lilies and the well-clipped bushes of lad's love. Before the time of roses I remember chiefly the Canterbury bells and pyrethrums, and earlier still the edge nearest the path was thick with wallflowers and daffodils. I have never seen hollyhocks grow as they grew at the back of those borders, and they were all single ones, ranging from pale yellow to the deepest claret. Beyond this path, on one side was the big lawn with four large and very old mulberry trees. As a child it frequently struck me that considering how small mulberries were compared to apples, plums and so forth, it was really little short of a miracle what a glorious mess one could get into with them in next to no time. Amongst the flowers great-aunt Lancilla loved most were evening primroses. I have never since then seen a large border, as she had, entirely given to them. She used to pick the flowers to float in finger bowls at dinner.

ELEANOUR SINCLAIR ROHDE,
The Scented Garden [1931]

SECRET GARDENS

Gardens and gardening loom large in the archetypal battlings for power between Lucia and Miss Mapp. In this encounter the parameters are neatly set between the contending women.

'My little plot,' said Miss Mapp. 'Very modest, as you see, three-quarters of an acre at the most, but well screened. My flower-beds: sweet roses, tortoise-shell butterflies. Rather a nice clematis. My Little Eden I call it, so small, but so well loved.'

'Enchanting!' said Lucia, looking round the garden before mounting the steps up to the garden-room door. There was a very green and well-kept lawn, set in bright flower-beds. A trellis at one end separated it from a kitchen-garden beyond, and round the rest ran high brick walls, over which peered the roofs of other houses. In one of these walls was cut a curved archway with a della Robbia head above it.

'Shall we just pop across the lawn,' said Miss Mapp, pointing to this, 'and peep in there while Withers brings our tea? Just to stretch the – the limbs, Mrs Lucas, after your long drive. There's a wee little plot beyond there which is quite a pet of mine. And here's sweet Puss-Cat come to welcome my friends. Lamb! Love-bird!'

Love-bird's welcome was to dab rather crossly at the caressing hand which its mistress extended, and to trot away to ambush itself beneath some fine hollyhocks where it regarded them with singular disfavour.

'My little secret garden,' continued Miss Mapp as they came to the archway. 'When I am in here and shut the door, I mustn't be disturbed for anything less than a telegram. A rule of the house: I am very strict about it. The tower of the church keeping watch, as I always say, over my little nook, and taking care of me. Otherwise not overlooked at all. A little paved walk round it, you see, flower-beds, a pocket-handkerchief of a lawn, and in the middle a pillar with a bust of good Queen Anne. Picked it up in a shop here for a song. One of my lucky days.'

'Oh Georgie, isn't it too sweet?' cried Lucia. 'Un giardino segreto. Molto bello!'

E. F. BENSON, *Mapp and Lucia*
[1931]

I heard this first as a serial on 'Children's Hour'. It still retains its magic.

Mary had stepped close to the robin, and suddenly the gust of wind swung aside some loose ivy trails, and more suddenly still she jumped towards them and caught them in her hand. This she did because she had seen something under them – a round knob which had been covered by the leaves hanging over it. It was the knob of a door.

She put her hands under the leaves and began to pull and push them aside. Thick as the ivy hung, it nearly all was a loose and swinging curtain, though some had crept over wood and iron. Mary's heart began to thump and her hands to shake a little in her delight an excitement. The robin kept singing and twittering away and tilting his head on one side, as if he were an excited as she was. What was this under her hands which was square and made of iron and which her fingers found a hole in?

It was the lock of the door which had been closed ten years, and she put her hand in her pocket, drew out the key, and found it fitted the keyhole. She put the key in and turned it. It took two hands to do it, but it did turn.

And then she took a long breath and looked behind her up the long walk to see if anyone was coming. No one was coming. No one ever did come, it seemed, and she took another long breath, because she could not help it, and she held back the swinging curtain of ivy and pushed back the door which opened slowly – slowly.

Then she slipped through it, and shut it behind her, and stood with her back against it, looking about her and breathing quite fast with excitement, and wonder, and delight.

She was standing *inside* the secret garden.

It was the sweetest, most mysterious-looking place anyone could imagine. The high walls which shut it in were covered with the leafless stems of climbing roses, which were so thick that they were matted together. Mary Lennox knew they were roses because she had seen a great many roses in India. All the ground was covered with grass of a wintry brown, and out of it grew clumps of bushes which were surely rose-bushes if they were alive. There were numbers of standard roses which had so spread their branches that they were like little trees. There were other trees in the garden, and one of the things that made the place look strangest and loveliest was that climbing roses had run all over them and swung down long tendrils which made light swaying curtains, and here and there they had caught at each other or at a far-reaching branch and had crept from one tree to another and made lovely bridges of themselves. There was neither leaves nor roses on them now, and Mary did not know whether they were dead or alive, but their thin grey or brown branches and sprays looked like a sort of hazy mantle spreading over everything, walls, and trees, and even brown grass, where they had fallen from their fastenings and run along the ground. It was this hazy tangle from tree to tree which made it look so mysterious. Mary had thought it must be different from other gardens which had not been left all by themselves so long; and, indeed, it was different from any other place she had ever seen in her life.

'How still it is!' she whispered. 'How still!'

Then she waited a moment and listened at the stillness. The robin, who had flown to his tree-top, was still as all the rest. He did not even flutter his wings; he sat without stirring and looked at Mary.

'No wonder it is still,' she whispered again, 'I am the first person who has spoken in here for ten years.'

She moved away from the door, stepping as softly as if she were afraid of awakening someone. She was glad that there was grass under her feet and that her steps made no sound. She walked under one of the fairy-like arches between the trees and looked up at the tendrils and sprays which formed them.

'I wonder if they are all quite dead,' she said. 'Is it all a quite dead garden? I wish it wasn't.'

But she was *inside* the wonderful garden, and she could come through the door under the ivy at any time, and she felt she had found a world all her own.

The sun was shining inside the four walls and the high arch of blue sky over this particular piece of Misselthwaite seemed even more brilliant and soft than it was over the moor. The robin flew down from his tree-top and hopped about or flew after her from one bush to another. He chirped a good deal and had a very busy air, as if he were showing her things. Everything was strange and silent, and she seemed to be hundreds of miles away from anyone, but somehow she did not feel lonely at all. All that troubled her was her wish that she knew whether all the roses were dead, or if perhaps some of them had lived and might put out leaves and buds as the weather got warmer. She did not want it to be a quite dead garden. If it were a quite alive garden, how wonderful it would be, and what thousands of roses would grow on every side!

Her skipping-rope had hung over her arm when she came in, and after she had walked about for a while she thought she would skip round the whole garden, stopping when she wanted to look at things. There seemed to have been grass paths here and there, and in one or two corners there were alcoves of evergreen with stone seats or tall moss-covered flower-urns in them.

As she came near the second of these alcoves she stopped skipping. There had once been a flower-bed in it, and she thought she saw something sticking out of the black earth – some sharp little pale green points. She remembered what Ben Weatherstaff had said, and she knelt down to look at them.

'Yes, they are tiny growing things and they *might* be crocuses or snow-drops or daffodils,' she whispered.

She bent very close to them and sniffed the fresh scent of the damp earth . . .   FRANCES HODGSON BURNETT,
The Secret Garden [1907]

SUNKEN GARDENS

Very much a garden type of this century.

THE SUNKEN GARDEN

Speak not – whisper not;
Here bloweth thyme and bergamot;
Softly on the evening hour,
Secret herbs their spices shower,
Dark-spiked rosemary and myrrh,
Lean-stalked, purple lavender;
Hides within her bosom, too,
All her sorrows, bitter rue.

Breathe not – trespass not;
Of this green and darkling spot,
Latticed from the moon's beams,
Perchance a distant dreamer dreams;
Perchance upon its darkening air,
The unseen ghosts of children fare,
Faintly swinging, sway and sweep,
Like lovely sea-flowers in its deep;
While, unmoved to watch and ward
'Mid its gloomed and daisied sward
Stands with bowed and dewy head
That one little leaden Lad.

     WALTER DE LA MARE [1873–1956]

TOWN GARDENS

Philemon Holland (1551–1636) provides a lively account in Elizabethan English of Roman town gardens in his translation of Pliny the Elder (AD 23–79)

In all the twelve tables throughout which containe our ancient lawes of Rome, there is no mention made so much as once of a Grange or Ferme-house, but evermore a garden is taken in that signification, and under the title of Hortus (*i.e.* Garden) is comprised Hoeredium, that is to say, an Heritage or Domaine; and hereupon grew by consequence, a certain religious or ridiculous superstition rather, of some, whom we see ceremoniously to sacre and bless their garden and hortyard dores onely, for to preserve them against the witchcraft and socerie of spightfull and envious persons. And therefore they use to set up in gardens, ridiculous and foolish images of Satyres, Antiques, and such like as good keepers and remedies against envie and witchcraft; howsoever *Plautus* assigneth the custodie of gardens to the protection of the Goddess *Venus*. And even in these our daies, under the name of Gardens and Hortyards, there goe many daintie places of pleasure within the very citie; and under the colour and title of them men are

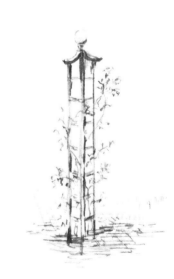

possessed of faire closes and pleasant fields, yea, and of proper houses with a good circuit of ground lying to them, like pretie fermes and graunges in the countrey: all which, they tearme by the name of gardens. The invention to have gardens within a citie came up first by *Epicurus*, the Doctor and master of all voluptuous idlenes, who devised such Gardens of pleasance in Athens: for before his time, the manner was not in my citie, to dwell (as it were) in the countrey, and so to make citie and countrey all one, but all their Gardens were in the villages without. Certes at Rome, a good Garden and no more was thought a poor man's chievance; it went (I say) for land and living. The Garden was the poore commoner's shambles, it was all the market-place he had for to provide himselfe of victuals . . .

That quarter of the Garden which serveth our house with poignant hearbs instead of sauce, to give a commendable tast and seasoning to our meat, sheweth plainly that the master and mistresse thereof were not woont to run in the Merchants' bookes for Spicerie, but chaunged the Grocer or Apoth-ecaries' shop, for the Garden . . . And as for the other quarters set out with beds of floures and sweet smelling hearbes, what reckoning was made of them in old time may appeare by this, that a man could not heretofore come by a commoner's house within the citie, but he should see the windowes beautified with greene quishins (cushions) wrought and tapissed with floures of all colours, resembling daily to their view the Gardens indeed which were in out-villages, as being in the very heart of the citie, they might think themselves in the countrey. Let us give therefore to Gardens their due honor; and let us not, (I say) deprive things of their credit and authoritie, because they are common and nothing costly, for I may tell you, some of our nobilitie, yea, and the best part of the citie, have not distain'd to take their surnames from thence . . . in the noble house and lineage of the Valerii, some were not abashed nor ashamed to be called Lactuncini in regard to the best kind of Lectuce that they either had in their gardens or affected most. And here I cannot chuse but mention by the way, the grace that hath growne to our name by occasion of some diligence employed and gaines taken this way; whereby certain cherries beare our name and are called Pliniana, in testimonie of our affection and love to that fruit.

PLINY THE ELDER, *The Natural History*, Book XIX, chap. iv [translated 1601]

Thomas Fairchild (1667?–1729), nurseryman and florist, wrote a book on town gardens describing which plants would prosper as 'everything will not prosper . . . because of the smoke of the sea-coal'.

I find that most persons whose business requires them to be constantly in town, will have something of a garden at any rate. One may guess the general love my fellow citizens have of gardening, in furnishing their rooms and chambers with basons of flowers and Bough pots, rather than not have something of a garden before them. THOMAS FAIRCHILD, *The City Gardener* [1722]

The town garden was largely a phenomenon of the eighteenth century when the new London squares were laid out with houses all of which had rectangular gardens behind them.

Ev'n in the stifling bosom of the town,
A garden, in which nothing thrives, has charms
That soothes the rich possessor; much consol'd,
That here and there some sprigs of mournful mint,
Or nightshade, or valerian, grace the well
He cultivates . . .
What are the casements lin'd with creeping herbs,
The prouder sashes fronted with a range
Of orange, myrtle, or the fragrant weed,
The Frenchman's darling? are they not all proofs
That man, immur'd in cities, still retains
His inborn inextinguishable thirst
Of rural scenes, compensating his loss
By supplemental shifts, the best he may?
The most unfurnish'd with the means of life,
And they that never pass their brick-wall bounds,
To range the fields and treat their lungs with air,
Yet feel the burning instinct: over head
Suspend their crazy boxes, planted thick
And water'd duly. There the pitcher stands
A fragment, and the spoutless tea-pot there;
Sad witness how close-pent man regrets
The country, with what ardour he contrives
A peep at Nature, when he can no more.

WILLIAM COWPER, *The Task*   [1785]

THE DESERTED GARDEN

There is a garden in our square,
    And householders can have the key,
    On payment of an annual fee;
        Yet no one enters there!

From August till the first of May,
    This garden is an empty place;
    No puppy-dogs their tails may chase,
        No children romp and play!

Here faithful pug or Pekinese
    With chain and collar must be led,
    Lest he disturb some flower-bed
        That no one ever sees!

Here ragged urchins from the street
  Peer through the bars with wistful eyes
  On a deserted Paradise,
    Untrod by children's feet!

Some day, I know, with guilty grin,
  That garden gate I shall unlock,
  Collect this squalid little flock
    And lead them gaily in!

And, 'spite of by-laws and decrees,
  Poor Ponto's collar I'll detach,
  And let him run about and scratch,
    And scamper at his ease!

What matter then that neighbours glare
  At happy dog or grubby boys,
  If somebody at last enjoys
    The garden in our square?

HARRY GRAHAM [1874–1936]

HER GARDEN

My grandmother grew tiny grapes and tiger-lilies,
But there is no sentimental cut to her garden
Through a fat album or remembered lane;
Only interior voyages made on London ferries

Paddling the Thames' wicked brew to Silvertown,
Where regular as boot boys, the factories
Blacked her house every day, obscured the skies
And the town's sweet name at the railway station.

Between ships parked at the end of the road
And factory gates, she kept her home against soot,
Kept her garden colours in spite of it –
Five square feet of bitterness in a paved yard

Turned to the silent flowering of her will,
Loaded with dusty beauty and natural odours,
Cinnamon lilies, and the vine roots hanging grapes,
Sour as social justice, on the wash-house wall.

FREDA DOWNIE [1929–]

VICTORIAN
GARDENS

Percy Lubbock takes us on a tour of the Victorian garden at its height. This one was in Norfolk.

It was superb, the great lawn at Earlham – it really was. I have described how it was lifted up, almost to the level, I should think, of the first-floor windows, by a steep bank of shaven grass, but there was a considerable expanse on the lower level too, before you reached the bank. On this lower lawn, to right and left, there was a fantastic medley of flower-beds, cut in queer shapes, coils and lozenges and loops; and the gardener's fancy ran strangely riot, year by year, in selecting and disposing the flowers that filled them. Geraniums roasting-red, French marigolds orange and mahogany-coloured, the tomato-note of waxen begonias, exotic herbage all speckled and pied and ring-staked, dahlias, calceolarias – they were marshalled and massed together, they fought it out as they would. But indeed they were mastered by the sunshine, by the blaze of light in which they flashed and twinkled; and they fell back, right and left, leaving a wide space of clear clean grass unbroken. And then there rose before you the green bank, so steep that I wonder how the mowing-machine contrived to sidle along it and keep it thus smoothly shaven.

To me, as I gained the crest of the bank, it seemed as though the huge flat of the lawn stretched away and ahead for a mile; so serene, so steady and peaceful . . .

Ah, but none the less I have found what I was looking for; it *can* be found after all, and not only in dreams. It was just a flash of sensation, not more, but I recognized it at once. Wait however – wait and look nearer at the flower-beds, which lie in a rambling cluster, you remember, under the lip of the steep bank of grass. Their coiling serpentine forms are all confused in the darkness, but I can easily thread the narrow grassy paths that separate each from each. The bright colours of the geraniums and the salvias are veiled by night; the brightest red and blue, even the flaring orange of the marigolds, are softened and obscured so that you hardly notice them among the deep grey of the tufts and bushes. But wait – the scent of the night-flower leads me on, where the narrow way between the beds goes turning and twisting. And there – where this morning you saw nothing but tall stalks, broad leaves, drooping and discoloured flower-trumpets, look now! Pure and cool and snow-white the clear stars have opened with the fall of the dusk, was, with nothing to break its even greenness till the eye, sweeping far, reached the shrubberies and trees that bordered it about. The broad silence made nothing of such trivialities as a lawn-tennis net, a few croquet hoops; they were lost in the quiet plain. Beyond it the horizon was bounded by clumped oaks, by dim woods more distant; out there was the park, and you could catch sight of the cows swinging their tails in the deep pasture. On either hand was a dense thicket, with an edging of bright flowers – a straight edge, on this side and that, so that the lawn was a great square. From the further side of it the view of the house was beautifully mellow and kindly, with its long rows of old windows and its high chimney-stacks. But that comes later; at this hour of the morning I should not set out on the journey across the lawn; I should turn aside to the thickets and shrubberies, to the shadowy corners and recesses of which there were so many to choose from . . . and whiter and whiter they grow as the night deepens. This is the flower which sends that wave of fragrance into the stillness, the flower that shines in the garden at Earlham from dusk to dawn. Far into an August night, till the first quiver of day-break stirs the hush of the darkness, the white stars hang motionless on their tall stalks, facing the sky. With the daylight they droop and fall; but in August the morning already delays, there are long hours after

midnight before the polar clouds begin to catch the advancing light. Till then the night-flower blooms in its white splendour, awake and alone.

PERCY LUBBOCK, Earlham [1922]

Disraeli's late novel Lothair *captures the Victorian cult of the olde worlde garden with its bastions of yew and cascades of traditional flowers. It is an evocation of the antithesis of the High Victorian bedding style.*

In the pleasure-grounds of Brentham were the remains of an ancient garden of the ancient house that had long ago been pulled down. When the modern pleasure-grounds were planned and created, notwithstanding the protests of the artists in landscape, the father of the present Duke would not allow this ancient garden to be entirely destroyed, and you came upon its quaint appearance in the dissimilar world in which it was placed, as you might in some festival of romantic costume upon a person habited in the courtly dress of the last century.

It was formed upon a gentle southern slope, with turfen terraces walled in on three sides, the fourth consisting of arches of golden yew. The Duke had given the garden to Lady Corisande, in order that she might practise her theory that flower-gardens should be sweet and luxuriant, and not hard and scentless imitations of works of art. Here, in their season, flourished abundantly all those productions of Nature which are now banished from our once delighted senses: huge bushes of honeysuckle, and bowers of sweet-pea and sweetbriar and jessamine, clustering over the walls, and gillyflowers scenting with their sweet breath the ancient bricks from which they seemed to spring. There were banks of violets, which the southern breeze always stirred, and mignonette filled every vacant nook.

As they entered now, it seemed a blaze of roses and carnations, though one recognized in a moment the presence of the lily, the heliotrope, and the stock. Some white peacocks were basking on the southern wall, and one of them, as their visitors entered, moved and displayed its plumage with scornful pride. The bees were busy in the air, but their homes were near, and you might watch them labouring in their glassy hives.

BENJAMIN DISRAELI, Lothair [1870]

VILLA GARDENS   *Already in the reign of George IV we have a type of garden which was to proliferate on a huge scale through the century. For Shenstone and The Leasowes, the somewhat strange source of its inspiration, see pp. 307–8.*

A PROVINCIAL VILLA GARDEN

LIME GROVE, 1828

I have erected a lofty and fanciful verandah – In the front is a small plot of Grass, and a figure of Flora or Pomona, about 3 feet high and elevated about 6 feet from the ground. At the back is a large rusticated Oaken Chair, and over that against the wall is a Sarcophagus in painted marble with this Inscription:

To

the creative Genius & amiable qualities of

SHENSTONE

in grateful remembrance of the intense delight I experienced at least half a Century ago, on my first visit to the Leasowes, and the pleasant recollections subsequently enjoyed . . . In the course of the next Season this monument will be embedded in Ivy, and will then exhibit its proper character.

The leading feature of the Garden next to the Lawn, and its decorations, consists of two bold and serpentine Walks somewhat parallel and reaching from top to bottom, the intersecting Walks at the extremes forming corners which are all of them raised as high as the size will admit, and filled with every variety of Evergreens and the bolder flowers which would less suit narrow borders. The undulations in the surface give a relief to the whole and may not unjustly be considered as producing the imaginary effect of so many Lilliputian Earthquakes.

Adjoining the yard are two beds about 10 yards wide & reaching all across and these form my little Orchard. They slope rapidly in consequence of a Turf embankment in front and contain as many Damson, Pear, and Plum Trees, as the space will allow, with a hedge of Filberts along the back. Last year we had a great abundance of Fruit, as much as we could consume and a considerable supply for winter preserves, but the produce this Season failed altogether . . .

I am no Florist, at least not a Scientific one, but I have enough independence of mind to judge for myself without asking the self-named Connoiseurs when I must be pleased and when I must criticize what they are pleased to denounce as the inferior works of Nature. All have their characteristic beauties & in my parterre, the humble Cowslip, or the unpretending Foxglove finds as hearty a welcome as the Crown Imperial or the Stately and exuberant Holyoake.

On this principle I have never felt any partiality for Hot or Green Houses — in my estimation, they violate the simplicity of Nature which constitutes the matchless & indescribable charm of a well-arranged garden. Formal beds of Anemonies & Tulips are therefore ill adapted to my Taste, variety of contrast being infinitely preferable. I have had an exquisite display of Tulips, but all scattered in little Clumps — the colours left to chance, and one year produced as fine a shew of Brompton Stocks as perhaps ever Garden contained.

JAMES LUCOCK, *My House and Garden (in manuscript)* [1828]

WHITE GARDENS

A fashion promoted above all by the famous one at Sissinghurst and now sadly a garden cliché.

The most beautiful all-white garden I ever saw was at Broadlands, in the days before the Mountbattens had it, when it was still the home of Lady Mount Temple. It was, and still is, the dream of a house, with wide lawns sloping down to a river which was curved like the neck of a swan. The white garden lay at about a quarter of a mile from the house, enclosed on all sides by walls of old red brick, and when one entered through the little gate one might have exclaimed that it was 'a veritable fairyland', if one were in the habit of using such expressions. It was laid out informally, with one very wide irregular border, which looked like a snow-drift in high summer — white delphiniums, drifts of white campanulas, white phlox, white Shirley poppies, phalanxes of white Madonna lilies rising from pools of white dianthus. The walls were a riot of that lovely rose, Madame Alfred Carrière, side by side with a magnificent old magnolia, whose white blossoms shone like lamps in the green leaves. On the furthest wall she had disposed a flight of white pigeons, which remained strangely still as though in a trance, which was hardly surprising as they were made of china.

BEVERLEY NICHOLS, *Garden Open Today* [1963]

PART
IV

ELEMENTS

A quintessential element in any Elizabethan, and later, garden.   ARBOUR

> I saw the object of my pining thought
>   Within a garden of sweete nature's placing,
> Wherein an arbour, artificiall wrought,
>   By workeman's wondrous skill the garden gracing,
> Did boast his glorie, glorie farre renowned,
>   For in his shadie boughs my Mistres slept,
> And, with a garland of his branches crowned,
>   Her daintie forehead from the sunne ykept.
>
> Thomas Watson, The Tears of
Fancie [1593]

Henry VIII built one at Nonsuch Palace, the forebear of many that   BANQUETING
adorned the gardens of Tudor and Stuart England. Even in those days,   HOUSE
minus the telephone, they had 'to get away from it all'.

Arbours, Benches, and Seats are very necessary, being present expedients for them that are weary, but that which Crowns the pleasures of a Garden is a place of repose, where neither Wind, Rain, Heat, nor cold can annoy you.

This small Edifice, usually term'd a Pleasure-house or Banqueting-house, may be made at some remote Angle of your Garden: For the more remote it is from your house, the more private will you be from the frequent disturbances of your Family or Acquaintance, and being made at an Angle part within your Garden and part without, you will have the priviledges and advantages of Air and View, which otherwise you will want, and which render it much more pleasant than to be without them.

The Windows and Doors, the one or other respecting every Coast, may be beglazed with the best and most transparent Glass, to represent every Object through it the more splendid, with Skreene of printed and painted Sarcenet, to prevent in the day, and shutters of thin Wainscot, in the Night, others from disturbing your Solitary repose.

Also you may reap the pleasure and advantage of the Air from either Coast, by opening that side of your small Ediface, from whence you would receive it, excluding on the other side that which might otherwise annoy you.

John Worlidge, Systema
Horticulturae [1677]

BEDDING PLANTS   *E. A. Bowles (1865–1954), who gave his name to many a plant, describes their use in a way now only seen in municipal parks.*

I remember a garden of twenty years ago that was the most bedded out I ever saw. Thousands of bedding plants were prepared for planting out in Summer, but always in straight lines in long, straight borders. It all began at the stable gates, and ran round three sides of the house, and continued in unbroken sequence, like Macbeth's vision of kings, for two sides of a croquet lawn, and then rushed up one side and down the other of a long path starting at right angles from the middle of the lawn, and if you began at the gates with blue lobelia, Mrs Pollock Pelargonium, Perilla, Yellow Calceolaria, and some Scarlet Pelargoniums in ranks according to their relative stature, so you continued for yards, poles, perches, furlongs, or whatever it was . . . and so you ended up when the border brought you back again to the lawn. I once suggested 'Why not paint the ground in stripes and have the effect all the year round, even if snow had to be swept off sometimes.'

E. A. BOWLES, *My Garden in Summer* [1914]

BEEHIVES   *Beehives, now a rare garden sight, were included in all early gardens.*

Store of Bees, in a dry and warme Bee-house, comely made of Fir-boards, to sing, and sit, and feede upon your flowers and sprouts, make a pleasant noyse and sight. For cleanly and innocent Bees, of all other things, love and become, and thrive in your Orchard. If they thrive (as they must needs if your Gardiner be skilfull, and love them: for they love their friends and hate none but their enemies) they will besides the pleasure, yeeld great profit, to pay him his wages; yea the increase of twenty Stocks or Stools with other bees, will keep your Orchard.

You need not doubt their stings, for they hurt not, whom they know, and they know their Keeper and acquaintance. If you like not to come among them, you need not doubt them; for but near their store, and in their own defence, they will not fight, and in that case only (and who can blame them?) they are manly, and fight desperately.

WILLIAM LAWSON, *A New Orchard and Garden* [1618]

By Evelyn's day they could be made of glass. The extraordinary speaking statue was in emulation of one described by Hero of Alexandria in the fifth century. The place is Wadham College, Oxford.

We all din'd, at that most obliging and universaly Curious Dr Wilkin's, at Waddum, who was the first who shew'd me the Transparent Apiaries, which he had built like Castles and Palaces and so ordered them one upon another, as to take the Hony without destroying the Bees. These were adorn'd in variety of Dials, little Statues, Vanes, etc; very ornamental, and he was abundantly civill, as finding me pleased with them, to present me one of these Hives, which he had empty, and which I afterwards had in my Garden at Says-Court, many Yeares after; and which his Majestie came on purpose to see and contemplate with much satisfaction. He also contrived an hollow Statue which gave a Voice and utter'd Words, by a long concealed pipe which went to its mouth, whilst one spake thro' it, at a good distance and which was at first very surprising.

JOHN EVELYN, *Diary*, 13 July 1654

John Lyly (1554?–1606) describes an Elizabethan border.

BORDERS

Gentleman, what floure like you best in all this border, heere be faire Roses, sweete Violets, fragrant primroses, heere wil be Jilly-floures, Carnations, sops in wine, sweet Johns, and what may either please you for sight, or delight you with savour: loth we are you should have a Posie of all, yet willing to give you one, not yat which shal looke best, but such a one as you shal lyke best.

JOHN LYLY, *Euphues and His England* [1580]

And borders appear in that classic of late Victorian humour, the Diary of a Nobody.

April 14. Spent the whole of the afternoon in the garden, having this morning picked up at a bookstall for fivepence a capital little book, in good condition, on *Gardening.* I procured and sowed some half-hardy annuals in what I fancy will be a warm, sunny border. I thought of a joke, and called out Carrie. Carrie came out rather testy, I thought. I said: 'I have just discovered I have got a lodging-house.' She replied: 'How do you mean?' I said: '*Look at the boarders.*' Carrie said: 'Is that all that you wanted me for?' I said: 'Any other time you would have laughed at my little pleasantry.' Carrie said: 'Certainly – *at any other time*, but not when I am busy in the house.'

GEORGE and WEEDON GROSSMITH, *Diary of a Nobody* [1892]

And no one has described better how to create one than that mistress of the art at its apogee, Miss Jekyll (1843–1932).

The planting of the border is designed to show a distinct scheme of colour arrangement. At the two ends there is a groundwork of grey and glaucous foliage – Stachys, Santolina, *Cineraria maritima*, Sea-Kale and Lyme-Grass, with darker foliage, also of grey quality, of Yucca, *Clematis Recta* and Rue. With this, at the near or western end, there are flowers of pure blue, grey-blue, white, palest yellow and palest pink; each colour partly in distinct masses and partly intergrouped. The colouring then passes through stronger yellow to orange and red. By the time the middle space of the border is reached the colour is strong and gorgeous, but, as it is in good harmonies, it is never garish. Then the colour strength recedes in an inverse sequence through orange and deep yellow to pale yellow, white and palest pink, again with blue-grey foliage. But at this, the eastern end, instead of the pure blues we have purples and lilacs.

Looked at from a little way forward, for a wide space of grass allows this point of view, the whole border can be seen as one picture, the cool colouring at the ends enhancing the brilliant warmth of the middle. Then, passing along the wide path next to the border, the value of the colour arrangement is still more strongly felt. Each portion now becomes a picture in itself, and every one is of such a colouring that it best prepares the eye, in accordance with natural law, for what is to follow. Standing for a few moments before the endmost region of grey and blue, and saturating the eye to its utmost capacity with these colours, it passes with extraordinary avidity to the succeeding yellows. These intermingle in a pleasant harmony with the reds and scarlets, blood-reds and clarets, and then lead again to yellows. Now the eye has again become saturated, this time with the rich colouring, and has therefore, by the law of complementary colour, acquired a strong appetite for the greys and purples. These therefore assume an appearance of brilliancy that they would not have had without the preparation provided by their recently received complementary colour.

GERTRUDE JEKYLL, *Colour Schemes for the Flower Garden* [1936]

Not everybody, however, loved the herbaceous border. Here is a surprising opponent.

Plaintive letters reach me from time to time saying that if I do not like herbaceous borders, what would I put in their place? It is quite true that I have no great love for herbaceous borders or for the plants that usually fill them – coarse things with no delicacy or quality about them. I think the only justification for such borders is that they shall be perfectly planned, both in regard to colour and to grouping; perfectly staked – and perfectly weeded.

VITA SACKVILLE-WEST, *Vita Sackville-West's Garden Book* [1968]

And everyone used to showing one off to visitors will know about this.

That border was a dream in June. It is going to be lovely again in October.

RUTH DRAPER as Mrs Guffer in *Showing the Garden*

BUILDINGS

John, 5th Earl of Orrery (1707–62) created a superb garden at Caledon, Co. Tyrone, in the 1740s. In 1747 he was exploring how to build a bone house like the one he had heard of at Kedleston and he goes on to describe his other buildings.

We have built, at the expence of five pounds, a root house, or hermitage, to which on Sunday the country people resort, as the Londoners to Westminster Abbey. For gayer scenes, I have a lodge near a mile distant from the hermitage, and large enough to contain a good number of friends at dinner or supper, or to entertain eight couples with a country dance. Behind this room are three little rooms, a kitchen, a bedchamber, and another room, besides a cellar . . . These buildings are in the form of Buckingham house. And the courtyard is filled with various fowls, and admits the most lively and innocent scene imaginable. All the buildings command a view of the river, of groves and of various agreeable objects . . . Caledon has changed me into a Hibernian. It is a charming place indeed.

Letter of JOHN, LORD ORRERY, *Orrery Papers, Houghton Library, Harvard College* [1747]

Oriel Temple Gardens, Co. Lowth, were the creation of the Hon. John Foster (1740–1828), the last Speaker of the Irish House of Commons. His daughter records the history of the various garden buildings.

About the year 1780 or '81 my Father made some additions to a garden house built in the Plantations at Oriel, to make it capable of receiving us to lodge there in the Summer months. The Drawing-room he built in the form of a Temple, dedicating it to my Mother. In that building were spent some of the happiest of my childish days, tho' when grown up, I hailed the day that brought us back to Collon House, where we had accommodation for friends which the Temple was too small to admit of. From being at first but the Summer Villa, it became our sole residence, leaving the house for visitors who passed to and fro in an old coach, passing their days at Oriel, their nights at Collon. This was so uncomfortable as soon to banish all visitors, even of our own family, yet for some years I thought no enjoyment greater than living in the grounds, following my Father on foot, and on horseback, when my lessons were over, (and sometimes when they were not) and sitting by my Mother at her work frame drawing, or at music, dancing in the evenings to Andrew Branigan's eternal fiddle, and enlisting such of the neighbourhood, or of our cousins in the same, as would be accommodated with Mother in the Temple, or were near enough to return home at night. The desire of increasing the accommodation – I believe it was – that first suggested to my Mother the thought of building that dear Cottage, that proved such a source of amusement to her for many years, and remains such a beautiful monument of the elegance and simplicity of her taste. She wished it to be of mud, to be built in one season, and made use of immediately as a Tea-rooms to the Temple. My Father, who was always desirous to make his work permanent, and was perhaps particularly so in an object that was to be exclusively hers, and on which she was to display her taste without any interference (for that was the agreement she made) persuaded her to let him build it of stone and mortar, with a strong projecting thatched roof. Whilst the building was going on she directed the furnishing of the walls, the recesses all to suit the plans she made from the first in her own mind, of what she wished it should be when finished. The very model of what a real cottage should be, – in the furniture the same plan was pursued. All was useful, simple, and well adapted. She composed some pretty lines for it, and selected others equally suitable. The prints with which the walls were hung she had been for some time collecting – and many friends, when they knew what she was about, contributed little decorations that they thought would gratify her. In this dear Cottage many happy hours were spent. We used often to drink tea there from the Temple and have dances in the evening, or stroll about the grounds surrounding it, till the close of evening sent us home. Sometimes with some of my cousins who were often with us, we used to dress in stuff gowns, and dear Mother in a stuff gown, used to call herself Madge of the Cottage, and tell how her old Master, the Speaker, had settled her and her daughters in that happy spot.

In the course of a few years she wanted something new to excite her to be as much in the open air as my Father thought would be good for her health. She took a fancy to a little stream, and some rocky ground, which he called Margate from her name. She proposed building a Grotto there, but soon found that it was too distant from the Temple for her to superintend it with any satisfaction. (The reversion of this was given to me.)

I built a seat there and laid out walks – a boy was given to me to carry on the work, the same, who has ever since been attached to Margate, and known to those who frequent it by the name of James Murphy.

A spot near the Cottage, an old gravel quarry, was then fixed on for the Grotto, and there my Mother converted the most incongruous materials into one of the most beautiful pieces of Grotto-work that could be imagined. Broken china, beads, lobster shells, coloured parchment, sealing wax, everything that had either colour or substance to suit the purpose were all combined, with specimens of spars and shells, and various descriptions of stones, and coloured glass and pieces of looking glass, and pebbles, and fish bones, and many more such materials, to cover the walls, which were broken across by diagonal arched partitions, which she still added, as she still wanted a fresh surface on which to display any newly acquired treasures. To the last years of her life, the working at this Grotto afforded her both health and pleasure. Latterly, by inducing her to go out, when merely taking the air would have been a dull pursuit, and previously, by dividing her leisure time with the embroidery frame, at which she was inclined to sit for hours together, without air or exercise.

ANNA DOROTHEA, LADY DUFFERIN,
Recollections of a Beloved Mother
[1824]

CARPET BEDDING

The supreme expression of Victorian gardening, we now only see it at roundabouts or on seafronts still cherished by municipal gardeners.

Another thing also much too commonly seen, is an aberration of the human mind which otherwise I should have been ashamed to warn you of. It is technically called carpet-gardening. Need I explain it further? I had rather not, for when I think of it, even when I am quite alone, I blush with shame at the thought.

WILLIAM MORRIS, *Hopes and Fears for Art: 'Making the Best of it', Oxford and Cambridge Magazine* [c. 1860]

CONTAINERS

I once visited an antique dealer in Burford who had a couple of Elizabethan pots. Here is a list of what they grew in them.

*For Those who have no Garden: Herbs, Branches, and
Flowers, for Windows and Pots*

1. Bayes sowe or set in plants in Ianuarie.
2. Batchelers buttens.
3. Botles blew, red and tawney.
4. Collembines.
5. Campions.
6. Daffadowndillies.
7. Eglantine or sweete bryer.
8. Fether few.
9. Flower armour sow in May.
10. Flower de luce.
11. Flower gentle, white and red.
12. Flower nyce.

13. Gelyflowers, red, white, and carnations, set in Spring, and Haruest in potts, pailles, or tubs, or for summer in bedds.
14. Holiokes, red, white, and carnations.
15. Indian eye, sowe in May or set in slips in March.
16. Lauender of all sorts.
17. Larks foot. '
18. Laws tibi.
19. Lilium cum halium.
20. Lilies red and white, sowe or set in March & September.
21. Marigolds double.
22. Nigella Romana.
23. Paunces or hartsease.
24. Paigles greene and yellow.
25. Pinkes of all sortes.
26. Queen's Gilliflowers.
27. Rosemary.
28. Roses of all sortes.
29. Snap dragons.
30. Sops in Wine.
31. Sweete Williams.
32. Sweet Johns.
33. Star of Bethlehem.
34. Star of Jerusalem.
35. Stock Gilliflowers of all sorts.
36. Tuft Gelliflowers.
37. Velvet flowers or French marigolds.
38. Violets yellow or white.
39. Wal geliflowers of all sorts.

THOMAS TUSSER, *Five Hundred Pointes of Good Husbandrie* [1580]

EYE-CATCHERS

The mania for eye-catchers – follies, obelisks, arches and so on – is satirized here at the expense of Archibald Campbell, Lord Islay, later 3rd Duke of Argyll (1682–1761). The garden was at Whitton, Middlesex.

Old Islay, to show his fine delicate taste,
In improving his gardens purloin'd from the waste,
Bade his gard'ner one day to open his views,
By cutting a couple of grand avenues;
No particular prospect his lordship intended,
But left it to chance how his walks should be ended.

With transport and joy he beheld his first view end
In a favourite prospect – a church that was ruin'd –
But also! what a sight did the next cut exhibit!
At the end of the walk hung a rogue on a gibbet!
He beheld it and wept, for it caus'd him to muse on
Full many a Campbell that died with his shoes on.
All amazed and aghast at the ominous scene,

He order'd it quick to be clos'd up again
With a clump of Scotch firs, that served for a Screen.

THE REVEREND JAMES BRAMSTON as
quoted by Horace Walpole to Horace
Mann, 3 June 1742

Twenty years later the fashion for eye-catchers was still providing good copy for the comic pen.

STERLING: I'll only show his lordship my ruins, and the cascade, and the Chinese bridge, and then we'll go in to breakfast.

LORD OGLEBY: Ruins, did you say, Mr Sterling?

STERLING: Ay, ruins, my lord! and they are reckoned very fine ones too. You would think them ready to tumble on your head. It has just cost me a hundred and fifty pounds to put my ruins in thorough repair. – This way, if your lordship pleases.

LORD OGLEBY *(going, stops)*: What steeple's that we see yonder? the parish church, I suppose.

STERLING: Ha! ha! ha! that's admirable. It is no church at all, my lord! it is a spire that I have built against a tree, a field or two off, to terminate the prospect. One must always have a church, or an obelisk, or a something to terminate the prospect you know. That's a rule in taste, my lord!

LORD OGLEBY: Very ingenious, indeed! For my part, I desire no finer prospect than this I see before me. (*Leering at the women.*) – Simple, yet varied; bounded, yet extensive.

GEORGE COLMAN, *The Clandestine
Marriage*, Act II, sc. i [1766]

FOUNTAINS

Fountains have always received a mixed press due to maintenance problems.

For Fountains, they are a Great Beauty and Refreshment, but Pools mar all, and make the Garden unwholesome, and full of Flies and Frogs. Fountains I intend to be of two Natures: the one that sprinkleth or spouteth Water, the other a fair Receipt of Water, of some thirty or forty foot square, but without Fish, or Slime or Mud. For the first, the Ornaments of Images Gilt, or of Marble, which are in use, do well; but the main matter is, so to convey the Water, as it never stay, either in the Bowls, or in the Cistern, that the Water be never by rest discoloured, Green or Red, or the like; or gather any Mossiness or Putrefaction. Besides that, it is to be cleansed every day by the hand; also some Fine Pavement about it, doth well. As for the other kind of Fountain, which we may call a Bathing Pool, it may admit much curiosity and Beauty, wherewith we will not trouble ourselves, as, that the Bottom be finely paved, and with Images, the Sides likewise; and withal Embellished with coloured Glass, and such things of Lustre; Encompassed also with fine Rails of low Statua's. But the main point is the same, which we mentioned in the former kind of Fountain, which is, that the Water be in perpetual Motion, fed by a Water higher than the Pool, and delivered into it by fair Spouts, and then discharged away under Ground by some Equality of Bores, that it stay little. And for fine Devices, of Arching Water without spilling, and making it rise in Several forms (of Feathers, Drinking Glasses, Canopies, and the like) they be pretty things to look on, but nothing to Health and Sweetness.

SIR FANCIS BACON, *Of Gardens*
[1625]

One of the greatest ornaments to a garden is a fountain, but many fountains are curiously ineffective. A fountain is most beautiful when it leaps high into the air, and you can see it against a background of green foliage. To place a fountain among low flower-beds, and then to substitute small fancy jets that take the shape of a cup, or trickle over into a basin of gold-fish; or toy with a gilded ball, is to do all that is possible to degrade it. The real charm of a fountain is, when you come upon it in some little grassy glade of the 'pleasaunce', where it seems as though it sought, in the strong rush of its waters, to vie with the tall boles of the forest-trees that surround it. Such was the fountain in Leigh Hunt's *Story of Rimini*, which shot up 'beneath a shade of darksome pines',

> 'And 'twixt their shafts you saw the water bright,
> Which through the tops glimmered with show'ring light.'

HENRY ARTHUR BRIGHT, *The English
Flower Garden* [1881]

The greenhouse proliferated in the gardens of the great houses of the eighteenth century in the main in the classical style. Poets celebrated their advent.

GREENHOUSE

> Here, far beyond
> That humble wish, her lover's genius form'd
> A glittering fane, where rare and alien plants
> Might safely flourish; where the citron sweet,
> And fragrant orange, rich in fruit and flowers,
> Might hang their silver stars, their golden globes,
> On the same odorous stem: yet scorning there
> The glassy penthouse of ignoble form,
> High on Ionic shafts he bad it tower
> A proud rotunda; to its sides conjoin'd
> Two broad piazzas in theatric curve,
> Ending in equal porticos sublime.
> Glass roof'd the whole, and sidelong to the south
> 'Twixt ev'ry fluted column, lightly rear'd
> Its wall pellucid. All within was day,
> Was genial Summer's day, for secret stoves
> Thro' all the pile solstitial warmth convey'd.

WILLIAM MASON, *The English
Garden* [1777]

This is the so-called Swan of Lichfield's response to the greenhouse at Shugborough.

> See
> Where the stately colonnade extends
> Its pillar'd length, to shade the sculpted forms
> Of Demigods or Heroes, and protect
> From the cold northern blast each tender plant,
> The fragrant progeny of milder climes.
> Orange and lime, and cedars from the banks
> Of Arno or Parthenope's soft shore,
> There in fair order rang'd, stage above stage,
> Rear to the lofty roof their green heads, crowned
> At once with flowers profuse and golden fruit,
> A sylvan theatre . . .
> Here while we breathe perfume, the ravish'd eye
> Surveys the miracles of Grecian art.
>
> ANNA SEWARD   [1747–1809]

William Cowper (1731–1800), the poet, was devoted to his greenhouse.

> Who loves a garden, loves a green-house too.
> Unconscious of a less propitious clime
> There blooms exotic beauty, warm and snug,
> While the winds whistle and the snows descend.
> The spiry myrtle with unwith'ring leaf
> Shines there and flourishes. The golden boast
> Of Portugal and western India there,
> The ruddier orange and the paler lime,
> Peep through their polish'd foliage at the storm,
> And seem to smile at what they need not fear.
> Th'amomum there with intermingling flow'rs
> And cherries hangs her twigs. Geranium boasts
> Her crimson honors, and the spangled beau
> Ficoides, glitters bright the winter long.
> All plants of ev'ry leaf that can endure
> The winter's frown if screen'd from his shrewd bite,
> Live there and prosper. Those Ausonia claims,
> Levantine regions these; th'Azores send
> Their jessamine, her jessamine remote
> Caffraia, foreigners from many lands . . .
>
> WILLIAM COWPER, *The Task*   [1785]

My green-house is never so pleasant as when we are just upon the point of being turned out of it. The gentleness of the autumnal suns, and the calmness of this latter season, make it a much more agreeable retreat than we ever find it in the summer; when the winds being generally brisk, we cannot cool it by admitting a sufficient quantity of air, without being at the same time incommoded by it. But now I sit with all the windows and the door wide open, and am regaled with the scent of every flower, in a garden as full of flowers as I have known how to make it.

WILLIAM COWPER to the REVEREND
JOHN NEWTON, 18 September 1784

My dear, I will not let you come till the end of May or beginning of June, because before that time my green-house will not be ready to receive us, and it is the only pleasant room belonging to us. When the plants go out we go in. I line it with mats, and spread the floor with mats; and there you shall sit with a bed of mignonette at your side, and a hedge of honeysuckles, roses, and jasmine; and I will make you a bouquet of myrtle every day.

WILLIAM COWPER to LADY
HESKETH, 9 February 1786

Written about 1913, Hardy is recalling an incident in the 1870s. 'She' is his wife Emma Gifford.

THE FROZEN GREENHOUSE
(ST JULIOT)

'There was a frost
Last night!' she said,
'And the stove was forgot
When we went to bed,
And the greenhouse plants
Are frozen dead!'

By the breakfast blaze
Blank-faced spoke she,
Her scared young look
Seeming to be
The very symbol
Of tragedy.

The frost is fiercer
Than then today,
As I pass the place
Of her once dismay,
But the greenhouse stands
Warm, tight, and gay.

While she who grieved
At the sad lot
Of her pretty plants –
Cold, iced, forgot –
Herself is colder,
And knows it not.

THOMAS HARDY [1840–1928]

GROTTO

Grottoes arrived in England in the Elizabethan period. Thomas Bushnell (1594–1674) was a servant of Francis Bacon and later created a spectacular garden and grotto in Oxfordshire which Charles I and Henrietta Maria visited in 1636. Here is Aubrey's account of what were known as the Enstone Marvels.

After his master the Lord Chancellor dyed, he maried, and lived at Enston, Oxon; where having some land lyeing on the hanging of a hill facing the South, at the foot wherof runnes a fine cleare stream which petrifies, and where is a pleasant Solitude, he spake to his servant, Jack Sydenham, to gett a Labourer to cleare some Boscage which grew on the side of the Hill, and also to dig a Cavity in the hill, to sitt and read, or contemplate. The Workman had not worked an hower before he discovers not only a Rock, but a rock of an unusuall figure with Pendants like Icecles as at Wokey Hole, Somerset, which was the occasion of making that delicate Grotto and those fine Walkes.

The Grotto belowe lookes just South; so that when it artificially raineth, upon the turning of a cock, you are enterteined with a Rainbowe. In a very little pond (no bigger than a Basin) opposite to the rock, and hard by, stood Neptune, neatly cutt in wood, holding his Trident in his hand, and ayming with it at a Duck which perpetually turned round with him, and a Spanniel swimming after her – which was very pretty, but long since spoyled.

Here in fine weather he would walke all night. Jack Sydenham sang rarely: so did his other servant, Mr Batty. They went very gent. in cloathes, and he loved them as his children.

He did not encumber himselfe with his wife, but here enjoyed himselfe thus in this Paradise till the War brake out, and then retired to Lundy isle . . .

In the time of the Civill Warres his Hermitage over the Rocks at Enston were hung with black-bayes; his bed and black Curtaines, etc, but it had no bed posts but hung by 4 Cordes covered with black-bayes instead of bed-postes. When the Queen-mother came to Oxon to the King, she either brought (as I thinke) or somebody gave her, an entire Mummie from Egypt, a great raritie, which her Majestie gave to Mr Bushell, but I beleeve long ere this time the dampnesse of the place haz spoyled it with mouldinesse.

JOHN AUBREY [1626–1697], *Brief Lives*

The most famous grotto constructed in pre-Civil War England was by Isaac de Caus (1590–1648) at Wilton. It was to remain intact until demolished in the early eighteenth century.

Grottoe is at the end of the garden just the middle off the house, its garnished with many fine figures of the Goddesses, and about 2 yards off the doore is severall pipes in a line that with a sluce spouts water up to wett the Strangers; in the middle roome is a round table, a large pipe in the midst, on which they put a crown or gun or a branch, and so it spouts the water through the carvings and poynts all round the roome at the Artists pleasure to wet the Company; there are figures at each corner of the roome that can weep water on the beholders, and by a straight pipe on the table they force up the water into the hollow carving of the roof like a crown or coronet to appearance, but is hollow within to retaine the water forced into it in great quantetyes, that disperses in the hollow cavity over the roome and descends in a shower of raine all about the roome; on each side is two little roomes which by the turning their wires the water runnes in the rockes you see and hear it, and also it is so contrived in one room that it makes the melody of Nightingerlls and all sorts of birds which engaged the curiosity of the Strangers to go in to see, but at the entrance off each room, is a line of pipes that appear not till by a sluce moved it washes the spectators, designed for diversion. The Grottoe is leaded on the top where are fish ponds, and just without the grottoe is a wooden bridge over the river, the barristers [balusters] are set out with Lyons set thick on either side with their mouths open and by a sluce spout out water each to other in a perfect arch the length of the bridge; there are fine woods beyond the house and a large parke walled in.

CELIA FIENNES, c. 1685–96; in
The Journeys of Celia Fiennes,
ed. Christopher Morris   [1947]

The poet Alexander Pope was to make a cult of his grotto which ran beneath his house and the road, enabling visitors to pass under it to the garden.

Let the young ladies be assured I make nothing new in my gardens without wishing to see the print of their fairy steps in every part of them. I have put the last hand to my works of this kind, in happily finishing the subterraneous way and grotto. I there found a spring of the clearest water, which falls in a perpetual rill, that echoes through the cavern day and night. From the river Thames, you see through my arch up a walk of the wilderness, to a kind of open temple, wholly composed of shells in the rustic manner; and from that distance under the temple you look down through a sloping arcade of trees, and see the sails on the river passing suddenly and vanishing, as through a perspective glass. When you shut the doors of this grotto, it becomes on the instant, from a luminous room, a *camera obscura*; on the walls of which all the objects of the river, hills, wood, and boats, are forming a moving picture in their visible radiations: and when you have a mind to light it up, it affords you a very different scene. It is finished with shells interspersed with pieces of looking-glass in angular forms; and in the ceiling is a star of the same material, at which when a lamp (of an orbicular figure of thin alabaster) is hung in the middle, a thousand pointed rays glitter, and are reflected over the place. There are connected to this grotto by a narrower passage two porches, one towards the river of smooth stones full of light, and open, the other toward the garden shadowed with trees, rough with shells, flints, and iron ore. The bottom is paved with simple pebble, as is also the adjoining walk up the wilderness to the temple, in the natural taste, agreeing not ill with the little dripping murmur, and the aquatic idea of the whole place. It wants nothing to complete it but a good statue with an inscription, like that beautiful antique one which you know I am so fond of,

Hujus Nympha loci, sacri custodia fontis,
    Dormio, dum blande sentio murmur aque.
Parce meum, quisquis tangis cava marmora, sommum
    Rupere; si bibas, sive lavere, tace.

Nymph of the grot, these sacred springs I keep,
And to the murmur of these waters sleep;
Ah spare my slumbers gently tread the cave!
And drink in silence, or in silence lave!

You will think I have been very poetical in this description, but it is pretty near the truth. I wish you were here to bear testimony how little it owes to art, either the place itself, or the image of it.

ALEXANDER POPE to EDWARD
BLOUNT [1725]

Mid-eighteenth-century grotto mania is caught in this doggerel verse accompanying a plate in which a gentleman, his architect, hermits and labourers are all at work.

Where Severn, Trent or Thames's Ouzy side
Pours the Smooth Current of their easy Tide,
Each will require a sameness to the Spot,
For this a Cell, a Cascade or a Grot;
The Moss, or gliding Streams productive Store,
To grace the Building on the Verdant Shore,
There the rough Tuscan, or the Rustic fix
Or Pebbles, Shells or calcin'd Matter mix,
The frozen Isicles resembled form
Or Sea-green Weed your Grotto must adorn.

WILLIAM WRIGHTE, *Grotesque
Architecture or Rural Amusement*
[1767]

Dr Johnson had a healthy aversion to them.

The Lincolnshire lady who showed him a grotto she had been making, came off no better, as I remember: 'Would it not be a pretty cool habitation in summer, Mr Johnson?' she said. 'I think it would, Madam,' replied he, '– for a toad.'

JAMES BOSWELL, *Life of Johnson*
[1781]

HA-HA *This somewhat bizarre account of its origin was current in the early eighteenth century.*

At present we frequently make Thorough-Views, call'd *Ah, Ah,* which are Openings in the Walls, without Grills, to the very Level of the Walks, with a large and deep Ditch at the Foot of them, lined on both Sides to sustain the Earth, and prevent the getting over, which surprizes the Eye upon coming near it, and makes one cry, *Ah, Ah!* from whence it take its Name.

A. J. DÉZALLIER D'ARGENVILLE,
The Theory and Practice of Gardening,
translated by John James [1712]

Horace Walpole eulogizes its invention which made the landscape style possible.

I call a sunk fence the leading step, for these reasons. No sooner was this simple enchantment made, than levelling, mowing and rolling, followed. The contiguous ground of the park without the sunk fence was to be harmonized with the lawn within; and the garden in its turn was to be set free from its prim regularity, that it might assort with the wilder country without. The sunk fence ascertained the specific garden, but that it might not draw too obvious a line of distinction between the neat and the rude, the contiguous out-lying parts came to be included in a kind of general design: and when nature was taken into the plan, under improvements, every step that was made, pointed out new beauties and inspired new ideas.

HORACE WALPOLE, The History of
the Modern Taste in Gardening
[1771–80]

An essential structural element in any garden. Evelyn advises the use of the yew, in the aftermath of the icy winters of late seventeenth-century England which had killed junipers, but reserves his greatest accolade for holly.

HEDGES

Above all the natural *Greens* which inrich our *home-born* store, there is none certainly to be compar'd to the *Agrifolium* (or *Acuifolium* rather) our *Holly*, insomuch as I have often wonder'd at our *curiosity* after forreign Plants, and expensive *difficulties*, to the neglect of the *culture* of this *vulgar*, but *incomparable* tree; whether we will propagate it for *Use* and *Defence*, or for *Sight* and *Ornament*.

> A Hedge of Holly, Thieves that would invade,
> Repulses like a growing *Palizade*;
> Whose numerous leaves such *Orient Greens* invest,
> As in deep *Winter* do the *Spring* arrest.

Is there under *Heaven* a more glorious and refreshing object of the kind, than an impregnable *Hedge* of *near three hundred foot* in length, *nine* foot high, and *five* in *diameter*; which I can shew in my poor *Gardens* at any time of the year, glitt'ring with its arm'd and vernish'd *leaves*? the taller *Standards* at orderly distances, blushing with their natural *Coral*: It mocks at the rudest assults of the *Weather, Beasts*, or *Hedge-breakers*,
Et illium nemo impunè lacessit.   JOHN EVELYN, *Sylva, or a Discourse on Forest-Trees* [1664]

A decade later Moses Cook gives us a list of the plants used for hedging. He was gardener to the Earl of Essex whose garden at Cassiobury was famous.

Holly makes a most stately and beautiful hedge; and had we but store of the white-berry'd holly to mix in the hedge with the red, it would make it the more ornamental. Its ground that it most delight on, is dry and gravelly . . . Had we but store of the striped (variegated) to make hedges with, it would be very noble indeed.

Hornbeam may be kept in good shape for a high hedge, and very thick, even to the ground. It is (alone) one of the very best home-bred natural forest trees that shed the leaf to make a hedge of, and is fencible, unless against the rudest sort of cattel.

Box maketh a good hedge, and lasting; I mean the *English*, though the others are pretty, both the gilded and the dwarf.

Laurel (as we call it) or bay-cherry, make a good hedge; and if well kept, very fine standards. Hard winters do pierce it on some grounds, but on most it is durable: it is easy to increase, and will grow well on most grounds; keep it but down, and it will grow strong below, and thick, and then make a very fine hedge.

Arbutus, or strawberry-tree, is a curious plant for a hedge, only it is very tender, especially . . . while young, for the leaves being constant, whilst life lasteth, and of a fair green, finely dented about the edges, and its pretty white in flower in summer, with its strawberry on, the beginning of winter, all together add a great deal of grace to this plant.

Cypress would make fine hedges, but for two faults: for first, in some grounds it is tender, and will not abide our hard winters; and secondly, it doth not love to be headed, for that makes it still more tender. Cut it not in late summer.

Mezereon, or Dwarf-Bay, both the red and the white together, make a pretty low hedge, and show very beautifully early in the spring.

Rhamnus alaternus, or evergreen Privet, makes a fine thick green hedge: it should be supported with a frame, especially when it is young.

Pyracantha, or prickly Coral, makes a good thick hedge, and a very fine show when it is full of its fine red berries, which appear like beads of red coral among the dark green leaves. It likes our entertainment so well, that it will grow well on most grounds; our winters disturb it not, and 'tis very easy to be multiply'd or increas'd by laying or cutting.

They that have store of ground, and are lovers of plants, I hope will not be without these few named, and many more that will be very acceptable; but they are not, some of them, so proper for hedges. Many more there be that would make very fine hedges for pleasures, if well kept; as the double-blossom Cherry, the *Laurus Tinus*, or wild Bay, Primme, Savin, etc.

These few are only for ornament, and make (any of them), fine hedges alone; or you may mix them with judgement, and they will then be very pleasant.

Now I shall show you a few of those that are for profit and ornament; such are the Summer-Pears on Quince-stocks; for that makes them the more dwarfish. Cherries make a fine hedge, but especially the small-leaved, and the several sorts of Flanders, etc.

Plumbs, Quinces, Codlins, Barberries, etc., all these make fine hedges, but must have supporters. In the three last there is this fault, that the better they be kept, I mean the handsomer, the worse they will bear.

MOSES COOK, *The Manner of Raising, Ordering and Improving Forrest-Trees* [1676]

HERMITAGE

No early eighteenth-century garden was complete without one amongst its collection of garden buildings. John, 5th Earl of Orrery (1707–1762) had one in his splendid garden at Caledon, Co. Tyrone.

Nothing is completed yet but an *hermitage*, which is about an acre of ground – an island, planted with all variety of trees, shrubs, and flowers that will grow in this country, abundance of little winding walks, differently embellished with little seats and banks; in the midst is placed an hermit's cell, made of the roots of trees, the floor is paved with pebbles, there is a couch made of matting, and little wooden stools, a table with a manuscript on it, a pair of spectacles, a leathern bottle; and hung up in different parts, an hourglass, a weatherglass and several mathematical instruments, a shelf of books, another of wooden platters and bowls, another of earthen ones, in short everything that you might imagine necessary for a recluse. *Four little gardens surround his house* – an ordchard, a flower-garden, a physick-garden, and a kitchen garden, with a kitchen to boil a teakettle or so: I never saw so pretty a *whim* so *thoroughly well* executed.

Mrs Delany to Mrs Dewes, 2nd August
1748

Queen Caroline filled hers at Richmond with busts of her intellectual heroes and mentors. Others acquired suitable live occupants in various ways.

Hermits were obtained by advertisement, and it never seems to have been difficult to get one; indeed one young man, Mr Laurence from Plymouth, did not merely answer advertisements but himself advertised in 1810 that he wished to retire as a hermit (to a convenient spot) and was willing to engage (for a gratuity) to any nobleman or gentleman who was desirous of having one. One advertisement demanded a hermit who would live underground invisible, silent, unshaven and unclipped for seven years, in a comfortable room with books, an organ and delicious food. The reward was to be a pension for life of £50 a year, and a hermit accepted, but lasted for only four years. Mr Hamilton's terms at Pain's Hill were similar, again the mystic seven years, again no cutting of hair, nails or beard, again food from the house and no speech. But he could walk in the grounds, and was provided with a Bible, optical glasses, a mat, a hassock and an hourglass. The recompense was to be seven hundred pounds, but the chosen hermit was caught at the end of three weeks going down to the pub.

So what with hermits who were invisible, and hermits who gave notice, and doubtless hermits who were rude to visitors, or posed badly, we must commend the gentleman said to have used a clockwork hermit and also Sir Richard Hill, who built at Hawkstone a very dimly-lit hermitage and solved all employment problems by having his hermit stuffed.

BARBARA JONES, *Follies and Grottoes*
[1974 ed.]

And Cowper viewed his hermitage in this wry light.

INSCRIPTION
FOR AN HERMITAGE IN THE AUTHOR'S GARDEN
This cabin, Mary, in my sight appears,
Built as it has been in our waning years,
A rest afforded to our weary feet,
Preliminary to – the last retreat.

WILLIAM COWPER [1793]

KNOTS

Knots were the fundamental ingredients of all gardens before the advent of the parterre. They went on being planted by the middle classes until well on into the seventeenth century. John Parkinson (1567–1650) gives a lively account of the materials used to set out the pattern.

It is necessary also, that I shew you the seuerall materials, wherewith the knots and trayles are set forth and bordered; which are two sorts: The one are liuing herbes, and the other are dead materials; as leade, boords, bones, tyles &c. Of herbes, there are many sorts wherewith the knots and beds in a Garden are vsed to bee set, to shew forth the forme of them, and to preserue them the longer in their forme, as also to be as greene, and sweete herbes, while they grow, to be cut to perfume the house, keeping them in such order and proportion, as may be most conuenient for their seuerall natures, and euery man's pleasure and fancy: Of all which, I intend to giue you the knowledge here in this place; and first, to begin with that which hath beene most anciently receiued, which is Thrift. This is an euerliuing greene herbe, which many take to border their beds, and set their knots and trayles, and therein much delight, because it will grow thicke and bushie, and may be kept, being cut with a paire of Garden sheeres, in some good handsome manner and proportion for a time, and besides, in the Summer time send forth many short stalkes of pleasant flowers, to decke up an house among other sweete herbes: Yet these inconueniences doe accompany it; it will not onely in a small time ouergrow the knot or trayle in many places, by growing so thicke and bushie, that it will put out the forme of a knot in many places: but also much thereof will dye with the frosts and snowes in Winter, and with the drought in Summer, whereby many voide places will be seene in the knot, which doth much deforme it, and must therefore bee yearely refreshed: the thickness also and bushing thereof doth hide and shelter snayles and other small noysome wormes so plentifully, that Gilloflowers, and other fine herbes and flowers being planted therein, are much spoyled by them, and cannot be helped without much industry, and very great and daily attendance to destroy them. Germander is another herbe, in former times also much vsed, and yet also in many places; and because it will grow thicke, and may be kept also in some forme and proportion with cutting, and that the cuttings are much vsed as a strawing herbe for houses, being pretty and sweete, is also much affected by diuers: but this also will often dye and grow out of forme, and besides that, the stalkes will grow too great, hard and stubby, the rootes doe so farre shoote vnderground, that vpon a little continuance thereof, will spread into many places within the knot, which if continually they be not plucked vp, they will spoile the whole knot it selfe;

and therefore once in three or foure yeares at the most, it must be taken vp and new set, or else it will grow too roynish and cumbersome. Hyssope hath also been vsed to be set about a knot, and being sweet, will serue for strewings, as Germander: But this, although the rootes doe not runne or creep like it, yet the stalkes doe quickly grow great aboue ground, and dye often after the first yeares setting, whereby the grace of the knot will be much lost. Marierome, Sauorie, and Thyme, in the like manner being sweete herbes, are vsed to border vp beds and knots, and will be kept for a little while, with cutting, into some conformity; but all and euery of them serue most commonly but for yeares vse, and will soone decay and perish: and therefore none of these, no more than any of the former, doe I commend for a good bordering herbe for this purpose. Lauander Cotton also being finely slipped and set, is of many, and those of the highest respect of late daies, accepted, both for the beauty and forme of the herbe, being of a whitish greene mealy colour, for his sent smelling somewhat strong, and being euerliuing and abiding greene all the Winter, will, by cutting, be kept in as euen proportion as any other herbe may be. This will likewise, soone grow great stubbed, notwithstanding the cutting, and besides will now and then perish in some places, especially if you doe not strike or put off the snow, before the Sunne lying vpon it dissolue it: The rarity & nouelty of this herbe, being for the most part but in the Gardens of great persons, doth cause it to be of the greater regard, it must therefore be renewed wholly euery second or third yeare at the most, because of the great growing thereof. Slips of Iuniper or Yew are also receiued of some & planted, because they are alwayes green, and that the Iuniper especially hath not that ill sent that Boxe hath, which I will presently commend vnto you, yet both Iuniper and Yew will soon grow too great and stubbed, and force you to take vp your knot sooner, than if it were planted with Boxe. Which lastly, I chiefly and aboue all other herbes commend vnto you, and being a small, lowe, or dwarfe kinde, is called French or Dutch Boxe, and serueth very well to set out any knot or border out any beds: for besides that it is euer greene, it being reasonable thicke set, will esily be cut and formed into any fashion one will, according to the nature thereof, which is to grow very slowly, and will not in a long time rise to be of any height, but shooting forth many small branches from the roote, will grow very thicke, and yet not require so great tending, nor so much perish as any of the former, and is onely receiued into the Gardens of those that are curious. This (as I before said) I commend and hold to bee the best and surest herbe to abide faire and greene in all the bitter stormes of the sharpest Winter, and all the great heates and droughts of Summer, and doth recompence the want of a good sweet sent with his fresh verdue, euen proportion, and long lasting continuance . . .

JOHN PARKINSON, *Paradisi in sole*
paradisus terrestris [1629]

Open knots were filled with flowers, closed ones with various coloured materials running from sand to coal-dust. They were not appreciated by everyone.

As for the making of Knots or Figures, with Divers coloured Earths, that they may lie under the Windows of the House, on that Side which the Garden

stands, they be but Toys, you may see as good sights many times in Tarts.

Sir Francis Bacon, Of Gardens
[1625]

LAWNS   *An American perspective.*

Home would not be home to me without a lawn, and if there are, as I've recently read, twenty-five million home lawns in the United States, at least fifty million other Americans must agree with me. Yet the more one considers the never-ending labor a lawn represents, the more astonishing it is that in every small city, suburb, town, and village, our patches (or wide expanses) of greensward are so lovingly tended year after year. The effort and expense of making a lawn – grading, topsoiling, rolling the ground, and sowing the seed – are minor compared to the week-by-week, year-by-year fatigues of keeping the grass fertilized, free of weeds, watered, and shorn. Why so many of us consider this green velvet ground cover essential to the beauty and tranquillity of our homes is a question to which I have never seen a satisfactory answer. The sociologists call the lawn a 'status symbol,' and it is, to a degree, since nearly everybody wants his bit of ground to look as neat and pretty as the next man's. Yet I think there is much more to it than that. We could have chosen, in the European or Oriental tradition, to pave or cobble our yards and garden areas, and modern landscape architects, even in humid England whose turf is our envy, are urging everyone to do just that. To me it would be a great loss.

Consider the many special delights a lawn affords: soft mattress for a creeping baby; worm hatchery for a robin; croquet or badminton court; baseball diamond; restful green perspectives leading the eye to a background of flower border, shrubs, or hedge; green shadows – 'This lawn, a carpet all alive/With shadows flung from leaves' – as changing and as spellbinding as the waves of the sea, whether flecked with sunlight under trees of light foliage, like elm and locust, or deep, dark, solid shade, moving slowly as the tide, under maple and oak. This carpet! What pleasanter surface on which to walk, sit, lie, or even to read Tennyson?

> *Sweeter thy Voice, but every sound is sweet;*
> *Myriads of rivulets hurrying thro' the lawn,*
> *The moan of doves in immemorial elms*
> *And murmuring of innumerable bees.*

The familiar lines are perhaps as apt for England today as when Tennyson wrote them, but our immemorial elms are fast dying, our bees, thanks to poison sprays, are now only too easily numbered, and for the same reason our doves may soon no longer moan or our robins hop about the lawn and cock their heads to listen for the good earthworms underneath the grass. It is a rare American lawn, too, through which rivulets hurry, and the weary American businessman (or, for that matter, the weary American plowman) must wend his way home after a hard day to turn on the hose and the sprinkler, and, more often than not, must also be prepared to give a part of his precious weekend leisure to cutting the grass.

Katharine S. White in the New
Yorker [1962]; reprinted in Onward
and Upward in the Garden [1979]

A garden feature for centuries, no account excels Jerome K. Jerome's narrative of one of the famous Three Men's visit to Hampton Court.

MAZE

A Maze

Harris asked me if I'd ever been in the maze at Hampton Court. He said he went in once to show somebody else the way. He had studied it up in a map, and it was so simple that it seemed foolish – hardly worth the twopence charged for admission. Harris said he thought that map must have been got up as a practical joke, because it wasn't a bit like the real thing, and only misleading. It was a country cousin that Harris took in. He said:

'We'll just go in here, so that you can say you've been, but it's very simple. It's absurd to call it a maze. You keep on taking the first turning to the right. We'll just walk round for ten minutes, and then go and get some lunch.'

They met some people soon after they had got inside, who said they had been there for three-quarters of an hour, and had had about enough of it. Harris told them they could follow him, if they liked; he was just going in, and then should turn round and come out again. They said it was very kind of him, and fell behind, and followed.

They picked up various other people who wanted to get it over, as they went along, until they had absorbed all the persons in the maze. People who had given up all hopes of ever either getting in or out, or of ever seeing their home and friends again, plucked up courage at the sight of Harris and his party, and joined the procession, blessing him. Harris said he should judge there must have been twenty people, following him, in all; and one woman with a baby, who had been there all the morning, insisted on taking his arm, for fear of losing him.

Harris kept on turning to the right, but it seemed a long way, and his cousin said he supposed it was a very big maze.

'Oh, one of the largest in Europe,' said Harris.

'Yes, it must be,' replied the cousin, 'because we've walked a good two miles already.'

Harris began to think it rather strange himself, but he held on until, at last, they passed the half of a penny bun on the ground that Harris's cousin swore he had noticed there seven minutes ago. Harris said: 'Oh, impossible!' but the woman with the baby said, 'Not at all,' as she herself had taken it from the child, and thrown it down there, just before she met Harris. She also added that she wished she never had met Harris, and expressed an opinion that he was an impostor. That made Harris mad, and he produced his map, and explained his theory.

'The map may be all right enough,' said one of the party, 'if you know whereabouts in it we are now.'

Harris didn't know, and suggested that the best thing to do would be to go back to the entrance, and begin again. For the beginning again part of it there was not much enthusiasm; but with regard to the advisability of going back to the entrance there was complete unanimity, and so they turned, and trailed after Harris again, in the opposite direction. About ten minutes more passed, and then they found themselves in the centre.

Harris thought at first of pretending that that was what he had been aiming at; but the crowd looked dangerous, and he decided to treat it as an accident.

Anyhow, they had got something to start from then. They did know where they were, and the map was once more consulted, and the thing seemed simpler than ever, and off they started for the third time.

And three minutes later they were back in the centre again.

After that, they simply couldn't get anywhere else. Whatever way they turned brought them back to the middle. It became so regular at length that some of the people stopped there, and waited for the others to take a walk round, and come back to them. Harris drew out his map again, after a while, but the sight of it only infuriated the mob, and they told him to go and curl his hair with it. Harris said that he couldn't help feeling that, to a certain extent, he had become unpopular.

They all got crazy at last, and sang out for the keeper, and the man came and climbed up the ladder outside, and shouted out directions to them. But all their heads were, by this time, in such a confused whirl that they were incapable of grasping anything, and so the man told them to stop where they were, and he would come to them. They huddled together, and waited; and he climbed down, and came in.

He was a young keeper, as luck would have it, and new to the business; and when he got in, he couldn't find them, and he wandered about, trying to get to them, and then *he* got lost. They caught sight of him, every now and then, rushing about the other side of the hedge, and he would see them, and rush to get to them, and they would wait there for about five minutes, and then he would reappear again in exactly the same spot, and ask them where they had been.

They had to wait till one of the old keepers came back from his dinner before they got out.

Harris said he thought it was a very fine maze, so far as he was a judge; and we agreed that we would try to get George to go into it, on our way back.

JEROME K. JEROME, Three Men in a Boat [1889]

MOUNTS   *These were features of Tudor and Stuart gardens facilitating a prospect of both garden and countryside beyond. This mount was created by Charles Seymour, the 'Proud' Duke of Somerset (1662–1748), on the site of what is now Marlborough College.*

. . . this leads to the foote of the Mount and that you ascend from the left hand by an easye ascent bounded by such quick set hedges cut low, and soe you rise by degrees in 4 rounds bounded by the low cutt hedge and on the top is with same hedge cut in works, and from thence you have a prospect of the town and country round and two parishes two mile off in view, and the low grounds are water'd with ditches and this mount is encompass'd about with such a cannal which emptys its self into a fish pond, then it emptys it self into the river; there is a house built over the fish pond to keep the fish in; at the foote of the mount as I began out of a green walke on the left hand to ascend it so on the right hand leads to another such a walk quite round by the cannall to the other side of the bowling-green; in the midst of the top of the mount was a house built and pond, but thats fallen down; halfe way down is a seate opposite to the dwelling house which is brick'd.

CELIA FIENNES, c. 1701–c. 1712; in The Journeys of Celia Fiennes, ed. Christopher Morris [1947]

John Worlidge in 1676 gives a repertory which three centuries on remains virtually unchanged.

ORNAMENTS

OF STATUES, OBELISKS, DYALS, AND OTHER INVEGETATIVE ORNAMENTS.

In all places where there is a Summer and a Winter, and where your Gardens of pleasure are sometimes clothed with their verdant garments, and be-spangled with variety of Flowers, and at other times wholly dismantled of all these; here to recompence the loss of past pleasures, and to buoy up their hopes of another Spring, many have placed in their Gardens, Statues, and Figures of several Animals, and great variety of other curious pieces of Workmanship, that their walks might be pleasant at any time in those places of never dying pleasures.

Herein the ancient *Romans* were excessively prodigal, sparing of no cost, to adorn their avenues with curious figures for their Winter diversions, as well as with rare plants for their Summer delights. Which vanity (although one of the most excusable) is descended on the *Italians*, whose Gardens are the mirrors of the world, as well for those ornaments as for their excellency of the Plants that are propagated in them.

This mode of adorning Gardens with curious workmanship is now become *English*, how many Statues made by excellent Art, are there to be seen in his Majesties Gardens, and in the Gardens of divers of the nobility of *England*? But what great pity is it that in many places remote from Cities and great Towns, these Statues should drive out of their view, those natural Beauties that so far exceed them?

Much more ornamental are Statues placed in Groves and Shades, and in or near your borders of the choicest Plants than on the naked surface of the Earth, which beget not that surprise in the Spectators, as the others.

Statues are commendable in the midst of Fountains, and Green Squares, in Groves, and at the ends of obscure walks.

In the room of Statues in the midst of your Green Squares, Obelisks or single Columns may not be improper, so that the Workmanship be accord-ingly. Neither can there be a more proper use for an obelisk, than to support a Globe with its Axis duely placed respecting both Poles, and its circum-ference on the Equinoctial Line, exactly divided into twenty four parts, and marked with twice twelve hours, that on it at a distance by the shadow only of the Globe on its self, you may discern the hour of the day, and observe how the Day and Night, and Summer and Winter happen throughout the Universe.

Many Dials of various and curious Workmanship are made, and may be placed on Pedestals in the midst of the Squares instead of Statues, which better become the shades.

Dials of Glass, were it not for the casualties they are subject unto, pre-excel any other for Beauty, especially the Globe with its Axis through the midst and duely elevated with small Beads on it, placed at their due distances according to the lines of the Celestial Globe, painted on the superficies of your orbicular Glass, which will not only give you the true hour of the day, but all other variations that a Dial can direct: But more of these things in another place.

Other ancient Ornaments of a Garden are Flower-pots, which painted white and placed on Pedestals, either on the ground in a streight line on the edges of your Walks, or on your Walls, or at the corners of your Squares, are exceeding pleasant.

They are usually made of Potters Clay and burnt, which when full of Earth and frozen in the Winter are apt to break, unless you place another ordinary pot of Earth in the inside of it wherein to plant your Flowers, you design to propagate in them.

But to prevent that casualty of breaking, some are made of Lead which are much to be preferred.   JOHN WORLIDGE, *Systema Horticulturae* [1677]

Today we seek out what was newly made in Worlidge's day in architectural graveyards.

It was well on in the afternoon before I reached Syon Lodge, which is the home of Bert Crowther; however, the hour did not seem to matter, for this is a place where time stands still. When you visit it you are caught up in a dream . . .

And you walk into the strangest garden in the world, or rather, a whole series of gardens, leading to leafy groves and shadowed lawns and trellised walks, crowded with the strangest collection of creatures that can ever have met together. Battalions of leaden cupids flock under the trees and sport on the old stone parapets; fauns and satyrs grimace from the undergrowth; round the ancient fountains a chorus of grey stone figures extend their arms and point their toes, gazing at the dancing water with eyes that see nothing and yet see everything, as they gazed, long ago, in the gardens from which they have been transported . . . the gardens of Versailles, of Rome, of Athens, and of many of the stately homes of England. There are scores of sundials, some of them thickly encrusted with moss, for whole decades had passed since the sun filtered through the mulberry branches to tell them the time of day; there are Palladian summer-houses, dusty and deserted; there are plinths and porticoes and balustrades and marble columns; and there is a whole Noah's Ark of animals, from elegant Chinese cockerels to plaster Victorian dogs which still manage to look respectable.

And there are urns. And urns. And still more urns. There are so many urns, in fact, urns of lead and marble and stucco and porphyry and terracotta, that one could walk off with a cartload of them without anybody being any the wiser. Indeed, that is one of the charms of Crowther's; nobody ever seems to be there. It takes ages before you find some young man in a shed who is reassembling an Adam mantelpiece and ask him the price of – say – an iron gate, and he never knows, and has to wander off to find our Mr Smith, and then you spend a delightful hour waiting for our Mr Smith who, at last, comes drifting along, and delivers a long and graceful exposition on Georgian ironwork, and finally, with the utmost reluctance, informs you of the sum for which the gate may be yours.

So I went to Crowther's and walked through the groves and the alleys to the sunken garden where most of the urns were grouped together. For nearly half an hour I prowled about among them; it was like stepping through the pages of a fairy-tale, so quiet was the garden, so rich the influences of the

past. At last I found the pair I wanted. They were lying on the grass in the shadow of one of the old mulberries; the fruit from the branches had fallen on them and around them so thickly that they were stained with the juice, and the lips of the maidens engraved on them glistened scarlet in the dying sunlight. They were delicately carved in lead, and on the sides of each urn four heads were embossed, two of youths and two of maidens. The faces of the maidens were placid and resigned, but the faces of the youths were scowling and passionate, maybe because they had been condemned by their creator to stare in front of them for all time, with never a chance to turn their heads to glance at their fair companions. Round the lips of the urns were clusters of grapes and at the base a frieze of acanthus leaves.

They had to be mine. Whatever they cost they had to be mine. Repairing of roof could wait; mending the cracks in the ceiling could wait, the peculiar smell in the woodshed could, and almost certainly would, wait. I had to have those urns. And after the customary search for our Mr Smith, who seemed even vaguer and more distant than usual, a bargain was struck, the urns were reverently placed in the back of the car, and I drove off.

BEVERLEY NICHOLS, *Merry Hall*
[1951]

PARTERRES

Parterres succeeded knots until swept away by the exponents of the landscape school. In their day they included quite a complex repertory of forms.

There are divers Sorts of Parterres, which may be all reduced to these Four that follow; namely, Parterres of Embroidery, Parterres of Compartiment, Parterres after the English Manner, and Parterres of Cut-work. There are also Parterres of Water, but at present they are quite out of Use.

Parterres of Embroidery are so called, because the Box wherewith they are planted, imitates Embroidery upon the Ground. These are the finest and most magnificent of all, and are sometimes accompanied with Knots and Scrolls of Grass-work. Their Bottom should be sanded, the better to distinguish the Foliage and Flourish'd-work of the Embroidery, which is usually filled with Smiths-Dust, or Black Earth. [In a note he says: 'Dross, or Scales of Iron. Smiths-Dust is either the Scales beaten off at the Anvil, or Iron Filings.']

Parterres of Compartiment differ from those of Embroidery, in that the same Symmetry of Design is repeated, as well in respect of the Ends as of the Sides. These Parterres are made up of Scrolls and other Grass-works, Knots, and Borders for Flowers, with a little well-disposed Embroidery, which Mixture produces an Effect very agreeable to the Eye. The Ground of these should be very well made, and filled with Sand between the Leaves; the narrow Paths that separate the Compartiments, we usually distinguish with Tile-shards, or Brick-dust. [In a note, 'powdered Tile or Brick, mix'd with Lime, which makes excellent Mortar, and is used by the French in Works under Water.']

Parterres after the English Manner are the plainest and meanest of all. They should consist only of large Grass-plots all of a Piece, or cut but little, and be encompassed with a Border of Flowers, separated from the Grass-work by a Path of Two or Three Foot wide, laid smooth, and sanded over, to make the greater Distinction. We give it the Name of Parterre à l'Angloise,

because we had the Manner of it first from England. [In a note, 'The French understand a Path raked over only, and not rolled, as 'tis generally translated, to comply with our Custom of Rolling, which is not so much used by the French, their Gravel rarely binding, as ours does.']

Parterres of Cut-work, tho' not so fashionable at present, are however not unworthy our Regard. They differ from the others, in that all the Parts which compose them should be cut with Symmetry, and that they admit neither of Grass nor Embroidery, but only Borders edged with Box, that serve to raise Flowers in; and by means of a Path of convenient Breadth that runs round each Piece, you may walk through the whole Parterre without hurting any Thing: All these Paths should be sanded.

A. J. DÉZALLIER D'ARGENVILLE,
The Theory and Practice of Gardening,
translated by John James [1712]

Although Southey confuses the parterre and the knot, he catches how much of a curiosity such a feature had become by his day. Within years J. C. Loudon was to revive the art for the Victorians.

The fashion which this buxom Flora introduced had at one time the effect of banishing flowers from what should have been the flower-garden; the ground was set with box in their stead, disposed in patterns more or less formal, some intricate as a labyrinth and not little resembling those of Turkey carpets, where Mahommedan laws interdict the likeness of any living thing, and the taste of Turkish weavers excludes any combination of graceful forms. One sense at least was gratified when fragrant herbs were used in these 'rare figures of composures,' or knots as they were called, hyssop being mixed in them with thyme, as aiders the one to the other, the one being dry, the other moist. Box had the disadvantage of a disagreeable odour; but it was greener in winter and more compact in all seasons. To lay out these knots and tread them required the skill of a master-gardener: much labour was thus expended without producing any beauty. The walks between them were sometimes of different colours; some would be of lighter or darker gravel, red or yellow sand: and when such materials were at hand, pulverized coal and pulverized shells.

Such a garden Mr Cradock saw at Bordeaux no longer ago than the year 1785; it belonged to Monsieur Rabi, a very rich Jew merchant, and was surrounded by a bank of earth, on which there stood about two hundred blue and white flower-pots; the garden itself was a scroll-work cut very narrow and the interstices filled with sand of different colours to imitate embroidery; it required repairing after every shower, and if the wind rose, the eyes were sure to suffer. Yet the French admired this and exclaimed, *Superbe magnifique!'*　　　　　　　ROBERT SOUTHEY [1774–1843]

PATHS　*The landscape style brought with it the meandering walk to replace the straight paths of the old formal style. Such paths became symbolic of British liberties.*

Smooth, simple path! whose undulating line
　With sidelong tufts of flow'ry fragrance crown'd,
　'Plain in its neatness' spans my garden ground;

What, though two acres thy brief course confine,
Yet sun and shade, and hill and dale are thine,
  And use with beauty here more surely found
  Than where, to spread the picturesque around,
Cast ruts and quarry holes their charms combine!
  Here, as thou lead'st my step through lawn or grove,
Liberal though limited, restrain'd though free,
  Fearless of dew, or dirt, or dust, I rove,
And own those comforts, all deriv'd from thee!
  Take then, smooth path, this tribute of my love,
Thou emblem pure of legal liberty!

THE REVEREND WILLIAM MASON,
The English Garden [1783 ed.]

Practical advice on front paths from a great Victorian popularizer.

Then we have winding paths, to make butcher-boys giddy, and perplex the stranger . . . and which compel the visitor to make half a tour of the grounds, when his chief object is to get inside the house, to take off his hat and gloves, and sit at the table punctual to a moment. Depend upon it, the best taste for an approach to a house, is to have it as direct as possible.

SHIRLEY HIBBERD, *The Town
Garden* [1859]

Too frequently an aberration of suburban gardening.   POND

We have three goldfish in our pond
Of whom my father's very fond,
And they were given by his choice
The names of Julia, Edith, Joyce.

(Since many a year they did abide,
Nor added nor yet multiplied
It seemed a safe thing to report
They all were of one sex or sort.)

And Father feeds them every day,
And often has been heard to say
That Edith looked a little wan
Or Joyce more weight was putting on.

But Julia was his special friend;
She swam the pond from end to end,
So long, so strong, so golden-red –
The finest fish, so Father said.

The poet Herrick loved and sung
A Julia when he was young;
And Father knew a Julia too –
His cousin, hence his tribute true.

But now a sudden doubt arises,
One of life's tragical surprises:
A friend points out with sceptic air
That goldfish (girls) alas are rare.

A gloom across our pond is shed,
The water-lily droops its head,
The reeds are wilting on the brink
And nobody knows what to think.

Though Father still by word of voice
Addresses Julia, Edith, Joyce,
His tones the sad conviction carry
They might be Thomas, Dick and Harry.

MARGARET LODGE, *Our Goldfish* [1935]

PROSPECT   *A letter of Robert, Lord Molesworth (1656–1725) gives a delightful account of the mighty prospect achieved by his Italian designer, Alessandro Galilei, at his estate at Breckdenstown, Co. Dublin. The 'Mr Switzer' was, of course, Stephen Switzer (1682–1745).*

I amuse my self with ye business of my estate & the diversions of my Grounds & gardens. I dare averr that I have by much the finest Canal near compleated in the Kings dominions, with regard to ye situation, in respect to ye house & gardens & to ye Sea & to all ye prospects, tis not much less than that in St James's Park, but tis infinitely more beautifull & herein I do not exaggerate & I shoud be glad yr Ldp had such a just occasion as I wish for, to view it upon ye spott & disprove me if you coud: I have a great many chimerical designs of my own & of others for yr large parterre wch leads down to it from whence I have ye noblest prospect of the main ocean, of ye Harbour of Malahide, & ye Sand Downs beyond it of Severall rising rocks & Islands, (such as Lambay, Hoath, Irelands Eye, Feltrim Hill, Malahide Hill, with many castles & churches & Wind mills &c), that I my self who have bin so long used to it am charmd with it. I can see ye Fleets of Shipps pass by to ye Bay of Dublin as I lye in my bed: yet I am above 3 miles from ye Wide Sea & have no manner of ill influence from it lying so much above it as I do, with a gentle descent all ye way to it, & ye harbour (wch is within 2 long miles of my house) & where at this instant I have a Ship of 80 tunns laden wth Coales for my use lying ready to be unloaded to morrow so that yr Ldp may see I do not intend to lye idle this summer but shall be deep in mortar & other work too chargeable for a purse like mine, wch gett's nothing to speak of from a Government I have served all my Life. However I can not refrain doing, tho I spend my whole income, & I coud wish for Mr Switzer to joyn his maggots to mine, & I am vain enough to think he would learn as much here as he woud teach us. I have & shall manage a little water to as great advantage as any man in Britain, tho I want proper workmen & instruments for the execution of my designs, this Kingdom affording none good . . .

LORD MOLESWORTH to LORD CONINGSBY, 26 May 1719

RUINS

No self-respecting landscape garden was devoid of a ruin, either castle or abbey, to complete a prospect. Sanderson Miller (1717–1780) and other garden architects were also only too willing to oblige in building one. Those whose estates embraced the remains of a dissolved monastery had no need to build but were provided with an instant ruin. Here Alexander Pope describes one of the earliest garden responses to the cult of ruins, those in Lord Digby's garden at Sherborne, Dorset.

On the left, full behind these old Trees, which make this whole Part inexpressibly awful & solemn, runs a little, old, low wall, beside a Trench, coverd with Elder trees & Ivyes; which being crost by another bridge, brings you to the Ruins, to compleat the Solemnity of the Scene. You first see an old Tower penetrated by a large Arch, and others above it thro which the whole Country appears in prospect, even when you are at the top of the other ruins, for they stand very high, & the Ground slopes down on all sides. These venerable broken Walls, some Arches almost entire of 30 or 40 ft deep, some open like Portico's with fragments of pillars, some circular or inclosd on three sides, but exposd at top, with Steps which Time has made of disjointed Stones to climb to the highest points of the Ruin: These I say might have a prodigious Beauty, mixd with Greens & Parterres from part to part, and the whole Heap standing as it does on a round hill, kept smooth in green turf, which makes a bold Basement to show it. The open Courts from building to building might be thrown into Circles or Octagons of Grass or flowers, and even in the gaming Rooms you have fine trees grown, that might be made a natural Tapistry to the walls, & arch you over-head where time has uncoverd them to the Sky. Little paths of earth, or sand, might be made, up the half-tumbled walls; to guide from one View to another on the higher parts; & Seats placd here and there, to enjoy those views, which are more romantick than Imagaination can form them . . .

What should induce my Lord D. the rather to cultivate these ruins and do honour to them, is that they do no small honour to his Family; that Castle, which was very ancient, being demolishd in the Civil wars after it was nobly defended by one of his Ancestors in the cause of the King. I would sett up at the Entrance of 'em an Obelisk, with an inscription of the Fact: which would be a Monument erected to the very Ruins.

ALEXANDER POPE TO MARTHA
BLOUNT [c. 1724]

Here a writer later in the century explains both their purpose and attraction.

To this great variety must be added the many changes which may be made by the means of *ruins*; they are a class by themselves, beautiful as objects, expressive as characters, and peculiarly calculated to connect with their appendages into elegant groupes: they may be accommodated with ease to irregularity of ground, and their disorder is improved by it; they may be intimately blended with trees and with thickets, and the interruption is an advantage; for imperfection and obscurity are their properties; and to carry the imagination to something greater than is seen, their effect. They may for any of these purposes be separated into detached pieces; contiguity is not necessary, not even the appearance of it, if the relation be preserved; but straggling ruins have a bad effect, when the several parts are equally considerable. There should be one large mass to raise an idea of greatness, to attract the others about it, and to be a common centre of union to all: the smaller pieces then mark the original dimensions of one extensive structure; and no longer appear to be the remains of several little buildings.

All remains excite an enquiry into the former state of the edifice, and fix the mind in a contemplation on the use it was applied to; besides the characters expressed by their style and position, they suggest ideas which would not arise from the buildings, if entire. The purposes of many have ceased; an abbey, or a castle, if complete, can now be no more than a dwelling; the memory of the times, and of the manners, to which they were adapted, is preserved only in history, and in ruins; and certain sensations of regret, of veneration, or compassion, attend the recollection: nor are these confined to the remains of buildings which are now in disuse; those of an old mansion raise reflections on the domestic comforts once enjoyed, and the ancient hospitality which reigned there. Whatever building we see in decay, we naturally contrast its present to its former state, and delight to ruminate on the comparison. It is true that such effects properly belong to real ruins; but they are produced in a certain degree by those which are fictitious; the impressions are not so strong, but they are exactly similar; and the represen-tation, though it does not present facts to the memory, yet suggests subjects to the imagination: but in order to affect the fancy, the supposed original design should be clear, the use obvious, and the form easy to trace; no fragments should be hazarded without a precise meaning, and an evident connection; none should be perplexed in their construction, or uncertain as to their application. Conjectures about the form, raises doubts about the existence of the ancient structure: The mind must not be allowed to hesitate; it must be hurried away from examining into the reality, by the exactness and the force of the resemblance . . .   THOMAS WHATELY, *Observations on Modern Gardening* [1770]

Ruins as a feature ran happily on through the picturesque phase of the landscape movement.

It is not every man who can build a house, that can execute a ruin. To give the stone its mouldering appearance – to make the widening chink run naturally through all the joints – to mutilate the ornaments – to peel the facing from the internal structure – to shew how correspondent parts have once united; though now the chasm runs wide between them – and to scatter heaps of ruin around with negligence and ease; are great efforts of art; much too delicate for the hand of a common workman; and what we very rarely see performed.

Besides, after all that art can bestow, you must put your ruin at last into the hands of nature to finish. If the mosses and lychens grow unkindly on your walls – if the streaming weather-stains have produced no variety of tints – if the ivy refuses to mantle over your buttress; or to creep among the ornaments of your Gothic window – and if the ash cannot be brought to hang from the cleft; or long, spiry grass to wave over the shattered battle-ment – you may as well write over the gate, Built in the year 1772.

Nor is the expence, which attends the construction of such a ruin, a trifling difficulty. The picturesque ruin must have no vulgarity of shape; and must convey the idea of grandeur. And no ruins that I know, except those of a real castle, or abbey, are suited to this purpose; and both these must be works of great expence.

THE REVEREND WILLIAM GILPIN,
*Observations on Several Parts of
England* . . . [1772]

But Gilpin (1724–1804) did censure those who dare tamper with a real ruin, as at Fountains Abbey.

The very idea of giving finished splendor to a ruin, is absurd. How unnatural, in a place, evidently forlorn and deserted by man, are the *recent* marks of human industry! . . . the *restoration* of parts is not enough; *ornaments* must be added: and such incongrous ornaments, as disgraced the *scene*, are disgracing also the *ruin*. The monk's *garden* is turned into a trim parterre, and planted with flowering shrubs: a view is opened, through the great window, to some ridiculous figure, (I know not what; Ann Bolein, I think, they called it) that is placed in the valley; and in the central part of the abbey-church, a circular pedestal is raised out of the fragments of the old pavement; on which is erected – a mutilated heathen statue!!!

THE REVEREND WILLIAM GILPIN,
*Observations on Several Parts of
England* . . . [1772]

Every garden needs seats upon which to linger, but here is an entire outdoor study erected each summer in the garden at Dyrham Park laid out for William Blathwayt (1649–1717), Secretary of State to William III.

SEATS

From this Seat you descend again to a flourishing Wilderness, on an easy Slope, cut out into the utmost Variety of Walks, especially solitary Walks, and beautify'd with Statues: In the Middle there is a delightful square Garden having four large Seats at the Corners, and a Seat round an aspiring Fir-Tree in the Center, from whence your Prospect terminates in a large old Church, at a very great Distance. I never in my whole Life did see so agreeable a Place for the sublimest Studies, as this is in the Summer, and here are small Desks erected in Seats for that Purpose.

STEPHEN SWITZER, *Ichnographia
Rustica* [1718 and 1742]

John, Lord Orrery (1707–62) describes how a garden seat placated his tenants in the large garden he was creating at Caledon, Co. Tyrone in the 1740s.

. . . To tell you the truth, my tenants have a notion that I am atheistically inclined, by putting up heathen statues and writing upon them certain words in an unknown language. They immediately suspected me for a papist, and my statues had been demolished, my woods burnt and my throat cut had not I suddenly placed a seat under an holly bush with this plain inscription, SIT DOWN AND WELCOME. I have assured them that all the Latin mottoes are to this purpose, and that in places where they cannot sit down, I have desired them in the old Norman dialect to go to the lodge, and drink whisky.

Letter of JOHN, LORD ORRERY,
*Orrery Papers, Houghton Library,
Harvard College* [1747]

And no garden seat is complete without a planting.

ON
A PLANT OF VIRGIN'S BOWER
Designed to Cover a Garden-seat

Thrive gentle plant! and weave a bow'r
   For Mary and for me,
And deck with many a splendid flow'r
   Thy foliage large and free.

Thou cam'st from Eartham, and wilt shade
   (If truly I divine)
Some future day th'illustrious head
   Of him who made thee mine.

Should Daphne show a jealous frown
   And envy seize the bay,
Affirming none so fit to crown
   Such honour'd brows as they,

Thy cause with zeal we shall defend,
   And with convincing pow'r;
For why should not the Virgin's Friend
   Be crown'd with Virgin's-bow'r?

WILLIAM COWPER [1793]

SHRUBBERY   *No garden anthology would be complete without this passage.*

She went, however, and they sauntered about together many an half hour in Mrs Grant's shrubbery, the weather being unusually mild for the time of year, and venturing sometimes even to sit down on one of the benches now comparatively unsheltered, remaining there perhaps till, in the midst of some tender ejaculation of Fanny's on the sweets of so protracted an autumn, they were forced by the sudden swell of a cold gust shaking down the last few yellow leaves about them, to jump up and walk for warmth.

'This is pretty, very pretty,' said Fanny, looking around her as they were thus sitting together one day; 'every time I come into this shrubbery I am more struck with its growth and beauty. Three years ago this was nothing but a rough hedgerow along the upper side of the field, never thought of as anything, or capable of becoming anything; and now it is converted into a walk, and it would be difficult to say whether most valuable as a convenience or an ornament; and perhaps in another three years we may be forgetting – almost forgetting what it was before.' . . .

'It may seem impertinent in me to praise, but I must admire the taste Mrs Grant has shewn in all this. There is such a quiet simplicity in the plan of the walk! Not too much attempted!'

'Yes,' replied Miss Crawford, carelessly, 'It does very well for a place of this sort. One does not think of extent *here*; and between ourselves, till I came to Mansfield, I had not imagined a country parson ever aspired to a shrubbery, or anything of the kind.'

'I am so glad to see the evergreens thrive!' said Fanny, in reply. 'My uncle's gardener always says the soil here is better than his own, and so it appears from the growth of the laurels and evergreens in general. The evergreen! How beautiful, how welcome, how wonderful the evergreen! When one thinks of it, how astonishing a variety of nature! In some countries we know that the tree that sheds its leaf is the variety, but that does not make it less amazing, that the same soil and the same sun should nurture plants differing in the first rule and law of their existence.'

JANE AUSTEN, *Mansfield Park*   [1814]

STATUARY

Henry Peacham (1576–1643) records exactly the moment when statuary arrived in England and was utilized to adorn gardens.

And here I cannot but with much reverence, mention the every way Right honourable *Thomas Howard* Lord high Marshall of *England*, as great for his noble Patronage of Arts and ancient learning, as for his birth and place. To whose liberall charges and magnificence, this angle of the world oweth the first sight of Greeke and Romane Statues, with whose admired preference he began to honour the Gardens and Galleries of Arundel-House about twentie yeeres agoe, and hath ever since continued to transplant old Greece into *England*. King *Charles* also ever since his coming to the Crowne, hath amply testified a Royall liking of ancient statues, by causing a whole army of old forraine Emperours, Captaines, and Senators all at once to land on his coasts, to come and doe him homage, and attend him in his palaces of Saint *Iames*, and Sommerset-house. A great part of these belonged to the late Duke of *Mantua*: and some of the Old-greeke-marble-bases, columnes, and altars were brought from the ruines of *Apollo's* Temple at *Delos*, by that noble and absolutely compleat Gentleman Sir *Kemhelme Digby* Knight. In the Garden at St *Iames* there are also halfe a dozen brasse statues, rare ones, cast by *Hubert le Sueur* his Majesties Servant now dwelling in Saint *Bartholomewes* London, the most industrous and excellent Statuary in all materials that ever this Countrey enjoyed.

The best of them is the Gladiator, molded from that in Cardinall *Borgheses Villa*, by the procurement and industry of ingenious Master *Gage*. And at the present the said Master *Sueur* hath divers other admirable molds to cast in brasse for his Majestie, and among the rest that famous *Diana* of *Ephesus* above named. But the great Horse with his Majestie upon it, twice as great as the life, and now well-nigh finished, will compare with that of the New-bridge at *Paris*, or those others at *Florence* and *Madrid*, though made by *Sueur* his Master, *Iohn de Bolonia* that rare workeman, who not long since lived at *Florence*. At Yorke-house also, the Galleries and Roomes are ennobled with the possession of those Romane Heads, and Statues, which lately belonged to Sir *Peter Paul Rubons* Knight, that exquisit Painter of *Antwerp*: and the Garden will bee renowned so long as *Iohn de Bologna's Cain* and *Abel* stand erected there, a peece of wondrous Art and Workemanship. The King of *Spaine* gave it his Majestie at his being there, who bestowed it on the late Duke of *Buckingham*.

HENRY PEACHAM, *Compleat Gentleman*   [1634]

Today we forget that many of the figures were polychrome and aimed to deceive the visitor. Woburn Abbey had a famous one in a cherry orchard.

... in the midst ... stands a figure of stone resembling an old weeder woman used in the garden, and my Lord would have her Effigie which is done so like and her clothes so well that at first I tooke it to be a real living body ...

CELIA FIENNES, 1697; in The Journeys of Celia Fiennes, ed. Christopher Morris, [1947]

John James (1672–1746), in his translation of Dézallier d'Argenville's book of 1709, tells us the principles that governed their placing in the baroque garden.

These figures represent all the several deities, and illustrious persons of antiquity, which should be placed properly in gardens, setting the river gods, as the *Naiades, Rivers* and *Tritons*, in the middle of fountains and basons; and those of the woods, as *Sylvanes, Faunes*, and *Dryads* in the groves; sacrifices, bacchanals and children's sports, are likewise represented in bass-relieve, upon the vases and pedestals, which may be adorn'd with festoons, foliage moldings, and other ornaments.

The usual places of figures and vases are long the palisades, in the front, and upon the sides of a parterre; in the niches and sinkings of hornbeam, or of latticework made for that purpose. In groves, they are placed in the centre of a star, or S. *Andrew's* Cross; in the spaces between the walks of a goose-foot, in the middle of halls and cabinets, among the trees and arches of a green-gallery, and at the head of a row of trees, or palisades, that stand free and detached. They are also put at the lower end of walks and vistas, to set them off the better; in porticos, and arbors of trellis-work; in basons, cascades, &c.

In general, they do well everywhere; and you can scarce have too many of them in a garden but, as in the business of sculpture, it should be excellent, as well as in paintings and posesy (which are its two sisters). I think it more advisable for a private gentleman to be content without figures, than to take up with such as are but indifferent, which do but create a continual longing after this perfection; the expense of which is fit only for princes, and great ministers.

A. J. DÉZALLIER D'ARGENVILLE, The Theory and Practice of Gardening translated by John James [1712]

William Robinson (1838–1935), the apostle of the wild garden, hated statues.

... the scattering of numerous statues of a low order of merit, or of no merit at all, which we see in some Italian gardens, often gives a bad effect and the dotting of statues about both the public gardens of Paris and London is destructive of all repose.

W. ROBINSON, The English Flower Garden, 6th edn, [1898]

And Sir George Sitwell, champion of the Italian formal garden, loved them.

Statues of marble seldom look well in Italy, never in England, and of all discords none can be so jarring as to place among the flowers dreadful forms

of disease and suffering, cripples or beggars, or the monstrous dwarfs that look down from the Valmarana garden as if to symbolize the starved and stunted life of the wall-coping. Art, like laughter, should be the language of happiness, and those who suffer should be silent. Time and Care may wait without the gateway, but Time the ungracious guest, who is always late for the wedding feast and early for the funeral – envious Time the spoiler of the roses, who lays his hateful scythe to the root of the fairest flowers, should have no image, no altar, in the garden, for it is by events and not by the measure of them that we grow old, and hours spent in a garden are stolen from Death and from Time. Only health and strength and beauty are at home among the flowers, shepherds and shepherdesses, youths and maidens in the garb of long ago, portly noblemen in periwigs and armour, warriors and Amazons, nymphs and satyrs, virtues and graces. We may personify the particular place in a figure or bust, taught by the gate at Capua and the pulpit at Ravello, or commemorate an historic event by reference as in the cavalier's garden at Norton Conyers where a leaden warrior speaks discreetly of the Edgehill fight. We may represent the great elemental forces of nature, the higher motives which sway the human drama, the hoped-for triumph of Love over Death. We may build in some secluded nook a Cupid's altar, where many generations of lovers shall carve their names and make their offerings of flowers, or may set in the four quarters of the garden our pageant of the Seasons: Spring, as a winged youth, primrose-crowned, with flute and flower-embroidered robe; proud Summer as a weary king; spendthrift Autumn with open purse and lifted cup and gathered fruit; hoary Winter having a sealed casket under his foot, his beard hung with icicles and his mantle broidered with double-faced jests. No statue, however bad, should be condemned to a desolate old age. In a decorative landscape the figures are never happy unless they are enjoying themselves, and in a portrait even ugliness is rendered charming by the presence of a child, a dog or bird. Diana in a garden should not be without a hound, nor Neptune without his sea-monster; Mars may be mated with Venus, Flora with Vertumnus, Cupid with Psyche; every Amazon should have her warrior and every nymph her satyr.   Sir George Sitwell, *On the Making of Gardens* [1909]

SUNDIAL

Now merely an ornament, before the advent of clocks and watches the garden sundial had a practical purpose as well as offering moral overtones.

What a collegiate aspect has that fine Elizabethan hall, where the fountain plays, which I have made to rise and fall, how many times! to the astoundment of the young urchins, my contemporaries, who, not being able to guess at its recondite machinery, were almost tempted to hail the wondrous work as magic! What an antique air had the now almost effaced sun-dials, with their moral inscriptions, seeming coevals with that Time which they measured, and to take their revelations of its flight immediately from heaven, holding correspondence with the fountain of light! How would the dark line steal imperceptibly on, watched by the eye of childhood, eager to detect its movement, never catched, nice as an evanescent cloud, or the first arrests of sleep!

> Ah yet doth beauty like a dial hand
> Steal from his figure, and no pace perceived!

What a dead thing is a clock, with its ponderous embowelments of lead and brass, its pert or solemn dulness of communication, compared with the simple altar-like structure and silent heart-language of the old dials! It stood as the garden god of Christian gardens. Why is it almost everywhere vanished? If its business-use be superseded by more elaborate inventions, its moral uses, its beauty, might have pleaded for its continuance. It spoke of moderate labours, of pleasures not protracted after sunset, of temperance, and good hours. It was the primitive clock, the horologe of the first world. Adam could scarce have missed it in Paradise. It was the measure appropriate for sweet plants and flowers to spring by, for the birds to apportion their silver warblings by, for flocks to pasture and be led to fold by. The shepherd 'carved it out quaintly in the sun'; and, turning philosopher by the very occupation, provided it with mottoes more touching than tombstones.

CHARLES LAMB, *Essays* [1823]

A friend in London who knew my desire for a sun-dial and heard that I could not obtain the old one which had told me so important a story in my childhood, presented me with one to stand on the grass under my terrace wall and above the quarry which was already beginning to fill with shrubs and wild flowers. The design of the dial is beautiful -- being a copy of an ancient font; and in grey granite, to accord with the grey-stone house above it. The motto was an important affair. A neighbour had one so perfect in its way as to eclipse a whole class, -- the class of Bible-sayings about the shortness of life and the flight of time, -- 'The Night Cometh'. In asking my friends for suggestions, I told them of this, and they agreed that we could not approach this motto in the same direction. Some good Latin ones, to which I inclined, were put aside because I was besought, for what I considered good reasons, to have nothing but English. It has always been my way to ask advice very rarely, and then to follow it. But on this occasion I preferred a motto of my own to all that were offered in English; and Wordsworth gave it his emphatic approbation. 'Come! Light! Visit me!' stands emblazoned on my dial; and it has been, I believe, as frequent and impressive a monitor to me as ever was any dial which bore warning of the fugacious nature of life and time.

HARRIET MARTINEAU,
Autobiography [1877]

> 'Tis an old dial, dark with many a stain;
>   In summer crowned with drifting orchard bloom,
> Tricked in the autumn with the yellow rain,
>   And white in winter like a marble tomb;
>
> And round about its gray, time-eaten brow
>   Lean letters speak -- a worn and shattered row:
> *I am a Shade: a Shadowe too arte thou:*
>   *I marke the Time: saye, Gossip, dost thou soe?*

Here would the ringdoves linger, head to head;
    And here the snail a silver course would run,
Beating old Time; and here the peacock spread
    His gold-green glory, shutting out the sun.

AUSTIN DOBSON (1840–1921),
The Sundial

TOPIARY

Although topiary was a feature of the medieval garden, it was developed as a garden element to its highest pitch in the Tudor and Stuart periods.

Your Gardiner can frame your lesser wood to the shape of men armed in the field, ready to give battell: or swift running Grey hounds: or of well sented and true running Hounds, to chase the Deere, or hunt the Hare. This kinde of hunting shall not waste your corne, nor much your coyne.

WILLIAM LAWSON, *A New Orchard
and Garden* [1618]

It was Addison (1672–1719) who began the attack, viewing topiary in a political light as a symbol of the absolutism of the French monarchy.

Our *British* Gardeners, on the contrary, instead of humouring Nature, love to deviate from it as much as possible. Our Trees rise in Cones, Globes, and Pyramids. We see the Marks of the Scissars upon every Plant and Bush. I do not know whether I am singular in my Opinion, but, for my own part, I would rather look upon a Tree in all its Luxuriancy and Diffusion of Boughs and Branches, than when it is thus cut and trimmed into a Mathematical Figure; and cannot but fancy that an Orchard in Flower looks infinitely more delightful, than all the little Labyrinths of the most finished Parterre. But as our great Modellers of Gardens have their Magazines of Plants to dispose of, it is very natural for them to tear up all the Beautiful Plantations of Fruit Trees, and contrive a Plan that may most turn to their own Profit, in taking off their Evergreens, and the like Moveable Plants, with which their Shops are plentifully stocked.

JOSEPH ADDISON, *The Spectator*,
No. 414, 25 June 1712

And Pope's famous satire followed a year later to strike the death knell of the art.

I believe it is no wrong Observation, that Persons of Genius, and those who are most capable of Art, are always most fond of Nature, as such are chiefly sensible, that all Art consists in the Imitation and Study of Nature. On the contrary, People of the common Level of Understanding are principally delighted with the Little Niceties and Fantastical Operations of Art, and constantly think that *finest* which is least Natural. A Citizen is no sooner Proprietor of a couple of Yews, but he entertains Thoughts, of erecting them into Giants, like those of *Guild-hall*. I know an eminent Cook, who beautified his Country Seat with a Coronation Dinner in Greens, where you see the Champion flourishing on Horseback at one end of the Table, and the Queen in perpetual Youth at the other.

For the benefit of all my loving Country-men of this curious Taste, I shall here publish a Catalogue of Greens to be disposed of by an eminent Town-Gardiner, who has lately applied to me upon this Head. He represents, that for the Advancement of a politer sort of Ornament in the Villas and Gardens adjacent to this great City, and in order to distinguish those Places from the meer barbarous Countries of gross Nature, the World stands much in need of a Virtuoso Gardiner who has a Turn to Sculpture, and is thereby capable of improving upon the Ancients of his Profession in the Imagery of Ever-greens. My Correspondent is arrived to such Perfection, that he cuts Family Pieces of Men, Women or Children. Any Ladies that please may have their own Effigies in Myrtle, or their Husbands in Horn beam. He is a Puritan Wag, and never fails when he shows his Garden, to repeat that Passage in the Psalms, *Thy Wife shall be as the fruitful Vine, and thy Children as Olive Branches round thy Table.* I shall proceed to his Catalogue, as he sent it for my Recommendation.

ADAM and *Eve* in Yew; *Adam* a little shatter'd by the fall of the Tree of Knowledge in the great Storm; *Eve* and the Serpent very flourishing.

THE tower of *Babel*, not yet finished.

St GEORGE in Box; his Arm scarce long enough, but will be in a Condition to stick the Dragon by next *April.*

A green *Dragon* of the same, with a Tail of Ground-Ivy for the present. N.B. *These two not to be Sold separately.*

EDWARD the *Black Prince* in Cypress.

A *Laurustine* Bear in Blossom, with a Juniper Hunter in Berries.

A Pair of Giants, *stunted*, to be sold cheap.

A Queen *Elizabeth* in Phylyraea, a little inclining to the Green Sickness, but of full growth.

ANOTHER Queen *Elizabeth* in Myrtle, which was very forward, but Miscarried by being too near a Savine.

AN old Maid of Honour in Wormwood.

A topping *Ben Johnson* in Lawrel.

DIVERS eminent Modern Poets in Bays, somewhat blighted, to be disposed of a Pennyworth.

A Quick-set Hog shot up into a Porcupine, by its being forgot a Week in rainy Weather.

A Lavender Pig with Sage growing in his Belly.

NOAH's *Ark* in Holly, standing on the Mount; the Ribs a little damaged for want of Water.

A Pair of *Maidenheads* in Firr, in great forwardness.

ALEXANDER POPE, *Essay from
'The Guardan'* [1713]

Having been swept away by the Georgians, the Victorians revived the art, but not everyone was delighted.

. . . What right have we to deform things given us so perfect and lovely in form? No cramming of Chinese feet into impossible shoes is half so wicked as the wilful and brutal distortion of the beautiful forms of trees.

W. ROBINSON, *The English Flower
Garden* [6th edn 1898]

In the summer of 1955 Sir Cecil Beaton visited Elsie Mendl at her house at Versailles.

I decided to go for a walk in the park of Versailles. The Hubert Robert avenues of vast dark trees were a triumph of symmetry; at certain points one came to the junction of eight avenues stretching to the statue-adorned horizons. Surely the French in the eighteenth century had reached their peak in ordering nature to current fashion? Returning to Elsie's entirely green garden, I wondered if she had not beaten even the eighteenth century at its own game? The lawns were like billiard cloth, the overhanging trees were 'set' in place by a great scene designer so that not a branch dare move. But the *clous* of Elsie's topiary garden were the trees cut into the shape of oversize elephants. These green animals were Elsie's last defiance at the contempt with which the Germans had maltreated her garden during the Occupation.

CECIL BEATON, *The Restless Years, Diaries 1935–63* [1976]

WALKS

The Elizabethans had wonderful enclosed walks from which to view their gardens.

The commodities of these Alleis and walkes serve to good purposes, the one is that the owner may diligently view the prosperities of his herbes and flowers, the other for the delight and comfort of his wearied mind, which he may be himself or fellowship of his friends conceyve in the delectable sightes and fragrant smelles of the flowers, by walking up and downe, and about the Garden in them, which for the pleasant sights and refreshing of the dull spirites, with the sharpening of the memorie, many shadowed over with vawting or herbes, having windowes properly made towards the Garden, whereby they might the more fully view and have delight in the whole beautie of the Garden.

THOMAS HILL, *The Gardener's Labyrinth* [1577]

WALLS

Any gardener lucky enough to have old ones will echo these sentiments.

An old garden wall is a very precious possession to a gardener. If he finds himself placed in a new garden surrounding a new house he may by much expenditure of labour and money soon get a well-filled garden, but if ever he goes into the garden of a friend who owns an old garden, surrounded or bounded by an old wall, he feels that his own garden wants something which only time can give him. For an old wall is, or may be, very useful to gardeners; I do not mean for training trees – a new wall will do for that as well, or better – but for planting on it many things which there find their most congenial home. Nature teaches us the lesson by the way she clothes, and clothes rapidly, old ruins; but I do not wish to say anything of this natural clothing of old walls, except that it is well worth noting how many plants seem to prefer these old walls even to well-tilled ground near them. I never saw the beautiful small white periwinkle (an uncommon plant any-where, and even doubtfully native) so luxuriant as I once saw it on the walls of Tintern Abbey. As it grew there I could easily fancy that it was an escape from, and perhaps the last remnant of, the old Abbey garden, and for the first time I realized how well adapted the plant was to form the 'garlands of

Pervenke set on his heaed' that Chaucer and other old writers sing of; but the plant is no longer there, having been destroyed by a succession of admiring and greedy visitors. And many of us recollect with pleasure the South European *Senecio squalidus* at Oxford. It probably escaped from the botanic garden, and now clothes, not only the grand old cop wall of the gardens (a wall that is almost unequalled as a garden wall), but also the walls of the park of Magdalen, and even grows freely on the stringcourses of Magdalen tower.

CANON ELLACOMBE, *In a Gloucestershire Garden* [1895]

WATER   *Without which, in some form, no garden is truly complete.*

If the river run by your door, and under your Mount, it will be pleasant. You might sit in your Mount, and Angle a speckled Trout, sleighty Eele, or some other dainty Fish. Or Moate, whereon you may row with a Boat, and fish with Nets.

WILLIAM LAWSON, *A New Orchard and Garden* [1618]

Thomas Whately (d. 1772), a minor politician and a miscellaneous writer, produced one of the best descriptions of the delights of water in the garden.

OF THE EFFECTS AND SPICIES OF WATER

Water . . . which though not absolutely necessary to a beautiful composition, yet occurs so often, and is so capital a feature, that it is always regretted when wanting; and no large place can be supposed, a little spot can hardly be imagined in which it may not be agreeable; it accommodates itself to every situation; is the most interesting object in a landscape, and the happiest circumstance in a retired recess; captivates the eye at a distance; invites approach, and is delightful when near; it refreshes an open exposure; it animates a shade; chears the dreariness of a waste, and enriches the most crouded view; in form, in style, and in extent, may be made equal to the greatest compositions, or adapted to the least; it may spread in a calm expanse to sooth the tranquillity of a peaceful scene; or hurrying along a devious course, add splendour to a gay, and extravagance to a romantic, situation. So various are the characters which water can assume, that there is scarcely an idea in which it may not concur, or an impression which it cannot enforce: a deep stagnated pool, dank and dark with shades which it dimly reflects, befits the seat of melancholy; even a river, if it be sunk between two dismal banks, and dull both in motion and colour, is like a hollow eye which deadens the countenance; and over a sluggard, silent stream, creeping heavily along all together, hangs a gloom, which no art can dissipate, nor even the sun-shine disperse. A gently murmuring rill, clear and shallow, just gurgling, just dimpling, imposes silence, suits with solitude, and leads to meditation: a brisker current, which wantons in little eddies over a bright sandy bottom, or babbles among pebbles, spreads chearfulness all around: a greater rapidity, and more agitation, to a certain degree are animating; but in excess, instead of wakening, they alarm the senses: the roar and the rage of a torrent, its force, its violence, its impetuosity, tend to inspire terror; that terror, which, whether as cause or effect, is so nearly allied to sublimity.

Abstracted, however, from all these ideas, from every sensation, either of depression, composure, or exertion; and considering water merely as an object, no other is so apt soon to catch, and long to fix, the attention: but it may want beauties of which we know it is capable; or the marks may be confused by which we distinguish its species; and these defects displease: to avoid them, the properties of each species must be determined.

THOMAS WHATELY, *Observations on Modern Gardening* [1770]

But perhaps Sir George Sitwell's is even better.

I have left almost to the last the magic of water, an element which owing to its changefulness of form and mood and colour and to the vast range of its effects is ever the principal source of landscape beauty, and has like music a mysterious influence over the mind. It was, perhaps, of this that Wagner was thinking when he wrote that music is like a power of nature which men perceive but do not understand. In the sound of rushing or of falling water there is beauty of reflection, for it repeats and by repeating deepens the joy or sorrow of the listener's mood; but to those who hearken more intently water will speak with a voice of its own, a message of peace or strength or freedom, in the careless ease of its flowing, the lulling monotony of rhythmic sound, the exhilaration of power. But its chief appeal is through the avenue of sight. Movement representing to the eye the essential character of living things, the quality by which they reveal themselves, just as inanimate objects are recognized by form, a fountain or rivulet will be to the garden a well of living water. On the other hand, the reflections in still basins have a strangely restful effect. They are associated, as Ruskin points out, with the idea of quiet succession and continuance; that one day should be like another, one life the echo of another life, being a result of quietude, part of that great rhythm of harmonious change through birth and death to birth again which is the heart-beat of the universe. In lake or pool or river, water emphasizes the prevailing note of the landscape, harmonizes the picture by distributing or echoing colours and forms, by 'reviving' the tints of sky, foliage and flowers, and whether in movement or repose it fascinates the eye which returns to it again and again; it should therefore, both in park and garden, be found at the focus of beauty and interest. These water reflections are actually more delightful than the views they repeat in the softness of the lights, the depth, transparency and intricacy of the shadows, the freshness and tenderness of the colouring; for the gloss of the water-film is like the coat of old varnish which mellows a picture; like the twilight it gives breadth, connection and unity; and the reversal of the image by baffling perception makes the colours richer and the contrasts of light and shade more conspicuous. The effect goes even further than this. We have not merely an improved presentment but an altered composition. The landscape is repeated from a fresh point of view, that is to say from one as much below the surface of the water as the spectator is above it, and all the objects which make it up are seen under different lights and in different relative positions. It may thus happen that the foreground, instead of being merged in soft meadow or shadowy foliage is silhouetted upon the sky; is relieved, as in Turner's drawing of Nottingham, not against the dark base of a hill but against its sunlit summit. The middle distance is cut out of the picture, there is a sharper gradation of values from the nearer to the more distant reflections, and the shadows are not merely a lower tone but spaces of an entirely different hue, to which the heightened power of reflection gives depth and variety. The blue of the sky is darkened and other colours are altered or omitted. If there is the least movement of the surface, vertical lines will be lengthened and rendered more emphatic, while horizontal lines will tend to disappear.

But the distant view in a water landscape can never be so beautiful as a simple rendering of reeds and foliage. The grandest effect of all is produced by formal canals, not too large, which reflect the pavilion at the further end and the lime avenues which edge them in. For smaller pools, the first object must be to give the water-artist something to play with – richly carved balustrades as at Frascati with fountain masks of bearded river-gods that drop tiny runlets of crystal into the basin, or mossy crevices, or the golden bloom of lichened stone, or plants, if any such exist, whose leaves are dark above and light below. Baby faces may lean to meet the reflections or, as in D'Annunzio's novel, Love and Death may kiss each other. The larger or more vertical the angle at which one looks down, the greater is the difference between the scene and its echo. We may thus, by slightly sinking the pool, reflect beauties of carving and surface invisible from above; phantom forms may reveal themselves, or sculptured figures in the water may be springing up to grasp the shadows. The effect may be complicated by strange effects of light admitted through a crevice between bank and balustrade.

In water the two pictures always contend, reflection and transparency being in inverse ratio to each other, and in some positions it may be better to abandon the surface and cultivate the beauties of the underworld. With a fountain basin, sculpture must necessarily be above the water, but in dealing with a still reservoir no such law is imposed upon us. We may have a merman's pool, fringed with floating lilies, where below the water-film are sea-maidens and gold-red fish and underwater palaces, and that strange power the eye has of clearing away reflections by the change to a longer focus will enhance the effect by a sudden thrill of surprise. Columns and opposing mirrors may give endless vistas of pillared halls, and if the pool is near the upper edge of a cliff a strange light may be thrown into it through an opening protected by glass. We may build up a dark screen of masonry behind it and illuminate it through a water passage from a pool beyond, or make the still more interesting experiment of 'total internal reflection,' admitting the sun's rays in the late afternoon between the stems of a great hedge of beech or ilex at such an angle that the returning rays will lie along or actually under the surface of the water. Some of these will appear to be bizarre suggestions, and indeed it is likely enough that, except in great conservatories or winter gardens, under-water mirrors may produce an unquiet effect. But until such experiments have been tried, an opinion is of little value. There are no rules in art which some great artist has not shown us how to break with advantage, and every new adventure is a voyage of discovery, the outcome of which no man may foresee. Nature has 'thousands of exquisite effects of light which are absolutely inexplicable,' which can be believed only while they are seen, and by good fortune we may reap a larger harvest than we have sown.

Elsewhere the designer may prefer to play with the colour of the water,

seeking to reproduce those lovely hues of blue and green which the Italians of an earlier age caught and fixed in garden reservoirs, and even in small fountain basins. Water absorbs the red rays of the spectrum and is therefore a blue transparent medium, its colour when distilled being a tint of Prussian blue, as may be seen in the pure ice of the glacier crevasses. All that is necessary to bring out the natural beauty of the element by transmitted light is, firstly, a flood of strong sunshine; secondly, to look down from above as nearly vertically as possible; thirdly, to cut off reflections of the sky by trees or hedges or other dark objects. Suspended particles of glacier dust or chalk or lime add much to the brilliance of the effect, and in a country where the stone is red or yellow should give a tint of green or purple or violet. In England one may sometimes see blue or green pools at the bottom of a deserted stone-quarry: if experiment should show that good colour is unattainable at a higher level under these grey skies, we shall be justified in helping it out by the use of coloured tiles.

SIR GEORGE SITWELL, *On the Making of Gardens* [1909]

All of those tempted to embark on a water-garden should read this first.

Advice to those about to build a Water-garden – DON'T. Not that the Water-garden is not a joy and a glory; but that it is cruelly hard to keep in order and control unless you are master of millions and of broad ample acres of pool and pond. Water, like fire, is a good servant, perhaps, but is painfully liable to develop into a master . . . How many little ponds are unguardedly built, only to become mere basins of slime and duckweed? How many larger pools are made, only to fill with *Chara, Potamogeton*, and the other noxious growths that make its depths a clogged, waving forest of dull brown verdure? The fact is a pool, not an easy thing to build and set going – is of all things in the garden the hardest of all to keep in decent order. Some of its choice inmates devour and despoil the smaller ones; water weeds increase and multiply at a prodigious rate; dead leaves drift thick upon it in autumn, slime and green horrors make a film across it in summer.

R. J. FARRER, *Alpines and Bog Plants* [1908]

Triumphs of Renaissance hydraulic engineering, the passion for infantile water pranks was also a standard ingredient of the gardens of the great. Both Chatsworth had and Petrodvorets, Peter the Great's palace, still has a weeping tree fountain of a type described here as having been at Dyrham Park.

WATER WORKS

At the Bottom of the Steps are planted two Thorns encompass'd with Seats, which are arriv'd to a large Stature, and being kept of a round regular form with frequent Clippings, make a very good Figure: There are small Pipes which twine round the Bodies of these Trees, and appear more like Ivy on the rough Bark, (being painted Green) than leaden Pipes, which on the Turn of a Cock discharge Water from a vast Number of small Nosils in the Head of the Trees, all round as natural as if it rain'd; and in a cloudy Day I have been inform'd, Spectators setting down here to rest themselves, the more these Pipes have play'd, the closer they have embrac'd the Tree for Shelter, supposing it had really rain'd, 'till the gardener has convinc'd them of their Error, after they had partaken of a sufficient Sprinkling to imprint in their Memories the pleasurable Mistake.   STEPHEN SWITZER, *Ichnographia Rustica* [1718–42]

WILDERNESS   *A garden feature above all of the Stuart period, not in the least like we would now conceive it, for it was a geometrical planting of hedges to form paths leading to bowers and bosquets. This is a rare glimpse of its use. Every morning Mary Rich, Countess of Warwick (1625–78), retired to it to pray and meditate. Hence the grief at its radical pruning. The garden was at Leighs Priory, near Felstead, Essex.*

UPON THE CUTTING DOWN OF THE WILDERNESS

This sweet place that I have seen the first sprouting growth and flourishing of for above twenty years together, and almost daily taken delight in, I have also now to my trouble seen, by my lord's command, the cutting down of, in order to hasten its after growing again thicker and better, though I often interceded with him to have it longer spared.

This brought to my sad remembrance afresh the death of my only son, whom I had also seen the first growth of in his childhood, and the flourishing of, to my unspeakable satisfaction, for almost twenty-one years; and, in a short space of time, to my unexpressible grief, by my Great Lord's command, cut down by death, that he might rise again in a better and more flourishing condition, though I often implored, if it was agreeable with the divine will, he might be longer continued to me.

MARY RICH, COUNTESS OF WARWICK, *Journal*, quoted by her biographer, C. Fell Smith

A Border of Beds

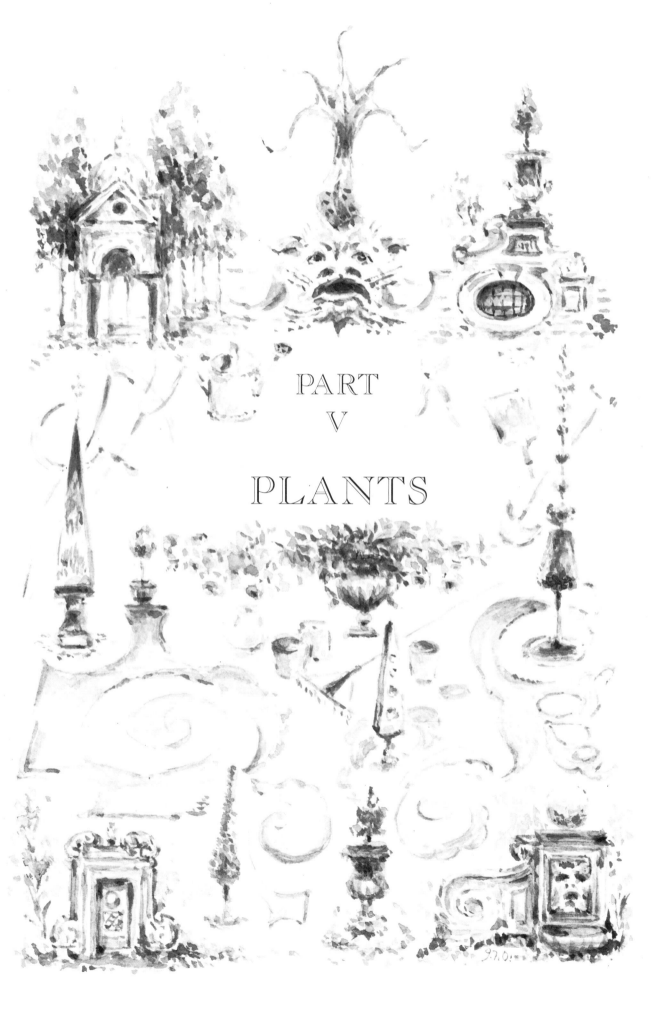

PART
V

PLANTS

Just as an un-assorted assemblage of mere words, though they may be the best words in our language, will express no thought, or as the purest colours on an artist's palette – so long as they remain on the palette – do not form a picture, so our garden plants, placed without due consideration or definite intention, cannot show what they can best do for us.

GERTRUDE JEKYLL, 'A Definite
Purpose in Gardening', *The World*,
15 August 1905

No one has ever written so hilariously about these as Katharine S. White whose pieces first appeared in the New Yorker, *in this instance in 1958.*

PLANT CATALOGUES

For gardeners, this is the season of lists and callow hopefulness; hundreds of thousands of bewitched readers are poring over their catalogues, making lists for their seed and plant orders, and dreaming their dreams. It is the season, too, when the amateur gardener like myself marvels or grumbles at the achievements of the hybridizers and frets over the idiosyncrasies of the editors and writers who get up the catalogues. They are as individualistic – these editors and writers – as any Faulkner or Hemingway, and they can be just as frustrating or rewarding. They have an audience equal to the most popular novelist's, and a handful of them are stylists of some note. Even the catalogues with which no one man can be associated seem to have personalities of their own.

Before we examine the writers and editors, let us consider the hybridizers, and the horticulturalists in general. Their slogan is not only 'Bigger and Better' but 'Change' – change for the sake of change, it seems. Say you have a nice flower like the zinnia – clean-cut, of interesting, positive form, with formal petals that are so neatly and cunningly put together, and with colors so subtle yet clear, that they have always been the delight of the still-life artist. Then look at the W. Atlee Burpee and the Joseph Harris Company catalogues and see what the seedsmen are doing to zinnias. Burpee, this year, devotes its inside front cover to full-color pictures of its Giant Hybrid Zinnias, which look exactly like great, shaggy chrysanthemums. Now, I *like* chrysanthemums, but why should zinnias be made to look like them? From Harris, you can buy the seed of what it calls New Super *Cactus* Flowered Zinnias, and they certainly do look like cactuses, or you can buy the seed of Fantasy Zinnias, which are the counterpart of asters. And both companies offer zinnias that look like dahlias. It is all very confusing. The Burpee people, who have always been slightly mad on the subject of marigolds, this

year devote their outside front cover to their New Giant Fluffy Marigolds, which they describe as 'large, round, fluffy, double chrysanthemum-like blooms'; this is just what they appear to be – chrysanthemums, not marigolds. In the Harris book, similar marigolds go by the *name* of Mum Marigolds. Meanwhile, what is happening to chrysanthemums? Well, some of *them* are being turned into cactuses, too; Wayside Gardens offers plants of one it describes as 'Bronze Cactus – rare new mums with new style flowers.' What is happening to cactuses this year I can't say, since I don't belong to the Succulent Society (a very active group, by the way) and have no cactus catalogues at hand, but I do own – among my other cactuses – a cactus a friend gave me years ago called a *poinsettia* cactus, and a miserable old thing it is, full of mealy bugs.

It is not only these transmogrifications of old favorites that trouble me; I am equally bothered by the onward-and-upward cry of the seedsmen and plant growers. Of course, this is nothing new; the trend since almost the beginning of time has been to grow things that are bigger and better. Better I go for: roses that blossom all summer, day lilies that stay open longer, lettuce with less tendency to bolt, corn that will not wilt, string beans without strings. The hybridizers – with an assist, perhaps, from the chemists – are responsible for all these blessings. But as for flowers, I have never been able to persuade myself that the biggest blooms are necessarily the most beautiful. Take the rose called Peace – 'the rose of the century,' one cataloguer terms it. Everybody knows this huge, rosy-yellow rose, and nearly everybody admires it and tries to grow it. In spite of its lovely colors, I don't like Peace. Even a small vaseful of Peace roses is grotesque, and on the bush the blossoms look to me like the cabbagy Tenniel roses of the Queen's Croquet Ground – the white ones Alice found the card gardeners hurriedly painting red against the arrival of the Queen. Lewis Carroll was prophetic; today the garden men are quite as busy changing the colors of flowers as they are changing their size and shape. KATHARINE S. WHITE, *Onward and Upward in the Garden* [1979]

Plant catalogues are beguiling reading for all gardeners in the winter months. Catalogues of old roses always have for me a poetry. Here are a few entries for damask roses.

Celsiana. Small, clusters of large open semi-double flowers of freshest pink, with golden stamens. A graceful shrub with grey-green foliage. Very beautiful and excellent in every way.
5 ft. × 4 ft. (Prior to 1750).

Comte de Chambord. (Portland Rose). Flat, quartered flowers of bright, warm-pink and plenty of foliage producing its blooms recurrently throughout the season. Excellent for small gardens.
4 ft. × 3 ft. (Moreau-Roberts 1860).

Glorie de Guilan. Cupped blooms opening flat and quartered in a beautifully clear pink, it forms a nice sprawling shrub with fresh green leaves. Grown in Persia for Attar of Roses.
4 ft. × 4 ft. (Int. N. Linday. 1949).

Ispahan. 'Pompon des Princes'. Exquisite half open blooms of lovely clear

pink opening to form a loosely reflexed flower. Free flowering, one of the first old roses to flower and last to finish. Very fragrant.
5 ft. × 4 ft.

Jacques Cartier. (Portland Rose). Similar to Comte de Chambord but rather less perpetual, not quite so neat a flower, but very beautiful, with large rich pink blooms and a very strong fragrance.
4 ft. × 3 ft. (Moreau-Robert 1868).

La Ville de Bruxelles. Very large, rich pink flowers, in the highest quality, perhaps the largest of the old roses, bending down the branches with their weight. Very fragrant, luxuriant foliage.
5 ft. × 4 ft. (Moreau-Robert 1849).

Mme. Hardy. A most beautiful white rose, with flowers of exquisite perfection, opening cupped, later becoming flat, with the outer petals turning down while the inner petals remain incurved. These are medium-sized. There is a suggestion of lemon in the fragrance. Vigorous with good foliage.
6 ft. × 5 ft. (Hardy 1832).

Marie Louise. Enormous, full-petalled flowers, of intense pink, opening flat and later reflexing. Arching growth with plenty of good foliage. A sumptuous beauty, fitting nicely into the smaller garden.
4 ft. × 4 ft. (Malmaison 1813).   DAVID AUSTIN, *A Handbook of Roses* [1984]

PLANT NAMES

Here is an American perspective on plant names. Louise Beebe Wilder's (1878–1938) garden writing stems from that of Mrs Earle and Miss Jekyll but gives it an American voice.

Nowadays we are become so learned in the matter of Latin plant names that there is some danger that the familiar English names, their pet names, will disappear from our garden vocabulary and finally, perhaps, be altogether forgotten. More and more often do we hear the words Dianthus, Digitalis, Lychnis tripping easily from the tongues of young gardeners, and less and less the friendly, time-endeared appellations – Pink, Foxglove, Campion; and our garden conversations lose much of piquancy and agreeable intimacy in consequence. It is, of course, essential that we know the Latin names of our plants, for by no other means may we accurately designate them, but the passing of the old vernacular names would be a real loss. They are the connecting links between us and the flower lovers of all the ages – men, women, and children, a long line of them – stretching across the years through countless gardens, high and humble, through woods and meadows and marshes to the little gatherings of potent herbs and edible roots nestled against the protecting walls of ancient monasteries wherein were kept the first records of flowers and their names. Out of the simplicity and sweetness of each age these names were born and linger yet with the freshness and charm of the flowers themselves.

In 'English Plant Names' the Rev. John Earl says: 'The fascination of plant names is founded on two instincts – love of nature and curiosity about language.' It lies deeper than this, it seems to me; these old names are a bond between the gardeners of to-day and generations of congenial spirits who

loved and laboured in their gardens as do we; they are the artless records of centuries of pleasant work, of country-spent leisure, and they reach us across the years like messages from old friends. More than this, many of these quaint titles – Gillyflower, None-so-pretty, London Tufts, Sops-in-wine, Honesty, to take a few at random – have the power to spread a magic carpet for the mind and send it voyaging into the gardens of the past. They not only place us on a more friendly footing in our own gardens, but open the gate of many a one long claimed by oblivion, and even acquaint us somewhat with the gardener, his fancy and his station in life.

One may not search old horticultural works without gleaning the knowledge that it was the housewife who in most cases had the garden under her jurisdiction; and it seems highly probable that her mind and the minds of her children, fitted to the narrow circumference of home and garden, blossomed into many of the pretty whimsical titles with which we are familiar to-day. One seems to detect a woman's fancy in many of them, a woman's note of detail. There is ample testimony in the old flower books in support of this supposition. The ancient writers again and again give 'our women' or our 'English Gentlewomen' credit for the fanciful christenings of flowers. 'Some English Gentlewomen' says Parkinson, 'call the white Grape-flower Pearles of Spain,' and of the gay scarlet Poppy 'Our English women call it by a name, Ione Siluer Pinne: sub-auditor, Faire without and fowle within.' Here, too, is the case of the 'Frenticke or Foolish Cowslip,' 'come lately into our gardens whose floures are curled and wrinkled after a most strange manner, which our women have called Jacknapes-on-horse-back.' 'Our women' it was, too, one feels sure, whose tender scrutiny caught the resemblance between another Cowslip and a sort of old-fashioned foot-gear and called it the Cowslip, Galligaskins; and fitted the double Cowslips, whose rounds of petals set one within the other, so nicely with the name of Hose-in-hose.

The burnished little Hawkweed (Hieracium aurantiacum), a traveller to our roadsides and meadows from over seas, was once a garden flower in good standing with a string of friendly names to its credit. One of these names is Grim-the-colliar – seemingly obscure enough as to origin – and yet here we have old John Gerarde informing us across three hundred years in this wise: 'The stalkes and cups of the floures are all set thick with a blackish downe or hairiness as it were the dust of coles; whence the women who keep it in gardens for noueltie sake, have called it Grim the Colliar.'

Mr Frederick Hulm offers further elucidation of the origin of this curious name by telling us that during the reign of Queen Elizabeth a comedy called 'Grim the Colliar of Croydon' enjoyed wide popularity and from this seeming coincidence he assumes that 'the grimy hero of the populace stood god-father to our plant.' If we may accept this supposition we have, not only Gerade's account of its derivation, but we learn that the woman who bestowed the name belonged, not to a remote rural neighbourhood, but was more or less urban in her associations and while spending at least part of the year in the country, was no stranger to the gay doings of London Town.

How fascinating to trace out the beginnings of these old plant names! The origin of some is, of course, obvious enough as for instance, Shepherd's Warning and Poor-man's-weather-glass, for the Scarlet Pimpernell, that closes its tiny blossoms at the approach of a storm; Butter and Eggs for such

flowers as display the fresh colours of those good country products; Guinea-hen-flower and Checker Lily for the Little Fritillary whose bell is well checkered over with deeper colour; Hod-the-rake (hold-the-rake) and Rest Harrow (Arrest harrow) for meadow plants having such growing roots that they impede the operation of rakes and harrows.

Many plants have received names indicatory of their habits; thus Four-o'clocks, Morning Glory, Evening Glory, John-go-to-bed-at-noon, Ten o'clock Lady, Flower-of-an-hour, Good-night-at-noon; and also Turnesol (turning toward the sun), Catch-fly, Fly-Trap, and so on.

Creeping plants with insistent colonizing proclivities usually receive some such name as Meg-many-feet, Gill-over-the-ground, Robin-run-in-the-hedge, Roaming Charlie, Creeping Jenny, Jack-jump-about, or Mother-of-thousands. Hundreds were named from some real or fancied resemblance to some object; thus Monkshood, Bluebell, Turtle-head, Ladies-tresses, Snow-in-summer, Adder's-tongue, Snowdrop, Quaker Bonnets, Dutchman's-breeches, Maltese Cross, Larkspur, Bird's-foot, Pussy-toes, and so on indefinitely. The words Bull or Horse used as a prefix to certain others, as Bull-rush and Horse-mint, simply indicate a coarser variety of rush or mint. Many twining plants were christened by sentimentalists Love-bind and Bind-with-love.

Several centuries ago John Parkinson wrote 'I would not two things should be called by one name, for the mistaking and misusing of them.' If there was this danger in Parkinson's day, it has increased a hundredfold in ours. Few of these old plant names are at all fixed in their application, many doing duty for numerous quite different and unrelated plants and others making part of a string of names of anywhere from two or three to fifty or sixty designating the same plant. Nearly all neat, rather small, round flowers have been called at some time or in some locality Bachelors Buttons; many flowers with soft whitish leaves Dusty Miller, and those having fringed petals were frequently called Ragged Robin or Ragged Sailor. There are countless Prince's Feathers, Bird's-eyes, Sweet Nancys, Cowslips, London Prides, Nonesuch, Cuckoo Flowers, Honeysuckles, Long-purples, Sweet Marys, Ladders-to-heaven, Forget-me-nots, Buttercups, Roses of Heaven, Butter and Eggs, Willow-herbs, Sweet Williams, and Ox-eyes – to name but a few; and the number of Meadow Pinks, Indian Pinks, Squaw-roots, and May-flowers that flourish in our own floral kingdom would astonish the curious searcher into such matters.

The word Gillyflower, one of the softest and prettiest of all flower names, plunges us into a most pleasurable confusion. It seems to have been a sort of pet name given to many greatly admired flowers having no attributes in common save a delightful fragrance. The Clove Carnation was, I believe, preëminently the Gillyflower, though the Wallflower and the Stock, and numerous others, shared with it the distinction of the pretty name. The Carnation's claim lies in the assumption that from the Latin Caryophyllum, a clove, grew the Italian garofalo, the French giroflée, and finally by way of the capricious spelling common to those days, the English Gillofer or Gillyflower.

July-flower was another corruption of Gillyflower. Drayton wrote of the 'curious, choice Clove July-flower,' probably meaning the Carnation; and Wallflowers also came to be known as July-flowers.

Old Gervasie Markham in 'The Country Housewife's Garden' (1626) speaks of 'July-flowers (I call them so because they flower in July), they have the name of cloves of their scent.' These must have been Carnations, but he also notes 'July-flowers of the wall, or Bee-flowers, or winter July-flowers, because growing in the walls even in Winter, and good for Bees.'

The name Carnation comes from coronation because of the constant use of this flower in garlands and wreaths. In France the Pink is Oeillet – Petite Oeillet, or Oeillet de Poete, but the fragrant flowers sold to-day in the Paris markets as Giroflé are Wallflowers, 'Gold blossoms frecked with iron brown.' A friend tells me that in her grandmother's garden in New York State Wallflowers were always called Gillyflowers.

Stocks were also called Gillyflowers and sometimes also White Wall-flowers; and our Sweet Rocket (Hesperis matronalis) was known as Queen's Gillyflower. A sort of Campion was the Marsh Gillyflower, and the great Thrift was known as Sea Gillyflowers; and there were doubtless many others that shared the name.

I think the flower with the greatest number of names must be the Marsh Marigold. Mrs Earl says it is the proud possessor of fifty-six. The Pansy, a loved flower of all ages, has attached to itself almost as many. The flower that comes down the years without winning one or more pet names has somehow failed to draw close to the lives of the human beings beside whom it has grown. There are not many old-fashioned flowers of which this may be said, but it is a curious fact that a flower so appealing and distinctive as the Crocus should be one. Crocuses have been grown in gardens since the early part of the seventeenth century but none as far as I can ascertain has acquired a common name save Crocus sativus, which was called Saffron or Saff-flower. Its relative the Colchicum, on the other hand, boasts quite a number, the quaintness and intimate character of which seem to imply a special affection for the jaunty little autumn flower.

LOUISE BEEBE WILDER, *Color in My Garden* [1918]

PLANT HUNTERS

A breed of plant-hunting writers emerged in the late Victorian and Edwardian periods whose works are still 'a good read'. Reginald Farrer's books read more like Rider Haggard than the tales of an Edwardian plant-hunter. His account of discovering 'swathes' of Harebell poppies in the mountainous region between China and Tibet in 1914 reads like someone having alighted upon the lost treasure of the Incas.

And now, immediately, the beauty of the Harebell Poppy began to break upon us. It was everywhere, flickering and dancing in millions upon millions of pale purple butterflies, as far as eye could see, over all the enormous slopes and braes of the grass. The sun was now coming up, and its earliest rays slanted upon the upland in shafts of gold-dust; in the young fresh light the whole alp was a glistering jewel-work with dew in a powdered haze of diamond, with the innumerable soft blue laughter of the Poppies rippling universally above a floor of pale purple Alpine Asters, interspersed with here and there the complacent pinkness of the Welcome Primula. In the far-off memory of that scene I have to rein myself in, for fear a flux of words should ensue: but do not be embittered, all you who incline to be jealous, scornful, or incredulous of lovelinesses you have never shared (and possibly never could) if I tell you coldly that even I, in those moments, was stricken dumb and helpless by the sight of a glory surpassing, as I do truly think, all that I have ever seen elsewhere. Stupid with a blank delight, I wandered spellbound over those unharvested lawns, agonizing with the effort to contain without breaking the infinite flood of glory they were so mercilessly pouring into so frail and finite a vessel. One did not dare speak. It was indeed a pain almost like the water-torture of Madame de Brinvillers. And at my side walked Bill, silent as I. What was he thinking then? How was this sight striking home to him? But who can ever know what even these dearest and nearest are doing and enduring in the secret inmost rooms of the soul? We continued together, voiceless and smitten.

And then at last he turned to me, and in the awe-stricken whisper of one overwhelmed by a divine presence, he said: 'Doesn't it make your very soul ache?' It was the right, the absolute and final word. It did. It twisted one's very being, in the agony to absorb that sight wholly, to get outside it, possess it, delay its passing, tear it away from its native hills and keep it with one for ever – flesh of one's flesh, and brain of one's brain. But beauty is so big and enduring, and we so small and evanescent, that for us the almost physical pain of trying to pack the incommensurable inside the infinitesimal is, indeed, as if one should try to decant the Yellow River into a thimble. Let us hope that even a drop remains inside the poor little vessel round which so titanic an overflow goes inevitably lost, roaring and seething in a spate that would baffle any holding capacity.

Meconopsis quintuplinervia! Will anybody wonder that even I, hating as I do the Wardour Street popular names with which Ruskin tried to 'affubler' such known beauties as Saxifrage and Campanula should now yield to the same weakness, and try to give my beloved Tibetan Poppy an English name to which she has no right at all? But I hope it is only proleptically that I forge the name of Harebell Poppy. I hope that the plant's beauty and its charm and its permanence will so ensure its popularity in gardens as to make a popular name inevitable. And, that being so, there will be 'Harebell Poppy' ready made. For indeed, to cherish or even to purchase, a plant called Meconopsis quintuplinervia is as impossible as to love a woman called Georgiana: mitigating substitutes inevitably have to be invented. So, as the 'Harebell Poppy,' may my Tibetan treasure long enrich our gardens, luxuriant and enduring in rich moist ground, and inimitably lovely in the well-bred grace of its habit, as well as in the serene and tranquil loveliness of its lavender bells.

REGINALD FARRER, Rainbow Bridge [1921]

Frank Kingdon-Ward (1885–1958) is another who writes in the same rapturous vein. Over the top might be an apter description of their floral ecstasies.

. . . then we pitched the sodden tents, and having lit a fire made some tea. There was ample time before dusk to climb the steep rock stairway which led towards the upper valley and the pass; and with my rucksack on my back I started off. A thin mist, gelid with half-frozen moisture, was driving gustily over the ridge, and every now and then a shower of rain swooped down, blotting out the mountains and chilling me to the bone. Between the showers, the pale winding-sheet of the mountain gleamed bleakly.

But if the weather was discomfiting, the scene which revealed itself to me as soon as I had ascended the first flight of rocks, compensated for every inconvenience. I was breathless, not merely with the ascent: the valley was alight with flowers! Rhododendrons, dwarf in stature, yet hoary with age, sprawled and writhed in every direction. I trod them underfoot, priceless blooms which many men have yearned to see. You could not walk without crushing them, the whole rock floor was hotly carpeted, and over the cliffs poured an incandescent stream of living lava. When I saw that I looked down on twenty-five distinct species of Rhododendron, more than half of which had never been noticed by man – nor had been since, for that matter – I speak the cold truth. It was immense. Aladdin's cave contained nothing to equal this glut of treasure. Could one but reproduce a pale imitation of that scene in England, scarcely would men believe their eyes. Though almost sick with excitement I proceeded methodically. I collected on the spot each species, gave it a serial number, wrote a description of it, and then pressed and dried my specimens. Then in October, I collected ripe seed of every one: aromatic *anthopogons*, wide-flowered *saluenses*, scalding scarlet *neeriiflorums*, apple-blossom *glaucums*, the whole tide-rip of them. Finally I brought the seeds home and they were soon in a hundred English gardens.

F. KINGDON WARD, *The Romance of Gardening* [1935]

INDOOR PLANTS

Our house is embowered with something like a hundred pots on its windowsills crammed with geraniums, pelargoniums, passion flowers, Scarborough lilies, amaryllis let alone ivies and, in winter, agapanthus. These mercifully are the province of my wife. Hence my sympathy with the following.

. . . I become, in winter, a sort of floor nurse in my spare moments – taking temperatures, rubbing backs, and making a thousand small adjustments when my patients summon me. Here in summer, I recall the anxieties of those midwinter mornings: Were the cyclamens in a strategic place – near, but not touching, a cold windowpane that provided sun but not too much sun? Were the African violets, whose forebears had come from the tall forests of East Africa, getting their filtered forest sunshine and their seventy-degree heat? Was the bottom heat from a radiator under the pots of starting amaryllis enough to encourage growth and still not cook the bulbs? Was it the day to raise the humidity of the plant room by adding water to the pebbled trays? Did the rubber plant need its weekly bath and the sulking clivia miniata its fortnightly shot of chemical fertilizer? Had the mealy bags moved over from the infested cactuses to the poinsettia? My patients were scattered all over the house, upstairs and down, and I had a ward of many pots in the plant room, which is really part of the kitchen. Some of these ward patients were there because I had raised them or sought them out; some, like the Christmas and orchid cactuses, were there because they were aging members of the family whom sentiment forbade me to abandon; others were accident cases – that is, unexpected gifts, always welcome but sometimes hard to find space for. My floor duty started before breakfast, when I watered the plants in the upstairs rooms, and ended at bedtime, when

I checked night temperatures and adjusted the thermostat and the radiators. Baths could not be worked in until mid-afternoon, when the kitchen sink was free of cooking utensils. Pillow plumping and words of cheer same at any old time as I passed through a room and paused just long enough to remove a withering leaf from a geranium or loosen the earth in a packed pot or move a plant to a window where it would catch a few rays of the pale winter light.

It is an agreeable life, but it calls for dedication. There was one morning, I remember, when I realized that the temperature I ought to be taking was my husband's; a tendril of the grape ivy on the piano had reached out, as he walked by, and seized him lightly by the wrist. It is all too easy for house plants to take over a home, leaving no room for the owner. Already I am worrying about where to put the pots that must soon be moved in from the terrace – plants like White Flower Farms' lovely trailing lantanas (I have the lavender species, Selloviana, and the pale-yellow hybrid, Cream Carpet). And I have a mammoth six-year-old strelitzia from the Park Seed Company, in its huge tub; where am I going to put *that*? And my loyal old rhizomatous begonias, which have grown so portly – where do *they* fit in? Then there are the terrace fuchsias, but these I can defoliate and store in the cellar.

KATHARINE S. WHITE in the *New Yorker* (1959); reprinted in *Onward and Upward in the Garden* [1979]

It is difficult to think that Shelley could have written this without the revival of interest in flower gardens pioneered by Humphry Repton and the gardenesque style. He wrote it not in England but while in Pisa, however.

THE SENSITIVE PLANT

A sensitive plant in a garden grew,
And the young winds fed it with silver dew,
And it opened its fan-like leaves to the light,
And closed them beneath the kisses of night.

And Spring arose on the garden fair,
Like the Spirit of Love felt everywhere;
And each flower and herb on Earth's dark breast
Rose from the dreams of its wintry rest.

But none ever trembled and panted with bliss
In the garden, the field, or the wilderness,
Like a doe in the noontide with love's sweet want,
As the companionless Sensitive Plant.

The snowdrop, and then the violet,
Arose from the ground with warm rain wet,
And their breath was mixed with fresh odour, sent
From the turf, like the voice and the instrument.

Then the pied wind-flowers and the tulip tall,
And narcissi, the fairest among them all,

Who gaze on their eyes in the stream's recess,
Till they die of their own dear loveliness;

And the Naiad-like lily of the vale,
Whom youth makes so fair and passion so pale,
That the light of its tremulous bells is seen
Through their pavilions of tender green;

And the hyacinth purple, and white, and blue,
Which flung from the bell a sweet peal anew
Of music so delicate, soft, and intense,
It was felt like an odour within the sense;

And the rose like a nymph to the bath addrest,
Which unveiled the depth of her glowing breast,
Till, fold after fold, to the fainting air
The soul of her beauty and love lay bare:

And the wand-like lily, which lifted up,
As a Maenad, its moonlight-coloured cup,
Till the fiery star, which is its eye,
Gazed through clear dew on the tender sky;

And the jessamine faint, and the sweet tuberose,
The sweetest flower for scent that blows;
And all rare blossoms from every clime
Grew in that garden in perfect prime.

And on the stream whose inconstant bosom
Was prankt under boughs of embowering blossom;
With golden and green light, slanting through
Their heaven of many a tangled hue,

Broad water lilies lay tremulously,
And starry river-buds glimmered by,
And around them the soft stream did glide and dance
With a motion of sweet sound and radiance.

And the sinuous paths of lawn and of moss
Which led through the garden along and across,
Some open at once to the sun and the breeze,
Some lost among bowers of blossoming trees,

Were all paved with daisies and delicate bells
As fair as the fabulous asphodels,
And flowrets which drooping as day drooped too
Fell into pavilions, white, purple, and blue,
To roof the glow-worm from the evening dew.

And from this undefiled Paradise
The flowers (as an infant's awakening eyes
Smile on its mother, whose singing sweet
Can first lull, and at last must awaken it),

When Heaven's blithe winds had unfolded them,
As mine-lamps enkindle a hidden gem,
Shone smiling to Heaven, and every one
Shared joy in the light of the gentle sun;

For each one was interpenetrated
With the light and the odour its neighbour shed,
Like young lovers whom youth and love make dear
Wrapped and filled by their mutual atmosphere.

Percy Bysshe Shelley,
The Sensitive Plant [1820]

Beware of all garden gimmicks.

FLOWERAMA

Speaking of gardening with less labor, a device called Flowerama burst upon a wondering world a year ago come May. You probably saw the exclamatory full-page ad in the *Times*. A scientific breakthrough! Amazing! Just unroll the Magic Carpet! No topsoil needed! No weeding! No work at all! Hundreds of gorgeous flowers all summer long or your money back! So ran the pretty story. The carpet, it seemed, was a 'self-contained medium,' and there was 'a hundred and one ways to use it!' You could cut it with scissors, place it around trees in circles, make figure eights, grow flowers in the shape of your initials. Although an unbeliever, I unlimbered my scissors and sent off my order for one carpet and my check for $4.95 to Horticulture, Inc., the firm behind the new wonder.

In due course the carpet arrived. It was eighteen feet long, medium gray, and looked like the stuff you put under wall-to-wall carpeting. It also looked a little like the messy interior lining of the soft modern book-mailing envelope. And it was bursting with seed. I cut it in half, thinking to plant one half for a solid mass of bloom and to spell out something with the other half – probably the word WELCOME, though I also considered KEEP OFF. The dry seeds sprang out of the carpet so alarmingly at my first attempt to fashion a letter that I abandoned the idea and decided we would settle for only a nine-foot 'riot of color.' On a damp, warm evening in early June, attended by a cloud of mosquitoes, I unrolled the half length of magic carpet and laid it down, as tenderly as if it were a baby, on good soil at the edge of the vegetable garden. Following directions carefully, I watered it. Then nature took over, and we had the wettest June in years, bringing with it a crop of weeds that despite the advertisement's claims did not appear to be in the least cowed by the mulch of Flowerama's carpet.

Our first magic flower was a lone eschscholtzia; it struggled up painfully through the gray fibers in July. By mid-August, there was a small patch of tiny purple-and-brown pea-like blossoms, which I did not recognize. The first week in September gave us a handsome stand of Shirley poppies, about a

foot long. A solitary annual chrysanthemum followed. That was all. The carpet has a tendency to scuff up in spite of the continuous wetness, and from June until frost the long blanket lay there looking as if a couple of Boy Scouts had spent the night in our garden, end to end. Eventually our dachshund, who is always inflamed by a stray rag, discovered it and carried bits of the blanket about with him from place to place. Well, considering all, it probably wan't a fair test, but there can be no doubt that *our* Flowerama was a flop. Perhaps I didn't really want this form of magic. I didn't approve of it, and I notice that plants I don't approve of seldom do well.

> KATHERINE S. WHITE in the *New Yorker* [1959]; reprinted in *Onward and Upward in the Garden* [1979]

FLOWERS   *Some viewpoints.*

> Still
> in a way
> nobody sees a flower
> really
> it is so small
> we haven't the time
> and to see takes time
> like to have a friend takes
> time
>
> GEORGIA O'KEEFFE (*1887–1986*)

How astonishingly does the chance of leaving the world improve a sense of its natural beauties upon us! Like poor Falstaff, though I do not 'babble,' I think of green fields; I muse with the greatest affection on every flower I have known from my infancy – their shapes and colours are as new to me as if I had just created them with a superhuman fancy. It is because they are connected with the most thoughtless and the happiest moments of our lives. I have seen foreign flowers in hothouses, of the most beautiful nature, but I do not care a straw for them. The simple flowers of our Spring are what I want to see again.

> JOHN KEATS to JAMES RICE, 16 February 1820

In truth, nothing can be more vulgar than my taste in flowers, for which I have a passion. I like scarcely any but the common ones. First and best I love violets, and primroses, and cowslips, and wood anemones, and the whole train of field flowers; then roses of every kind and colour, especially the great cabbage rose; then the blossoms of the lilac and laburnum, the horse-chestnut, the asters, the jasmine, and the honeysuckle; and to close the list, lilies of the valley, sweet peas, and the red pinks which are found in cottagers' gardens. This is my confession of faith.

> MARY RUSSELL MITFORD to WILLIAM ELFORD, 17 April 1812

What more delightsome than an infinite varietie of sweet smelling flowers? decking with sundry colours the greene mantle of the Earth, the universall Mother of us all, so by them bespotted, so dyed, that all the world cannot sample them, and wherein it is more fit to admire the Dyer, than imitate his workemanship. Colouring not onely the earth, but decking the ayre, and sweetning every breath and spirit.

The Rose red, damaske, velvet, and double province Rose, the sweet muske Rose double and single, and double and single white Rose. The faire and sweet senting Woodbind, double and single. Purple Cowslips, and double Cowslips. Primrose double and single. The Violet nothing behinde the best, for smelling sweetly. And 1000 more will provoke your content.

WILLIAM LAWSON, *A New Orchard and Garden* [1618]

Brave flowers, that I could gallant it like you
And be as little vaine,
You come abroad, and make a harmlesse shew,
And to your bedds of Earthe againe;
You are not proud, you know your birth
For your Embroidered garments are from Earth:

You doe obey your moneths, and timis, but I
Would have it ever springe,
My fate would know noe winter, never dye
Nor thine of such a thing;
O that I could my bedd of Earth but view
And Smile, and look as Chearefully as you.

HENRY KING, *A Contemplation upon Flowers* [1657]

Some persons may think, that *Flowers* are things of no *use*; that they are *nonsensical* things. The same may be, and, perhaps with more reason, said of *pictures*. An Italian, while he gives his fortune for a picture will laugh to scorn a Hollander, who leaves a tulip-root as a fortune to his son. For my part, as a thing to keep and not to sell; as a thing, the *possession* of which is to give me pleasure, I hesitate not a moment to prefer the plant of a fine carnation to a gold watch set with diamonds.

WILLIAM COBBETT, *The American Gardener* [1821]

GWENDOLEN [*Looking round.*] Quite a well-kept garden this is, Miss Cardew.
CECILY So glad you like it, Miss Fairfax.
GWENDOLEN I had no idea there were any flowers in the country.
CECILY Oh, flowers are as common here, Miss Fairfax, as people are in London.

OSCAR WILDE, *The Importance of Being Earnest* [1895]

Canon Ellacombe provides a useful reflection on the British obsession with flowers.

I doubt if any national literature has been so full of flowers as our own, and especially in our poetry. Among the older writers, Gower, Chaucer, Spenser, and Shakespeare, and, indeed, almost all, love to speak of gardens and flowers. The plants named by them are far more than most people are aware of, and a very slight acquaintance with their writings will add much to the pleasure of a garden. And this love of gardens and flowers was not confined to the older poets; it rather languished in the eighteenth century, but in our day flowers have been fully honoured by our poets. Of course, modern poets have naturally loved the old flowers, but they have not hesitated to speak lovingly also of the newer introductions. The latest addition to the flora of the poets is the yucca, and, as I have always grown this plant largely, I am glad to see it so honoured. I wonder it has so long remained unsung, for it was a very early introduction from the New World, and was grown in England by Gerard in 1597; yet, as far as I know, no poet has noticed it before the late poet-laureate, and he has done so in his latest work:—

> 'My Yucca which no winter quells,
>   Although the months have scarce begun,
>   Has pushed towards our faintest sun
> A spike of half-accomplished bells.'
>
> *To Ulysses. Demeter, p. 113*

. . . Of all the associations which flowers keep for us, none can equal those connected with persons or places. Of the way in which flowers bring back the memory of friends little can be said; in the pleasure they thus bring they must vary according to the memories they recall, and in not a few cases these memories may be full of sadness and sorrow. But the memories of places which flowers bring back to us must always, I think, be more or less pleasant; and to pick flowers or to collect plants in various places, and then to be able to grow them in our own garden, adds much to the pleasure of travelling. My beech-fern recalls Cader Idris to me, and my oak-fern Snowdonia, though it is many years since I collected them; and my Osmunda recalls North Donegal, and Slieve League, not because my plants come from there, but because I never saw them elsewhere so beautiful; my saxifrages recall Switzerland, and my pinks the Castle of Falaise; my pulsatilla recalls the beautiful hillside near Thring, which I once saw studded with the flower in a luxuriance that I fear is now a thing of the past; while my sedums recall a pleasant afternoon in the Botanic Gardens at Angers, where the pleasant old curator, M. Boreau, made that family his special study, and gave me an excellent collection; and as to other gardens, both public and private, they are recalled to me most pleasantly in almost every yard of my garden. And these associations have what I may call a reflex character that doubles the pleasure. I can remember my delight when I first saw the beautiful *Campanula barbata* in the Swiss valleys; it had always been a special favourite with me as a garden beauty; and now, when I see it, I call to mind a delightful walk up the Flegère, where this lovely flower grows in the greatest abundance, in all shades of white and blue, from the commencement of the ascent in the valley of the Arve till the pine woods are passed. Tennyson records the

same double pleasure brought to him in connection with one small flower:—

> 'We took our last adieu,
> And up the snowy Splugen drew,
> But ere we reached the highest summit,
> I plucked a daisy, I gave it you;
> It told of England then to me,
> And now it tells of Italy.'

And these memories and associations that our flowers give us are independent of seasons or of age. They come to us as well in autumn and winter, in spring and summer; and as to age, the older we get the more, from the very nature of things, do these memories increase and multiply.

I have said nothing of the legendary associations of flowers, they are too numerous; but I will just name the forget-me-not, that with it I may bring this paper to a close. All admire the pretty flower, and like to tell of the pretty, though modern, legend. But in my garden, and I know it is the same in the gardens of all who love flowers, nine-tenths of my plants and flowers are forget-me-nots, and have their legends, which they tell to me over and over again, and which I often like to repeat to others. There are trees on my lawn which were planted when children were born; there are hundreds of plants which tell me of the liberal help given by such gardens as Kew, Edinburgh, Dublin, and many other public gardens, both British and foreign; there are hundreds of others which speak to me of delightful private gardens, and of the pleasant freemasonry that exists among true gardeners; there are flowers which tell of pleasant travels, and long walks and beautiful spots which I shall probably never see again; there are others which bring to memory voices which I shall never hear, and faces which I shall never see again in this world; and hundreds more which in their several ways have their own memories, and their own associations, which make each and all forget-me-nots of the highest value and beauty. And in looking on our flowers with these thoughts there is nothing mawkish or sentimental, the thoughts are good and wholesome; and though some of the memories connected with our flowers may be sad, and some of the associations may be even painful, yet *meminisse juvat* is written upon them all; and that our flowers can give us such memories, and can be linked with such associations, we may, indeed, be thankful.

CANON ELLACOMBE,
In a Gloucestershire Garden [1895]

And the redoubtable E. A. Bowles does not hesitate to list those flowers he really couldn't stand.

I can admire and enjoy most flowers, but just a few I positively dislike. Collarette dahlias and those superlatively double African marigolds that look like india rubber bath sponges offend me most of all. I dislike the cheap thin texture of godetias almost as much as I do the sinful magenta streaks and splotches that run in the blood of that family. I loathe celosias especially with dyed pampas-grass; and coxcombs, and spotty, marbled, double balsams I should like to smash up with a coal-hammer; and certain great flaunting mauve and purple cattleyas cloy my nose and annoy my eye till I conjure up a vision of them expiating their gaudy double-dyed wickedness with heads impaled on stiff wires like those of criminals on pikes, in a sea of *Asparagus sprengeri*, and forming the bouquet presented to the wife of a provincial Mayor on the occasion of his opening the new sewage works.

E. A. BOWLES, *My Garden in Summer* [1914]

And again describing a close relation of the Dragon Arum.

. . . the most fiendish plant I know of, the sort of thing, Beelzebub might pluck to make a bouquet for his mother-in-law . . . [it] looks as if it had been made out of a sow's ear for spathe, and the tail of a rat that died of Elephantiasis for the spadix. The whole thing is mingling of unwholesome greens, livid purples, and pallid pinks, the livery of putrescence in fact, and it possesses an odour to match the colouring. I once entrapped the vicar of a poor parish into smelling it, and when he had recovered his breath he said it reminded him of a pauper funeral. It only exhales this stench for a few hours after opening, and during that time it is better to stand afar off and look at it through a telescope.

E. A. BOWLES, *My Garden in Spring* [1914]

FLOWER LISTS   *English poetry and prose of the Tudor and Stuart periods abound with luscious listings of flowers. Edmund Spenser is an early example.*

> Bring hether the Pincke and purple Cullambine,
>   With Gelliflowres.
> Bring Coronations, and Sops in wine,
>   Worne of Paramoures.
> Strowe me the ground with Daffadown dillies,
> And Cowslips, and Kingcups, and lovéd lillies
>   The pretie Pawnce,
>   And the Chevisaunce,
> Shall match with the fayre flowre Delice.

EDMUND SPENSER, *The Shepheardes Calendar* [1578]

Shakespeare is another.

> . . . the fairest flowers o' the season
> Are our carnations and streaked gillyvors,
> Which some call nature's bastards. Of that kind
> Our rustic garden's barren, and I care not
> To get slips of them.
>
> . . . O Proserpina,
> For the flowers now, that frighted thou let'st fall
> From Dis's waggon daffodils,
> That come before the swallow dares, and take
> The winds of March with beauty; violets (dim,
> But sweeter than the lids of Juno's eyes
> Or Cytherea's breath); pale primroses,
> That die unmarried, ere they can behold

Bright Phoebus in his strength (a malady
Most incident to maids); bold oxlips and
The crown imperial; lilies of all kinds
The flower-de-luce being one O, these I lack,
To make you garlands of – and my sweet friend,
To Strew him o'er and o'er . . .

WILLIAM SHAKESPEARE,
The Winter's Tale, Act IV, sc. iv

There's rosemary, that's for remembrance;
pray you, love, remember; and there is pansies,
that's for thoughts.

There's fennel for you, and columbines;
there's rue for you; and here's some for me;
We may call it herb of grace o'Sundays; oh,
you must wear your rue with a difference.
There's a daisy; I would give you some
violets, but they withered all when my father
died; they say he made a good end . . .

WILLIAM SHAKESPEARE,
Hamlet, Act IV, sc. vi

*And Ben Jonson a third. This one comes from a masque in celebration of
James I's birthday.*

The first presentation is of three nymphs strewing several sorts
of flowers, followed by an old shepherd with
a censer and perfumes.

1st NYMPH   Thus, thus begin the yearly rites
Are due to Pan on these bright nights;
His morn now riseth and invites
To sports, to dances and delights:
    All envious and profane, away;
    This is the shepherds' holiday.

2nd NYMPH   Strew, strew the glad and smiling ground
With every flower, yet not confound
The primrose drop, the spring's own spouse;
Bright day's-eyes and the lips of cows;
    The garden star, the queen of May
    The rose to crown the holiday.

3rd NYMPH   Drop, drop, you violets, change your hues,
Now red, now pale, as lovers use,
And in your death go out as well
As when you lived, unto the smell,
    That from your odor all may say
    This is the Shepherds' holiday.

SHEPHERD
Well done, my pretty ones; rain roses still,
Until the last be dropped. Then hence, and fill
Your fragrant prickles for a second shower;
Bring corn-flag, tulips and Adonis' flower,
Fair ox-eye, goldilocks and columbine,
Pinks, goulands, king-cups and sweet sops-in-wine,
Blue harebells, paigles, pansies, calaminth,
Flower-gentle, and the fair-haired hyacinth;
Bring rich carnations, flower-de-luces, lilies,
The checked and purple-ringèd daffodillies,
Bright crown-imperial, king's spear, hollyhocks,
Sweet Venus' navel, and soft lady's-smocks;
Bring too some branches forth of Daphne's hair,
And gladdest myrtle for these posts to wear
With spikenard weaved, and marjoram between,
And starred with yellow-golds and meadow's queen.
Then when the altar, as it ought, is dressed,
More odor come not from the Phoenix's nest;
The breath thereof Panchaia may envy,
The colors China, and the light the sky.

BEN JONSON, *Pan's Anniversary, or
the Shepherd's Holiday* [1620]

FLORIST'S FEASTS

*These apparently were very popular in the eighteenth century and
remind us that the improving hand of 'Capability' Brown had not wiped
flowers off the face of the garden totally.*

On Tuesday last a great Feast of Gardiners Call'd Florists was held at the
Dog in Richmond Hill, at which were present about 130 in Number; after
Dinner several shew'd their Flowers (most of them Auricula's) and five
ancient and judicious Gardiners were judges to determine whose Flowers
excell'd; on this Occasion two Silver Spoons and Ladles were given to the
Gardiners that had the best Flowers; a Gardiner of Barnes in Surrey was so
well furnish'd with good Flowers, that the Judges in that affair, ordered him
two Spoons and one Ladle. At the same Feast a Dish of Garden Beans with
Bacon was given to the Society by a Gardiner near Leatherhead but he was
no ways intitled to the above Plate by Reason he had brought no Flowers.
The Beans were full as big as common Horse-Beans when out of the Shells.

THE CRAFTSMAN, 16 April 1729

SINGLE FLOWERS

Avriculas or Bear's Ears.

See how the Bears Eares in their several dresses,
(That yet no Poet's pen to hight expresses.)
Each head adornèd with such rich attire,
Which Fools and Clowns may slight, whilst skil'd admire.
Their gold, their purples, scarlets, crimson dyes,
Their dark and lighter hair'd diversities.
With all their pretty shades and Ornaments,
Their parti-colour'd coats and pleasing scents.

Gold laid on scarlet, silver on the blew
With sparkling eyes to take the eyes of you.
Mixt colours, many more to please that sense,
Other with rich and great magnificence,
In double Ruffs, with gold and silver laced,
On purple crimson and so neatly placed.
Ransack Flora's wardrobes, none sure can bring
More taking Ornaments t' adorn the spring.

THE REVEREND SAMUEL GILBERT,
The Florist's Vade-Mecum [1683]

Chrysanthemums

. . . Oh, that you could see my chrysanthemums I have one out now unlike any I ever saw. It is the shape and size of a large honeysuckle,* and the inside filled up with tubes. Each of the petals or florets (which are they?) is, on the outside, of a deep violet colour, getting, however, paler as it approaches the end, and the inside shows itself much like the inside of a honeysuckle tube, of a shining silver white, just, in some particular lights, tinged with purple. I never saw so elegant a flower of any sort; and my jar of four kinds, golden, lemon, yellow, purple, lilac, crimson, and pink, exceeds in brilliancy any display that I ever witnessed. The brightest pot of dahlias is nothing to it. My father, who has been twice in London lately (about my American 'Children's Books' and your friend 'Inez'), says that they have nothing approaching it in splendour in the new conservatories at Covent Garden. I am prodigiously vain of my chrysanthemums, and so is Clarke.

MARY RUSSELL MITFORD to EMILY
JEPHSON, December 1830

THE LAST CHRYSANTHEMUM

Why should this flower delay so long
    To show its tremulous plumes?
Now is the time of plaintive robin-song,
    When flowers are in their tombs.

Through the slow summer, when the sun
    Called to each frond and whorl
That all he could for flowers was being done,
    Why did it not uncurl?

It must have felt that fervid call
    Although it took no heed,
Walking but now, when leaves like corpses fall,
    And saps all retrocede.

Too late its beauty, lonely thing,
    The season's shine is spent,

---

* This, by-the-way, is the shape and size of the tassel white, only that that flower is still more curved and curled and all of one colour.

> Nothing remains for it but shivering
> In tempests turbulent.
>
> Had it a reason for delay,
> Dreaming in witlessness
> That for a bloom so delicately gay
> Winter would stay its stress?
>
> — I talk as if the thing were born
> With sense to work its mind;
> Yet it is but one mask of many worn
> By the Great Face behind.

THOMAS HARDY [1840–1928]

Cowslips

The Franticke, Fantasticke, or Foolish Cowslip, in some places is called by Country people, Iacke an Apes on Horsebacke, which is an vsuall name with them, giuen to many plants, as Daisies, Marigolds, etc. if they be strange or fantasticall, differing in the forme from the ordinary kinde of the single ones. The smallest one vsually called through all the North Country, Birds eyen, because of the small yellow circle in the bottomes of the flowers, resembling the eye of a bird.

The Common Field Cowslip

The common fielde Cowslip I might well forbeare to set downe, being so plentifull in the fields: but because many take delight in it, and plant it in their gardens, I will giue you the description of it here. It hath diuers green leaues, very like vnto the wild Primrose, but shorter, rounder, stiffer, rougher, more crumpled about the edges, and of a sadder greene colour, euery one standing vpon his stalke, which is an inch or two long: among the leaues rise vp diuers round stalkes, a foote or more high, bearing at the toppe many faire yellow single flowers, with spots of a deeper yellow, at the bottome of each leafe, smelling very sweete . . .

The Primrose Cowslip

The leaues of this Cowslip are larger than the ordinary fielde Cowslip, and of a darke yellowish greene colour: the flowers are many, standing together, vpon the toppes of the stalkes, to the number of thirty sometimes vpon one stalke, as I haue counted them in mine owne Garden, and sometimes more, euery one hauing a longer roote stalke than the former, and of as pale a yellowish colour almost as the fielde Primrose, with yellow spots at the bottome of the leaues, as the ordinary hath and of as sweete a sent.

The single Greene Cowslip

There is little differences in leafe or roote of this from the first Cowslip, the chiefest varietie in this kinde is this, that the leaues are somewhat greener, and the flowers being in all respects like in forme vnto the first kinde but somewhat larger, are of the same colour with the greene huskes, or rather a little yellower, and of a very small sent; in all other things I finde no diuersitie, but that it standeth much longer in flower before it fadeth, especially if it stand out of the Sunne.

Curl'd Cowslips or Gallegaskins

There is another kinde, whose flowers are folded or crumpled at the edges, and the huskes of the flowers bigger than any of the former, more swelling out in the middle, as it were ribbes, and crumpled on the sides of the huskes, which doe somewhat resemble men's hose that they did weare, and tooke the name of Gallegaskins from thence.

The Franticke or Foolish Cowslip
or Iacke an Apes on Horsebacke

We haue in our Gardens another kinde, not much differing in leaues from the former Cowslip, and is called Fantasticke or Foolish, because it beareth at the toppe of the stalke a brush or turf of small long greene leaues, with some yellow leaues, as it were peeces of flowers broken, and standing among the greene leaues. And sometimes some stalkes among those greene leaues at the toppe (which are a little larger then when it hath but broken peeces of flowers) doe carry whole flowers in huskes like the single kinde.

ANONYMOUS, *The Garden of Pleasant Flowers* [1629]

Daffodils

The double white Daffodil of Constantinople was sent into England vnto the right honourable the Lord Treasurer, among other bulbed flowers: whose roots when they were planted in our London gardens, did bring forth beautiful flowres, very white and double, with some yellownesse mixed in the middle leaues, pleasant and sweet to smell.

JOHN GERARD, *The Herball* [1597]

DAFFODILS

Faire Daffodils, we weep to see
    You haste away so soone:
As yet the early-rising Sun
    Has not attain'd his Noone.
    Stay, stay,
Until the hasting day
    Has run
But to the Even-song;
And having pray'd together, we
    Will go with you along.

We have short time to stay, as you,
    We have as short a Spring;
As quick a growth to meet Decay,
    As you, or any thing.
    We die,
As your hours doe, and drie
    Away,

Like to the Summer's raine;
Or as the pearles of Morning's dew
Ne'er to be found againe.

ROBERT HERRICK [1591–1674]

Elizabeth Lawrence recalls the old-fashioned daffodils of the Southern States.

The 'early trumpet' is one of the traditional types of the South, and is unidentified. Mr Wister describes it as the 'common early naturalized trumpet of our Southern states.' A Virginia grower lists it (characteristically as 'early Virginia') with the statement that this and *Narcissus biflorus* have been naturalized in the state for over two centuries. This small and charming trumpet is as pale as early sunlight and as graceful as a wild flower. It should be sought out and planted in great quantities to bloom with the early shrubs. I like it for planting in grass because the sparse thin foliage withers soon and allows the passage of the lawn mower.

Other charming old-fashioned daffodils have become naturalized in the South. They come up spring after spring, to bloom for generation after generation. If you think back to quiet gardens in little towns passed by in modern time (you will have to go off the main highways to find them) you will remember the pale delicate pattern of the Silver Bells against dark cedar trees. I have seen them in dooryards in Hillsboro, and in drifts under the oaks and along the box-bordered terraces of Cooleemee plantation, and in gardens in the country. They came to me from an apple orchard. To the orchard they had come from an old colored woman who traded them for an apple tree. I do not know their proper name, although they are similar to, if not identical with, William Goldring, an old white trumpet called the swan's-neck daffodil. The slender buds are so bent, like a swan's neck, that the tips point to the ground. They rise slowly as they expand, but they never become horizontal. The twisted sea-foam petals are held forward over the crown. The best way to get a stock of Silver Bells is to watch the farm markets in February when they appear among the cut flowers brought in to add a little to the butter money. The farmers' wives are reluctant to part with the bulbs, for they are slow of increase, but they can be coaxed to sell you a few later on when the tops die down. I bought some from the butter woman this year. She said she had them from her grandmother. The fact that I was eager to buy, and she was not eager to sell, did not raise the price. In fact, she said that they would be thirty cents a dozen, and when she brought them told me that she had made a mistake, that they were only a quarter.

ELIZABETH LAWRENCE, *A Southern Garden* [1942]

Dahlias

I should like to be strong-minded enough to dislike Dahlias and to shut the garden gate on one and all of them as a punishment to them and the raisers who have produced some of the horrors of modern garden nightmares. But as it would not make much stir in the world of Dahlias however tightly I barred it, and as I have a great affection for single Dahlias and all the true species I have been able to get, the family is still admitted. I cannot believe I shall ever be converted to a taste for Collarette Dahlias. The crumpled little pieces of flower that form the frill cause an itching in my fingers to pick them all out to see what the flower would look like without them; and latterly they have taken to themselves such appallingly virulent eye-jarring combinations of colour that I long to burn them, root and all. A screeching magenta Dahlia with a collarette of lemon yellow, or a mixture of cerise and yellow, I think only fit to be grown in the garden of an asylum for the blind. Even the name annoys me; it suggest a sham affair, a dickey or some lace abomination, a middle-class invention to transform useful work-a-day clothes into a semblance of those of afternoon leisure.

Then we have a new race of Paeony-flowered Dahlias that get larger and more violently glaring each season, and their poor stalks seem more and more unable to hold up the huge targets that grow out of them. They must be matchless for saving labour in decorating for Harvest Thanksgiving, one pumpkin with two Paeony Dahlias and one bud would be enough for the pulpit, and an extra large one would be all-sufficient for the font. I saw some magnificently grown last season, but so huge that I could not resist asking, in as innocent a tone as I could manage, whether they fried or steamed them, and if the latter, were they best with a white sauce or brown gravy.

E. A. BOWLES, *My Garden in Autumn and Winter* [1915[

Forget-me-nots

> When to the flowers so beautiful,
> The Father gave a name,
> Back came a little blue-eyed one,
> All timidly it came,
> And standing at its Father's feet,
> And gazing in His face,
> It said in low and trembling tones,
> 'Dear God, the name Thou gavest me,
> Alas! I have forgot.'
> Kindly the Father looked Him down,
> And said, 'Forget-me-not.'
>
> ANON.

Gentians

> Thou blossom, bright with autumn dew,
> And coloured with the heaven's own blue,
> Thou openest, when the quiet light
> Succeeds the keen and frosty night.
>
> Thou comest not when violets lean
> O'er wandering brooks and springs unseen,
> Or columbines in purple dress'd,
> Nod o'er the ground-bird's hidden nest.

Thou waitest late, and com'st alone,
When woods are bare and birds are flown,
And frosts and shortening days portend
The aged year is near his end.

Then doth thy sweet and quiet eye
Look through its fringes to the sky,
Blue – blue – as if that sky let fall
A flower from its cerulean wall . . .

WILLIAM CULLEN BRYANT
[1794–1878]

Geraniums

In the window beside which we are writing this article, there is a geranium shining with its scarlet tops in the sun, the red of it being the more red for a background of lime-trees which are at the same time breathing and panting like airy plenitudes of joy, and developing their shifting depths of light and shade, of russet browns and sunny inward gold.

It seems to say, 'Paint me!' so here it is. Every now and then some anxious fly comes near it: – we hear the sound of a bee, though we see none; and upon looking closer at the flowers, we observe that some of the petals are transparent with the light, while others are left in shade; the leaves are equally adorned, after their opaquer fashion, with those effects of the sky, showing their dark brown rims; and on one of them a red petal has fallen, where it lies on the brighter half of the shallow green cup, making its own red redder, and the green greener. We perceive, in imagination, the scent of those good-natured leaves, which allow you to carry off their perfume on your fingers; for good-natured they are in that respect, above almost all plants, and fittest for the hospitalities of your rooms. The very feel of the leaf has a household warmth in it something analogous to clothing and comfort . . . .

LEIGH HUNT, 'A Flower for your
Window' in *The Seer, or Common-
Places Refreshed* [1840]

And further on the delights of the sweet-scented variety.

Some months ago I read an article in the Bulletin of the Garden Club of America which delighted me, for it was by a lover of sweet-scented geraniums, and I felt that if I met the writer we should be friends at once, because in our childhood we had both loved these sweet-leaved plants. There must be thousands of folk who associate the scent with their childhood, for with the exception of lemon-scented verbena, and 'cherry pie,' there are, I suppose, no scents which attract one more when one is very young. I think this must be because, although sweet, yet they are so pungent and vigorous and surprisingly unexpected from such delicately cut leaves. The writer of the article in question described how, when a child, she used to go with her father on winter Sunday afternoons to see a friend who was renowned for his collection of sweet-leaved geraniums. She used to follow 'the two flower-lovers, the one so tall and straight, the other old and bent, up and down the narrow aisles between the benches of plants, pausing when they paused, moving slowly forward when they advanced filled with beatitude by the

warm, sweet odours given off by the moist earth and the growing green
things. No notice was taken of me, and so, left to my own devices, I would
snip as I went, a leaf here, a leaf there, until finally with my hands and
pockets full of aromatic leaves I would subside on an upturned tub in a
corner and sniff and compare the different scents to my heart's content. It
was a very good game indeed, as well as valuable nose training. It always
seemed amazing that just leaves could have such a variety of odours. Some
had the scents of oranges or lemons, some were spicy, others had a rose-like
fragrance, and many were vaguely familiar but tantalizingly elusive. One
that especially ravished my youthful nose smelled exactly like the pennyroyal that grew in our woods. The leaves of this kind were large and soft, and
the bush was lax and ungainly in habit. I know it now for *Pelargonium
tomentosum*, usually called the peppermint geranium.

ELEANOUR SINCLAIR ROHDE,
The Scented Garden [1931]

Gillyflowers

*John Gerard attempts to clear up for us what these were. In modern
terms they are dianthus, pinks and carnations.*

There are at this day under the name of *Caropbyllus*, comprehended divers
and sundrie sorts of plants, of such variable colours, and also severall shapes,
that a great and large volume would not suffice to write of every one at large
in particular; considering how infinite they are, and how every yeere, every
climate and countrie bringeth foorth new sorttes, such as have not been
heretofore written of; somewhereof are called Carnations, other Clove
Gilloflowers, some Sops in wine, some Pagiants or Pagion colour, Horse-
flesh, blunket, purple, white, double and single Gilloflowers, as also a
Gilloflower with yellow flowers. The which a worshipfull marchant of
London Master *Nicholas Lete*, procured from Poland, and gave me thereof
for my garden, which before that time was never seen nor heard in these
countries. Likewise there be sundrie sorts of Pinks, comprehended under the
same title, which shall be described in a severall chapter. There be under the
name of Gilloflowers also those flowers, which we do call Sweet Johns, and
Sweete Williams. JOHN GERARD, *The Herball* [1597]

Here is a list of varieties available early in the reign of Charles I.

The lustie Gallant or Westminster (some make them to be one flower, and
others to be two, one bigger than the other) at the first blowing open of the
flower sheweth to be a reasonable size and comelinesse, but after it hath
stood blowen some time it sheweth smaller and thinner: it is of a bright red
colour, much striped and speckled with white.
The red Douer is a resonable great Gilloflower and constant, being of a faire
red, thicke powdered with white spots . . .
The light or white Douer is for forme and all other things more comely than
the former, the colour of the flower is blush, thicke spotted with very small
spots, that it seemeth all gray, and is very delightfull.
The Faire Maid of Kent, or Ruffling Robin, is a very beautiful flower, and as

large as the white Carnation almost: the flower is white, thicke powdered with purple, wherein the white hath the maistrie by much, which maketh it the more pleasant.

The Daintie is a comely fine flower, although it be not great, and for the smallnesse and thinnesse of the flower being red so finely marked, striped and speckled, that for the livelinesse of the colours it is much desired, being inferiour to very few Gilloflowers.

The Brassill Gilloflower is but of a meane size, being of a sad purple colour, thicke powdered and speckled with white, the purple herein hath the maistrie, which maketh it shew the sadder, it is vnconstant, varying much and often to bee all purple . . .

The Turkie Gilloflower is but a small flower, but of great delight, by reason of the well marking of the flower, being most vsually equally striped with red and white.

The light or pale Pageant is a flower of a middle size, very pleasant to behold, and is both constant and comely, and but that it is so common, would be much more respect than it is: the flower is of a pale bright purple, thicke powdered, and very euenly with white, which hath the mastery, and maketh it the more graceful.

Master Bradshawe his dainty Lady may bee well reckoned among these sorts of Gilloflowers, and compare for neatnesse with most of them: the flower is very neate, though small, with a fine small iagge, and of a fine white colour on the vnderside of all the leaues, as also all the whole iagge for a pretty compasse, and the bottome or middle part of the flower on the vpperside also; but each leafe is of a fine bright red colour on the upperside, from the edge to the middle, which mixture is of great delight.

The stamell Gilloflower is well knowne to all, not to differ from the ordinary red or cloue Gilloflower, but only in being of a brighter or light red colour: there is both a greater and a lesser of this kinde.

Iohn Wittie his great tawny Gilloflower is for forme of growing, in leafe and flower like vnto the ordinary tawny, the flower onely, because it is the fairest and greatest that any other hath noursed vp, maketh the difference, as also it is of a faire deepe scarlet colour.

Of Reds likewise there are some varieties, but not so many of the other colours; for they are most dead or deepe reds, and few of a bright red or stamell colour; and they are single like Pinkes either striped or speckled, or more double striped and speckled variably . . .

The striped Tawny are either greater or lesser, deeper or lighter flowers twenty sorts and aboue, and all striped with smaller or larger stripes, or equally diuided, of a deeper or lighter colour, and some also for the very shape or forme will bee more neate, close and round: others more loose, vnequall, and sparsed.

The marbled Tawny hath not so many varieties as the striped, but is of as great beauty and delight as it, or more; the flowers are greater or smaller, deeper or lighter coloured than one another, and the veines or markes more conspicuous, or more frequent in some than in others; but the most beautiful that euer I did see was with Master Ralph Tuggie, which I must needes

therefore call Master Tuggies Princesse, which is the greatest and fairest of all these sorts of variable tawnies, or seed flowers, being as large fully as the Prince or Chrystall, or something greater, standing comely and round, not loose or shaken, or breaking the pod as some other sorts will; the marking of the flower is in this manner: It is of a stamell colour, striped and marbled with white stripes and veines quite through euery leafe, which are as deeply jagged as the Hulo: sometimes it hath more red than white, and sometimes more white than red, and sometimes so equally marked that you cannot discerne which hath the mastery; yet which of these hath the predominance, still the flower is very beautifull, and exceeding delightsome.

The Flaked Tawny is another diuersity of these variable or mixt coloured flowers, being of a pale reddish colour, flaked with white, not alwaies downeright, but often thwart the leaues, some more or lesse than others; the marking of them is much like vnto the Chrystall: these also as well as others will be greater or smaller, and of greater or lesse beauty than others.

The Feathered Tawny is more rare to meete with than many of the others; for most vsually it is a faire large flower and double equalling the Lombard red in his perfection: the colour hereof is vsually a scarlet, little deeper or paler, most curiosly red and streamed with white throughout the whole leave.

The Speckled Tawny is of diuers sorts, some bigge, some lesse, some more, and some lesse spotted than others: Vsually it is a deepe scarlet, speckled or spotted with white, hauing also some stripes among the leaues.

Master Tuggie his Rose Gilloflower is of the kindred of these Tawnies, being raised from the seede of some of them, and onely possessed by him that is the most industrious preseruer of all nature's beauties, being a different sort from all other, in that it hath round leaues, without any iagge at all on the edges, of a fine stamell full colour, without any spot or streake therein, very like vnto a small Rose, or rather much like vnto the red Rose Campion, both for forme, colour, and roundnesse, but larger for size.

ANON., The Garden of Pleasant Flowers [1629]

Hellebores

'Know ye the flower that just now blows,
In the middle of winter – the Christmas rose –
Though it lack perfume to regale the nose,
To the eyes right fair is the Christmas rose –
A fiddlestick's end for the frost and snows;
Sing hey, sing ho, for the Christmas rose.'

Punch, 30 December 1882

Hostas

One Sunday, in the days of my youth, I was 'volunteered' with my younger brother to superintend the family garden which was opening up for a Red Cross Sunday. We had been weeding all morning, and at lunch time handed over to the various dignitaries who set up card tables, arrows to the lavatory, the tea tent and so on. Meanwhile, my brother and I lurked in the rhodo-

dendrons, ready to tackle cuttings pinchers, retrieve lost children, banish unwelcome dogs and generally see to the needs of the public. One of the first to arrive was a famous local Brigadier (retd.) who had a short fuse and tended to speak in telegrams. He obviously disliked teenagers intensely, for he glared at my brother and shouted 'Hostas!'

'Sorry?' queried my brother, who didn't know a dahlia from a damson.

'Where are your hostas?' The Brigadier's face was turning crimson. Clearly, with words at a premium he disliked having to repeat himself.

'They're not here, sir,' said my brother.

'Can see that! That's why I'm asking.'

'They've gone to India. They'll be back next week.'

'Good God!' said the Brigadier and strode off looking perplexed. I looked at my brother.

'What on earth did you say that for?' I asked.

'I thought "hosta" must be a military word for "parent".' He shuffled more deeply into the rhododendrons to hide his embarrassment. Inevitably, the military gent found the hostas and strode back to berate us.

'India be dammed!' be roared. 'Down by pond! Hostas! Dozens! Pretty sight. Love kalmias too! Very pretty. That boy your gardener? Useless! No clue!'

NIGEL COLBORN, *Take Me to Your Hostas* [1989]

Hyacinths

There are great diversity of these . . . differences in colour and greatnes, and seasons of bearing. The fairest and largest we call ORIENTALL, because they came first out of Turkey and the Eastern countreys, whereof there are some blew, pale and deepe, smelling sweet, and some white, all which flower betimes, and some of the same colours which flower later, amongst which the rarest is the DOWBLE WHITE, and the FLESH color, and the ASH color. And after all these come the VIOLET color polyanthes, single and dowble, the sweet pale WATCHET, called in Italy Januarius, from a gardener's name, and the dowble Sky or Blew, called there Roseus, from the figure like a rose blowne, and the Rosemary color.

SIR THOMAS HANMER, *Garden Book* [1659]

Lilies

Next to the rose, there is not a fairer flower than the Lillie, nor of greater estimation. The oiles also and ointments made of them both, have a resemblance and an affinitie one to the other. As touching the oile of Lillies, the Physicians call it Lirinon. And if a man should speak truly, a Lillie growing among Roses, becommeth and beautifieth the place very well; for it beginneth then to flower when the Roses have halfe done. There is not a flower in the garden again that groweth taller than the Lillie, reaching otherwhile to the height of three cubits from the ground: but a weak and slender necke it hath, and carried it not streight and upright, but it bendeth and noddeth downeward, as being not of strength sufficient to beare the weight of the head standing upon it. The flower is of incomparable whiteness, devided into leaves, which without-forth are chamfered, narrow at the bottome, and by little and little spreading broader toward the top: fashioned all together in manner of a broad mouthed cup or beaker, the brims and lips wherof turne up somewhat backward round about and lie very open. Within these leaves there appeare certaine fine threds in manner of seeds: and just in the middest stand yellow chives, like as in Saffron.

Now Lillies be set and sowed after the same manner in all respects as the roses, and grow as many waies. This vantage moreover they have of the roses, that they will come up of the very liquor that distilleth and droppeth from them, like as the hearb Alisanders: neither is there in the world an hearb more fruitfull insomuch as you shall have one head of a root put forth oftentimes five hundred bulbs or cloves.

PLINY THE ELDER, *The Natural History*, translated by Philemon Holland [1601]

The rose sleeps in her beauty, but the lily seems unaware of her own exceeding loveliness. The rose is never so glorious as in cultivation and fares sumptuously, with every care lavished on her but, given rich food instead of the sharp drainage and leaf mould to which she is accustomed, the lily withdraws her gracious presence. The purity of the lily is not only in her outward form, but it is characteristic of the food she requires. No members of the lily family tolerate manure, artificial or otherwise. The lily is at her fairest in the waste places of the earth, where human eyes rarely see her in her beauty. Think of the splendour of *Lilium regale* in her native haunts where her discoverer, the late Mr E. H. Wilson, found her, in that little-known, wild territory which separates China proper from mysterious Thibet. In narrow valleys bordering on the roof of the world, in a region dominated by lofty peaks crowned with eternal snows, subjected to intense cold in winter and terrific heat in summer, in solitudes where only a few intrepid explorers and wild tribesmen venture, the regal lily reigns. Both in summer and winter these regions are swept by storms of awe-inspiring violence, yet in June the precipitous, arid mountain-sides blossom with countless thousands of these glorious lilies filling the air with their wondrous perfume. And from her mountainous fastness this radiant queen has been transported to our gardens. When one looks at her with the rich wine-colour shining through the snow-white inner surface of her petals and her golden anthers in this exquisite setting, and bearing sometimes as many as fifteen flowers on each slender stalk, it seems as though one so gorgeously apparelled must live delicately in Kings' courts, yet her dwelling is amidst the bleakest solitudes of this planet. Still stranger is it that this lily ripens seed freely in this country, the seeds germinate in a few weeks and the plants flower after their second year.

ELEANOUR SINCLAIR ROHDE, *The Scented Garden* [1931]

Lobelia

Today I should like to put in a good word for the lobelia, dear to the heart of some suburban and most municipal gardeners, but despised by those who pride themselves on a more advanced taste. The poor lobelia has suffered terribly and most unjustly from its traditional use and from association.

Association has been the worst enemy of many plants. I suppose that the first time anybody saw pink tulips coming up through forget-me-nots they may have exclaimed in delight. Similarly, the Victorian-Edwardian combination of lobelia and sweet alyssum may once have given pleasure. No longer now.

But can you discard all your preconceived ideas and think of the lobelia as though you had never seen it before? What a fine blue, as good as a gentian, is it not? And so dense, so compact, such a rug, such a closely woven carpet, you could put a pin though not a finger into the mat of flower. Think of it in this way, and you will instantly begin to see it in a different light and full of different possibilities.

Think of it as a great blue pool. Think of it in terms of waves and washes; think of it in terms of the Mediterranean at its best; think of it in spreads and sweeps and wapentakes and sokes and bailiwicks and tithings. Or, if you have not quite so much space at your disposal, do at least plant it in really generous patches, not just as an edging, and remember the variety called Cambridge Blue, which lives up to its name.

If you must have it as an edging, and if you must combine it with alyssum, try it with the alyssums called Lilac Queen, Violet Queen, and Royal Carpet, instead of the traditional white. The blue of the lobelia mixes into something very sumptuous with their mauves and purples. And I did observe an amusing and original use of lobelia last summer. The dark blue and the bright blue were planted in neat squares up either side of a narrow path leading from the garden gate to the front door. It was like a slice of chessboard; an Oxford and Cambridge chess-board.

V. SACKVILLE-WEST, *More for Your Garden*, [1955]

Love-in-a-mist

Light Love in a Mist, by the midsummer morn misguided,
  Scarce seen in the twilight garden if gloom insist,
Seems vainly to seek for a star whose gleam has divided
    Light Love in a Mist.
All day in the sun, when the breezes do all they list,
  His soft-blue raiment of cloud-like blossom abided
Unrent and unwithered of winds and of rays that kissed,
  Blithe-hearted or sad, as the cloud on the sun subsided.
Love smiled in the flower with a meaning whereof none wist,
  Save two that beheld as a gleam that before them glided,
    Light love in a mist.

ALGERNON CHARLES SWINBURNE
[1837–1909]

Pansies

OBERON That very time I saw – but thou could'st not –
        Flying between the cold moon and the earth,
        Cupid all arm'd: a certain aim he took
        At a fair vestal, throned by the west,

And loosed his love-shaft smartly from his bow,
As it should pierce a hundred thousand hearts:
But I might see young Cupid's fiery shaft
Quench'd in the chaste beams of the watery moon:
And the imperial votaress pass'd on,
In maiden meditation, fancy-free.
Yet mark'd I where the bolt of Cupid fell:
It fell upon a little western flower;
Before, milk-white; now purple, with love's wound
And maidens call it, love-in-idleness.
Fetch me that flower; the herb I showed thee once:
The juice of it, on sleeping eye-lids laid,
Will make or man or woman madly dote
Upon the next live creature that it sees.
Fetch me this herb; and be thou here again
Ere the leviathan can swim a league.

> WILLIAM SHAKESPEARE,
> *A Midsummer Night's Dream*, Act II,
> sc. i

Poppies

BIG POPPY

Hot-eyed Mafia Queen!
At the trim garden's edge

She sways towards August.
A Bumble Bee
Clambers into her drunken, fractured goblet –

Up the royal carpet of a down-hung,
Shrivel-edged, unhinged petal, her first-about-to-fall.
He's in there as she sways. He utters thin

Sizzling bleats of difficult enjoyment.
Her carnival paper skirts, luminous near-orange,
Embrace him helplessly.

Already her dark pod is cooking its drug.
Every breath imperils her. Her crucible
Is falling apart with its own fierceness.

A fly, cool, rests on the flame-fringe.

Soon she'll throw off her skirts
Withering into vestal afterlife,

Bleeding inwardly
Her maternal nectars into her own
Coffin – (cradle of her offspring).

Then we shall say:
'She wore herself in her hair, in her day,
And we could see nothing but her huge flop of petal,

Her big, lewd, bold eye, in its sooty lashes,

And that stripped, athletic leg, hairy,
In a fling of abandon –'

TED HUGHES [1930–   ]

Primroses

TO PRIMROSES FILLED WITH MORNING DEW

Why doe ye weep, sweet Babes? can Teares
Speak griefe in you,
Who were but borne
Just as the modest Morne
Teem'd her refreshing dew?
Alas! you have not known that shower,
That marres a flower;
Nor felt th'unkind
Breath of a blasting wind;
Nor are ye worne with yeares;
Or warpt, as we,
Who think it strange to see
Such pretty flowers (like the Orphans young),
To speak by Teares, before ye have a Tongue.

Speak, whimp'ring Younglings, and make known
The reason why
Ye droop, and weep;
Is it for want of sleep?
Or childish Lullabie,
Or that ye have not seen as yet
The *Violet*?
Or brought a kisse
From that Sweet-heart, to this?
No, no, this sorrow shown
By your teares shed,
Who'd have this Lecture read,
That things of greatest, so of meanest worth,
Concei'd with grief are, and with teares brought forth.

ROBERT HERRICK [1591–1674]

Welcome, pale primrose! starting up between
Dead matted leaves of ash and oak that strew
The every lawn, the wood, the spinney, through
'Mid creeping moss, and ivy's darker green.
How much thy presence beautifies the ground –
How sweet thy modest unaffected pride
Glows on the sunny banks and woods' warm side.

JOHN CLARE [1793–1864]

Roses

I smelt and prays'd the fragrant rose,
Blushing, thus answer'd she:
    The praise you gave,
    The scent I have,
    Doe not belong to mee;
    This harmlesse odour, none
    but only God indeed does owne;
    to be his keepers, my poor leaves he chose;
    And thus reply'd the rose . . .

        PATRICK CAREY, *Trivial Poems and*
        Triolets [1651]

And if you voz to see my roziz
As is a boon to all men's noziz, –
You'd fall upon your back and scream –
'O Lawk! O criky! it's a dream!'

        EDWARD LEAR, Postscript to a letter to
        Lord Carlingford, 30 April 1885

In a gracious, small and ancient town near where I live, someone has had the imagination to plant a hedge of rambler roses. It occupies the whole of his road frontage, about one hundred and fifty yards I believe, and in the summer months people come from all over the country to see it. I must admit that it is an impressive sight; a blaze of colour; a long angry, startling streak, as though somebody had taken a red pencil and had scrawled dense red bunches all over a thicket-fence of green. A splendid idea; very effective; but, oh, how crude! I blink on seeing it, and having blinked, I weep. It is not only the virulence of the colour that brings tears to my eyes, but the regret that so fine an idea should not have been more fastidiously carried out.

The hedge is made of *American Pillar*, a rose which, together with *Dorothy Perkins*, should be forever abolished from our gardens.

        VITA SACKVILLE-WEST, *In Your*
        Garden Again [1953]

    The rose is a rose,
    And was always a rose.
    But the theory now goes
    That the apple's a rose,
    And the pear is, and so's
    The plum, I suppose.
    The dear only knows
    What will next prove a rose.
    You, of course, are a rose –
    But were always a rose.

        ROBERT FROST [1875–1963]

Tulips

I do verily thinke that these are the Lillies of the field mentioned by our Saviour for He saith that Solomon in all his royaltee was not arrayed like one of these. The reasons that induce me to thinke thus are these: First their shape, for their flowers resemble Lillies, and in these places whereas our Saviour was conversant they grow wilde in the fields. Secondly, the infinite varietie of colour, which is to be founde more than in any other sorte of flowre: and thirdly the wondrous beautie and mixtures of these flowres.

    This is my opinion, which any may either approue or gainsay as he shall thinke goode.

JOHN GERARD, The Herball [1597]

As I sat in the porch, I heard the voices of two or three persons, who seemed very earnest in discourse. My curiosity was raised when I heard the names of Alexander the Great and Artaxerxes; and as their talk seemed to run on ancient heroes, I concluded there could not be any secret in it; for which reason I thought I might very fairly listen to what they said.

    After several parallels between great men, which appeared to me altogether groundless and chimerical, I was surprised to hear one say, that he valued the Black Prince more than the Duke of Vendosme. How the Duke of Vendosme should become a rival of the Black Prince, I could not conceive: and was more startled when I heard a second affirm, with great vehemence, that if the Emperor of Germany was not going off, he should like him better than either of them. He added, that though the season was so changeable, the Duke of Marlborough was in blooming beauty. I was wondering to myself from whence they had received this odd intelligence: especially when I heard them mention the names of several other generals, as the Prince of Hesse and the King of Sweden, who, they said, were both running away. To which they added, what I entirely agreed with them in, that the Crown of France was very weak, but that the Marshal Villars still kept his colours. At last, one of them told the company, if they would go along with him, he would show them a Chimney-Sweeper and a Painted Lady in the same bed, which he was sure would very much please them. The shower, which had driven them as well as myself into the house, was now over; and as they were passing by me into the garden, I asked them to let me be one of their company.

    The gentleman of the house told me, 'if I delighted in flowers, it would be worth my while; for that he believed he could show me such a blow of tulips as was not to be matched in the whole country.'

    I accepted the offer, and immediately found that they had been talking in terms of gardening, and that the kings and generals they had mentioned were only so many tulips, to which the gardeners, according to their usual custom, had given such high titles and appellations of honour . . .

    I accidentally praised a tulip as one of the finest I ever saw; upon which they told me it was a common Fool's Coat. Upon that I praised a second, which it seems was but another kind of Fool's Coat . . . The gentleman smiled at my ignorance. He seemed a very plain honest man, and a person of good sense, had not his head been touched with that distemper which Hippocrates calls the Tulippomania; insomuch that he would talk very rationally on any subject in the world but a tulip.

    He told me, 'that he valued the bed of flowers that lay before us, and was

not above twenty yards in length and two in breadth, more than he would the best hundred acres of land in England,' and added, 'that it would have been worth twice the money it is, if a foolish cook-maid of his had not almost ruined him the last winter, by mistaking a handful of tulip roots for a heap of onions, and by that means,' says he, 'made me a dish of pottage that cost me above a thousand pounds sterling.' . . .

JOSEPH ADDISON, The Tatler [1710]

A battle of flowers between the tulip and the rose.

In this solemn randevoux of flowers and herbs, the Rose stood forth, and made an oration to this effect.

It is not unknown to you, how I have precedency of all flowers, confirmed unto me under the patent of a double sence, sight and smell. What more curious colours? how do all diers blush, when they behold my blushing as conscious to themselves that their art cannot imitate that tincture, which nature hath stamped upon me. Smell, it is not lusciously offensive, nor dangerously faint, but comforteth with a delight, and delighteth with the comfort thereof: yea, when dead, I am more soveraigne than living: what cordials are made of my syrups? how many corrupted lungs (those fans of nature) sore wasted with consumption that they seem utterly unable any longer to cool the heat of the heart, with their ventilation, are with conserves made of my stamped leaves, restored to their former soundness again. More would I say in my own cause, but that happily I may be taxed of pride, and self-flattery, who speake much in mine own behalf, and therefore I leave the rest to the judgement of such as hear me, and pass from this discourse to my just complaint.

There is lately a flower (shall I call it so? in courtesie I will tearme it so, though it deserve not the appellation) a Toolip, which hath engrafted the love and affections of most people unto it; and what is this Toolip? a well complexion'd stink, an ill favour wrapt up in pleasant colours; as for the use thereof in physick, no physitian hath honoured it yet with the mention, nor with a Greek, or Latin name, so inconsiderable hath it hitherto been accompted; and yet this is that which filleth all gardens, hundred of pounds being given for the root thereof, whilst I the Rose, am neglected and contemned, and conceived beneath the honour of noble hands, and fit only to grow in the gardens of yeomen.

THOMAS FULLER, Antheologia, or the Speech of Flowers [1660]

Simon Schama gives a brilliant account of that unique phenomenon in the history of floriculture, tulipomania.

There is nothing mysterious about the tulip's arrival in western Europe. It came to the Netherlands in the sixteenth century at a time when commercial and cultural contacts between the Ottoman Levant and the Habsburg empire flourished notwithstanding their official bellicosity. Ambassador Busbeq saw it growing in Adrianople and agents and diplomats as well as merchants brought the bulbs to the gardens of courtiers, scholars and bankers in Antwerp, Brussels and Augsburg in the 1560s. Joris Rye, who was a botanist as well as a merchant, cultivated varieties at Malines, and by the 1590s it had appeared in gardens in the north, perhaps even the *Hortus*

Botanicus at Leiden University, where Clusius and Johan van Hooghelande both experimented with different hues and sizes. In this early period, its cultivation was essentially an aristocratic taste – a novelty that caught on from Paris to Prague, where that passionate innovator the emperor Rudolf II indulged his curiosity. Both Boisot, the admiral of the Beggar Fleet, and Philip van Marnix, among the entourage of William the Silent, were fanciers, but it was not until the publication of the first substantial catalogues that admiration of the flower moved out from court and humanist circles to a wider group of aficionados. Emmanuel Sweerts's *Florilegium*, published in Frankfurt in 1612, included around a hundred plates reflecting the varieties that he was already selling in Amsterdam. But it was Chrispijn van de Pas's *Hortus Floridus*, published in both Dutch and Latin editions in 1614, that promoted the reputation of the flower throughout Dutch and German towns on the lower Rhine.

By the early 1620s, tulips were established as the unrivaled flower of fashion throughout northern France, the Netherlands and western parts of Germany. In an age extremely conscious of hierarchy, it was not long before an informal system of classification arranged varieties according to rank, from the most noble to the most common. Superior ranking did not necessarily (though often did) indicate rarity, but rather flamboyance and subtlety of color combinations. It was the flamed and irregularly striped varieties that were most admired and were grouped into three aristocratic estates according to dominant hue: the roses (red and pink on white-ground), the violets (lilac and purples on white ground) and *bizarden* (red or violet on yellow ground). At the very head of this nobility were the imperial rarities, the Semper Augustus (red flames on white) and the attempted clone, the Parem Augustus. There were also Viceroys, but in the Netherlands, where royalty had gone out of favor, inventive growers appropriated heroic titles for their flowers that cast a reflected patriotic luster on themselves. Thus admirals and generals (for the tulip was always anthropomorphized as male) sprang up everywhere. General Bol and Admiral Pottebacker were not, then, named for military heroes but rather admiral and general tulips named for the growers Pieter Bol of Haarlem and Henrik Pottebacker of Gouda. Tulips could inspire even fancier conceits from poets, one comparing *Tulipa clusiana*, with its carmine-tinted white petals, to the 'faint blush on the cheek of chaste Susannah.'

In this stage of the flower's debut in northern Europe, tulips were either admired or scorned as an elegant extravagance. Those critics (especially Calvinist preachers) who attacked the follies of outrageous ruffs and beribboned hose or overwrought bedsteads, saw the tulip as yet another dangerous addition to the lengthy catalogue of vanities that were subverting the godly Republic. There are, it is true, occasional exceptions to their hostility in the iconography of moralizing texts. One emblem seems to have imported the oriental Sufi association of tulips with eternity. It shows an image of virtue rather than vice: an elderly widow awaiting her end with her attribute of honorable industry, the distaff, and that of fidelity, her (equally aged) dog. The imminence of her end is symbolized in the scaly hand of death grasping the stem of the tulip. A connotation of virtuous resignation, however, is rare. Much more typical was the association of the tulip with worldly folly. Roemer Visscher's *Sinnepoppen* used it for the motto 'A fool and his money are soon parted' almost twenty years *before* the speculative mania got under way. At a time when a single bulb of Semper Augustus might easily fetch a thousand guilders, the sentiment was easily understandable.

Even by the late 1620s, the tulip remained for the most part a costly flower, produced either by gentlemen botanists for themselves or a small number of professional growers for their patrician clientele. Adriaan Pauw, the Pensionary of Amsterdam immediately after Oldenbarneveld's demise, was typical in planting out beds at his rural retreat at Heemstede soon after its purchase in 1623, and became an enthusiast in his own right, producing new red-and-white-striped hybrids. The most inventive and prolific among the professional growers, like Abraham Catoleyn in Amsterdam and Pieter Bol and Jan Quackel in Haarlem, established specialist reputations, both from the bulbs named for them in the catalogues and through their well-connected clientele. But around the beginning of the 1630s, a second generation of horticulturalists began to break out from this relatively genteel and circumscribed trade and to change the conditions of distribution and sale. Some of these men had served their apprenticeship as gardeners to the older professionals and now struck out on their own with rented lots and aggressively entrepreneurial ambitions . . .

The new dealers geared themselves to supplying a much broader range of stock, from the high-price hybrids to the gaudier, single-color varieties like the Switsers and the Yellow Crowns that sold for a few stuivers the ace. Differences in both weight and price were enormous, so that potential customers could pick and choose according to their means . . .

The result of deliberate market innovations and the extension of production to cover cheaper varieties had produced something like an explosion of demand during the course of 1634 and 1635. The popularization of the tulip had touched a deep well of consumer hunger in the Dutch that could only be assuaged by colorful novelty and conspicuous expenditure at home. The growers had succeeded beyond their wildest expectations. They had invented a national cliché. The effect on prices was extraordinary. Initially, during 1634, the introduction of many new varieties had the effect of depressing prices to the point at which they became accessible to the popular market. The sudden surge of demand then swung them abruptly in the opposite direction. Seasonal unavailability, as well as the strain on production to keep pace with demand, further accelerated the price rise. By lifting time in 1636, many varieties – even common ones – had trebled in price. A Gouda that had cost thirty stuivers in December 1634 fetched more than fl. 3 two years later. An Admiral de Maan that had sold for fl. 15 cost fl. 175 after the same period. A fl. 40 Centen went for fl. 350 just a few months later; a Scipio bought for fl. 800 sold weeks later for fl. 2,200. Such cases could be multiplied indefinitely.

Before long, payment was made in kind, partly as a reflection of downmarket customers who could offer more in the way of stock than ready cash to snap up desirable buys. Quite frequently they were obliged to part with their goods on making the purchase and then promised to pay a balance in cash on delivery of the bulb. A quarter of a pound of White Crowns, for example, were bought for fl. 525 to be paid on delivery together with four cows paid at once. A one-pound Centen was paid for by fl. 1,800 and immediate transfer of a 'best shot coat, one old rose noble and one coin with

a silver chain to hang round a child's neck.' A Viceroy that had been bought for fl. 900 was resold while still planted out for fl. 1,000 on delivery and the immediate exchange of a suit and coat. The different kinds of goods offered give some indication of the wide range of occupations and social status of buyers. In all likelihood it was a farmer who paid fl. 2,500 for a single Viceroy in the form of two *last* of wheat and four of rye, four fat oxen, eight pigs, a dozen sheep, two oxheads of wine, four tons of butter, a thousand pounds of cheese, a bed, some clothing and a silver beaker. Tools and stock in trade were commonly offered. Just as van Heemskerck had bought his lottery ticket with a painting, so Jan van Goyen – on the very eve of the crash – paid a Hague burgomaster fl. 1,900 for ten bulbs, and promised, in addition, a picture by Salomon van Ruysdael and a history painting of Judas by himself. By 1641, four years later, he had still not delivered the picture nor had discharged his debts and died insolvent. At the top end of the speculators' market extraordinary deals were made, all carefully notarized. A Semper Augustus of 193 aces was bought for fl. 4,600 and a coach and dapple gray pair (around fl. 2,000 value on their own). The few bulbs of that most prized variety were thought to fetch fl. 6,000 each at the height of the mania. Tracts of land, houses, silver and gold vessels and fine furniture were all commonly traded as part of the increasingly feverish tempo of transactions.

SIMON SCHAMA, *The Embarassment of Riches* [1987]

Snowdrops

Of all the February flowers I suppose the snowdrop is the most popular. Its thorough hardiness, its patience under any ill-treatment, its easy cultivation, and, above all, its pure beauty, make it welcome to every garden, and there is no more valued plant in the garden of the poor, and in children's gardens. I suppose no flower brings so many associations and past remembrances with it; certainly it does to me, for it has always been a favourite flower here . . .

Something must be said about the pretty name, or rather the pretty names, of the snowdrop. The common name is not the old name, and certainly, to nearly the end of the seventeenth century, it was described as the white bulbous violet. Such a cumbrous name might do when the plant was only a garden plant, and probably not a common one, but when it increased and multiplied so as to be found in every garden, and was becoming naturalized in many places, another name was wanted, and none more fitting could be found that the pretty name of snowdrop, which was creeping in Gerard's time (he gives the name very doubtfully), but which only came into general use by very slow degrees. I suppose it was adopted from the common names of the flower in its native countries, such as France and Germany. Its German names may be translated as snowflake, February flower, naked maiden-snow-violet, and snowdrop; and its French names as the white bell, the bell of the snows, the bell of winter, and the snow-piercer.

CANON ELLACOMBE, *In a Gloucestershire Garden* [1895]

Sunflowers

THE SUNFLOWER COMPARED

The sunflower hangs its heavy head of seed
Like a wide standard-lamp that has gone out;
Its only enemy has been the wind;
Sun-like it shone that shame-faced dinner plate.
Eleven feet – too high for any room;
Its lower leaves, when withered, left their print;
Throughout its haughty progress I can claim
It stood assisted by my string and splint.
But now I snip the string and heave it up,
Its clotted root no bigger than the head
Which wildly wags without the help of wind:
A schizophrenic dumb-bell which I snap
To make an earth-mace and a pole-borne load
Like young mayoral hopes swung on the road.

ALAN DIXON [1974]

Violets

As long as my grandmother lived,
The sweet white violets that grew
On either side of the garden path
Bloomed every spring, and when in bloom
Made sweet the garden and the lane,
And scented all the avenue;
While in the house, from room to room,
Their fragrance travelled with the breeze.
They thrived until she died, and then
Survived her death another spring.
And after that nobody knew
The words she said to make them bloom,
When walking up and down the path
She poked among them with her cane.

Quoted by ELIZABETH LAWRENCE,
A Southern Garden [1942]

FLOWER ARRANGING

My sentiments exactly on the abominable direction taken by too many flower arrangers.

Despite my reservations about the National Council and the heavy hand it lays on American flower arranging, I love to go to flower shows, even standard flower shows conducted under the Council's aegis. A couple of winters back, I went to one held by the flourishing garden club of a medium-sized Florida city. It was staged in the city's biggest auditorium and was called 'A World Tour of Gardens.' The flower-arrangement section, so big it occupied more than half of a fifty-page catalogue, came under the heading 'Artistic Division: Round the World with Flora.' Well, as usual in recent years, there were mighty few flora in the arrangements so lovingly and

painstakingly devised by the devoted ladies of the many chapters of the club. Backgrounds and what are called in flower-show language 'accessories' ruled the day. There were nineteen classes under this heading of 'Artistic,' with such titles as 'Australia – Land of the Boomerang,' 'France – Pomp and Elegance,' 'Korea – Country of the Morning Calm,' even 'Never Never Land.' For each class there were strict requirements. Five of the classes allowed only dried or painted material, seven specified fresh. The others called for a mixture of fresh and dried material, but far more dry stuff than green stuff was in evidence, and this in a flower-laden city at the height of its semitropical bloom. No wonder that when my husband accompanied me to an earlier show in the same building he looked around the vast hall and asked, 'Where are the flowers?' This year he waited outside – said he'd seen enough dry-ki to last him – while I fought my way in. (The show had been open an hour and my ticket number was three thousand and something.)

Here, reconstructed from almost illegible notes, is a rundown of a few of the entries:

Iceland: Rules requiring an abstract to interpret the feeling of cold. Some fresh plant material must be used. The blue-ribbon winner's fresh material was one white chrysanthemum inserted in a piece of twisted cedar that had been painted white and rested on a heap of broken pale-green glass. (I own a pair of pale-green glass bookends, and I couldn't help wondering whether the exhibitor had taken a hammer to a similar pair of her own.) This exhibit won the Creativity Award.

Never Never Land: Requirements: 'Avant-Garde – Some fresh plant material must be used.' A paper-covered cardboard cylinder had been painted red and peppered with red sequins stuck on while the paint was wet. Cylinder held some flowers and artificially curled papyrus. 'Camp, perhaps,' I noted, 'but not Avant-Garde.' Won a blue ribbon. Another exhibit was fashioned of two long coils of half-inch copper tubing that had been tortured into intertwining circles. Out of each of the four sawed-off ends of the tubing one small magenta-pink rose dropped, already sadly wilted – the 'fresh plant material.' Intended, no doubt, as an abstract – the current rage.

England: The exhibit to interpret a Shakespearean character, the name of the character to be printed on a card. When I couldn't get near enough to read the cards, the fun was to guess the characters. Often it wasn't hard. Juliet was represented by three red roses and a paper-cutter shaped like a dagger, and the balcony was an ivy vine with a mass of green podocarpus at the base. Shylock (or maybe it was Portia; I couldn't get near enough to see) was suggested by a postal scale (or maybe it was a fish scale), a heap of imitation gold-wrapped coins, and a branch of prickly Crown of Thorns, with its pink blossoms.

Peru – Lost Culture of the Incas: Required 'a design using gold and other rich colors with dried, painted, or treated materials.' The blue ribbon went to an entry involving gold-painted palm fronds, fungus, dried red celosia, and a figurine. A real beaut.

Italy – The Fountains of Rome: 'Must give the illusion of water or use water as part of the composition, featuring fresh aquatic material.' One entry consisted of a shallow oblong lead container holding half an inch of water, some green water plants, and the fleshless headbone of a catfish. The last was aquatic material, all right, but could hardly be called 'fresh.' Another lady, though, had ingeniously suggested a fountain by the curled, unfolding fronds of ferns, and the arrangement was pleasing. But is this arranging flowers? To me it's more like playing a game – a game little girls might play on a rainy afternoon.

France – Pomp and Elegance: Required roses and permitted accessories. Led to an absolute orgy of the latter – opera glasses, kid gloves, fans, lace, jewelry, yards and yards of artificial pearls. In contrast to the other classes, the bouquets were fairly opulent – usually a big vaseful of roses with gloves, pearls, fans, or whatever, ranged round the base. One was against a purple velvet background. I heard one spectator say as she passed a handsome jar of roses and other flowers, 'That's the only thing she knows how to do – an absolutely *stuffed* vase.'

Some exhibits were beautiful; the majority were modernistic, extremely studied designs. Old dried vines, I discovered, are particularly beloved for the abstracts. Design is now everything; flowers, as such, don't count. The old idea of bringing flowers into the house and preserving their natural beauty for several days in a bowl of water is forgotten. In the same show, the growing plants, not the arrangements, were what interested me; they were lovely, and they at least indicated that most of the exhibitors were capable of growing a good potted plant, a hanging basket, an orchid, or a cactus. The 'Horticultural Classes' – i.e., specimen flowers of almost everything from a humble ageratum to a Eucharis lily or a Bonsai – showed that the ladies of the garden club also knew how to garden. How the exhibitors have time to grow anything, though, and still spend the days it must take to gather accessories is a mystery. Bad, cheap statuettes of animals, wrack from the beaches, pseudo-Oriental figurines, junk from the junk-jewelry counters, plunder from the drugstores, the notion counters, the wastelands – these were much in evidence in the exhibits. Some of the ladies must have traveled to distant lands for their exotic accessories – hemp and straw and grass mats from Tahiti, brass and copper pots from India, bits of carved ivory from Taiwan, a temple bell from Thailand.

KATHARINE S. WHITE in the *New Yorker* [1967]; reprinted in *Onward and Upward in the Garden* [1979]

Two contrasting views of the same event.

FLOWER SHOWS

From Mrs Peters, The Hall, Ditton-Bishop, to her Sister:
My Dear, As usual, the flower show was a huge success and William actually managed to collect six firsts. You'll never guess who came down for it. Penelope Masters! It was actually her first *real* flower show. Naturally she'd been to the Chelsea one, but that hardly counts, does it? – none of the *fun* there is at ours. I don't think dear Penelope quite realized the *kind* of clothes to wear. If it had been a fine day – of course it never is for the flower show – her suede shoes and lovely Ascot frock would have been *most* appropriate. But it just chanced to be rather wet and I really don't quite know where Penelope thought one *has* flower shows, but she seemed a bit upset when she found we had to go right across the vicarage field to reach the tents. I had my

brogues and burberry, and William was really very good about holding an umbrella over Penelope. Once we got inside she seemed quite interested in the peas and beans, and she was really most amusing about the marrows, though I was rather glad the rector could not quite catch what she said. Of course I'm thoroughly broad-minded myself, and marrows have sometimes struck me as being rather *coarse*. Penelope must have been rather overdoing it with all those night clubs because, just as we were talking about potatoes, she suddenly clutched my arm and said, 'My dear, I'm afraid I'm going to faint.' Of course I offered to go home with her, but she said it was just through being shut up in the tent, and might William drive her home? It meant poor William missing my judging but he was *very* good about it.

Ever

Maud

Penelope Masters to Her Cousin:
Sylvia. If ever your life depends on going to a flower show, just die. It's quicker. My dear, can you imagine it? I thought the wretched affair was in the *town hall*! I did wonder why Maud wound herself up in her old burberry, but you know what she is. Of course it was raining, but I thought that going by car and being indoors it would rather cheer up the squires and people to see some clothes that weren't home-grown. Well, we'd only gone a little way when the car stopped. Maud shouted in that dreadful *hearty* way of hers, 'Here we are' and I found we had to squelch our way over the most enormous field. I nearly lost both my heels and I was smothered in mud and simply soaked. William *thought* he was holding an umbrella over me, but being him it just dripped. As last we got to a floppy tent. My dear, you never smelt such a smell of hot, wet people, mixed up with earth. Crowds of women in tweeds with faces like horses and not a lick of paint among them – just as God and the weather made them. Why do they call it a flower show? There were little piles of vegetables and the most obscene-looking marrows. Well, my dear, we counted every pea and measured every bean, and Maud told me some tale about Pike having no business to have won first prize for cottage potatoes because he grew them in his master's bed. As if I'd have cared if he'd grown them in his pyjamas. Anyhow William seemed to have won every other prize and no one could call the Hall a cottage. When Maud started talking about another tent it finished me. I looked all googly-eyed and said I thought I was going to faint. William drove me home. When we got there we sat by the library fire, and he didn't seem at all in a hurry to get back. Really, my dear, the woman's an imbecile! *Quelle vie!*

MRS PETERS and PENELOPE
MASTERS, *The Flower Show* in The
Countryman Gardening Book [1973]

Water Butt on wheels

FRUIT   *Apples*

'Here's to thee, old apple-tree;
Hence thou mayst bud, and whence thou mayst blow,
And whence thou mayst apples bear enow!
Hats full! caps full!

Bushel, bushel sacks full!
And my pockets full, too! Huzza!'
                                    Traditional

George Bernard Shaw's rubbish tip apple!

In June, 1931, G.B.S. complained, in a letter to his district council, of the nuisance caused in Ayot St Lawrence and its neighbourhood by a refuse dump at Wheathampstead. 'In March,' he wrote, 'I was cruising the Mediterranean, where I was very strongly reminded of the dump by the fumes of the island volcano of Stromboli, which is believed by the islanders to communicate directly with hell, and to be, in fact, one of the chimneys of that establishment. I was able to assure them that this could not be the case, as our Wheathampstead volcano, which has no crater, is a much greater nuisance.' On his return he found the dump 'in full blast', but a much more dangerous nuisance than the smell had developed. 'To explain its gravity is beyond my literary powers: therefore, I will ask the District Council to allow me to quote the Eighth Chapter of the Book of Exodus, verses 21–4: "Behold I will send swarms of flies upon thee".' Shaw had already had cause in previous years to complain about the nuisance. 'What happens every four years is, evidently, that the covering up is allowed to fall behind the dumpings; and the uncovered refuse catches fire and Strombolizes us, while the unburnt stuff breeds billions of flies.'

The letter was forwarded to the Islington Borough Council, who owned the dump, and after an inspection, they denied the nuisance. In reply, Shaw pointed out that his first letter was not written in the interests of 'merry Islington', so that 'the perfect satisfaction of its Cleansing Superintendent and Medical Officer is no satisfaction to me'. He went on: 'The Wheathampstead dump is twenty miles north of Islington; and at that distance its fragrance is lost. It is about a mile south of my house; and when the wind is in that quarter I am not reminded of Shakespeare's "Sweet south that breathes upon a bank of violets"; I am reminded of Stromboli, of Etna, of Vesuvius and of hell. My famous neighbour, My Cherry-Garrard, sole survivor of "the worst journey in the world", after the horrors of which one would suppose that no discomfort possible in these latitudes could seem to him worth mentioning, has written a letter implying plainly that there is little to choose between midwinter at the South Pole and midsummer at Lamer Park when the dump is in eruption.'

In May 1932, when I was employed at Rothamsted on problems of water pollution, I visited the dump out of curiosity and found it inoffensive, but I was impressed by the wealth of blossom on a young apple tree about 6 ft in height growing out of the rubbish. When I went to see the tree again in August to examine the fruit, I was disappointed to find only a few deformed specimens, the tree having been considerably damaged. But I was still curious as to the possible merits of such a potentially fruitful tree, so I grafted cuttings on Type IX rootstocks the following spring.

Three years later the tree bore a single apple, which weighed 24 oz. When I sent this to G.B.S. it brought in reply the characteristic postcard ... Although Mrs Shaw's appreciation was from the culinary point of view only, it has since proved to be a worthy dessert apple. After the war I planted up to

two acres with it, and now that the trees are coming into bearing, I find that the fruit has a ready sale in competition with well-established varieties.

N. W. BARRITT, *Shaw's Pippin* in *The Countryman Gardening Book* [1973]

Behold the apples' rounded worlds:
juice-green of July rain,
the black polestar of flower, the rind
mapped with its crimson stain.

The russet, crab and cottage red
burn to the sun's hot brass,
then drop like sweat from every branch
and bubble in the grass.

They lie as wanton as they fall,
and when they fall and break,
the stallion clamps his crunching jaws,
and starling stabs his beak.

In each plump gourd the cidery bite
of boys' teeth tears the skin;
the waltzing wasp consumes his share,
the bent worm enters in.

I, with as easy hunger, take
entire my season's dole;
welcome the ripe, the sweet, the sour,
the hollow and the whole.

LAURIE LEE, 'Apples' from *My Many-coated Man* [1955]

Strawberries

Another incident from Reginald Arkell's charming tale of a gardener.

One afternoon, about the end of April, there was a pleasant little tea-party at the Manor. Nothing formal, of course, but not quite the casual affair that might happen on any day in the week. Just a gathering together of old friends to meet the estate solicitor who was down from London. Mrs Garlick had been asked to put her best foot forward and, though she was getting on a bit now, had not done so badly. Having removed their cloaks and warmed themselves before the big open fireplace, the visitors were settling down to enjoy the good things when old General Henderson, his eyes popping out of his head, gave tongue like an old hound in cover.

'My god, Charlotte!' he cried, 'where in heaven's name did you find *those*?'

Everyone turned to the General, except the hostess, who, warned by past experience, cast a furtive eye towards her tea-table. Everything seemed in order. The best tea-service, the silver kettle, Mrs Garlick's admirable buttered scones . . . What was the matter with the man?

'Strawberries!' roared the General. 'Strawberries in April! What will you be giving us next?'

Mrs Charteris thought the old warrior had gone mad – and then she saw them: a dish of such heavenly strawberries as neither Mr Fortnum nor Mr Mason had dreamed of in their most expensive moments. It was as though the year had taken a giant's stride forward, landing you suddenly in the last week of June. If the General was seeing things, so was his hostess. But she kept her head.

'Strawberries, General,' she replied coolly, 'just a few strawberries. Won't you try one?'

'But where did you get them?' asked three ladies in chorus.

Mrs Charteris was asking herself the same question. But once again she kept her head. She rang her little silver bell and the housekeeper, surprisingly on the alert, appeared in the doorway, to be asked, in tones that tried to appear casual, where the strawberries had come from.

'Pinnegar brought them in from the greenhouse five minutes ago,' said Mrs Garlick.

'Tell Pinnegar I wish to speak to him,' said Mrs Charteris; and, when Bert Pinnegar duly appeared in that holy of holies, wishing that the fine Bokhara carpet on which he was standing would waft him away to other climes, his mistress turned to the General:

'This is my gardener, General, he is in charge of the greenhouses and he knows all about such things . . . Pinnegar, General Henderson would like to know how you manage to have strawberries ready for the table so early in the season.'

So Bert Pinnegar explained, carefully and in simple terms, as you would to an intelligent child, how it had all happened. How it was no use starting the runners under glass in the autumn, because they got all dried up like, however much you watered them. What you had to do was to pot the runners in the autumn, leave them out in the open like the rest of the strawberries, and bring them into the greenhouse about February, so as to have them well under cover before they began to think about flowering. That was all there was to it.

General Henderson thanked Mr Pinnegar for his very lucid explanation and Mr Pinnegar was about to shuffle out backwards when his mistress landed her broadside before he could get out of range.

'Just a minute, Pinnegar,' she said. 'Which greenhouse did you use for this – interesting experiment?'

'The little one at the end, ma'am; next to the dump, ma'am.'

'Strange. I've never seen strawberries growing there,' said Mrs Charteris.

'I put them under the bench whenever you were about,' explained Mr Pinnegar.

'Why did you do that?' asked Mrs Charteris.

'Because,' said Mr Pinnegar, 'I wanted it to be a surprise, like.'

'Very well, Pinnegar, you may go.'

Mr Pinnegar went.
REGINALD ARKELL, *Old Herbaceous* [1950]

FLOWERING
SHRUBS

Katharine S. White remembers the flowering shrubs of her Boston childhood at the turn of the century.

. . . a garden of flowering shrubs seems wonderfully easy and peaceful. Shrubs grow slowly. They need less care, less adjudication, less ruthless cutting back than perennials. We have never grown many shrubs here, probably because a well-landscaped shrubbery does not seem to suit our rural countryside. We do have a few, but they are the common ones, seen on almost every farm – lilacs, spiraea, honeysuckle bush, and shrub roses. Yet flowering shrubs are dear to me. I grew up in a house where the beauty of the shrubbery far surpassed that of the flower beds. We actually lived on a Hawthorn Road, in a suburb of Boston, and the street was named for the three huge English hawthorn trees that grew in our own yard – a red, a pink, and a white. Towering above the lilacs in the curving bed of shrubs, they were a sight to see in May. Only the most ambitious nursery catalogues seem to list hawthorn any more, and when they do they are apt to spell it 'hawthorne,' such is the carrying power of Nathaniel. To reach our May blossoms, we children had to carry a stepladder into the empty lot next door, use it for the first boost up, and then scramble the rest of the way to a narrow ledge on top of an enormously high lattice fence that backed our shrubbery. Standing there perilously, trying to keep our balance, we had to reach *up* to break the branches. Memory makes the fence at least twenty feet high, and the hawthorn trees many feet higher, but remembered Boston snowdrifts still tower way over my head, so perhaps our hawthorns were only the average height of eighteen or twenty feet. At that, they were the tallest of the shrubs.

Most people do not pick their flowering shrubs, but we always did. I can remember the succession of flowering branches, plucked by the adults of the household and arranged by them in a tall gray Chinese jar, in our gold-and-green parlor. My sister and I and our friends had a game we played with the shrubbery. It was called Millinery. All the little girls in the neighborhood would bring to our lawn their broad-brimmed straw school hats, which, because they were Boston girls' hats, had only plain ribbon bands for decoration. Then each of us would trim her straw with blossoms from the shrubs. There was a wide choice of trimmings – forsythia, Japanese crab, Japanese quince, mock orange, flowering almond, lilac, hawthorn, bridal wreath, weigela, deutzia, with its tiny white bells, and, in June, altheas and shrub roses. We were not allowed to pick the rhododendrons or the azaleas, but nothing else was forbidden. When our flowery concoctions were completed, we put them on our heads and proudly paraded into the house to show them off to our elders; it seems to me now that we must have made quite a gay sight. By dusk the trimmings were dead, and the next day we could start all over again.

KATHARINE S. WHITE in the *New Yorker* [1960]; reprinted in *Onward and Upward in the Garden* [1979]

Lilac

We reach'd a meadow slanting to the North;
Down which a well-worn pathway courted us
To one green wicket in a privet hedge;

This, yielding, gave into a grassy walk
Thro' crowded lilac-ambush trimly pruned;
And one warm gust, full-fed with perfume, blew
Beyond us, as we enter'd in the cool.
The garden stretches southward. In the midst
A cedar spread his dark-green layers of shade.
The garden-grasses glanced, and momently
The twinkling laurel scatter'd silver lights.

ALFRED, LORD TENNYSON, [1809–
1892] *The Gardener's Daughter*

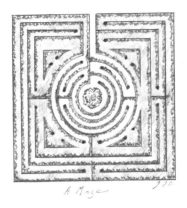

A Maze

Walt Whitman's (1819–1892) tribute to President Lincoln is linked to a poignant evocation of lilac.

When lilacs last in the dooryard bloom'd,
And the great star early droop'd in the western sky in the night,
I mourn'd, and yet shall mourn with ever-returning spring.

Ever-returning spring, trinity sure to me you bring,
Lilac blooming perennial and drooping star in the west,
And thought of him I love.

And then, surely, one of the most vivid visual pictures in poetry:

In the dooryard fronting an old farm-house near the white-wash'd
palings,
Stands the lilac-bush tall-growing with heart-shaped leaves of rich
green,
With many a pointed blossom rising delicate, with the perfume strong I
love,
With every leaf a miracle – and from this bush in the dooryard,
With delicate-color'd blossoms and heart-shaped leaves of rich green,
A sprig with its flower I break.   WALT WHITMAN's tribute to President
Lincoln, *Leaves of Grass*   [1865]

Rhododendrons

I am a sucker for rhododendrons and if I were limited to only one flower in
the garden I should unhesitatingly choose them – for their grandeur and their
delicacy; their fantastic range of colour, from almost black to glistening
white; for their exquisite variety of design, from the clustering coral bells of
Lady Chamberlain to the flamboyant trusses of Pink Pearl; for the many
months in which they delight us, from early February, when the 'Praecox'
opens its buds of palest mauve, to the dusty days of August when the
branches of the Polar Bear are laden with scented snow. Even for their
fragrance. One of my annual pilgrimages is to the cool house at Kew, to
stand alone by the *Rhododendron 'Fragrantissimum'*, which fills the whole
house with the perfume of frozen incense.
   I am aware that some people do not 'get' them. Even as sensitive a spirit as

John Betjeman once described them to me as a 'stockbrokers' flower'. If this is indeed the case, the stockbrokers are to be felicitated.

BEVERLEY NICHOLS, *Garden Open Today* [1963]

TREES Trees are the best monuments that a man can erect to his own memory. They speak his praises without flattery, and they are blessings to children yet unborn. Every gentleman in Ireland is become a Planter. I doubt the spirit is not so universal in England.

LORD ORRERY to THOMAS CAREW, 15 May 1749

The planters of trees, with few very notable exceptions, have been men whose age might seem a sound reason for refraining from so doing; but the appeal of trees would seem to bear some subtle relationship to that of Chinese art, and to share with Fame the claim of being 'that last infirmity of noble mind': this being so, young men may rightly deem it sound to being where the old and wise leave off.

Experience will prove that there is something personal and insistent in the claims of trees and shrubs (as opposed to herbaceous plants) on those who love them. A tree, young or old, if admired, remains a definite vision, and when after long absence it is visited again, the meeting place is approached with feelings of pleasure and of curiosity as to how one's friend has fared, even with thoughts as to what changes may have come to tree or visitor since first they met; this may seem like foolish sentiment – perhaps it is. But, after all, sentiment is mingled with most that's best in life.

CHARLES ELEY, *Gardening for the Twentieth Century* [1923]

The Cedar

There is none like her, none.
Nor will be when our summers have deceased.
O, art thou sighing for Lebanon
In the long breeze that streams to thy delicious East,
Sighing for Lebanon,
Dark cedar, though thy limbs have here increased,
Upon a pastoral slope as fair,
And looking to the South, and fed
With honeyed rain and delicate air,
And haunted by the starry head
Of her whose gentle will has changed my fate,
And made my life a perfumed altar flame;
And over whom thy darkness must have spread
With such delight as theirs of old, thy great
Forefathers of the thornless garden, there
Shadowing the snow-limbed Eve from whom she came.

ALFRED, LORD TENNYSON [1809–1892]

The Holly

> O reader! hast thou ever stood to see
>   The Holly tree?
> The eye that contemplates it well perceives
>   Its glossy leaves,
> Ordered by an Intelligence so wise
> As might confound the atheist's sophistries.
>
> Below a circling fence its leaves are seen,
>   Wrinkled and keen;
> No grazing cattle through their prickly round
>   Can reach to wound;
> But as they grow where nothing is to fear,
> Smooth and unarmed the pointless leaves appear.
>   ROBERT SOUTHEY [1774–1843]

The Judas Tree

*In one of Denton Welch's unnerving stories a middle-aged man opens up
a conversation with an art student which leads on to this.*

'Do you know what a Judas tree is?' He stared straight into my eyes, then
added, very surprisingly, 'I've been a schoolmaster for thirty years, and I can
always tell when a boy is lying.'

'I was going to say that I didn't know.' I felt repulsed at once by this
flashing glimpse of another side of his character. I recognized the schoolmaster's unnecessary parade, the over-emphasis.

'Well,' he said sweetly, returning to his earlier manner, 'it is a wonderful
tree that bears great rose-coloured flowers; and the amazing thing is that the
flowers appear before the leaves! Judas, you know, after he had betrayed our
Lord, repented and took back the thirty pieces of silver to the chief priests.
But when he had told them that he had betrayed innocent blood, they gave a
terrible answer; they said, "What is that to us? See thou to that." So he threw
down the silver in the temple and went to hang himself. He found a bare tree,
climbed up into the branches, tied a rope; then jumped. The next morning
the whole tree was lighted and hung with marvellous Judas-coloured
flowers. And the Judas tree, from that day to this, always bears its flowers
before its leaves.'
                     DENTON WELCH, 'The Judas Tree' in
                     Brave and Cruel [1948]

The Magnolia

> Woman has no seductions for the man who cannot
> take his eyes from his magnolias.
>   Old Saying

The Maple

The maple with its tassel flowers of green,
That turns to red a staghorn-shaped seed,
Just spreading out its scolloped leaves is seen,
Of yellowish hue, yet beautifully green;
Bark ribbed like corduroy in seamy screed,
That farther up the stem is smoother seen,
Where the white hemlock with white umbel flowers
Up each spread stoven to the branches towers;
And moss around the stoven spreads, dark green,
And blotched-leaved orchis, and the bluebell flowers;
Thickly they grow and 'neath the leaves are seen;
I love to see them gemmed with morning hours,
I love the lone green places where they be,
And the sweet clothing of the maple-tree.

JOHN CLARE [1793–1864]

The Monkey Puzzle

Mention has already been made of the well-known monkey puzzle (*Araucaria imbricata*), a native of Chile that withstands wind splendidly, is impatient of shade, and thrives best in districts with a heavy rainfall.

This tree may be compared to the Bolshevists, insomuch that at the commencement of its career, when quite a young plant, it has appeared attractive and well-favoured to the thoughtless; thus encouraged in unsuitable places, it takes the form of an ungainly monster, impossible to control and destined sooner or later to be destroyed. But though araucarias and Bolshevists may both be puzzles to species of the mammalia, it does not necessarily follow that either of them would really be much worse than (or very different from) those whom they puzzle, if only they were both kept in their proper places and compelled to exercise their great energy in a right sphere. The right sphere of both araucarias and Bolshevists is surely to live by themselves either singly or in the mass, and thus to work out their own salvation, unhindered by interference or by encroachment upon the liberty of others. Under such circumstances, at any rate the much-abused araucaria may be trusted to fulfil a worthy destiny, for no grander embodiment of sombre dignity can greet the eye than that of an ancient monkey puzzle, clothed to the ground, standing in solitary splendour at the bottom of a sheltered valley or in some mountain glen.

CHARLES ELEY, *Gardening for the Twentieth Century* [1923]

The Oak

All trees have a character analogous to that of men: Oaks are in all respects the perfect image of the manly character: In former times I should have said, and in present times I think I am authorized to say, the British one. As a brave man is not suddenly either elated by prosperity, or depressed by adversity, so the oak displays not its verdure on the sun's first approach; nor drops it, on

his first departure. Add to this its majestic appearance, the rough grandeur of
its bark and the wide protection of its branches.

WILLIAM SHENSTONE, *Unconnected*
Thoughts on Gardening [1764]

Winter-flowering prunus

Not a bee left on the wing,
Not even a fly
Blown by,
Not a bird yet come to sing,
Nor other glint of Spring.

This dauntless blossoming
Flings out its rose-cheeked snow
Its gauntlet resolute
Defying *Time*
For all who Him refute:
Usurper *Time*
Old Canceller, cancelled so.

This tree of trees,
Twirling and tossing in the breeze
(Sheer emblem of His vagaries),
Here bequeaths
With these wild wreaths
To those whose hearts are now
Set on what *Time* denies,
Their Everything.

Frail *Time*;
As *was*, with *is* and *shall be*, dies
Poor *Time*;
Outwitted by a bough
Or rime . . .   I. A. RICHARDS [1975]

Artichoke   VEGETABLES

The very basic virtues of which are here celebrated by an Elizabethan.

Artochoke reformeth the savour of the mouth.
Artochoke causeth urine and veneriall act.
Artochoke amendeth the hardness of making water and the
rank savour of the armpits.
Artochoke strengtheneth the stomacke, & helpeth the privie
places that men children may be conceived.

DIDYMUS MOUNTAIN, *The*
Gardener's Labyrinth [1586]

And a contemporary tribute.

NOTES ON THE GLOBE ARTICHOKE

You look as though you'd been invented by
Da Vinci: a detail maybe
Of some engine of assault.

Squamous: scaly.
You are green brother to
Fish, lily-bulb and armadillo.

Venus is your planet.

Pliny, that informed Roman,
Scorned thistle-eaters and deplored
Six thousand sesterces a year
Spent on you, but left
Rules for your cultivation.

The Maltese carved your head
In stone on palaces and places where
We'd have an acorn or a pineapple.

Left to your own devices,
Like N. Bonaparte you crown yourself:
No purple more imperial than yours.

With what inheritance of fervour we devour
Your delicate pale heart,
Your noble armour.

SUSANNE KNOWLES [1972]

Asparagus

They say that doggs drincking ye decoction of them will dye. And some have
related that if one hauing beaten rammes hornes in pieces do bury them,
Asparagus commes vp, which yet is incredible to mee. Now this Asparagus is
a plant of many branches, hauing many leaues long, like vnto Fennill; with a
round roote, great, hauing a knob, of which the stalke being beaten small
with white wine, doth assuage the griefs of the kidnies.

The Greek Herbal of Dioscorides,
translated by John Goodyer [1655]

Lettuce

Lettuce procureth sleepe, causeth good bloude, helpeth digestion, looseth
the belly, causeth plentifulness of milk in the breastes, sharpneth the sight,
cooleth impostumes, helpeth the dropsy, cureth the shedding of sperm,
procureth sleep being laid under the coverlet, and profiteth Cholericke
persons.

Lettuce is noisome unto married men: it dulleth the sight of the eies. It
abateth the venerealle acte, it harmeth the fleumaticke; the overmuch eating
of Lettuce is as perilous as Hemlocke.

DIDYMUS MOUNTAIN,
The Gardener's Labyrinth [1586]

There are not many references in English literature to lettuces. Apart from their soporific effect on the Flopsy Bunnies, readers would be hard put to it to find mention of their qualities. Certainly few would ascribe a satanic nature to them. Yet one of our earliest books describes the devil as dwelling in a lettuce.

In her biography of Alfred the Great, Eleanor Duckett tells how the king, in order to fortify the faith of his sorely-tired subjects, caused Bishop Werferth to translate the dialogues of St Gregory into the native Anglo-Saxon tongue. First among the stories which the saint relates to his doubting deacon Peter is that of a nun who ate a lettuce without first blessing it. She was seized with a violent stomach-ache which was diagnosed as a case of demonic possession. The other sisters straightway sent for a certain Holy Equitus, who came at great speed. No sooner had he arrived than the devil called out from the poor nun's mouth: 'What have I done? I was merely sitting in the lettuce and she came and ate me.' The Holy Equitus thereupon bade the devil in the name of God to depart and he did so, never to return.

On reading this simple tale my thoughts went back to the time during the war when I lay in a military hospital next to a captain. He held a commission in the Iraq levies, who were of mixed races and religions. 'Our Christians, mostly Assyrians, give little trouble and will eat anything,' he said. 'The Moslems will not touch pork, of course. Then there are the Yezidis; they will not eat lettuce.' They are devil worshippers dwelling near Mosul. The founders of their religion decided that it was better to come to terms with the powers of evil than actively to seek the power of good; and for this faith they are prepared to face persecution and martyrdom at the hands of true believers.

'But why eschew lettuce?' I asked.

'It is like this,' my friend replied. 'They believe that Satan was originally one of the angels, but that he fell from grace. He was chased from Heaven by the Archangel Gabriel with a sharp spear and, on reaching Earth, took refuge in the heart of a lettuce. Gabriel's spear easily pierced the frail leaves, and the wounded devil had to flee. He then found safety in a large onion whose slippery scales were proof against the darts of the Archangel.' Thus the father of lies survived to carry on his mischief, and his worshippers came to despise the lettuce and hold the onion in the highest regard.

'Those Yezidis are a strange lot,' went on the captain. 'Although they worship the devil they are most trustworthy and honest. They think it best never to mention the name of the evil one; and instead of representing him in a grotesque form they humour him by depicting him as a peacock.'

MICHAEL BIRD, *The Devil Among the Lettuces* in *The Countryman Gardening Book* [1973]

Radishes

Garden Raddishes are in wantonness by the gentry eaten as a sallad, but they breed but scurvy humours in the stomach, and corrupt the blood, and then send for a physician as fast as you can.

NICHOLAS CULPEPER, *The Compleat Herbal* [1653]

PART
VI

DELIGHTS

Everyone knows the incalculable debt a garden owes to the random hand of time and nature.

ACCIDENTAL EFFECTS

All and every part is untrimmed, antique, weather-stained and homely as can be imagined – gratifying the eye by its exceeding picturesqueness, and the mind by the certainty that no pictorial effect was intended – that it owes all its charms to 'rare accident'. My father laughs at my passionate love of my garden – and perhaps you will laugh too; but I assure you it's a 'bonny bit' of earth as was ever crammed full of lilies and roses . . .

MARY RUSSELL MITFORD to
BENJAMIN ROBERT HAYDON [1824]

Both physical and intellectual are described here by John Evelyn.

BENEFITS

We will endeavour to shew how the aire and genious of Gardens operat upon humane spirits towards virtue and sancitie, I meane in a remote, preparatory and instrumentall working. How Caves, Grotts, Mounts, and irregular ornaments of Gardens do contribute to contemplative and philosophicall Enthusiasms; how *Elysium, Antrum, Nemus, Paradysus, Hortus, Lucus,* &c., signifie all of them *rem sacram et divinam*; for these expedients do influence the soule and spirits of man, and prepare them for converse with good Angells; besides which, they contribute to the lesse abstracted pleasures, phylosophy naturall and longevitie.

JOHN EVELYN to SIR THOMAS
BROWNE [1657]

The appreciation of birdsong in the garden is a long one. Chaucer had it at the close of the fourteenth century.

BIRDS AND BIRDSONG

> In many places were nightingales,
> Alpes, finches, and wodewales,
> That in her swete song delyten
> In thilke place as they habyten.
>
> Ther mighte men see many flokkes
> Of turtles and of laverokkes.
> Chalaudres fele saw I there,
> That wery, nigh forsongen were.
> And thrustles, terins, and mavys,
> That songen for to winne hem prys,

And eek to sormounte in hir song
These other briddes hem among.
By note made fair servyse
These briddes, that I you devyse;
They songe hir song as faire and well
As angels doon espirituel.
Swich swete song was hem among,
That me thoughte it no briddes song,
But it was wonder lyk to be
Song of mermaydens of the see;
That, for her singing is so clere,
Though we mermaydens clepe hem
  here
In English, as in our usaunce,
Men clepen hem sereyns in France . . .

GUILLAUME DE LORIS, *Romaunt de
la Rose* (c. 1240), translated by
Geoffrey Chaucer

So did the Jacobeans . . .

One chiefe grace that adornes an Orchard I cannot let slippe. A broode of
Nightingales, who with their several notes and tunes, with a strong delightsome voyce, out of a weake body, will beare you company night and day. She
loves (and lives in) hots of wood in her heart. She will help you to cleanse
your trees of Caterpillars, and all noysome wormes and flyes. The gentle
Robbin-redbrest will helpe her, and in Winter in the coldest stormes will
keepe a part.

Neither will the Silly Wren be behind in Summer, with her distinct whistle
(like a sweet Recorder) to cheere your spirits.

The Black-bird and Threstle (for I take it the Thrush sings not, but
devoures) sing loudly in a May morning, and delight the Eare much (and you
neede not want their company, if you have ripe Cherryes or Berries, and
would as gladly as the rest doe you pleasure:) But I had rather want their
company than my fruit. WILLIAM LAWSON, *A New Orchard
and Garden* [1618]

Addison had exactly the same view a century on.

There is another circumstance in which I am very particular, or, as my
Neighbours call me, very whimsical: As my Garden invites into it all the
Birds of the Country, by offering them the Conveniency of Springs and
Shades, Solitude and Shelter, I do not suffer any one to destroy their Nests in
the Spring, or drive them from their usual Haunts in Fruit-time. I value my
Garden more for them being full of Blackbirds than Cherries, and very
frankly give them Fruit for their Songs. By this Means I have always the
Musick of the Season in its Perfection, and am highly delighted to see the Jay
or the Thrush hopping about my Walks, and shooting before my Eye across
the several little Glades and Alleys that I pass through.

JOSEPH ADDISON, *The Spectator*,
No. 477, 6 September 1712

Only in this century is there a shift from the constant euphoria.

Feeding birds induces 'good' feelings, like sending CARE packages to poor countries. It may or may not be helpful to the birds themselves, whose life-cycles aren't an analog of our own. Wildlife can't be allowed to become wholly dependent on man – if it does, it ceases to be wildlife and other arrangements have to be made. I can't even be certain that feeding has helped the immediately endangered species.

Certainly it isn't they who come to the feeders but an idle race of lazy gastronomes who increasingly pick and choose. No thistle seed? The goldfinches, who don't care that it costs about $1 a pound, pass me by. The cardinals on the other hand, want sun-flower. Standard mixtures no longer attract this fastidious clientele, which is far from doing its job of clearing the garden of insects. Soon they will have lost the habit of foraging for themselves. In short, and as far as I can make out, I am either in the business of feeding a barbarian horde of cowbirds, starlings, etc., or I am spoiling a number of pets; and in either case I am doing more harm than good.

Just how serious the situation was I hadn't realized until the recent death of a beloved cat. He had never hunted – like all my creatures he was too well-fed to bother. But his presence had obviously inhibited the birds to some extent because the news of his death all but brought them into the house. Cardinals built a nest within a few feet of the porch where we constantly sit. Purple finches actually built another inside a Tunisian birdcage that hangs on the porch itself. The weeks that followed were nerve-wracking. We couldn't cut the hedge or mow the lawn; a long standing arrangement to paint the house had to be put off. Nobody dared sit on the porch – it made the parent finches nervous. The launching of the baby cardinals was agony enough, but they finally made it. Not the finches, who liked their wire mosque so well they refused to leave it. They even learned to use the swings and retreated piteously into the dome when their parents tried to coax them out. Naturally I fed them seeing that the parents sensibly wouldn't. And it was then I saw where the St Francis-of-Assisi complex was leading. I stopped putting worms on their threshold, and one afternoon the cage was empty. Just in time. Another week, and the little finches would have tamed themselves, knocked at the door every morning, become my pets and dependants forever.

ELEANOR PERÉNYI, Green Thoughts
[1981]

It is easy to forget how much pleasure we get from being able to see 'over the garden wall'.

BYPASSING

In crossing the country to Strathfieldsaye, we observed a remarkably large yew tree in the churchyard at Sulhampstead. At Mortimer Street, the vicarage house has a very beautiful flower-garden and shrubbery, with a piece of water, the beauty of which may be fully enjoyed by passengers on the road. The grounds consist of two banks of turf which slope down to the pond, and the whole is considerably below the eye of a person walking along the road. It would be easy to shut it out by a hedge of ordinary height, but we recommend the taste and good feeling of the proprietor, in wishing his neighbours and the public to participate in his enjoyments. We know nothing of this vicar, not even his name; but we have little doubt that he is a good man. It seems to us that every man, in ornamenting his house, his garden, or his estate, however small it may be, ought to consider not only his own gratification, but the ornament and benefit of his country. He ought always to ask himself, what the passers by will think of what he is doing.

JOHN CLAUDIUS LOUDON, *Calls in Hertfordshire, Bedfordshire, Berkshire, Surrey, Sussex and Middlesex* [1833]

CATS   *The gardening world is inevitably divided between those who would or would not categorize a cat in the garden as a delight. I belong to the former category as indeed do two famous gardeners, William Cowper . . .*

Puss grew presently familiar, would leap into my lap, raise himself upon his hinder feet, and bite the hair from my temples. He would suffer me to take him up, and to carry him about in my arms, and has more than once fallen fast asleep upon my knee. He was ill three days, during which time I nursed him, kept him apart from his fellows, that they might not molest him (for, like many other wild animals, they persecute one of their own species that is sick), and by constant care, and trying him with a variety of herbs, restored him to perfect health. No creature could be more grateful than my patient after his recovery; a sentiment which he most significantly expressed by licking my hand, first the back of it, then the palm, then every finger separately, then between all the fingers, as if anxious to leave no part of it unsaluted: a ceremony which he never performed but once again upon a similar occasion. Finding him extremely tractable, I made it my custom to carry him always after breakfast into the garden, where he hid himself generally under the leaves of a cucumber vine, sleeping or chewing the cud till evening; in the leaves also of that vine he found a favourite repast. I had not long habituated him to this taste of liberty, before he began to be impatient for the return of the time when he might enjoy it. He would invite me to the garden by drumming upon my knee, and by a look of such expression as it was not possible to misinterpret. If this rhetoric did not immediately succeed, he would take the skirt of my coat between his teeth, and pull it with all his force. Thus Puss might be said to be perfectly tamed; the shyness of his nature was done away, and on the whole it was visible by many symptoms, which I have not room to enumerate, that he was happier in human society than when shut up with his natural companions.

WILLIAM COWPER, *The Gentleman's Magazine* [June 1784]

. . . and Gertrude Jekyll, who devotes a whole chapter to the creatures in one of her books.

My garden would not be half the pleasure it is to me without the pussies . . . They are perfect garden companions. When I am out at work there is sure to be one or other of them close by, lying on my jacket or on a bench if there is one near. When it is Tabby, if there is an empty basket anywhere handy he is certain to get into it . . . Like most cats he is devoted to the pretty catmint. It is in several places in the garden. He knows where every plant is and never passes one when we are walking together without stopping to nuzzle and nibble it . . . when he has had his first taste he will push himself right down into the middle of the plant and sometimes lie down and roll in it to get all he can of the sweet smell.

GERTRUDE JEKYLL, *Children and Gardens* [1908]

JEREMIAH, THE TABBY CAT, STALKS IN THE SUNLIT GARDEN

While you clamber over the blue gate in the garden,
In the sunlit garden I
Already arrived am before you: while
In a flash of the eye,
You are suspended in your leap
Against the blue ground of the gate. And then,
Unconscious cinema-actor, you cross your stage,
The plot where light cuts the shade like a jewel
On what intent?
Your eyes are amber in the sun, flashing
From the cushioned tuft of harebells
And calceolarias.
Now you thread the intricate pattern
Of garden stems and stems of shadow,
And cross the lawn:
Your supple flanks serpentine, your tread
Stealthy and secret, of who knows
What generations of jungle cats?
And so you reach the undergrowth of the sycamore;
Nor pause to hear me calling from my window
Whence sight of you I lose,
Your dappled side lost in the camouflage of shadow;
And you have left the sunlit garden
For who knows what memories of lost generations of great cats?

A. L. ROWSE [1903–   ]

COLOUR

Those who believe that the symphony of gradient colour began with Miss Jekyll and the herbaceous border should read this.

But though other *Countreys* have more benefit of Sun than we, and thereby more properly tyed to contemplate this delight; yet have I seen in our *own*, a delicate and diligent *curiosity*, surely without *parallel* among foreign *Nations*: Namely, in the Garden of Sir *Henry Fanshaw*, at his Seat in *Ware-Park*; where I well remember, he did so precisely examine the *tinctures* and *seasons* of his *flowers*, that in their *settings*, the *inwardest* of which that were to come up at the same time, should be always a little *darker* than the *outmost*, and so serve them for a kind of gentle *shadow*, like a piece not of *Nature*, but of *Art*: which mention (incident to this place) I have willingly made of his *Name*, for the dear *friendship*, that was long between us: though I must confess, with much wrong to his other *vertues*; which deserve a more solid *Memorial*, then among these vacant Observations. So much of *Gardens*.

SIR HENRY WOOTTON, *The Elements of Architecture* [1624]

William Morris, that great exponent of the Arts and Crafts Movement, gives voice to the ideas on colour that Miss Jekyll was to achieve in her work and spread through her writings.

As to colour in gardens. Flowers in masses are mighty strong colour, and if not used with a great deal of caution are very destructive to pleasure in gardening. On the whole, I think the best and safest plan is to mix up your flowers, and rather eschew great masses of colour – in combination, I mean. But there are some flowers – inventions of men, *i.e.*, florists – which are bad colour altogether, and not to be used at all. Scarlet geraniums, for instance, or the yellow calceolaria, which, indeed, are not uncommonly grown together profusely, in order, I suppose, to show that even flowers can be thoroughly ugly.

WILLIAM MORRIS, *Hopes and Fears for Art: 'Making the Best of it', Oxford and Cambridge Magazine* [c. 1860]

Here Miss Jekyll, the high priestess of colour control, enunciates her guiding principles.

To plant and maintain a flower-border, *with a good scheme for colour*, is by no means the easy thing that is commonly supposed.

I am strongly of the opinion that the possession of a quantity of plants, however good the plants may be themselves and however ample their number, does not make a garden; it only makes a *collection*. Having got the plants, the great thing is to use them with careful selection and definite intention. Merely having them, or having them planted unassorted in garden spaces, is only like having a box of paints from the best colourman, or, to go one step further, it is like having portions of these paints set out upon a palette.

GERTRUDE JEKYLL, *Colour Schemes for the Flower Garden* [1908]

But even Miss Jekyll was flexible.

It is a curious thing that people will sometimes spoil some garden project for the sake of a word. For instance, a blue garden, for beauty's sake, may be hungering for a group of white Lilies, or for something of palest lemon-yellow, but it is not allowed to have it because it is called the blue garden, and there must be no flowers in it but blue flowers. I can see no sense in this; it seems to me like fetters foolishly self-imposed. Surely the business of the blue garden is to be beautiful as well as to be blue. My own idea is that it should be beautiful first, and then just as blue as may be consistent with its best possible beauty. Moreover, any experienced colourist knows that the blues will be more telling – more purely blue – by the juxtaposition of rightly placed complementary colour.

GERTRUDE JEKYLL, *Colour Schemes for the Flower Garden* [1908]

Advocates of good taste gardening and the use of soft orchestrated colour compositions will sympathize with this encounter.

During May I was particularly pleased with one part of the garden because the graded lilacs and purples of the spring perennials – *Lunaria rediviva* and *Latbyrus vernus* among others – were looking especially harmonious. We

had planted the marvellous mauve, lily-flowered tulip 'Maytime' spor-
adically among them and the results were, I felt, good enough for a *Homes
and Gardens* photograph. But while I was admiring the show, one Sunday
afternoon, a chap in a cloth cap sidled up and said: 'Not much colour, is
there, mate? Yorta plant more toolips. All different colours. That'd liven it
up a bit.'

NIGEL COLBORN, Take Me to Your
Hostas [1989]

FRIENDSHIP

*The exchange of plants between gardeners is an expression of binding
friendship, that plant becoming also the person in the garden. Here is an
exchange between two famous seventeenth-century gardeners.*

SIR,

I send you herewith some rootes of severall sorts: the bears ears and some
of the anemones and ranunculus are very good but the tulips (except *Agat
Hanmer* and the *Ariana* and some others) are not extraordinary; indeed my
garden affords not now such varieties of rare tulips as I had formerly; most
of my best died the first yeare I came to live at this place, and I have not
furnisht my selfe anew, because I thinke neither this ayer nor earth agrees
with them.

I suppose your flower garden, being new, is not very large, and therefore I
send you not many things at this tyme, and I wish the beares eares doe not
dry too much before you receave them; they will be a fortnight at least before
they come to Deptford, and therefore sett them as soone as may be, and
water them well (if it raine not) for three or fower days, and plant them not in
too hott a sun. I thought once to have ventur'd some gilliflowers, having two
years since raised some very good ones from seed (w.h I never did before, nor
I thinke never shall againe, because the wett in England hinders the ripening
of the seed more than in Holland and Flanders) but there is such store of
excellent ones all about London that I had not the confidence to adventure
any to your view; – and I doubted whether being soe long on the way would
not kill them.

Sir, I wish I were better able to serve you either in these bagatelles or more
weighty occasions: I should with great alacrity and satisfaction, I assure you,
lay hold on all opportunityes to express myselfe how really I am.

S.r
Your affectionate servant
THO. HANMER
SIR THOMAS HANMER to JOHN
EVELYN, 21 August 1671

*A century and a half later the novelist Mary Russell Mitford catches
exactly the mood of happy recognition that envelops any plant in the
garden from a friend.*

. . . I like geraniums better than anything; and it is lucky that I do, since they
are comparatively easy to rear and manage, and do not lay one under any
tremendous obligation to receive, for I never buy any. All my varieties
(amounting to at least three hundred different sorts) have been either
presents, or exchanges, or my own seedlings – chiefly exchanges; for when

once one has a good collection, that becomes an easy mode of enlarging it; and it is one pleasant to all parties, for it is a very great pleasure to have a flower in a friend's garden. You, my own Emily, gave me my first plants of the potentilla, and very often as I look at them I think of you. You must send me some little seed in a letter, as a return for these plants, seeds of your own gathering and from your own garden; and it shall go hard but I will make them grow: any seed that you think pretty.

MARY RUSSELL MITFORD to EMILY
JEPHSON, 18 May 1835

. . . I send you, my dearest Emily, the four white oenotheras, the blue pea, the *Salpiglossis picta*, the white Clarkia, a new lupine, the most beautiful that I have ever seen, similar to the *Lupinus mutabilis*, in kind and fragrance, but a clear lilac and clear white, and of far larger spikes of flowers (I enclose a flower), a new annual chrysanthemum (Cape marigold) with yellow outer leaves, and two little packets of seeds from Madeira, sent me by a gentleman whom I have never either seen or even heard of till now, but who, having been ordered there for his health, took my books with him, and found them of so much amusement to him that he sent me some seeds on his arrival by way of return, and we are likely to become great friends.

MARY RUSSELL MITFORD to EMILY
JEPHSON, 3 September 1835

Here the tradition is cheerfully caught in a Victorian parsonage garden by the Reverend Farrer.

. . . what pleasure is there greater than to go round one's garden on a sunny day with a fellow-enthusiast, and to sing that cheering Litany which runs, in strophe and antistrophe, 'Oh, wouldn't you like a bit of this?' – 'And I could send you a bulb of that'. Down delves the glad trowel into a clump, and it is halved – like mercy, blessing him that gives and him that takes . . . There are few greater pleasures in life than giving pleasure with a plant; or getting pleasure again with a plant. And certainly there is none more bland and blameless.

THE REVEREND R. J. FARRER,
In a Yorkshire Garden [1909]

Some givers are more generous than others. The famous Miss Ellen Willmott's friendship left something to be desired.

As gardeners go she was not considered generous, and one looked carefully at gift plants for fear they might be fearful spreaders.

A reminiscence in AUDREY LE LIÈVRE,
Miss Willmott of Warley Place [1981]

HAPPINESS   *One of the founder members of the Garden Club of America catches a precious moment all gardeners have known.*

This very evening, in the dusk, I was walking in my garden alone. The air was full of sweetness from great walls or cascades of the mock orange, from heavy peonies in full bloom, whose white or rose-colored petals weighed the plants almost to the ground, from valerian or garden heliotrope, white with flowers. Outside the wall of green made by tall spruces, I heard voices. One said: 'Do look at those peonies – aren't they wonderful!' I called to the strangers, asking them to enter, to wander where they would. In they came, and we spent a few moments together enjoying the soft sight of many blooming flowers, the sweet scents in the dew, the rich greens of foliage and turf in the fading light; then I left them still exclaiming over the beauty of what they saw. But we had had together, these three unknown women and I, that satisfaction of the common beauty of the common things of the common life; and such moments leave one happier. They make for friendships through a common and rarely fine interest, an interest in the things that grow, an interest than which there is no better for body, mind, or spirit. Each one has his own most real thing. Mine is the garden. And the best I can wish for any one is that he may have a garden of his own, a little garden in which, through work and sweet imaginings he may find a creative happiness unknown to those without this dear possession.

LOUISA YEOMANS KINGS, *Chronicles of the Garden* [1925]

LONGEVITY

No doubt a similar collection could be made of short-lived gardeners but Eleanor Perényi's long-lived list is not only impressive but persuasive.

. . . Before the era of pesticides and atomic fallout a garden was about the healthiest place on earth and gardeners' longevity in impressive defiance of the actuarial tables. Theophrastus, Aristotle's heir at the Athens Lyceum, teacher, botanist and gardener, lived to be eighty-five – something of a feat in the second century B.C. But then so did Cato the Censor, the harsh old Sabine farmer who was devoted to cabbages and wrote excellent directions for growing them in his *De re rustica*. Marcus Terentius Varro, who produced *his* book on horticulture when he was over eighty, lived another nine years after that but didn't set a record. Pliny describes for us the Roman botanist Antonius Castor, spry as a cricket among his specimens and sound in mind and body: He was over one hundred when Pliny visited him.

Lives in the Middle Ages were briefer than those of the sturdy Romans and those of saints apt to be briefer still. Yet Albertus Magnus, theologian and horticulturist whose success at forcing plants under glass attracted charges of witchcraft, went to his reward at eighty-seven. Petrarch, who among other things was the first gardener to have what we would call a modern sensibility, died at the relatively youthful age of seventy – youthful, that is, for a gardener; he still outlived most of his contemporaries, and that continued to be the rule rather than the exception. Pirro Ligorio, creator of the Villa d'Este, survived all his noble patrons and lived to be eighty-seven. All the Mollets, gardeners to two generations of French kings (Claude, who worked for Henri IV, introduced box edging), lived longer than their masters. Le Nôtre did not, but he had a longer life than Louis XIV did, expiring after eighty-seven years of perfect health.

. . . Henry Wise, gardener to Queen Anne, and one of the founders of the first commercial nursery in England, died at eighty-three. George Russell, who gave us the finest of the lupin race, was hard at work at his hybridizing at the age of ninety-four. Gertrude Jekyll and William Robinson survived to eighty-nine and ninety-six respectively.

The record in this country is less salubrious – perhaps because the climate

is; perhaps because, for all our tremendous contribution to botany and hybridizing science, we have been rather notably short on great gardeners as such. Only two American presidents have taken a serious interest in gardens (as opposed to innumerable kings and statesmen in other countries, not forgetting Winston Churchill), and Jefferson (Washington was the other) lived to be eighty-three. Our designers of note haven't been many, but let Frederick Olmsted, designer of Central Park and some forty others, go into the longevity book. He lived from 1822 to 1903. Among plantsmen, include Charles S. Sargent (1841–1927), whose leadership made the Arnold Arboretum near Boston the best of its kind in America. But famous amateurs among us have been few, so it is a pleasure to report that Ruth Stout, the doyenne of organic gardening in America, inventor of the permanent hay mulch and contributor to *Organic Gardening*, died only recently at age ninety-six.

ELEANOUR PERÉNYI, *Green Thoughts*
[1981]

NIGHT   *There seems to be very little written about gardens at night which become places of shrouded mystery. Marvell's hymn to the glow worms is a rare exception.*

THE MOWER TO THE GLOW-WORMS

Ye living Lamps, by whose dear light
The Nightingale does sit so late,
And studying all the summer-night,
Her matchless Songs does meditate;

Ye Country Comets, that portend
Nor War, nor Princes funeral,
Shining unto no higher end
Than to presage the grasses fall;

Ye Glo-Worms, whose officious Flame
To wandring Mowers shows the way,
That in the Night have lost their aim,
And after foolish Fires do stray;

Your courteous Lights in vain you wast,
Since *Juliana* here is come,
For She my mind hath so displac'd
That I shall never find my home.

ANDREW MARVELL [1621–1678]

SEASONS   *For a true gardener every season brings its delights from the first flowers of spring to the tracery of twigs in winter sunlight. Francis Bacon's approach is to attempt a* ver perpetuum *rather than to revel in the special qualities which each season brings.*

God Almighty first planted a Garden; and indeed it is the purest of humane pleasures. It is the greatest refreshment to the Spirits of Man, without which Buildings and Palaces are but gross Handy-works. And a Man shall ever see, that when Ages grow to Civility and Elegancy, Men come to build stately, sooner than to garden finely: as if Gardening were the Greater Perfection. I do hold it in the Royal Ordering of Gardens, there ought to be Gardens for all the Months in the year, in which, severally, things of Beauty may be then in season.

For December and January, and the latter part of November, you must take such things as are green all Winter: Holly, Ivy, Bays, Juniper, Cypress-Trees, Yews, Pine-Apple Trees, Fir-Trees, Rosemary, Lavender, Periwincle, the White, the Purple, and the Blue, Germander, Flags, Orange-Trees, Limon-Trees, and Myrtles, if they be striped, and Sweet Marjoram warm set.

There followeth, for the latter part of January and February, the Mezerion Tree, which then blossoms, Crocus Vernus, both the Yellow and the Grey, Prim-Roses, Anemones, the Early Tulippa, Hiacynthus Orientalis, Chamarïris, Fretttellaria.

For March, there come Violets, specially the Single Blue, which are the Earliest, the yellow Daffadil, the Daisy, the Almond-Tree in blossom, the Peach-Tree in blossom, the Cornelian-Tree in blossom, Sweet Briar.

In April follow the double White Violet, the Wall-Flower, the Stock-Gilly-Flower, the Cowslip, Flower-de-Lices, and Lilies of all natures. Rosemary-Flowers, the Tulippa, the Double Piony, the pale Daffadill, the French Honey-Suckle, the Cherry-Tree in blossom, the Dammasin and Plum-Trees in blossom, the White Thorn in leaf, the Lelack Tree.

In May and June, come Pinks of all Sorts, specially the Blush-Pink Roses of all kinds (except the Musk, which comes later), Honey-Suckles, Straw-berries, Bugloss, Columbine, the French Marygold, Flos Africanus, Cherry-Tree in fruit, Ribes, Figs in fruit, Rasps, Vine-Flowers, Lavender in Flowers, the Sweet Satyrion with the White Flower, Herba Muscaria, Lillium Convallium, the Apple-Tree in blossom.

In July come Gilly-Flowers of all Varieties, Musk-Roses, and the Lime-Tree in blossom, Early Pears and Plumbs in Fruit, Ginnitings, Quodlings.

In August, come Plumbs of all sorts in Fruit, Pears, Apricocks, Barberries, Filberds, Musk-Melons, Monkshoods of all Colours.

In September come Grapes, Apples, Poppies of all Colours, Peaches, Melo-Cotones, Nectarines, Cornellians, Wardens, Quinces.

In October and the beginning of November come Servises, Medlars, Bullaces; Roses Cut or Removed to come late, Hollyoaks, and such like.

These particulars are for the climate of London: But my meaning is perceived, that you may have *Ver Perpetuum*, as the place affords.

SIR FRANCIS BACON, *Of Gardens*
[1625]

Ji Cheng (see above p. 48), writing in the fourth decade of the seventeenth century, gives a Chinese perspective on the delights of the seasons.

There are no fixed rules for designing gardens but there are certain principles in making use of the natural scenery. The essential thing is to keep in mind all the four seasons; at which point of the compass any feature is placed is of little importance. Woods and marshes are suitable for lingering in, since in them are bamboo groves and whispering forests. The clamour of cities should be avoided, so you must choose an area with few local residents.

From a high plateau you can gaze to the horizon, and the distant peaks surround you like a screen. Your hall sends forth a gentle breeze to welcome the visitor, and your gate brings in a springtime stream to feed the marsh. Amid lovely red and purple blossoms you will be happy to meet the Angel of the Flowers. Enjoy the Saint and savour the Sage, and you can compare yourself to the Prime Minister in the Mountains.

Spring will embody the poem on 'Living as a Hermit' by Pan Yue, or Qu Yuan's affection for the fragrant herbs. When sweeping your paths take care of the orchid shoots, and they will send their fragrance into your retreat. Roll up your blinds and greet the swallows who slice through the light breeze like shears. Everywhere float drifting petals and the drowsy threads of willows. If the cold still makes you shiver, hang up a high swing. You can enjoy yourself at leisure and delight in the hills and valleys. Your thoughts will travel beyond the confines of this world of dust, and you will feel as though you were wandering within a painting.

From the summer shade of the woods the song of the oriole starts; in the folds of the hills you suddenly hear a wood-cutter singing and, as a breeze springs up from the cool of the forest, you feel as though you were transported back to the realm of the Emperor Fuxi. The hermit recites poetry in his pine-wood hut, and the gentleman of leisure plucks his lute in a grove of bamboo. The red garments of the lotuses are newly washed, and the green jade of the bamboos gently chimes. You can gaze at the bamboo by a bend in the stream, and watch the fish from the banks of the Hao. Mist drifts through the mountains, and the floating clouds sink down as you lean on the railing. Ripples cover the surface of the water, and you feel a cool breeze as you recline on your pillow. On the southern verandah you express your exalted emotions, and by the northern shutters you enjoy the mid-day shade. Beyond the half-open window lies the emerald shade of plantains and paulownias, and vines and creepers spread their turquoise over the surrounding wall: lean over the stream and enjoy the moon; sit on a rock and savour the spring-water.

Your light summer clothes can no longer withstand the fresh chill of autumn, but the scent of the lotuses in the pond still draws you to them. The phoenix-tree leaves are startled into their autumn fall, and the insects cry, hidden in the grasses. The level surface of the lake is a boundless expanse of floating light; the outline of the hills is of delicious beauty. There comes into view a skein of white egrets, and rank upon rank of crimson maples flushed with wine. You gaze afar from a high terrace, rub your eyes and wonder at the clear sky; leaning over the void from a spacious pavilion, you raise your glass and hail the bright moon. Imperceptibly a heavenly fragrance steals around as the osmanthus seeds sadly fall.

You notice that beside the withered hedge the chrysanthemum flowers are over; it is winter now, time to explore the warmer hillsides to see if the first plum blossoms are out. You should tie a little money to your staff and invite your rustic neighbours to a drink. The plum flower is like a lovely woman coming from the moonlit woods, while the gentleman of high ideals lies in his snow-covered cottage. The lowering clouds are wintry grey; the few leaves left on the trees rustle together. Wind-blown crows perch on some sparse trees in the setting sun; cold-driven geese utter a few cries under the waning moon. Waking from a dream by the window of his study, a solitary figure recites poetry to himself. The brocade curtain huddles round the glowing brazier; the six-petalled flowers of snowflakes offer their benison. You can set out in a boat as if passing the stream of Yan, or sweep up snow and boil it, making tea better than the wine of the Dang clan. Elegant activities can still be carried on in the winter's cold, and you can equal famous men of refinement in the past. There are few flowers that do not wither, but fresh scenes can be enjoyed all year round.

JI CHENG, *The Craft of Gardens*
[1631–4]; translated by Alison Hardie,
1988

Vita Sackville-West catches the magic moment of the first flush of spring flowers though still in winter.

SPRING

The yellow crocus through the grass will bring
Her light as pointed as a candle flame,
Not there at sunrise, but at midday there.
And snowdrops that increase each year,
Each leaf so tipped with white
As though it too desired to bear a flower.

Now in odd corners you may find
Enough for little bunches, as a child
Will bring you in hot hand a drooping gift
Dragged from the hedges and the cranny wild,
The daisy and the campion and the thrift,
Too dead to save, but if your heart be kind
Too dear to throw away
Until the giver on some other quest
Darts off to find a blackbird on her nest
Or, dropped along the road, a wisp of hay.

But these your winter bunches, jealously
Picked on a February morning, they
Are dearer than the plenteous summer. See,
One coloured primrose growing from a clump,
One Lenten rose, one golden aconite,
Dog Toby in his ruff, with varnish bright,
One sprig of daphne, roseate or white,
One violet beneath a mossy stump,
One gold and purple iris, brave but small
Child of the Caucasus, and bind them all
Into a tussie-mussie packed and tight
And envy not the orchid's rich delight.

VITA SACKVILLE-WEST,
The Garden [1946]

Tusser's doggerel records how the Elizabethan housewife set about her garden in springtime.

In Marche, and in Aprill, from morning to night:
   in sowing and setting, good huswives delight.
To haue in their gardein, or some other plot:
   to trim up their house, and to furnish their pot.

The nature of flowers dame Physick doth shew,
   she teacheth them all to be knowne to a few.
To set on to sowe, or else sowne to remove,
   now that should be practised, learne if ye love.

Land falling or lieing full South or southwest,
   for profit by tillage is lightly the best.
So garden with orchard and hopyarde I finde,
   that want the like benefit, growe out of kinde.

If field to beare corne a good tillage doth craue,
   what thinke ye of garden, what garden would haue?
In field without cost be assured of weedes,
   in garden be suer thou loosest thy seedes.

At Spring (for the sommer) sowe garden ye shall,
   at harvest (for winter) or sowe not at all.
Oft digging, remoouing and weeding (ye see)
   makes herbe the more holesome and greater to bee.

Time faire, to sowe or to gather be bold,
   but set or remooue when the weather is cold.
Cut all thing or gather, the moone in the wane,
   but sowe in encreasing, or give it his bane.

Now set doo aske watering with pot or with dish,
   new sowne doo not so, if ye doo as I wish.
Though cunning with dible, rake, mattock and spade,
   by line and by leavell, trim garden is made.

Who soweth too lateward, hath seldome good seed,
   who soweth too soone, little better shall speed.
Apt time and the season so diuers to hit,
   let aier and laier helpe practise and wit.

Good person and leekes, to make porridge in Lent,
   and peascods in July, saue fish to be sent.
Thus hauing with other things plentifull than,
   thou winnest the hart of the labouring man.

THOMAS TUSSER, *Five Hundred Pointes of Good Husbandrie* [1573]

A late Victorian lady creating an English garden in Germany was just as busy.

We have been very busy till now getting the permanent beds into order and planting the new tea-roses, and I am looking forward to next summer with more hope than ever in spite of my many failures. I wish the years would pass quickly that will bring my garden to perfection! The Persian Yellows have gone into their new quarters, and their place is occupied by the tea-rose Safrano; all the rose beds are carpeted with pansies sown in July and transplanted in October, each bed having a separate colour. The purple ones are the most charming and go well with every rose, but I have white ones with Laurette Messimy, and yellow ones with Safrano, and a new red sort in the big centre bed of red roses. Round the semicircle on the south side of the little privet hedge two rows of annual larkspurs in all their delicate shades have been sown, and just beyond the larkspurs, on the grass, is a semicircle of standard tea and pillar roses. In front of the house the long borders have been stocked with larkspurs, annual and perennial, columbines, giant poppies, pinks, Madonna lilies, wallflowers, hollyhocks, perennial phloxes, peonies, lavender, starworts, cornflowers, lychnis, chalcedonica, and bulbs packed in wherever bulbs could go. These are the borders that were so hardly used by the other gardener. Spring boxes for the veranda steps have been filled with pink and white and yellow tulips. I love tulips better than any other spring flower; they are the embodiment of alert cheerfulness and tidy grace, and next to a hyacinth look like a wholesome, freshly tubbed young girl beside a stout lady whose every movement weighs down the air with patchouli. Their faint, delicate scent is refinement itself; and is there anything in the world more charming than the sprightly way they hold up their little faces to the sun? I have heard them called bold and flaunting, but to me they seem modest grace itself, only always on the alert to enjoy life as much as they can and not afraid of looking the sun or anything else above them in the face. On the grass there are two beds of them carpeted with forget-me-nots; and in the grass, in scattered groups, daffodils and narcissus. Down the wilder shrubbery walks foxgloves and mulleins will (I hope) shine majestic; and one cool corner, backed by a group of firs, is graced by Madonna lilies, white foxgloves, and columbines. Oh, I could dance and sing for joy that the spring is here.

Countess Russell, Elizabeth and
Her German Garden [1898]

SUMMER

The best time for gardens in England is late May and June when that quintessential flower of the English garden, the rose, opens its petals. These are some of the most precious weeks of the gardener's year when every day must be savoured as new delights unfold.

My Dear Friend

We rejoice to hear that you are well and in England, and with friends whom you love so much – Oh how I wish you were passing near us! I have been sitting all the morning in my little garden, with its roses and stocks of all kinds, and rich peonies and geraniums, and purple irises and periwinkles, and yellow laburnums and globe anemones, and greens vivid and beautiful even as flowers, making altogether the finest piece of colour I ever saw – and I really yearned after you – you would have liked it so much. It is provoking to show such a thing to common eyes, which go peeping about into the detail, pulling the effect to pieces as children do daisies – Besides the nightingale and the scent of lilies of the valley and honeysuckles – my garden, on which my father rallies me so much, is my passion. But you will forgive me for over-rating it. It is, at least, a mistake on the right side, to be too fond of one's own poor home – and no mistake at all to wish you in it.

MARY RUSSELL MITFORD to EMILY
JEPHSON, 27 May 1825

Matthew Arnold encapsulates exactly the poignant transience of that apogee.

So, some tempestuous morn in early June,
When the year's primal burst of bloom is o'er,
Before the roses and the longest day –
When garden-walks and all the grassy floor,
With blossoms, red and white, of fallen May.
And chestnut-flowers are strewn –
So have I heard the cuckoo's parting cry,
From the wet field, through the vext garden-trees,
Come with the volleying rain and tossing breeze:
The *bloom is gone, and with the bloom go I,*

Too quick despairer, wherefore wilt thou go?
Soon will the high Midsummer pomps come on,
Soon will the musk carnations break and swell,
Soon shall we have gold-dusted snapdragon,
Sweet-William with his homely cottage-smell,
And stocks in fragrant blow;
Roses that down the alleys shine afar,
And open, jasmine-muffled lattices,
And groups under the dreaming garden-trees,
And the full moon, and the white evening star.

MATTHEW ARNOLD [1822–1888]
Thyrsis

Vita Sackville-West describes the anti-climax of midsummer in the English garden.

Heavy July. Too rampant and too lush;
High Summer, dull, fulfilled, and satiate,
Nothing to fear, and little to await.
The very birds are hush.
Dark over-burdened woods: too black, their green.

No leaping promise, no surprise, no keen
Difficult fight against a young, a lean
Sharp air and frozen soil; no contest bright
Of fragile courage winning in despite.
Easy July, when all too warmly blows

The surfeit of the rose
Risking no harm;
And those aggressive indestructible
Bores, the herbaceous plants, that gladly take
Whatever's given and make no demand
Beyond the careless favour of a stake;
Humble appeal, not arrogant command,
Like some tough spinster, doughty, duteous,
All virtue and no charm.

VITA SACKVILLE-WEST,
The Garden [1946]

After the dull days of late summer comes the finale of the garden's floral AUTUMN
year. It too is transient.

Now thin mists temper the sloe-ripening beams
Of the September sun: his golden gleams
On gaudy flowers shine, that prank the rows
Of high-grown hollyhocks, and all tall shows
That Autumn flaunteth in his bushy bowers;
Where tomtits, hanging from the drooping heads
Of giant sunflowers, peck the nutty seeds;
And in the feathery aster bees on wings
Seize and set free the honied flowers.
Till thousand stars leap with their visiting:
While ever across the path mazily flit,
Unpiloted in the sun,
The dreamy butterflies
With dazzling colours powdered and soft glooms,
White, black and crimson stripes, and peacock eyes,
Or on chance flowers sit,
With idle effort plundering one by one
The nectaries of deepest-throated blooms.

With gentle flaws the western breeze
Into the garden saileth,
Scarce here and there stirring the single trees,
For his sharpness he vaileth:
So long a comrade of the bearded corn,
Now from the stunnels whence the shocks are borne,
O'er dewy lawns he turns to stray,
As mindful of the kisses and soft play
Wherewith he enamoured the light-hearted May,
Ere he deserted her;
Lover of fragrance, and too late repents;
Nor more of heavy hyacinth now may drink,
Nor spicy pink,
Nor summer's rose, nor garnered lavender,
But the few lingering scents
Of streaked pea and gillyflower, and stocks
Of courtly purple, and aromatic phlox.

And at all times to hear are drowsy tones
Of dizzy flies, and humming drones,
With sudden flap of pigeon wings in the sky,
Or the wild cry
Of thirsty rooks, that scour ascare
The distant blue, to watering as they fare
With creaking pinions, or on business bent.
If aught their ancient policy displease, –
Come gathering to their colony, and there
Settling in ragging parliament,
Some stormy council hold in the high trees.

ROBERT BRIDGES, *The Garden
in September* [1894]

*The poets who celebrate the garden in autumn never do so without
overtones of sadness and loss.*

AN OCTOBER GARDEN

In my Autumn garden I was fain
    To mourn among my scattered roses;
    Alas for that last rosebud that uncloses
To Autumn's languid sun and rain
When all the world is on the wain!
    Which has not felt the sweet constraint of June,
    Nor heard the nightingale in tune.

Broad-faced asters by my garden walk,
    You are but coarse compared with roses:
    More choice, more dear that rosebud which uncloses,
Faint-scented, pinched, upon its stalk,
That least and last which cold winds balk;
    A rose it is though least and last of all,
    A rose to me though at the fall.

CHRISTINA ROSSETTI,
Poems [1878]

The air is damp and hushed and close,
As a sick man's room when he taketh repose
    An hour before death –
My very heart faints and my whole soul grieves
At the moist rich smell of the rotting leaves,
    And the breath
    Of the fading edges of box beneath,
And the year's last rose.

ALFRED, LORD TENNYSON [1809–
1892]

Today I think
Only with scents, – scents dead leaves yield,
And bracken, and wild carrot's seed,
And the square mustard field.

Odours that rise
When the spade wounds the root of tree,
Rose, currant, raspberry, or goutweed,
Rhubarb or celery;

The smoke's smell, too
Flowing from where a bonfire burns
The dead, the waste, the dangerous,
And all to sweetness turns.

It is enough
To smell, to crumble the dark earth,
While the robin sings over again
Sad songs of Autumn mirth.

EDWARD THOMAS, *Collected Poems* [1936]

Addison pays tribute to the garden in winter. Like Bacon, however, he is still concerned not so much with enjoying the effects of winter for their aesthetic delights in their own right as much as planting to nullify the course of nature.

WINTER

What I am now going to mention will, perhaps, deserve your Attention more than any Thing I have yet said. I find that in the Discourse which I spoke of at the Beginning of my Letter, you are against filling an *English* Garden with Ever-Greens; and indeed I am so far of your Opinion, that I can by no Means think the Verdure of an Ever-Green comparable to that which shoots out annually, and cloaths our Trees in the Summer Season. But I have often wondered that those who are like myself, and love to live in Gardens, have never thought of contriving a *Winter Garden*, which should consist of such Trees only as never cast their Leaves. We have very often little Snatches of Sun-shine and fair Weather in the most uncomfortable Parts of the Year, and have frequently several Days in *November* and *January* that are as agreeable as any in the finest Months. At such Times, therefore, I think there could not be a greater Pleasure, than to walk in such a *Winter Garden* as I have proposed. In the Summer Season the whole Country blooms, and is a Kind of Garden, for which Reason we are not so sensible of those Beauties that at this Time may be every where met with; but when Nature is in her Desolation, and presents us with nothing but bleak and barren Prospects, there is something unspeakably chearful in a Spot of Ground which is covered with Trees that smile amidst all the Rigours of Winter, and give us a View of the most gay Season in the Midst of that which is the most dead and melancholy. I have so far indulged my self in this Thought, that I have set apart a whole Acre of Ground for the executing of it. The Walls are covered with Ivy instead of Vines. The Laurel, the Hornbeam, and the Holly, with many other

Heather thatched Summerhouse

Trees and Plants of the same Nature, grow so thick in it, that you cannot imagine a more lively Scene. The glowing Redness of the Berries, with which they are hung at this Time, vies with the Verdure of their Leaves, and are apt to inspire the Heart of the Beholder with that vernal Delight which you have somewhere taken Notice of in your former Papers. It is very pleasant, at the same Time, to see the several Kinds of Birds retiring into this little green Spot, and enjoying themselves among the Branches and Foliage, when my great Garden, which I have before-mentioned to you, does not afford a single Leaf for their Shelter.

JOSEPH ADDISON, *The Spectator*,
No. 477, 6 September 1712

Not every gardener was enamoured of winter. For some its depredations called for the comforts of the bottle.

To see one's urns, obelisks and waterfalls laid open; the nakedness of our beloved mistresses, the Naiads and the Dryads, exposed by that ruffian Winter to universal observations; is a severity scarcely to be supported by the help of blazing hearths, chearful companions, and a bottle of the most grateful burgundy.

WILLIAM SHENSTONE, *Unconnected
Thoughts on Gardening*　[c. 1745]

The onset of winter in the southern states of America produces its own special garden beauty.

Today is the fourteenth of November. I have been sitting in the sun eating my lunch and staring at the barbaric scarlet of Tithonia Fireball against the cold blue sky. The low retaining wall of the terrace is a study in values: bright silver leaves of *Veronica incana*, dull gray mounds of santolina, scattered flowers of white verbena against dark foliage. The path to the summer house, framed in a green arch, is as gay as ever from a little distance, even though the edging of *Zinnia linearis* and sweet alyssum proves, on closer view, to be a little ragged. Against the dark temple fir the scarlet berries and glossy foliage of the Formosa firethorn have assumed the brilliance that they will carry well into the winter. Along the fence there are still a few pale butterfly flowers on the climbing rose, Mermaid. The flowers of the tall yellow crotalaria and of the dwarfer bronzed one have become discolored during the cold nights, but one plant – protected by the hedge – still lifts tender yellow spires against the green. Throughout the garden the ageratum volunteers have come into their own, covering bare beds with the intense blue that they take on with the first cool weather. The strawberry pink reflection of a neighbouring maple lies on the black water of the pool. Already the leaves are falling from the trees.

Any night now frost may blacken the last crotalarias, zinnias, marigolds, and chrysanthemums. But, when the dead branches have been cleared away, there will still be the green of the ivy, the gray of santolina, and the scarlet fruit of the firethorn. Already sweet violets are in bloom, and before long there will be buds on the Paper White narcissus and the Algerian iris.

ELIZABETH LAWRENCE, *A Southern
Garden*　[1942]

But here is a garden in winter at its most depressing: the orphanage garden with its tiny plots, chillingly evoked.

The garden was a wide enclosure, surrounded with walls so high as to exclude every glimpse of prospect: a covered verandah ran down one side, and broad walks bordered a middle space divided into scores of little beds: these beds were assigned as gardens for the pupils to cultivate, and each bed had an owner. When full of flowers they would doubtless look pretty; but now, at the latter end of January, all was wintry blight and brown decay. I shuddered as I stood and looked round me . . .

CHARLOTTE BRÖNTE, *Jane Eyre*
[1846–7]

Part of any garden's delight is its ability to satisfy all five senses. Ralph Austen (d. 1676) writing during the Commonwealth describes how an orchard brings such satisfaction.

SENSES

It is a pleasure to the Eare to heare the sweet notes and tunes of singing Birds, whose company a man shall be sure to have in an Orchard, which is more pleasant there, than elsewhere, because of other concurrent pleasures there; a Consort of Musicke is more pleasant than a single Instrument . . .

And besides, something more this sense may receive from an Orchard . . . by hearing the slow motion of Boughes and Leaves, by soft and gentle aires, sometimes (as it were) with a kind of singing or whistling noise, which will easily induce a sweet and pleasant sleep in sommer time (if a man be dispos'd) in some close coole Arbor or shady seat.

Secondly, the sence of Touch may have more Pleasure in an Orchard from the coole fruits, and leaves of Trees, smoothing and brushing the face therewith, which is refreshing and cooling in heat of Sommer. But this sense receives pleasure chiefly by the shade of Trees in Sommer time. Coole refreshing Ayres are found in close Walks, Seats and Arbours under and about the Trees, which keepe off the burning heat of the Sunne . . .

Thirdly, the sence of Sight partakes of Pleasure in an Orchard, in beholding the exact Order in planting of the Trees, their decent Fromes, the well composed Allies, Walks, Seats and Arbours therein; for order and curious formes of things much delight the sight: of this see L. Bacon at large.

Likewise the sight is delighted with pleasant and delicate Colours of the Leaves, Blossomes, and Fruits, that shew themselves in great variety. Curious Colours, especially the Colour greene is accounted helpfull to the sight . . .

Is it not a pleasant sight to behold a multitude of Trees round about, in decent forme and order, bespangled and gorgeously apparelled with greene Leaves, Bloomes, and goodly fruits, as with a rich Robe of imbroidered work, or as hanging with some pretious and costly Jewels, or Pearles, the Boughes laden, and burdened, bowing downe to you, and freely offering their ripe fruits, as a large satisfaction of all your labours? . . .

Fourthly, the sence of smell, may likewise have its share of pleasure in a Garden of Fruit-trees . . . Chiefly the Pleasure this sence meets with is from the sweet smelling blossomes of all the fruit trees, which from the time of their breaking forth, till their fall, breathe out a most pretious and pleasant odour; perfuming the aire throughout all the Orchard . . .

Fiftly, the sence of Taste has its pleasure in an Orchard. This sence meets with Pleasure at all times of the Yeare from the fruits of an Orchard . . . The ordinary food they afford all the yeare, and the more delicate for Banquets, are also good and healthfull to the body, as well as pleasant to the taste.

RALPH AUSTEN, *A Treatise on Fruit Trees* [1653]

And three centuries later.

I enjoy the use of all five senses. The look of a garden can be a great joy – the massing of trees and shrubs, the stretch of lawn, the detailed beauty of a flower, reflections in water and the dappling of shadows – but the other senses also should bring delight. I value the smells that come from working in the garden – bruised elder-twigs, the sawdust of apple-wood, cut logs of the bay-tree, fungus, damp earth and bonfires. I value also the taste of things picked and eaten at once, such as water-cress and blackberries; the feel of the bark, of cool snowdrop stems in the picking, of hot rough stones in the sun, of water when cleaning the spade; and, of course, the sounds of the garden – birds calling, house martins twittering as they swoop from the eaves of the house, bees humming up the full height of a flower-covered lime tree, a hen clucking after laying an egg, water falling into the pond. But most of all, the sound of the wind, soft through the leaves and sometimes roaring through the branches as through the rigging of a tall ship in a storm.

MICHAEL DOWER, in *The Countryman*, Summer 1974

SCENT   *One of gardening's great delights and a sophisticated one in an age which prizes size and colour in a flower above fragrance. Our ancestors in the pre-deodorant age were keenly sensitive to the delicacy of smells.*

And because the Breath of Flowers is far Sweeter in the Air (where it comes and goes, like the Warbling of Musick) than in the Hand, therefore nothing is more fit for that Delight, than to know what be the Flowers and Plants that do best perfume the Air. Roses, Damask and Red, are fast Flowers of their Smells, so that you may walk by a whole Row of them, and find nothing of their Sweetness; yea, though it be in a morning Dew. Bays likewise yield no Smell as they grow, Rosemary little, nore Sweet-Marjoram. That, which above all others, yields the sweetest Smell in the Air, is the Violet, specially the White double Violet, which comes twice a year, about the middle of April, and about Bartholomew-tide. Next to that is the Musk Rose, then the Strawberry Leaves dying with a most excellent Cordial Smell. Then the Flower of the Vines; it is a little Dust, like the Dust of a Bent, which grows upon the Cluster in the first coming forth. Then Sweet-Briar, then Wall-Flowers, which are very delightful to be set under a Parlour, or lower Chamber Window. Then Pinks, especially the Matted Pink, and Clove Gilly-Flower. Then the Flowers of the Lime-Tree. Then the Honey-Suckles, so they be somewhat afar off. Of Bean-Flowers I speak not, because they are Field-Flowers. But those which perfume the Air most delightfully, not passed by as the rest, but being Trodden upon and Crushed, are three: that is Burnet, Wild-Time, and Water-Mints. Therefore you are to set whole Alleys of them, to have the Pleasure when you walk or tread.

SIR FRANCIS BACON, *Of Gardens* [1625]

John Aubrey's cousin was Sir John Danvers (1588?–1655) 'who first taught us the way of Italian gardens'. He was a friend of Francis Bacon who would have appreciated this use of herbs.

Sir John, being my Relation and faithfull Friend, was wont in fair mornings in the Summer to brush his Beaver-hatt on the Hysop and Thyme, which did perfume it with its naturall Spirit; and would last a morning or longer.

JOHN AUBREY [1626–1697], *Brief Lives*

Mary Russell Mitford, wandering through her cottage garden with the dog given her by Christina Rossetti, records the garden's many perfumes in summer.

. . . I am just come from a walk – if walk it may be called, which was merely a zig-zag kind of progress from the rose bushes to the honeysuckles, from the honeysuckles to the syringa tree – from the syringa to the acacia, and from the acacia back to the roses. – I have been gathering sweets by night as the bee gathers them by day – the luxury of that fresh growing perfume a flowering shrub in full bloom is to me the greatest of all enjoyments – and of all flowers the white acacia is, I think, the most fragrant; and of all white acacias, one which is my pet tree is the most laden with blossoms; and of all evenings in which to stand under it, this has been the pleasantest – a light wind shaking down the loosely hung florets upon my pet Mossy's black neck – and Mossy looking up and half-suspecting some evil design till another shower seemed to explain the cause and remove his fears.

MARY RUSSELL MITFORD to SIR WILLIAM ELFORD, 14 June 1818

Scent can also be memory.

It is a well-known fact that nothing recalls the past like scents, and this is so especially true of the scent of flowers, that I suppose most of us can name instances in our own experience. I never gather a leaf of the fine-leaved form of the oak-leaf geranium without at once going back in memory to a pleasant home in the Midlands, where the genial host was so fond of the leaf that it always formed a part of the 'button-hole' of his guests. Elwanger, in *The Garden's Story*, carries this too far when he says that the 'perfume of *Lilium auratum*, stealing from the spotted petals, recalls the reedy jungle and the spotted tiger'. Mr Savage Landor says more truly –

> 'Sweet scents
> Are the swift vehicles of still sweeter thoughts,
> And nurse and mellow the dull memory,
> That would let drop without them her best stores.'

But best of all was the excellent use that the late Miss Hope, of Edinburgh, made of her sweet-scented flowers. She was indefatigable in providing comforts for the sick in hospitals, and among the comforts she included a plentiful supply of flowers, but with the proviso that the flowers should be common flowers, and always accompanied with a sprig of some woody, aromatic plant, for the special purpose of recalling memories of home.

CANON ELLACOMBE, *In a Gloucestershire Garden* [1895]

Many of the garden's best scents only come or intensify with dusk.

And what of the night-scented flowers. To many of us there is no time when the scents in the garden are more exquisite than at twilight. The scents of the roses and the lilies then seem sweeter than at any other hour. The scent of honeysuckle is richer, and lured by it the hawk-moths fly to extract the honey which lies too deep for the bees or wasps to reach. Nor do the jasmines exhale their richest perfumes until darkness falls and the bells of the yuccas turn to stars. The scents of those old favourites, the night-scented stock (*Hesperis tristis*) and the old double white Rocket (*H. matronalis*) and *Nicotiana affinis*, have rejoiced generations of scent-lovers with the sweetness of their perfumes in the evening. The old double white Rocket was formerly known as Dames Violets, for in the evening it exhales a violet-like fragrance, whereas as Parkinson noted three hundred years ago this 'pretty sweet scent' is almost absent during the day. One of the sweetest of all evening scents is that of one of our native catchflies, *Silene nutans*, sometimes called the Nottingham catchfly, because it formerly grew in such abundance near that town, and in still older days it was called the Dover catchfly, because the cliffs there for miles were starred in the evening with its fragrant flowers. It is, alas! not a common wild flower now, and for those who love its rich scent it is well worth growing in a garden where there is chalky soil. But the scent is never so strong as when in its wild state. Even when gathered and brought indoors this catchfly opens only in the evening, and the scent in a room is overpowering. The wild evening campion (*Lychnis vespertina*) opens its flowers during the day, but as its name implies it is only in the evening that it breathes forth its incense. The humble little *Linnaea boréalis*, which grows wild in parts of Norway and Scotland, scents the air round with its delicious fragrance in the evening. Sowerby gives the following account of this plant: 'For this most interesting addition to the British Flora we are indebted to Professor James Beattie, junior, of Aberdeen, who discovered it in an old fir wood at Mearns in that neighbourhood and communicated wild specimens, along with an accurate coloured drawing, to the Linnaean Society, June 2nd, 1795. The *Linnaea* grows in dry, stony, mossy woods. The flowers are said to be very fragrant at night, smelling like the meadowsweet. Linnaeus in *Critica Botanica*, p. 80, has traced a pretty fanciful analogy between his own early fate and this 'little northern plant, long overlooked, depressed, abject, flowering early,' and we may now add more honoured in its name than any other'.

No evening scents, I think, have the fascination of the delicate fragrance of the evening primroses, especially that of the commonest variety. Those pale moons irradiate the twilight with their sweet elusive perfumes. Like the flowers themselves their scent as night draws in becomes full of mystery and holds our imagination captive. And the scent of limes, what an exquisite scent this is – an exquisite as the music of the trees. To me the loveliest music in the world is the music of the evening breeze in the lime trees on a July evening.

ELEANOUR SINCLAIR ROHDE,
The Scented Garden [1931]

And in the American garden there is nostalgia too for scent.

The gardens of my youth were fragrant gardens and it is their sweetness rather than their patterns of their furnishings that I now most clearly recall. My mother's rose garden in Maryland was famous in that countryside and in the nearby city, for many shared its bounty. In it grew the most fragrant roses, not only great bushes of Provence, damask and Gallica roses, but a collection of the finest teas and Noisettes of the day. Maréchal Niel, Lamarque and Gloire de Dijon climbed high on trellises against the stone of the old house and looked in at the second-story windows. I remember that some sort of much coveted distinction was conferred upon the child finding the first long golden bud of Maréchal Niel. Once a week, on Friday, a great hamper of freshly cut roses was loaded into the back of the 'yellow wagon' – its physical aspect in no way bore out its sprightly name – and with 'old Tom' in the driver's seat we fared into the city and distributed to the sick, the sad and the disgruntled, great bunches of dewy fragrant roses . . .

Why do garden makers of today so seldom deliberately plan for fragrance? Undoubtedly gardens of early times were sweeter than ours. The green enclosures of Elizabethan days evidently overflowed with fragrant flowers and the little beds in which they were confined were neatly edged with some sweet-leaved plant – thyme, germander, lavender, rosemary, cut to a formal line. The yellowed pages of ancient works on gardening seem to give off the scents of the beloved old favorites – gilliflower, stock, sweet rocket, wallflower, white violet. Fragrance, by the wise old gardeners of those days, was valued as much as if not more than other attributes. Bacon said immortal things about sweet scented flowers in his essay, 'Of Gardens,' as well as in his less known curious old 'Naturall Historie.' Theophrastus devoted a portion of his *Inquiry Into Plants* to odors, chiefly floral and leaf odors. Our books of today make sadly little of the subject.

Our great grandmothers prized more highly than any others what they called their posy flowers, moss rose, southernwood, bergamot, marigold, and the like. Indeed it would seem that save in that strangely tasteless period of the nineteenth century, when all grace departed from gardens and hard hued flowers were laid down upon the patient earth in lines and circles of crude color like Berlin wool-work, geranium, calceolaria, lobelia, and again geranium, calceolaria, lobelia, no period has been so unmindful of fragrance in the garden as this in which we are now living. We have juggled the sweet pea into the last word in hues and furbelows, and all but lost its sweetness; we have been careless of the rose's scent, and have made of the wistful Mignonette a stolid and inodorous wedge of vulgarity. We plan meticulously for color harmony and a sequence of bloom, but who goes deliberately about planning for a succession of sweet during every week of the growing year?

LOUISE BEEBE WILDER, *The Fragrant Path* [1932]

GARDEN TOURS

Beverley Nichols echoes exactly my experience in our own garden and of any tour around a garden with its owner. Even Louis XIV dictated a set route for visitors around the gardens of Versailles!

Whenever I arrive in my garden, I Make The Tour. Is this a personal idiosyncrasy, or do all good gardeners do it? It would be interesting to know.

By Making The Tour, I mean only that I step from the front window, turn to the right, and make an infinitely detailed examination of every foot of ground, every shrub and tree, walking always over an appointed course.

There are certain very definite rules to be observed when you are Making The Tour. The chief rule is that you must never take anything out of its order. You may be longing to see if a crocus has come out in the orchard, but it is strictly forbidden to look before you have inspected all the various beds, bushes and trees that lead up to the orchard.

You must not look at the bed ahead before you have finished with the bed immediately in front of you. You may see, out of the corner of your eye, a gleam of strange and unsuspected scarlet in the next bed but one, but you must stare with cool eyes at the earth in front, which is apparently blank, until you have made certain that it is not hiding anything. Otherwise you will find that you rush wildly round the garden, discover one or two sensational events, and then decide that nothing else has happened. Which means that you miss all the thrill of tiny shoots, the first lifting of the lids of the wallflowers, the first precious gold of the witch-hazel, the early spear of the snowdrop.

BEVERLEY NICHOLS, *Down the Garden Path* [1932]

A Border of Pots

PART
VII

GARDEN
WORK

Labyrinth

The garden in question was Castle Hill, South Moulton, Devon.

Articles of Agreement for keeping the Pleasure Ground, Kitchen Garden and Hothouses at Castle Hill according to the following calculation exclusive of the Park.

1. For mowing and carrying the grass off the walk from the western iron gate to the end of the long fir walk four times a year exclusive the first which is done by the bailey.

2. For raking leaves and cutting the bushments against the walk in Addabeer road as often as they shall want.

3. For mowing the Platform before the Spa Bath House six times.

4. For mowing the Platform, cutting Yews, turning of borders before the House.

5. For cutting the thorn hedges each side of the fir walk three times and keeping the fence.

6. For planting trees in room of them that are dead.

7. Keeping the clumps of firs on the Oxford Down.

8. Cutting the shady walk from Squire's house to the Church and the evergreens the backside of the Church as often as they want.

9. Cutting the hedge in Barnstaple road six times a year.

10. Cutting the thorn hedges round the Paddock six times a year.

11. Keeping a good fence around the paddock.

12. Weeding and keeping the black gravel walks and platform before the great house in good order.

13. Mowing, sweeping and carrying the grass round the paddock walks twelve times a year.

14. Keeping of grass and the bushments cut and carried away in the walks of both paddock roads.

15. Weeding and keeping the nine pin alley and before Turkey sopha clean, and the cushions wiped and aired as they need.

16. Mowing and carrying the grass, raking of leaves and cleaning the trees in the green plot by the little serpentine river paddock.

17. Cutting the yews and that part of the paddock road that over drapes the yews and turning the borders of the yews all round.

18. Propping up trees that shall be pruned or thrown down.

19. Opening and cleaning all drains that shall choke.

20. Carrying in and out the urns.

21. Cutting the rushes in the paddock and great walk to the Arch as they appear in sight of the Hall Door.

22. Keeping all the edges of the serpentine rivers and canals.

23. Keeping all the vistas cut that point to the buildings.

24. Cutting the grass three times each side of the serpentine river in Dark Lane and carrying it away exclusive the first time which is to be done, by the bayley.

25. Mowing the walks and cutting the slopes in Dark Lane Wood twelve times a year and carrying the grass away.

26. Cutting the grass under the trees twice a year and carrying it away and cleaning the trees from twigs and annual shoots as often as they shall want in Dark Lane Wood.

27. Cutting the yews, turning the borders round the Chinese temple.

28. Cutting the bushments keeping the walk clean from the Chinese temple down to Sybil's Cave. Weeding of rockwork and walls for the Cave and Satyr's Temple.

29. Mowing the walk from the Chinese temple to the north park through Mr Burgess' ground six times a year.

30. Cutting the grass on the Castle Green twelve times a year.

31. Cutting the hedges to the park gate from the house twelve times a year and keeping it in repair.

32. Mowing, carrying the grass away, raking, carrying them away, six times a year in Clatworthy Wood.

33. For keeping the hoops in the paddock as usual.

34. Repairing all the cascades and sluices.

35. For a boy to roll before the house and other walks.

36. Raking the leaves in the park twice a year, carrying them away, mowing the walks all round the park three times a year and before the Hermitage four times, cleaning out and looking after the cascades in the park and taking away such trees as are dead and planting others in their place and carrying off the stocks and limbs where they fall.

£102-16-0
Instructions of MATTHEW, 2ND LORD
FORTESCUE, 13 October 1752

BONFIRES *Perhaps the most poignant act of autumn.*

THE BURNING OF THE LEAVES

Now is the time for the burning of the leaves.
They go to the fire; the nostril pricks with smoke
Wandering slowly into a seeping mist.
Brittle and blotched, ragged and rotten sheaves!
A flame seizes the smouldering ruin and bites
On stubborn stalks that crackle as they resist.

The last hollyhock's fallen tower is dust;
All the spices of June are a bitter reek,
All the extravagant riches spent and mean.
All burns! The reddest rose is a ghost;
Sparks whirl up, to expire in the mist: the wild
Fingers of fire are making corruption clean.

Now is the time for stripping the spirit bare,
Time for the burning of days ended and done,
Idle solace of things that have gone before:
Rootless hope and fruitless desire are there;
Let them go to the fire, with never a look behind.
The world that was ours is a word that is ours no more.

They will come again, the leaf and the flower, to arise
From squalor of rottenness into the old splendour,
And magical scents to a wondering memory bring;
The same glory, to shine upon different eyes.
Earth cares for her own ruins, naught for ours.
Nothing is certain, only the certain spring.

LAURENCE BINYON [1869–1943]

THE BONFIRE

God of gardeners, accept this coil
Of acrid smoke from nettle and weed,
This left-hand mound of sinful soil
That I have sifted from the seed.

With hoe and mattock, spade and rake,
From morning dew to evening grace,
My back has bended for Thy sake,
To bring sweet order to this place.

Thy fruits and tubers basketed,
Thy flowers lit from setting sun,
With fragrant heart and reverent head
I tend this altar gleaming red,
As my forefathers must have done.

RICHARD CHURCH, *Twelve Noon* [1936]

We manage eight but not even this number would tempt me into verse with these three ghastly poems as precedents.

COMPOST HEAPS

Of composts shall the Muse descend to sing,
Nor soil her heavenly plumes? the sacred Muse
Naught sordid deems, but what is base; naught fair
Unless true Virtue stamp it with her seal.
Then, planter, wouldst though double thine estate,

Never, ah never, be ashamed to tread
Thy dung-heaps, where the refuse of thy mills,
With all the ashes, all thy coppers yield,
With weeds, mould, dung and stale, a compost form,
Of force to fertilize the poorest soil . . .
Whether the fattening compost in each hole
'Tis best to throw, or on the surface spread,
Is undetermined: trials must decide.
Unless kind rains and fostering dews descend,
To melt the compost's fertilizing salts,
A stinted plant, deceitful of thy hopes,
Will from those beds slow spring where hot dung lies:
But, if 'tis scattered generously o'er all,
The cane will better bear the solar blaze;
Less rain demand; and, by repeated crops,
Thy land improved its gratitude will show.
Enough of composts, Muse . . .

DR JAMES GRAINGER, *The Sugar-Cane*, eighteenth century

The stable yields a stercorarious heap,
Impregnated with quick fermenting salts,
And potent to resist the freezing blast:
For ere the beech and elm have cast their leaf
Deciduous, and when now November dark
Checks vegetation in the torpid plant
Exposed to his cold breath, the task begins.
That where he builds
Th'agglomerated pile, his frame may front
The sun's meridian dusk, and at the back
Enjoy close shelter, wall, or reeds, or hedge
Impervious to the wind. First he bids spread
Dry fern or litter'd hay, that may imbibe
Th'ascending damps; then leisurely impose,
And lightly, shaking it with agile hand
From the full fork, the saturated straw.
What longest binds the closest, forms secure
The shapely side, that as it rises takes
By just degrees an overhanging breadth,
Shelt'ring the base with its projected eaves.
Th'uplifted frame compact at ev'ry joint,
And overlaid with clear translucent glass
He settles next upon the sloping mount,
Whose sharp declivity shoots off secure
From the dash'd pane the deluge as it falls.
He shuts it close, and the first labour ends.

WILLIAM COWPER, *The Task* [1785]

THIS COMPOST

I

Something startles me where I thought I was safest,
I withdraw from the still woods I loved,
I will not go now on the pastures to walk,
I will not strip the clothes from my body to meet my lover the sea,
I will not touch my flesh to the earth as to other flesh to renew me.

O how can it be that the ground itself does not sicken?
How can you be alive you growths of spring?
How can you furnish health you blood of herbs, roots, orchards, grain?
Are they not continually putting distemper'd corpses within you?
Is not every continent work'd over and over with sour dead?

Where have you disposed of their carcasses?
Those drunkards and gluttons of so many generations?
Where have you drawn off all the foul liquid and meat?
I do not see any of it upon you to-day, or perhaps I am deceiv'd,
I will run a furrow with my plough, I will press my spade through
    the sod and turn it up underneath,
I am sure I shall expose some of the foul meat.

II

Behold this compost! behold it well!
Perhaps every mite has once form'd part of a sick person – yet
    behold!
The grass of spring covers the prairies,
The bean bursts noiselessly through the mould in the garden,
The delicate spear of the onion pierces upward,
The apple-buds cluster together on the apple-branches,
The resurrection of the wheat appears with pale visage out of its
    graves,
The tinge awakes over the willow-tree and the mulberry-tree,
The he-birds carol mornings and evenings while the she-birds sit
    on their nests,
The young of poultry break through the hatch'd eggs,
The new-born of animals appear, the calf is dropt from the cow,
    the colt from the mare,
Out of its little hill faithfully rise the potato's dark green leaves,
Out of its hill rises the yellow maize-stalk, the lilacs bloom in the
    dooryards,
The summer growth is innocent and disdainful above all those
    strata of sour dead.
What chemistry!
That the winds are really not infectious,
That this is no cheat, this transparent green-wash of the sea which
    is so amorous after me,
That it is safe to allow it to lick my naked body all over with its
    tongues,

That it will not endanger me with the fevers that have deposited
  themselves in it,
That all is clean forever and forever,
That the cool drink from the well tastes so good,
That blackberries are so flavorous and juicy,
That the fruits of the apple-orchard and the orange-orchard, that
  melons, grapes, peaches, plums, will none of them poison me,
That when I recline on the grass I do not catch any disease,
Though probably every spear of grass rises out of what was once
  a catching disease.

Now I am terrified at the Earth, it is that calm and patient,
It grows such sweet things out of such corruptions,
It turns harmless and stainless on its axis, with such endless
  successions of diseas'd corpses,
It distills such exquisite winds out of such infused fetor,
It renews with such unwitting looks its prodigal, annual,
  sumptuous crops,
It gives such divine materials to men, and accepts such leavings
  from them at last.

WALT WHITMAN [1819–92]

DESTRUCTION

*The old formal garden at Brasenose College, Oxford, was destroyed not
without the comment of a famous antiquary.*

Last week they cut down the fine pleasant garden in Brasenose College
Quadrangle, which was not only a great Ornament to it, and was agreeable
to the quadrangles of our old monasteries, but was a delightful pleasant
Shade in Summer Time, and made the rooms, in hot seasons, much cooler
than otherwise they would have been. This is done, by the direction of the
Principal and some others purely to turn it into a grass Plot and erect some
silly statue there.   THOMAS HEARNE [1727]

Southey records the same fate meted out to that at New College.

We visited the gardens . . . The College arms were formerly cut in box, and
the alphabet grew round them; in another compartment was a sun-dial in
box, set round with true lovers' knots. These have been destroyed more
easily as well as more rapidly than they were formed; but as nothing
beautiful has been substituted in their places, it had been better if they had
suffered these old oddities to have remained. One proof of their predeces-
sors' whimsical taste, however, has been permitted to stand; a row of trees,
every one of which has its lower branches grafted into its next neighbour, so
that the whole are in this way united.

ROBERT SOUTHEY, *Letter of
Espriella* [1807]

*Queen Mary's interest in horticulture was minimal but her obsession
with order, though presented positively by her tactful biographer, must
have wrecked havoc at Badminton where she passed the war.*

As we know, it was not Queen Mary's habit to be idle. Within the shortest possible time of her arrival at Badminton she was hard at work . . . In this period of what was rather optimistically called 'the phoney war' – 'What a dreadful mysterious war', Queen Mary wrote in November 1939 – the Queen also embarked upon an activity which engrossed more and more of her time and attention and which ended by greatly improving whole tracts of the Badminton estate. The first modest references in her Diary to this activity are dated 25 and 26 September 1939, and read:

> Lovely morning which we spent clearing ivy off the trees in the grounds while Jack Coke hacked off branches off 2 chestnut trees & an elm not far from the house & the gardeners began to clear a wall of ivy near Mary B's bedroom.

and:

> Lovely morning which we spent clearing ivy off trees – We watched a whole wall of ivy of 50 years standing at the back of Mary B's bedroom being removed – most of it came down like a blanket –

Queen Mary's enmity towards ivy had long been proverbial at Sandringham, and she had never missed an opportunity to attack it wherever it appeared within the grounds. Badminton offered a wider field for this private battle against ivy – there was more of it to be attacked, it was older and stronger, and consequently, in Queen Mary's view, more destructive to stonework, brickwork and trees. She was soon busily engaged in the garden, from which her hosts tactfully diverted her farther afield to the long, low stone wall surrounding the estate. Her equerry, her current lady-in-waiting, her Private Secretary and anyone who was staying in the house were swiftly enrolled in the 'Ivy Squad'. Besides being useful and providing healthy exercise, this fight against ivy satisfied that urge to tidy up and to put in order which was, as we know, basic to Queen Mary's nature.

By September 1940, the Ivy Squad had so extended its range that it became a 'Wooding Squad'. Into this the Queen had incorporated first her own four despatch riders attached to her for the duration of the war, and then the men of the company of fighting troops which stood guard at Badminton to defend Queen Mary in the event of an invasion of this country by the Germans, or an enemy attempt to kidnap her by aeroplane. Amongst the Queen's immediate entourage the Wooding Squad, whose work was arduous in the extreme, aroused small enthusiasm; but, indefatigable and thorough, Queen Mary exacted from her Household the same effort which she threw into the work herself. Her Diaries contain many entries recording the progress of the squad's work, as well as notes of future projects: 'After luncheon walked with C., J.C. & Major Rooke to look at an overgrown plantation opposite Watson's house, which they want our wood "Squad" to clear out – It may be an interesting job – we picked up chestnuts later', for example; or 'Went for a walk to see the spinney near the Allan Grove which Master wants us to thin out for him – I think it will be amusing to do.'

At first, to save petrol, Queen Mary insisted on proceeding to the more distant working sites in a farm-cart, drawn by two horses and containing a couple of basket chairs for herself and her Lady. 'Aunt May', remarked her niece, 'you look as if you were in a tumbril!' 'Well, it may come to that yet,

one never knows', Queen Mary answered happily as the cart jolted off. Subsequently the Queen made use of her old green Daimler car, in which she would set off after luncheon each day, back-saws and other equipment tied on to the back. Among the durable results of this portion of Queen Mary's war-time presence at Badminton is 'Queen Mary's Plantation' of young firs, no less than sixteen and a half acres in extent and occupying ground cleared solely by the Queen and her Wooding Squad.

JAMES POPE-HENNESSY,
Queen Mary [1959]

DROUGHT

The one in question was during the summer of 1893. We, in England, will remember those of 1976, 1989 and 1990.

The garden record for May ought to be a record of abundance of flowers and rich greenery, both in field and garden. But the May of 1893 will long be remembered as a May in which the garden was burnt up, and everything was thrown out of its proper season. There were flowers in abundance; but the flowers of May owed nothing to the April showers, for the long drought was accompanied with brilliant sunshine, and for the most part of the time with dry easterly and north-easterly winds, making the earth, even in the most favoured soils, hard and parched, and with little or no refreshment from dews, 'the heaven over our head being as brass, and the earth beneath us as iron.' The result of this was that the gardens, and indeed the whole country, presented an appearance such as few of us could remember, and produced many curious sights which might rightly be called abnormal.

Among these curious abnormal sights, I should reckon the hawthorn, of which it is generally very difficult to pick a single blossom on May-day, but which in that year was in full flower at the same time as the blackthorn, on the 13th of April, and was even in flower before the first swallow was seen. The swallows were very late that year. I did not see the first in my garden till the 23rd of April, only one day before the cuckoo was heard for the first time; and on the same day appeared the pretty little redstart, which I always welcome as one of the truest harbingers of summer, almost as much so as the corncake, which I both heard and saw on April 25.

In the garden the chief effect was that the flowers were forced into premature blooming; we had in May the flowers of June. There was a wonderful abundance of flowers everywhere, but they were stunted, and starved, and dwarfed, and so were robbed on half their beauty . . .

On the whole, after reckoning up all the losses and disappointments, I do not think that the gardener has much cause to complain of a long drought. There will be losses, of course, and so, perhaps, many gaps in the garden, but these we must expect every year from many causes, and the drought may teach us some good lessons. It teaches us very forcibly how steadily plant-life goes on in spite of all hindrances. It is really sad to go round the garden during a long drought, with the lawn brown, the shrubs getting scorched, and the beds looking almost like dust-heaps. Yet no sooner does the rain come than all is at once changed, and we are taught that the garden was by no means dead, but only biding its time; it was like a man who from illness or other cause is driven into enforced idleness, but who, as soon as the cause is removed, shows that the idleness was only from temporary weakness, which ended in increased strength. Within a very few days after the rains come to us after a long drought the grass becomes of the finest green and shrubs put out fresh leaves, herbaceous plants begin to shoot upwards, and it is no exaggeration to say that all Nature rejoices.

CANON ELLACOMBE,
In a Gloucestershire Garden [1895]

FERTILIZER

There seems to be no holds barred when it comes to the weird ingredients deposited at a plant's roots.

Our own most valuable, original discovery as Old Wives was made, as surely most must have been, by mistake. The over-enthusiastic use of detergents when they first became available caused the grease in washing-up water, suspended in the bubbles, to form gradually a thick cake of fat under the manhole cover outside the kitchen window. We lifted it out, but this was in London when food rationing was still in force after the War, when the throwing in the dustbin of what looked like a mass of edible dripping, eighteen inches by twelve and at least two inches thick, was unthinkable. We buried it darkly at dead of night in the back garden – not far, as it chanced, from the roots of a climbing rose which had never done very well. That year the rose flowered stunningly, and it flourished ever after. We never planted a rose again without burying fat below it, begging extra from the surprised butcher.

When we moved to the country we continued, the first year, the same practice. Every single one of our beautiful new roses was instantly dug up by the foxes that abound in the neighbouring woods, and we have had to desist. For townsfolk, however, or those with walled gardens, it cannot be too highly recommended.

We once read of a family in France who were said to bury the unwanted babies of maidens of the villagery under their vines, presumably on the same principle, but let it not be said that we actually advocate this.

MAUREEN and BRIDGET BOLAND,
Old Wives' Lore for Gardeners [1976]

From England, too, I have this week received a new recipe for the plant that is sick or dispirited. It comes from Millie Panter-Downes. A friend of hers in Surrey was showing an ailing wisteria vine to a gardening acquaintance. 'Oh,' said the visitor, 'all that wisteria wants is a nice rice pudding. They *love* them!' Accordingly, a rice pudding was cooked, well sugared, and laid round the feet of the vine, which promptly sat up, regained its tone, and is now full of health and pudding. There is probably a chemical explanation for this, but I would rather not know about it.

KATHARINE S. WHITE in the *New Yorker* [1961]; reprinted in *Onward and Upward in the Garden* [1979]

A more sinister story was told me about another vicar, who could never be induced to part with the secret of how he grew such fabulous roses, until finally some ladies of the parish cornered him and bullied it out of him: 'I bury a cat under each bush,' he said.

MAUREEN *and* BRIDGET BOLAND,
Old Wives' Lore for Gardeners [1976]

FROST   *Evelyn records what every gardener has endured.*

I went to Say[e]s-Court to see how the frost and rigorous weather had dealt with my garden, where I found many of the greens and rare plants utterly destroyed; the oranges and myrtles very sick, the rosemary and laurel dead to all appearance, but the cypress like to endure it.

JOHN EVELYN, Diary, 4 February
1684

Vita Sackville-West encapsulates the paradox of frost for gardeners.

Frost! Use as friend; forestall as enemy.
A gardener's scrap of wisdom, simply learnt.
Rash maiden growth may be as truly burnt
By chill as fire, to dangle limp and lame.
Young leaves hang seared by frost as though by flame;
See the young tender chestnut in the wood
As though a Goth with torch had passed that way
When the three ice-saints hold their sway
In middle-May:
Saint Boniface, Saint Servais, and the boy
Saint Pancras, martyred long before he came
To manhood, with his fame
Still known to Canterbury in his church,
With legendary power to destroy
Orchards of Kent that wither at his name
At coming of his feast-day with the smirch
Of blossom browned and future apples trim
Lost at the touch of his aberrant whim.

VITA SACKVILLE-WEST,
The Garden [1946]

GARDEN DIARY   *Sooner or later a gardener will begin to make seasonal notes. Petrarch seems to have kept the first equivalent of a garden diary. Mine rests on the breakfast table to hand for daily notation as to weather and tasks done and to be done.*

Along with the urge to make a garden usually comes the urge to keep track of it in writing — to note planting dates and the weather, and the outcome. (Dorothy's peas turned out well; they were eating them all through July and into August. But I can't make out what happened to the broccoli, which on looking it up I find the English don't distinguish from cauliflower.) Once started, the habit is hard to break. It expands to include lists of plants ordered, maps of the vegetable garden (illusory because real vegetables won't conform to them), hints and comments. 'Frank says must cut back all raspberry canes longer than 4 ft., calls these rogues,' 'Try Epsom Salts on roses,' and, furiously underlined, 'Windstorm *laid corn flat*,' are random entries that strike my eye as I turn the pages of various journals kept over the last twenty years. I notice, too, the changing character of the handwriting. Some of these entries seem to have been written rather late at night, under the influence of Mr. Weston's good wine and a session of bad weather. Others flow as smoothly as a summer breeze. In both, the evidence of a state of mind is just as evident as the state of the garden and makes me wonder if the garden would exist without the journal, much as a life may appear half-lived without a diary to record it. I don't reread my notes as often as I should, and frequently find I would have saved myself considerable grief if I had. One forgets, repeats mistakes. Rereading a real diary won't, unhappily, prevent one from tumbling into the same pitfalls over and over again; a faithfully kept garden record can. And besides, one is in good company.

ELEANOUR PERÉNYI, *Green Thoughts* [1981]

Garden diaries don't change much over the centuries. Here are some entries from Gilbert White's (1720–93) which could have been written yesterday.

March

13. Planted 100 more Cabbage plants, in all 200; the rows two feet apart, & the plants one foot from each other in the rows: every other plant to be pulled up early in the summer.

14. Melon-plants begin to appear.

16. Planted Gallon of broad-beans in the lower field-garden, almost seven rows. Sowed pound of spinage, with some common radishes, which ought to have been sowed 5 weeks before, but was prevented by the wet, in the upper field garden. Sowed some celeriac between the Cucumber boxes. Sowed eight basons in the field with double-upright-larkspurs; & the two lowest with large-single-branching D.o:

19. Vast heavy rains most part of y.e day.

21. Great snow all the day, and most part of the night; which went off the next day in a stinking wet fog. Very trying weather for Hot-beds, more like Jan: than March. No sun for many Days.

23. Planted among the Holyoaks next the street in y.e New-Garden 2 Austrian Briars, 1 black Belgick rose, 1 York & Lancaster D.o: 1 marbled D.o: 1 monthly D.o: from M.r: Budd: & two large roots of the Aster – kind in the Border before the roses – very late-blowing sort.

GILBERT WHITE, *Garden Kalendar* [1758]

Across the Atlantic the future President of the United States was keeping a similar book just a few years later recording garden events at his parents' house, Shadwell.

Shadwell

1766

Mar.

30. Purple hyacinth begins to bloom.

Apr.

6. Narcissus and Puckoon open.

13. Puckoon flowers fallen.

16. A bluish colored, funnel-formed flower in low grounds in bloom.
30. Purple flag blooms, Hyacinth & Narcissus gone.

May

4. Wild honeysuckle in our woods open. – also the Dwarf flag and Violets.
7. Blue flower in low grounds vanished.
11. The purple flag, Dwarf flag, Violet & wild Honeysuckle still in bloom.

THOMAS JEFFERSON, *Garden Book*

GARDEN ROOM *Not actually a garden but a wonderful indoor adjunct of one. The author recalls her aunt's.*

The process of furnishing her Pocket was usually done in the garden-room. Like most garden rooms, that was a wholly delightful place. Comfortable, worn old chairs, a long table used for arranging flowers and countless other processes, a rocking chair which rocked to such a pitch that it was a joy for ever, a large desk containing many treasured recipes, and all those fascinating odds and ends which seem to collect themselves in old desks, and which are so much more attractive to childhood than any toys. I wonder what manner of folk invented those entrancing fittings in the desks and work-boxes of Victorian days . . .

And there was a store-cupboard in the garden-room, which was an overflow from the store-room proper. That was a store-cupboard! Apart from the home-candied rose-petals, violets, carnation-petals, cowslips, rosemary and borage flowers, the damson cheeses and so forth, to be found in every well-regulated store-room in those days, that cupboard contained triumphs of the culinary art not to be bought nowadays. Great-aunt Lancilla candied oranges whole, and when done they were like semi-transparent globes of orange gold. Before being candied a tiny hole was made in the place where the stalk was and every bit of the pulp was scraped out with a salt-spoon, a slow and delicate process. Then the oranges were steeped in a strong salt and water pickle for a week, then soaked in fresh water for two or three days, the water being changed every day. The oranges were then boiled in syrup till they cleared. (This recipe has been used for at least six generations in our family.) In candle-light, or indeed any artificial light, these candied oranges look exquisite.

And do you know whortleberry jam and jelly? Whortleberries have many different names in Britain. Scotch folk call them blaeberries, and in Surrey we call them 'hurts.' They are, I fancy, the only fruit one cannot buy in London, and so far as I know whortleberry jelly and jam are also not to be bought. I suppose the process of picking the tiny berries being so slow, added to the cost of transit, and the fact that they travel badly account for this. But is there a more delicate, delicious fruit, whether plainly stewed or made into a conserve? And I remember also the bunches of white and red currants candied whole. These were very attractive, for they looked as though they were made of glass. They seemed very 'superior' to the rose leaves, but the latter were sweet and the former very acid, in spite of their deceptive coating of sugar. Both rose and carnation petals were preserved by coating them on both sides with white of egg well beaten. It was a fascinating process, done with a tiny brush like a paint-brush. Then the petals were spread out on very

large dishes, and castor sugar carefully and evenly shaken over them. Then they were turned over, and the other side was sugared. My great-aunt invariably dried these rose petals *in the sun*, and perhaps that is why they were so sweet. When dry they were beautifully crisp and put away in layers with paper between each layer in air-tight boxes. Primroses done like this look very pretty, for the flowers are done whole. And such syrups! Elder syrup, which was very pungent and luscious, clove carnation syrup (the best of all), mint syrup (quince juice strongly flavoured with mint), and saffron syrup, of which I only remember that one of the ingredients was Canary wine. The name 'Canary wine' made an impression on me, for as a child I thought it must have something to do with canary birds, and I vaguely wondered why! The cupboard also contained many homely medicines in which in those days I took no interest at all. But I remember how often the village women came for these remedies. For great-aunt Lancilla was the trusted friend of every soul in the place. She had known all the young generation from their birth upwards, and for the scapegraces, of whom the village had quite its normal share, she had a very understanding heart. One of the scapegraces was the garden boy. Even as a child I was conscious that between such a luminary as, for instance, the coachman, and the garden boy there was a great gulf fixed, but I was equally conscious that between my great-aunt and 'the young limb' (the cook's epithet for him, not mine) there was a solid bond of comradeship.

ELEANOUR SINCLAIR ROHDE,
The Scented Garden [1931]

GRAFTING

Like so many tasks, unchanged for centuries.

> Wyth a saw thou schalt the tre kytte
> And *with* a knyfe smowth make hytte
> Klene a-tweyne the stok of the tre
> Where-yn that thy graffe schall be
> Make thy Kyttyng' of thy graffe
> By-twyne the newe & the olde staffe.

JOHN GARDENER, *The Feate of
Gardening* [c. 1440]

HEDGE TRIMMING

With mechanical hedge-trimmers, one of gardening's joys, I never know why people regard it as a chore.

> Whether the twiggy hornbeam or the beech,
> The quick, the holly, or the lime to pleach
> Or little box, or gavity of yew
> Cut into battlements to frame a view
> Before the frost can harm the wounded tips
> Throughout the days he trims and clips and snips
> As must the guardian of the child correct
> Distorted growth and tendencies to wrong,
> Suppress the weakness, countenance the strong,
> Shaping through craft and patience of the years

Into a structure seemly, firm, erect,
Batter and buttress, furious gales to scorn.

He is both gardener and architect
Working in detail on his walls and piers
Of green anatomy, his garden's frame,
Design his object, shapeliness his aim,
Yet, practical, will with big gloves protect
Plant not the vulgar privet, to your shame
Nor laurel far less noble than its name,
Lost to reminder of the Pythian game;
Nor macrocarpa, cheap, and evergreen,
And fast in growth, until some searing day
Of Winter turns it dead and bracken-brown
With nothing left to do but cut it down . . .
Plant box for edging; do not heed the glum
Advice of those unthinking orthodox
Gardeners who condemn the tidy box
As haven for the slug, through winter numb.
Slugs will find shelter, box or nany box,
Therefore plant straightly, and with August come
Clip neatly (you may also clip in May
If time allow, a double yearly trim
To make your edging thicker and more prim,)
And in the scent of box on genial day
When sun is warm as seldom in this isle,
Smell something of the South, as clippings pile . . .

VITA SACKVILLE-WEST,
The Garden [1946]

IMPROVEMENTS   *The eighteenth-century word for keeping up with the Joneses.*

(In Mr Sterling's garden)

LORD OGLEBY: Great improvements indeed, Mr Sterling! Wonderful improvments! The four Seasons in lead, the flying Mercury, and the basin with Neptune in the middle, are all in the very extreme of the fine taste. You have as many rich figures as the man at Hyde Park Corner.

STERLING: The chief pleasure of a country house is to make improvements, you know, my lord. I spare no expense, not I. – This is quite another-guess sort of a place than it was when I first took it, my lord. We were surrounded with trees. I cut down above fifty to make the lawn before the house, and let in the wind and the sun – smack-smooth, as you see. – Then I made a greenhouse out of the old laundry, and turned the brew-house into a pinery. The high octagon summer-house, you see yonder, is raised on the mast of a ship, given me by an East India captain who has turned many a thousand of my money. It commands the whole road. All the coaches and chariots, and chaises, pass and repass under your eye. I'll mount you up there in the afternoon, my lord. 'Tis the pleasantest place in the world to take a pipe and a bottle – and so you shall say, my lord.

LORD OGLEBY: Ay – or a bowl of punch, or a can of flip, Mr Sterling; for it looks like a cabin in the air. – If flying chairs were in use, the captain might make a voyage to the Indies in it still, if he had but a fair wind.

CANTON: Ha! ha! ha! ha!

MRS HEIDELBERG: My brother's a little comical in his ideas, my lord! – But you'll excuse him. – I have a little gothic dairy, fitting up entirely in my own taste – In the evening I shall hope for the honour of your lordship's company to take a dish of tea there, or a sullabub warm from the cow.

LORD OGLEBY: I have every moment a fresh opportunity of admiring the elegance of Mrs Heidelberg – the very flower of delicacy and cream of politeness.

MRS HEIDELBERG: O my lord!   *Leering at each other*

LORD OGLEBY: O madam!

> GEORGE COLMAN, *The Clandestine Marriage*, Act II, sc.i   [1766]

LABELLING

This is an example of being put down.

Do not pay much attention to labelling; if a plant is not worth knowing it is not worth growing.

> WILLIAM ROBINSON in *Gardening Illustrated*, quoted by Mea Allan, *William Robinson*   [1982]

MANURE

How lucky they were in the past to get it. The revolution in transport and modern plumbing combine to deny us such.

Stercoration Among the Ancients

Of the several Sorts of Dung us'd for Manuring of land in Italy . . .

From *Columella, Varro, Paladius*, and others of the Ancients I gather thus much concerning Stercoration, that there were three particular Sorts of Dung us'd for manuring of Land, *viz*. That of Birds, Men and Cattle.

The best Dung of Birds, is that of Pidgeons, or what is taken out of a Dove-House; the next to that is, what is voided by common Poultry; but the Dung of Water Fowl, such as Geese, Ducks, etc. is rather pernicious than helpful to Ground.

We chiefly approve of the Pidgeon Dung, because we find by Experience, that a small Quantity of it sprinkled upon Ground, enriches it extreamly.

As to that of Men, it must be mix'd with Soil taken out of the Streets, and then it will render Ground very fertile, for it is of a very hot Nature of itself, and therefore should not be us'd alone.

For the helping of bearing Vines, Man's Urine is much better; but it must first lye six Months to mellow, and digest before it be us'd; there is nothing which contributes more to the Welfare of Vines and Fruit-Trees, than this, when it has lain long enough to maturate, before we apply it to the Roots: This will make our Trees bear Abundance of Fruit; and above all, the Fruit will be much better relish'd than by any other Means we can use, especially Grapes and Apples . . .

The third Sort of Manure is the Dung of Cattle, the best of which, is that of

Asses; because those Creatures eat very slowly, and have a quick Digestion, and their food presently passes throw their bodies.

RICHARD BRADLEY, *A Survey of the Ancient Husbandry and Gardening* [1725]

Edward James always claimed that Edward VII was his father. He recalls an encounter as a child in the garden of their Sussex house, West Devon.

We were in the garden at West Dean, the King, my mother and myself, and the King said to my mother: 'Evie, how is it my gardener at Sandringham can't get the yellow arums you gave us to grow as golden as the ones here? What secret does your gardener have?'

Mr Smith, our head gardener, whose little grey moustache hung over his lower lip, standing in his Sunday best tweeds with gold watch-chain, and holding his tweed cap respectfully, looked very nervous at this question because he knew that I had discovered what was used to make the golden arums so golden. It was what he called 'night manure', human excrement which he collected from an earth closet, and my mother would have been absolutely horrified had she known because, not only were things like that never mentioned during the Edwardian era, but she herself had an especially strong phobia about the subject and, had she found out, would never have had another arum lily in the house. And I piped up, 'I know,' and Mr Smith, terrified, clapped a hand over my mouth, and my mother said, 'Smith, are you out of your mind? What are you doing stopping Master Edward talking?' The King roared with laughter because he had obviously guessed what it was that Mr Smith used to make the yellow arum lilies more yellow.

EDWARD JAMES, *Swans Reflecting Elephants* [1982]

PESTICIDES *Written it seems by an enemy of the ecological movement.*

In this situation the only adequate response is to thank God for chemical pesticides, and use them liberally. Unfortunately the strongest and most effective ones keep being withdrawn from the market on the grounds that they have been found to damage the environment. So when you hit on a really lethal sort it's a good plan to buy it in large supply, which will allow you to go on using it after it has been outlawed. I did this for several seasons with a splendid product, now also unobtainable, which wiped out everything from snails to flea beetles. It had no adverse effect on the bird population so far as I could see, though the neighbourhood cats did start to look a bit seedy. That, of course, was an advantage from my point of view, for cats are filthy, insanitary beasts, and a fearful nuisance to the gardener. One of the anomalies of English law is that whereas it would, as I understand it, be an offence to clamber over your neighbour's fence and defecate among his vegetables, you can send a feline accomplice on precisely the same errand with total impunity. It has always amazed me that manufacturers of slug bait and other such garden aids, should proudly announce on the label that their product is 'harmless to pets'. A pesticide that could guarantee to cause pets irreparable damage would, I'd have thought, sell like hot cakes.

JOHN CAREY, *The Pleasures of
Vegetable Gardening*, in *The Sunday
Times* [1980]

They are many: frogs and caterpillars are two . . .

PESTS

As touching remedies against the Frogges, which in the summer nyghtes are wont to be disquieters of the wearied husbandmen, by chyrping and loude noyse making, let the Husbandman burie in some banke fast by, the gaule of a Goat, the Frogs will not afterwarde gather in that place.

A Greek remedy against Caterpillars:

Take a few of the Caterpillars in the next Garden or Orchard, and seeth them in water with hearbe Dill, which being cold sprinkle on the hearbes or trees, or in such places where they be, and the same destroy them. But take verie diligent heede, that none of this water fall, either on your face or hands.

DIDYMUS MOUNTAIN,
The Gardener's Labyrinth [1586]

How to PRESERVE FLOWERS being PLANTED from HURTFULL things

Mole and garden Volcanoes

The worst ENEMYES to gardens are Moles, Catts, Earewiggs, Snailes and Mice, and they must bee carefully destroyed, or all your labor all the year long is lost.

Many storyes there are of pretty wayes to catch Moles, as by putting a pott in the earth with a live Mole in it, to which the rest will resort, and falling in cannot get out againe; by pouring of scalding or poyson'd waters upon their great hills where their nests are and constant dwellings; and diverse others; but I passe them over as fabulous or very little useful. The only assur'd means to destroy them is by watching them heave at sun rising & setting, and then casting them forth with a spade, or striking them with a Mole speare, but I leave this to the direction of the Mole catchers who are everywhere to bee found, and shall rather say something of preventing the mischiefes these creatures doe by well wall-in your ground, for if the foundation be anything deepe they cannot get under, for they ever run neare the face of the earth when they are underground, and if the doores shut close at the bottomes, and there bee no holes in the walls, they cannot possibly enter above ground, for they run not up precipices as ratts or mice.

As for Catts they doe much hurt in most places, espetially in Townes if not prevented, for when the earth hath beene lately digged up, as it must bee newly before the planting of your flowers, they delight to scrape in it, and urine and dung upon it. To help which there is no better way than to cover the new planted beds with netts fastned downe close upon them with pinns of wood, which must not bee removed till the earth bee well sadded, and then they are in no great danger.

Earewiggs hurt most Gilliflowers, and are taken best when they are newly podded (for they feed upon the yong pods most) with sheepes hooves stucke upon stickes by the flowers, into which they creepe in the morning to hide themselves all day, feeding all night, and then you shall bee sure of them every morning and may easily kill them.

Snayles doe the leaste harme, and may bee taken in the night in the sommer with a candle as they creepe about, or early in the morning, or after raine.

The Garden Book of Sir Thomas Hanmer [1653]

Here is a second for the same purpose.

Of a General Remedy against all Sorts of Animals Hurtful to Flowers

Here follows a Remedy which *Democritus* has left us, and which shortens the way towards destroying all Sorts of Animals that are Enemies to Plants. He bids you take about Eight or Ten Cray-fish, put them into an Earthen Pit with Water, set them out in the Air for Eight Days, and then take of the Water and sprinkle the Plants with it, for the first time, as they are peeping out of the Ground. Then Eight days after repeat the same, and, he says, you'll find your self freed from all Sorts of Insects whatsoever, for they never attempt to come near your Garden any more.

GEORGE LONDON and HENRY WISE, *The Retir'd Gard'ner* [1706]

Blackfly was just as active in the Georgian age.

As we have remarked that insects are often conveyed from one country to another in a very unaccountable manner, I shall here mention an emigration of small *Aphides*, which was observed in the village of Selborne no longer ago than August the 1st, 1785.

At about three o'clock in the afternoon of that day, which was very hot, the people of this village were surprised by a shower of *Aphides*, or smother-flies, which fell in these parts. Those that were walking in the street at that juncture found themselves covered with these insects, which settled also on the hedges and gardens, blackening all the vegetables where they lighted. My annuals were discoloured with them, and the stalks of a bed of onions were quite coated over for six days after. These armies were then, no doubt, in a state of emigration, and shifting their quarters; and might have come, as far as we know, from the great hop-plantations of Kent or Sussex, the wind being all that day in the easterly quarter. They were observed at the same time in great clouds about Farnham, and all along the vale from Farnham to Alton.

GILBERT WHITE, *Natural History of Selborne* [1788]

GREEN FLY

Of every single garden pest,
I think I hate the Green Fly best.
My hate for him is stern and strong:
I've hated him both loud and long.
Since first I met him in the spring
I've hated him like anything.

There was one Green Fly, I recall:
I hated him the most of all.
He sat upon my finest rose,
And put his finger to his nose.
Then sneered, and turned away his head
To bite my rose of royal red.

Next day I noticed, with alarm,
That he had started out to charm
A lady fly, as green in hue
As all the grass that ever grew.
He wooed, he won; she named the night –
And gave my rose another bite.

Ye gods, quoth I, if this goes on,
Before another week has gone,
These two will propagate their kind
Until one morning I shall find
A million Green Fly on my roses,
All with their fingers to their noses.

I made a fire, I stoked it hot
With all the rubbish I had got;
I picked the rose of royal red
Which should have been their bridal bed;
And on the day they twain were mated
They also were incinerated.

                    REGINALD ARKELL

GREEN FLY

Now, Mr Arkell, you're a poet,
It only needs your book to show it,
And so you must not think me mean,
But you depict on page nineteen
A Greenfly showing Sex Appeal,
While from your rose he takes his meal
And, with a further shock, I read
Something about a 'bridal bed'.
May I submit, with all respects,
You're wrong about the greenfly's sex.

Mole and garden Volcanoes

For through the summer there is none
Or else it's both rolled into one;
In fact, in language unpoetic
They call it partheno-genetic.
Its only when the autumn comes
That they develop 'dads' and 'mums'
And eggs are laid, not living young,
From which the next year's brood is sprung.
I grant you licence as a poet
But thought perhaps you'd like to know it.

F. E. PRIESTLAND, Both from
REGINALD ARKELL, *Green
Fingers* [1934]

Earwigs. The writer's father was blind.

FATHER: Roses . . . Not much of a show of roses.
SON: Not bad.
FATHER: Onions. Hardly a bumper crop would you say?
SON: I suppose not.
FATHER: Earwigs at the dahlias? You remember when you were a boy,
            you remember our great slaughter of earwigs?
SON: I remember.
FATHER: You see the dahlias?
SON: Yes.
FATHER: Describe them for me. Paint me the picture . . .
SON: Well, they're red . . . and yellow. And blowsy . . .
FATHER: (puzzled) Blowsy?
SON: They look sort of over-ripe. Middle-aged . . .
FATHER: Earwig traps in place are they?
SON: They're in place.
FATHER: When you were a boy, we often bagged a hundred earwigs in a
            single foray! Do you remember?
SON: I remember.

JOHN MORTIMER, *A Voyage Round
My Father* [1971]

At Sissinghurst the battle against pests also raged.

. . . with heedful eye
Quick as a hatching bird, the gardener roves
Precautionary, nipping mischief's bud.
For mischief buds at every joint and node,
Plentiful as the burgeon of the leaves:
Fungus and mildew, blight and spot and rust,
Canker and mould, a sallow sickly list;
The caterpillar that with hump and heave
Measures the little inches of his way;
And, pullulating more than Tartar hordes'
Despoiling as they travel, procreation
Calamitous in ravage, multitude
Unnumbered, come the insect enemies,

Tiny in sevralty, in union dire,
Clustered as dense as pile in plush – the aphis
Greening the hopeful shoot, the evil ant
Armoured like daimios, in horrid swarm
Blackening twigs, or hidden down their hole
Mining amongst the roots till flagging heads
Of plants betray their presence.
                               Gardener,
Where is your armistice? You hope for none.
It will not be, until yourself breed maggots.

Moles from the meadow will invade your plot;
Pink palm, strong snout, and velvet energy
Tunnel a system worthy of a sapper;
Heave monticules while you lie snug-a-bed,
And heave again, fresh chocolate, moist mould,
In mounds that show their diligent direction
Busy while you but break your nightly fast,
Visible evidence of secret work,
And overground the nimble hopping rabbit
Soft as a baby's toy, finds out the new
Cosseted little plants with tender hand
Set out in innocence to do their duty.
Poor gardener! poor stubborn simpleton,
Others must eat, though you be bent on
    beauty.
                        VITA SACKVILLE-WEST,
                        The Garden [1946]

For those who feel a lingering regret over extermination.

MOLE-TRAP

When we arrived the trap was empty.
An hour later, after we had talked
And admired the view, we walked
On the lawn and found him lying limply,
A fat prelatical mole
With pudgy pink hands.
While we were chatting politely, his sands
Had run out. His velvet was cool
Already to touch. He was a nuisance,
Spoiling the lawn with his heaps of earth,
Unlicensed upheavals like the birth
Of garden volcanoes. Sentence
Of death had to be passed, no doubt,
And had been carried out.
It was sentimental to regret
That clerical-looking rogue. And yet . . .
                        RUTH BIDGOOD, in *The Countryman*,
                        Winter 1968

Wooden Mole-Trap

And Beatrix Potter is responsible for every gardener's crise de conscience when eradicating the rodent rabbit.

'Now, my dears,' said old Mrs Rabbit one morning, 'you may go into the fields or down the lane, but don't go into Mr McGregor's garden: your Father had an accident there; he was put in a pie by Mrs McGregor.'

Flopsy, Mopsy, and Cottontail, who were good little bunnies, went down the lane to gather blackberries:

But Peter, who was very naughty, ran straight away to Mr McGregor's garden, and squeezed under the gate!

First he ate some lettuces and some French beans; and then he ate some radishes;

And then, feeling rather sick, he went to look for some parsley.

But round the end of a cucumber frame, whom should he meet but Mr McGregor!

Mr McGregor was on his hands and knees planting out young cabbages, but he jumped up and ran after Peter, waving a rake and calling out, 'Stop thief!'

Peter was most dreadfully frightened; he rushed all over the garden, for he had forgotten the way back to the gate.

He lost one of his shoes among the cabbages, and the other shoe amongst the potatoes.

After losing them, he ran on four legs and went faster, so that I think he might have got away altogether if he had not unfortunately run into a gooseberry net, and got caught by the large buttons on his jacket. It was a blue jacket with brass buttons, quite new.

BEATRIX POTTER, *The Tale of Peter Rabbit* [1902]

Mole and garden Voleanoes

A member of the panel of the BBC's admirable Gardeners' Question Time programme, speaking of identifying small creatures in the garden, said that as a lad he was told: 'If it moves slowly enough, step on it; if it doesn't, leave it – it'll probably kill something else.'

MAUREEN and BRIDGET BOLAND, *Old Wives' Lore for Gardeners* [1976]

I include 'Mrs M.' here amidst pests with deliberation. We have all experienced her in some form and her mental effect is far more deleterious to the gardeners than an army of aphid and blight.

Mrs M. lives not fifty miles from me, but whether to the North, South, East or West, I prefer not to say.

She is the only gardener I know who never, for one instant, recalls Ruth Draper. (I apologize for introducing that lady's name, but it had to come out, sooner or later.) Never does she walk down a border and say 'you should have seen this six weeks ago . . . the wallflowers were a *mass* . . . weren't they a mass, Ada? . . . a positive *mass*!' Nor does she pause in front of a collection of feeble shoots and say 'of course, if you'd only come next month, I don't know what you would have *said* about these dahlias . . . what could he have said about the dahlias, Ada? . . . nobody *knows* what to say about them!'

Mrs M. is not like that. I have tried to catch her garden off its guard, without success. I always seem to arrive at the crowning hour of something or other. I have a feeling that as the car draws up at the door the stocks blaze into their ultimate, purple flames, the last of the lilies open their scented lips, the final rosebud sheds its virginity and flaunts itself in a southern breeze. Things are always at their very best when I visit Mrs M. Perhaps if I stayed a little longer, till dusk fell, I might detect a weariness among the lilies, the stocks might droop, and on her hard pavements I might catch the echo of rose-leaves falling. But I can never stay long at Mrs M.'s. She annoys me too much.

She is damnably efficient. She spends next to nothing on her garden, and gets astonishing results. She shows you a blaze of delphiniums. 'All out of a penny packet,' she croons. You pass a bank flaming with golden broom. 'All from seed,' she declares. 'A shilling packet I bought years ago.' In the rockery in a sheet of purple cyclamen. It grows so profusely on the hills outside Rome that the little boys stuff bundles of them on the backs of their bicycles, in the same way that English little boys load their backs with bluebells. 'Just a few roots I stuffed into my suitcase after my visit to Italy last year,' she murmurs.

And one is sure that she went to Italy for about ten shillings, and picked up a Guardi or a Bronzino for a couple of lire, and had a suite of rooms for which she paid half a crown a night.

BEVERLEY NICHOLS, *Down the Garden Path* [1932]

POT POURRI

Every recipe for which reads like a reverie. Here is a late Victorian one.

Gather the roses on a dry day only, and lay them on sheets of newspaper to dry in the sun, then sprinkle them freely with finely powdered bay-salt. Pound smoothly together a small quantity of musk, storax, gum benjamin, dried Seville orange peel, angelica root, cloves, Jamaica pepper, coriander seed, and spirits of wine. Now take sun-dried rose leaves, clove carnations, lavender, woodruff, rosemary, and any fragrant flowers, such as orange blossom, violets, &c., and place them in layers in a china or earthenware jar, alternately with salt and the pounded spices mentioned above. Or, pound very fine 1 lb. bay-salt, 2 oz. saltpetre, ¼ oz. each of cloves and allspice, and mix these thoroughly with a grated nutmeg, the very finely pared rind of four lemons (being careful to omit all white pith), 1 dr. of musk, 1 oz. of bergamot, 6 dr. powdered orris root, and 1 dr. each of spirits of lavender, essence of lemon, and storax. Have ready minced a handful each of bay leaves, rosemary, myrtle, lemon thyme, and sweet verbena. Place these all, when well hand-mixed, into a jar with a close-fitting lid, adding to them, as you can get them, six handfuls of sweet-smelling and dried rose leaves, three of orange blossom, three of clove pinks, and two each of rosemary flowers, lavender flowers, jasmine flowers, and violets. The roses must be gathered on a perfectly dry day, and may then, if liked, be placed in the jar at once – and the same applies to the other blossoms, for all sweet-scented flowers (as long as they are not succulent) can be used for pot-pourri – stirring them all well into the mixture, for pot-pourri cannot be too much stirred, especially at first. But remember no flowers must be added while the least damp, either from rain or dew. If the pot-pourri appears to become too dry, add more

Umbrella Rose Trainer

bay-salt and saltpetre; if too moist, add more spice and orris root; but always start your beau-pot (as our grandmothers called it) with the quantities given above, adding more flowers from time to time, as the spice retains its strength for years. As to the best flowers for the purpose, the old cabbage roses are really the most fragrant, but any kinds will do as long as they are dry; still, to have the scent perfect, there should be a strong proportion of the old-fashioned blooms; the more modern tea-roses are almost too faint to be entirely relied on. The question of drying simply depends on how long it takes to remove any moisture from the rose leaves. If gathered on a hot, sunny day, when absolutely dry, they need little, if any, exposure to the sun.

Recipe dated 1890

POTTING SHED

In her account of life in a country house before the Second World War Lesley Lewis recalls the role of the potting shed. This particular hub of the garden was at Pilgrims' Hall, near Ongar in Essex, into which the family moved in 1913.

Just as the tack room was the nerve-centre of the stables, the potting shed was that of the garden. It was a lean-to of black boarding with a cement floor, up against one of the outside walls of the kitchen garden. As you entered you saw on your right a pit in which stood the coke stove providing heat for the vinery and two other greenhouses, and making the potting shed comfortable on cold days. So comfortable indeed was the place on the wall where the chimney came up that the peacock, named Gabriel Junks out of Surtees' *Handley Cross*, insisted on perching there nearly all the time, instead of displaying on the lawns. What with this, his screeching and his depredations on the garden, he was not replaced when he died a natural death, and the uninteresting peahen was returned to Kelvedon Hall, whence they had both come. The vinery, on which the head gardener spent a lot of time, stood outside the main walled garden, with a big manured area around it for the roots. The other greenhouses were within the walls and nurtured peaches, nectarines, the succession of pot plants for the porch and conservatory, bulbs and seedlings. On the left of the outer part of the shed was a wooden wheelbarrow; the top half of its container lifted off, according to whether the load to be carried was bulky and light, such as dead leaves, or heavy soil and gravel. Nearby were two boards, about fifteen inches by eight, for scraping up leaves after they had been swept into piles with birch brooms, which stood in a row. Here too were kept large tools not in frequent use; wooden hay rakes, pitchforks, the scythe and, very conspicuous, the four huge leather boots worn by Prospero when he pulled the big mowing-machine once a week. For a day or two afterwards the lawn would have wide regular stripes, demonstrating the great precision with which he was guided and turned. Neither fickle Lady Gay nor our spoilt riding ponies, Pedlar and Peter Pan, would have anything to do with this operation but started playing up as soon as they saw the boots, and would have kicked the machine to pieces.

The inner part of the potting shed was well lit by a window running the length of the high bench used for potting, sowing in boxes and pricking out. The one kitchen chair was seldom sat on, nearly everything being done standing at the bench. There was a cupboard for seeds, fertilizers, small tools, catalogues and string, while a hank of bass hung from the handle. Whole flowerpots of varying sizes were kept under the bench and on one end were the broken ones which provided the crocks put at the bottom of a pot for drainage. A hammer for reducing them to handy sizes lay near and this was a job for wet days. All round the boarded walls were hooks or large nails for tools – sharp-edged spades, the wider shovels, forks, iron rakes, hoes, trowels and sickles. They were kept oiled and rust-free in a beautiful orderliness, the art of which must have been instilled into gardeners for generations, and passed on by them to their juniors. It was rare for new tools to be bought and the handles of the old ones acquired an inimitable satiny finish from years of use. The potting shed régime was very strict but if you properly looked after any tools you used, cleaned and put them back in the right place, never touched the scythe and did jobs at the bench in the approved manner, your presence might be tolerated for long periods. I much preferred these sessions to working in my own patch of garden with the miniature tools provided for our special use.

LESLEY LEWIS, *The Private Life of a Country House* [1980]

SNUFF

Method of scenting snuff.

The Flowers that most readily communicate their flavour to Snuff are Orange Flowers, Jasmine, Musk Roses, and Tuberoses. You must procure a box lined with dry white paper; in this strow your Snuff on the bottom about the thickness of an inch, over which place a thin layer of Flowers, then another layer of Snuff, and continue to lay your Flowers and Snuff alternately in this manner, until the box is full. After they have lain together four and twenty hours, sift your Snuff through a sieve to separate it from the Flowers, which are to be thrown away, and fresh ones applied in their room in the former method. Continue to do this till the Snuff is sufficiently scented; then put it into a canister, which keep close stopped.

The Country Lady's Directory [1732]

SWEET BAGS

To make little cusshins of parfumed Roses.
Take buddes of redde Roses, their heades and toppes cut awaye, drie them in the shadowe upon a table, or a linnen cloath: water and sprinkle the sayde buddes with Rose water, and let them drie, doynge this five or sixe times, turning them alwayes, to the end they waxe not mouldy: than take the poudre of Cipre, Muske & Amber, made into a pouder according as you woulde make them excellent, for the more you put in of it the better they shal be: put to it also Lignum aloes well beaten in pouder. Let the saide pouder be put w.th the budds wete with rose water, mixing well the budds together with the pouder, to thend al may be wel incorporated, so shal you leave them so al a night, covering them w.th som linnen cloth or Taffeta that the musk may not breath or rise out. The whiche thing done, take finallye lyttle bagges of Taffeta of what bignesse you wil, and according to the quantitie of the buddes that you would put among all the pouder. Then close up the bagges, and for to stop up the seames, you must have your mixion of Muske, Amber, & Civette, made as it were to seare with, wherewith you shall rubbe all a longe the seames, to stoppe the holes made with the needle in sowinge: you

may also sowe ribande (of gold or silke, or what you will) over the said seames. These be the best that a man can make: and (as I have sayed) the more Musk, Amber, Civet & Aloe you put in the better thei will be. If you wyll make them with lesse cost, take such buddes as are spoken of before, prepared and ordered in the same sort, and in steede of Muske and Amber, put in the pouder of Cloves, Synamom, & a little Mace, observing such a manner of parfuming the buddes as before.

The secretes of the reverent Maister
Alexis of Piemont, in SIR HUGH PLATT
Delights for Ladies [1594]

SWEET WATER   *This recipe presupposes the desecration of a very large rose garden. To make sweet water of the best kind . . .*

Take a thousand Damask Roses, two good handfuls of Lavender tops, a three-penny weight of Mace, two ounces of Cloves bruised, a quart of running water: put a little water into the bottom of an earthen pot, and then put in your Roses and Lavender, with the Spices by little and little, and in the putting in, always knead them down with your fist, and so continue it untill you have wrought up all your Roses and Lavender, and in the working put in always a little of your water: then stop your pot close, and let it stand in four dayes, in which time every morning and evening put in your hand and pull .from the bottom of your pot the said Roses, working it for a time, and then distill it, and having in the glass of water a grain or two of Musk wrapt up in a piece of Sarcenet or fine cloth.   GERVASE MARKHAM, *The English House-Wife* [1625]

TOOLS   *How remarkably little these have changed.*

. . . a fork, a wide blade, a spade or shovel, a knife . . . a seed-basket for seed-time, a wheel-barrow (more often a little hand-cart), basket, pannier and trap for sparrow-hawks . . . a two-edged axe to uproot thorns, brambles, briars, prickles and unwanted shoots, and rushes and wood to mend hedges . . . timbers, palings, and stakes or hedging hurdles . . . he should also have a knife hanging from his belt to graft trees and seedlings, mattocks with which to uproot nettles or vetch, darnel, thistles, sterile oats and weeds of this sort, and a hoe for tare . . .

ALEXANDER OF NECKHAM,
De Utensilibus, twelfth century

TREE PLANTING

The "Godiva" Lawn Mower

On the slope behind the house today
I cut through roots and rocks and
Dug a hole, deep and wide,
Carted away from it each stone
And all the friable, thin earth.
Then I knelt there a moment, walked
In the old woods, bent down again, using
A trowel and both my hands to scoop
Black, decaying woods-soil with the warm
Smell of fungi from the trunk of a rotting
Chestnut tree – two heavy buckets full I carried

Back to the hole and planted the tree inside;
Carefully I covered the roots with peaty soil,
Slowly poured sun-warmed water over them,
Mudding them gently until the soil settled.
It stands there, young and small,
Will go on standing when we are gone
And the huge uproar, endless urgency and
Fearful delirium of our days forgotten . . .

HERMANN HESSE, *Page from a Journal* [1953], translated by Rika Lesser

---

Anyone who has attempted to save or fell a tree in a public place will know the emotions unleashed for which this poem is not a little responsible.

TREE FELLING

THROWING A TREE (New Forest)

The two executioners stalk over the knolls,
Bearing two axes with heavy heads shining and wide,
And a long limp two-handled saw toothed for cutting great boles,
And so they approach the proud tree that bears the death-mark on its
    side.

Jackets doffed they swing axes and chop away just above ground,
And the chips fly about and lie white on the moss and fallen leaves;
Till a broad deep gash in the bark is hewn all the way round,
And one of them tries to hook upward a rope, which at last he
    achieves.
The saw then begins, till the top of the tall giant shivers:
The shivers are seen to grow greater each cut than before:
They edge out the saw, tug the rope; but the tree only quivers,
And kneeling and sawing again, they step back to try pulling once
    more.

Then, lastly, the living mast sways, further sways: with a shout
Job and Ike rush aside. Reached the end of its long staying powers
The tree crashes downward: it shakes all its neighbours throughout,
And two hundred years' steady growth has been ended in less than two
    hours.   THOMAS HARDY [1840–1928]

All of us who have retreated drenched to the house for a change of clothes will recognize this.

WATERING

One would think that watering a little garden is quite a simple thing, especially if one has a hose. It will soon be clear that until it has been tamed a hose is an extraordinarily evasive and dangerous beast, for it contorts itself, it jumps, it wriggles, it makes puddles of water, and dives with delight into the mess it has made; then it goes for the man who is going to use it and coils itself round his legs; you must hold it down with your foot, and then it rears and twists round your waist and neck, and while you are fighting with it as

Water Butt on wheels

with a cobra, the monster turns up its brass mouth and projects a mighty stream of water through the windows on to the curtains which have been recently hung. You must grasp it firmly, and hold it tight; the beast rears with pain, and begins to spout water, not from the mouth, but from the hydrant and from somewhere in the middle of its body. Three men at least are needed to tame it at first, and they all leave the place of battle splashed to the ears with mud and drenched with water; as to the garden itself, in parts it has changed into greasy pools, while in other places it is cracking with thirst.

KAREL ČAPEK, *The Gardener's Year* [1909]

WEEDING *Weeders in the past were women (see pp. 22–5).*

Above all, be careful not to suffer weeds (especially nettles, dandelion, groundsel, and all downy-plants) to run up to seed; for they will in a moment infect the whole ground: wherefore, whatever work you neglect, ply weeding at the first peeping of ye Spring . . . Note that whilst the gardener rolls or rows, the weeder is to sweep and cleanse in the same method, and never to be taken from that work 'til she have finished: first the gravel walks and flower-borders; then the kitchen-gardens; to go over all this she is allowed one month every three-months, with the gardeners assistance of the haw, and rough digging: where curious hand-weeding is less necessary.

JOHN EVELYN, *Directions for the Gardener at Says-Court* [1686]

Weeding here seems to take on the role of some kind of therapy.

But father disregarded our protests and obstinately pursued his destructive activities. His enjoyment of weeding was a positive danger. He would begin dreamily enough plucking here and there a stray plaintain, a red groundsel, a mustard plant, all of them easy enough to get out. Then he would catch sight of a more tenacious foe, a buttercup or a wild sorrel, and would tug at it fiercely. Sometimes it would be a bind-weed with an interminable root, sometimes a cinquefoil, sometimes a dandelion refusing to budge. Then he would kneel down and begin to dig; first with the one hand and then with the other he would tug at the couch-grass, the euphorbias, and grasses. A sort of rage overmastered him, he seemed incapable of leaving the ground till he had got rid of every single weed. But suddenly I would hear him swear and see him stop dead as he realized that he had made a mistake and torn up a perfectly good plant, a strawberry or an innocent salad. Then he would begin again, laying wildly about him with a reaping-hook, and again I would hear him swear: another good plant sacrificed. Beside himself with fury he would pull and tug in all directions at the good and the bad plants alike with the same wrathful gesture.

Needless to say the garden suffered. My father paid no heed to our objections, but would look about the open spaces where his talent had had its way, and say in an offended tone: 'No matter how much trouble I take over the garden you children never seem pleased.' . . .

GEORGES DUHAMEL, *In Sight of the Promised Land*, translated by Béatrice de Holthoir [1935]

Here is someone with a sympathy for these invaders of garden order.

I am sorry to say that the April record of the garden would be very incomplete without some mention of the weeds; for it is in April they first show themselves, and some of them only in April. In new gardens it is possible, and not very difficult, to keep the weeds under; but in old gardens it is almost impossible. It is an old and very true gardening proverb, that one year's seed is many years' weed; or as Hamlet laments, 'An unweeded garden grows to seed,' and so 'things rank and gross in nature possess it merely.' In the history of an old garden there must have often been a one year's seed; and there must be in it from time to time many an unweeded corner. But I have almost an affection for weeds, a decided affection for some of them, and I have not much sympathy with those who say that a garden is not worth looking at unless it is as clean as a newly-swept floor; it is a counsel of perfection, which I have no great wish to reach. A weed is but a good plant in the wrong place; I say a *good* plant advisedly, having a full faith that where nature plants it, it fills a right place. Daisies are not perhaps in their right place in lawns, but I should be sorry to see my lawn quite free from them, and so I am sure would the children. Buttercups have a shining beauty of petal that is not surpassed by any flowers, and I do not think that Jean Ingelow's comparison of a field of buttercups to the Field of the Cloth of Gold, to the great advantage of the buttercups, is much exaggerated; but they must be kept out of the garden. The weeds that chiefly trouble me in April are the two veronicas, *V. agrestis* and *V. Buxbaumi*; either of them might lay claim to the title of 'the little speedwell's darling blue,' and they are so short-lived that they do little real harm; still, they give a good deal of trouble. But some weeds are so beautiful that I should certainly grow them in the garden, if only they could be kept in place, and if they were not already too abundant. I should be sorry to banish from my walls the creeping toad-flax and the yellow fumitory, and as long as they keep to the walls they do no harm. But there are two plants that are sad weeds, but which, if lost, would be sorely missed. The dandelion is one –

> 'The flower
> That blows a globe of after arrowlets.'

Surely no other flower can surpass it for beauty of foliage, beauty of shape, and rich beauty of colouring. The second weed that I often wish to transplant into my garden, but dare not, is the goosegrass, or silver weed, *Potentilla anserina*. Its beautiful leaves have a silver sheen that make it very attractive; but it is better kept outside the garden, and it grows everywhere. It is found in the Arctic regions and it is found in New Zealand, and so has as wide a range as almost any known plant, except, perhaps, the little fern *Cystopteris fragilis*, which not only grows as far north as lat. 76 deg., and as far south as New Zealand, but was also found by Whymper in the Equatorial Andes.

But it is not only for their beauty that I have an affection for some of the weeds, but, speaking as a gardener, I am sure that they are often very useful. We may see how in a hedgerow the most delicate plants nestle themselves close to and under those of the coarsest growth, and seem all the better for it; and I have seen many instances in which delicate seeds and young cuttings have been saved when protected by weeds, when those not so protected have

perished. One of the most interesting gardens and the most untidy I ever saw was Professor Syme's in Fifeshire. It was a mass of weeds, and rampant weeds; but among the weeds, and apparently rejoicing in them was a collection of some of the rarest plants, growing in greater luxuriance than I have ever seen elsewhere. The weeds keep the earth moist, and prevent the radiation of heat, and how much they do so most of us can see by observing the plantains on our lawns. I am not fond of plantains on lawns, and get rid of them; but some will remain, and on them I have often noticed that in a slight hoar-frost no hoar-frost is formed on the plantains; the broad leaves lying flat on the ground keep in the earth-heat. I am tempted to say more about weeds and their uses, but instead of doing so I will refer – and those who do not know the book will thank me for doing so – to one of Burroughs' charming little books, *Pepacton*, where there is a long chapter on the use and beauty of weeds. I will, however, quote another American writer, Hawthorne, who is quite enthusiastic in his praise of weeds. 'There is,' he says, 'a sort of sacredness about them. Perhaps if we could penetrate Nature's secrets we should find that what we call weeds are more essential to the well-being of the world than the most precious fruit or grain.' This is perhaps somewhat exaggerated, but there is a good truth in it.

CANON ELLACOMBE,
In a Gloucestershire Garden [1895]

That leader of fashion, the Duchess of Queensberry, found a use for them in what must have been a remarkable dress.

The Duchess of Queensberry's clothes pleased me best; they were white satin embroidered, the bottom of the petticoat *brown hills* covered with all sorts of weeds, and *every breadth* had *an old stump of a tree* that run almost to the top of the petticoat, broken and ragged and worked with brown chenille, round which twined nasturtians, ivy, honeysuckles, periwinkles, convolvuluses and all sorts of twining flowers which spread and covered the petticoat, vines with leaves variegated as you have seen them by the sun, all rather smaller than nature, which made them look very light; the robings and facings were little green banks with all sorts of weeds, and the sleeves and the rest of the gown loose twining branches of the same sort as those on the petticoat; many of the leaves were finished with gold, and part of the stumps of the trees looked like gilding of the sun. I never saw a piece of work so prettily fancied, and am quite angry with myself for not having the same thought, for it is infinitely handsomer than mine, and could *not* cost *much more*.

Mrs Delany to Mrs Dewes, February
1741

WINTER WORK   *Thomas Coke commissioned Henry Wise and George London in 1704 to create the gardens at Melbourne Hall, Derbyshire which still survive. Here, in an undated note, he gives instructions.*

Things to be done this Winter in my garden whilst I am away . . . To make a bed behind ye espalier but close to it of violetts . . . To make ye little Grove of trees on ye left hand of the lower garden fitt to walk in, to make Thicketts in it of Roses of severall sorts and hony Suckles, Lee Locks, Seringos and in ye middle a close arbour. To enquire what will grow up the soonest to cover it and what it was Verio planted at Windsor which grew up soe very fast to be a Shade.

Quoted in DAVID GREEN, Gardener to Queen Anne [1956]

The forgotten toilers of the garden and, above all, the compost heap.   WORMS

In their native soil, worms are so careful and so gentle. Under the apple trees in the garden the first flakes of blossom are lying; and, after dark, when the dew is falling, and condensing on the white petals, the worms move up their galleries from the lower earth and put out their heads and feel the night air. They listen – not with ears, but with their entire bodies, which are sensitive to light and to all ground vibration. Then, feeling that it is safe, one after another begins to move out of its tunnel, and with eager pointed head, to search for petals of fallen apple-blossom. When a petal is found, it is taken in the worm's mouth and the worm withdraws into the tunnel, and leaves the petal outside the hole. Then the worm moves out again in another direction, casting about until it finds another flake. This, too, is taken to the entrance of the tunnel . . .

When the worm has, and so carefully, gathered about a dozen petals at the mouth of its tunnel, it picks them up in its mouth, one after the other, and then goes down into the darkness and eats them. Thus the night-wanderer turns blossom into the finest soil, or humus, which feeds the roots of the tree once more. Worms are soil-makers; and their galleries and tunnels act as drains to the top-soil. They are poets, choosing at their annual spring festival the choicest food and converting it, after much enjoyment, into food for the trees again. Like poets, they are the natural priests of the earth.

HENRY WILLIAMSON, Goodbye West Country [1936]

PART
VIII

SOME

FAMOUS
GARDENERS

Eve was an early convert to the division of labour between husband and
wife in the garden.

> *Adam*, well may we labour still to dress
> This Garden, still to tend Plant, Herb and Flour.
> Our pleasant task enjoyn'd, but till more hands
> Aid us, the work under our labour grows,
> Luxurious by restraint; what we by day
> Lop overgrown, or prune, or prop, or bind,
> One night or two with wanton growth derides
> Tending to wilde. Thou therefore now advise
> Or hear what to my mind first thoughts present,
> Let us divide our labours, thou where choice
> Leads thee, or where most needs, whether to wind
> The Woodbine round this Arbour, or direct
> The clasping Ivie where to climb, while I
> In yonder Spring of Roses intermixt
> With Myrtle, find what to redress till Noon:
> For while so near each other thus all day
> Our task we choose, what wonder if so near
> Looks intervene and smiles, or object new
> Casual discourse draw on, which intermits
> Our dayes work brought to little, though begun
> Early, and th'hour of Supper comes unearn'd.

It was, however, at a cost for in the garden lurked the Serpent.

> . . . , *Eve* separate he spies,
> Veil'd in a Cloud of Fragrance, where she stood,
> Half spi'd, so thick the Roses bushing round
> About her glowd, oft stooping to support
> Each Flour of slender stalk, whose head though gay
> Carnation, Purple, Azure, or spect with Gold,
> Hung drooping unsustained, them she upstaies
> Gently with Mirtle band, mindless the while,
> Her self, though fairest unsupported Flour,
> From her best prop so farr, and storm so nigh.
> Neerer he drew, and many a walk travers'd
> Of stateliest Covert, Cedar, Pine, or Palme,
> Then voluble and bold, now hid, now seen

Among thick-wov'n Arborets and Flours
Imborderd on each Bank, the hand of *Eve*:
Spot more delicious then those Gardens feign'd
Or of reviv'd *Adonis*, or renowned
Alcinous, host of old *Laertes* son,
Or that, not Mystic, where the Sapient King
Held dalliance with his faire *Egyptian* Spouse.

JOHN MILTON, *Paradise Lost*,
Book IX [1667]

JOHN BARTRAM
(1699–1777)

John Bartram established what was the first botanical garden in what was to become the United States. He was to be a major source for the introduction of American trees and plants to England as this letter to him from the London Quaker merchant, Peter Collinson, reveals.

Please to remember those Solomon's Seals, that escaped thee last year.

The great and small Hellebore are great rarities here, so pray send a root or two of each next year. Please to remember all your sorts of lilies, as they happen in thy way; and your spotted Martagons will be very acceptable.

The Devil's Bit, or Blazing Star, pray add a root or two, and any of the Lady's Slippers.

My dear friend, I only mention these plants; but I beg of thee not to neglect thy more material affairs to oblige me. A great many may be put in a box 20 inches or 2 feet square, and 15 or 16 inches high; – and a foot in earth is enough. This may be put under the captain's bed, or set in the cabin, if it is sent in October or November. Nail a few small narrow laths across it, to keep the cats from scratching it . . .

Pray what is your Sarsaparilla? The May-apple, a pretty plant, is what I have had for some years sent to me per Doctor Witt. It flowers well with us; but our summers are not enough to perfect its fruit.

The pretty humble beautiful plant, with a spike of yellow flowers, I take to be a species of Orchis or Satyrion. What sort of roots it has thee hath not mentioned. If it is taken up with the earth about the roots, it will certainly flower the first, if not the second year. I wish thee'd send me two or three roots, if it is plenty.

The Ground Cypress is a singular pretty plant. If it bears berries or seeds, pray send some; and if it bears flowers or seeds, pray send some specimens in both states.

Pray send me a good specimen or two of the shrub, three feet high, that grows by the water courses. The shrub that grows out of the sides of rocks, sometimes five or six feet high, bearing red berries hanging by the husks, is called Euonymus, or Spindle tree. We have the same plant, with a small difference; grows plenty in England.

Your wild Senna, with yellow flowers, is a pretty plant. Send seeds of both this and Mountian Goat's Rue.

Thee need not collect any more of the White Thorn berries, than has prodigious long, sharp thorns. It is what we call the Cock-spur Thorn. I had a tree last year, that had at least a bushel of berries. But haws of any other sort of Thorns will be very acceptable.

Pray send me a root or two of cluster-bearing Solomon's Seal. It is in all appearance a very rare plant, – as is the Panax.

Pray send a root or two of Joseph Breintnall's Snake-root. Pray send a root of the grassy leaves, that bears pretty little blue flowers, – that's good against obstructions of the bowels. [probably *Sisyrinchium, L.*]

When it happens in thy way, send me a root or two of the little tuberous root called Devil's Bit, which produced one or two leaves yearly.

I only barely mention these plants; not that I expect thee to send them. I don't expect or desire them, but as they happen to be found accidentally: and what is not to be met with one year, may be another . . .

PETER COLLINSON TO JOHN
BARTRAM, 20 January 1735

WILLIAM BECKFORD (1759–1854)

The 'Caliph' of Fonthill expected the transformations to his garden to be carried out with a speed exceeding even that of the building of the famous Abbey.

In confirmation of our idea that Mr Beckford's enjoyments consisted of a succession of violent impulses, we may mention that, when he wished a new walk to be cut in the woods, or any work of that kind to be done, he used to say nothing about it in the way of preparation, but merely gave orders, perhaps late in the afternoon, that it should be cleared out in a perfect state by the following morning at the time he came out to take his ride. The whole strength of the village was then put in requisition, and employed during the night; and the next day, when Mr Beckford came to inspect what was done, if he was pleased with it, he used to give a 5*l.* or a 10*l.* note to the men who had been employed to drink, besides, of course, paying their wages, which were always liberal.

JOHN CLAUDIUS LOUDON, *Calls in
Hertfordshire, Bedfordshire, Berkshire,
Surrey, Sussex and Middlesex*   [1833]

JACOB BOBART (1641–1719)

A German visiting Oxford describes his encounter with the superintendent of the Physic Garden and the university's Professor of Botany.

We entered the Hortus Medicus and Professor Bobart was waiting for us. I was greatly shocked by the hideous features and generally villainous appearance of this good and honest man. His wife, a filthy old hag, was with him, and although she may be the ugliest of her sex he is certainly the more repulsive of the two. An unusually pointed and very long nose, little eyes set deep in the head, a twisted mouth almost without upper lip, a great deep scar in one cheek and the whole face and hands as black and coarse as those of the poorest gardener or farm-labourer. His clothing and especially his hat were also very bad. Such is the aspect of the Professor, who might most naturally be taken for the gardener. In point of fact he does nothing but work continually in the garden, and in the science of botany he is the careful gardener rather than the learned expert. Yet the industry of the man in publishing the works of his predecessor Morison, who far excelled him in learning, is as praiseworthy as his work in the garden.

ZACHARIAS VON UFFENBACH,
Oxford in 1710

A Border of Beds

CHARLES
BRIDGEMAN
(died 1738)

The creator of Stowe and Gardener to George II whose pioneering of the English landscape style won him the plaudits of Horace Walpole . . .

Bridgeman . . . banished verdant sculpture, and did not even revert to the square precision of the foregoing age. He enlarged his plans, disdained to make every division tally to its opposite; and though he still adhered much to straight walks with high clipped hedges, they were only his great lines; the rest he diversified by wilderness, and with loose groves of oak, though still within surrounding hedges . . . In the royal garden at Richmond [he] dared to introduce cultivated fields, and even morsels of a forest appearance, by the sides of those endless and tiresome walks, that stretched out of one into another without intermission.   HORACE WALPOLE, *The History of the Modern Taste in Gardening* [1771–80]

and, equally, the condemnation of Stephen Switzer.

This aiming at an incomprehensible Vastness, and attempting at Things beyond the reach of Nature, is in a great measure owing to a late eminent Designer in Gardening, whose Fancy could not be bounded; and this Notion has been in many Places carried so far, that no Parterre or Lawn that was not less than 50 or 60 Acres, some of them 80, 90, or 100, were by him esteemed capacious enough, though it sometimes took up the whole Area of Ground, and made the Building or Mansion-house in the middle look very small, and by no means proportionable to it.

   The same extravagant way of thinking prevailed also to a great degree, in that otherwise ingenious Designer, in his Plan of Lakes and Pieces of Water, without any regard to the Goodness of the Land, which was to be over-flowed: But which he generally designed so large, as to make a whole Country look like an Ocean.   STEPHEN SWITZER, *Ichnographia Rustica* [1718 and 1742]; from 'A Prooemial Essay' to vol. 1 [1742]

LANCELOT
'CAPABILITY'
BROWN
(1715–83)

Beautiful though 'Capability' Brown's landscapes strike us today, he was the 'great destroyer' of England's formal garden heritage. Even in his own time it is difficult to find much written in his favour.

Improvement too, the idol of the age,
Is fed with many a victim. Lo, he comes!
Th'omnipotent magician, Brown, appears!
Down falls the venerable pile, th'abode
Of our forefathers – a grave whisker'd race,
But tasteless. Springs a palace in its stead,
But in a distant spot; where, more expos'd
It may enjoy th'advantage of the north,
And anguish east, till time shall have transform'd
Those naked acres to a shelt'ring grove.
He speaks. The lake in front becomes a lawn;
Woods vanish, hills subside, and vallies rise:
And streams, as if created for his use,
Pursue the track of his directing wand,
Sinuous or straight, now rapid and now slow,

Now murm'ring soft, now roaring in cascades –
Ev'n as he bids! Th'enraptur'd owner smiles.
Tis finish'd, and yet, finish'd as it seems,
Still wants a grace, the loveliest it could show,
A mine to satisfy th'enormous cost.

WILLIAM COWPER, *The Task*,
Book III, *The Garden* [1785]

His great rival was Sir William Chambers who referred to him as amongst the 'kitchen gardeners well skilled in culture of salads' and also as one of the 'peasants [who] emerge from the melon ground to take the periwig and turn professor'.

Whole woods have been swept away to make room for a little grass and a few American weeds. Our virtuosi have scarcely left an acre of shade, nor three trees growing in a line, from Land's End to the Tweed, and if their humour for devastation continues to rage much longer there will not be a forest-tree left standing in the whole Kingdom.

SIR WILLIAM CHAMBERS,
*A Dissertation on Oriental
Gardening* [1772]

One of the most poignant of all the encounters in the Gospels.

CHRIST

But Mary stood without at the sepulchre weeping: and as she wept, she stooped down, and looked into the sepulchre, and seeth two angels in white sitting, the one at the head, and the other at the feet, where the body of Jesus had lain. And they say unto her, 'Woman, why weepest thou?' She saith unto them, 'Because they have taken away my Lord, and I know not where they have laid him.' And when she had thus said, she turned herself back, and saw Jesus standing, and knew not that it was Jesus. Jesus saith unto her, 'Woman, why weepest thou? whom seekest thou?' She, supposing him to be the gardener, saith unto him, 'Sir, if thou have borne him hence, tell me where thou hast laid him, and I will take him away.' Jesus saith unto her, 'Mary.' She turned herself, and saith unto him, 'Rabboni.'

ST JOHN'S GOSPEL, Chapter 20

A motif taken up by Kipling in his short story 'The Gardener'.

A men knelt behind a line of headstones – evidently a gardener, for he was firming a young plant in the soft earth. She went towards him, her paper in her hand. He rose at her approach and without prelude or salutation asked: 'Who are you looking for?'

'Lieutenant Michael Turrell – my nephew,' said Helen slowly and word for word, as she had many thousands of times in her life.

The man lifted his eyes and looked at her with infinite compassion before he turned from the fresh-sown grass toward the naked black crosses.

'Come with me,' he said, 'and I will show you where your son lies.'

When Helen left the cemetery she turned for a last look. In the distance she saw the man bending over his young plants; and she went away, supposing him to be the gardener.

RUDYARD KIPLING, *Debits and
Credits* [1926]

SIR JOHN DANVERS
(1588?–1655)

Creator of two famous gardens in the Renaissance style in the Jacobean period at Chelsea and at Lavington, Wiltshire.

The Pleasure and Use of Gardens were unknown to our great Grandfathers: They were contented with Pot-herbs: and did mind chiefly their Stables. But in the time of King Charles II Gardening was much improved, and became common. 'Twas Sir John Danvers of Chelsey (Brother and Heir to Henry Danvers Earle of Danby) who first taught us the way of Italian Gardens: He had well travelled France & Italy, and made good Observations: He had in a faire Body an harmonicall Mind: In his Youth his Complexion was so exceedingly beautifull and fine that Thomas Bond Esqr. (who was his Companion in his Travells) did say, that the People would come after him in the Street to admire Him. He had a very fine Fancy, which lay (chiefly) for Gardens, and Architecture. The Garden at Chelsey in Middlesex (as likewise the House there) doe remaine Monuments of his Ingenuity. He was a great acquaintance and Favorite of the Lord Chancellor Bacon, who took much delight in that elegant Garden.   JOHN AUBREY, *Brief Lives* [1626–1697]

ADRIAN GILBERT

Gilbert was gardener to William Herbert, 3rd Earl of Pembroke (1580–1630). His skills must have been remarkable as this description of the garden at Wilton even before the famous 1630s one (see pp. 324–5) reveals.

Amongst the rest, the pains and industry of an ancient gentleman, Mr Adrian Gilbert, must not be forgotten: for there he (much to my Lord's cost and his own pains) used such a deal of intricate setting, grafting, planting, inoculating, railing, hedging, plashing, turning, winding, returning, circular, triangular, quadrangular, orbicular, oval, and every way curiously and chargeably conceited: there hath he made walks, hedges and arbours, of all manner of most delicate fruit trees, planting them and placing them in such admirable art-like fashions, resembling both divine and moral remembrances, as three arbours standing in a triangle, having each a recourse to a greater arbour in the midst, resemble three in one and one in three; and he hath there planted certain walks and arbours all with fruit trees, so pleasing and ravishing to the sense, that he calls it 'Paradise', in which he plays the part of a true Adamist, continually toiling and tilling.

Moreover, he hath made his walks most rarely round and spaceous, one walk without another (as the rinds of an onion are greatest without, and less towards the centre) and withal the hedges betwixt each walk are so thickly set one cannot see through from one walk who walks in the other; that, in conclusion, the work seems endless; and I think that in England it is not to be followed, or in haste will be followed.

JOHN TAYLOR, *A New Discovery by Sea, with a Wherry from London to Salisbury* [1623]

THOMAS
JEFFERSON
(1743–1826)

Jefferson began keeping a garden book at the age of twenty-two and its contents cover half a century of gardening at Monticello. Here he writes to his horticultural friend, William Hamilton, of his admiration for the English landscape style.

Having decisively made up my mind for retirement at the end of my present time, my views and attentions are all turned homewards. I have hitherto been engaged in my buildings which will be finished in the course of the present year. The improvement of my grounds has been reserved for my occupation on my return home. For this reason it is that I have put off to the fall of the year after next the collection of such curious trees as will bear our winters in the open air.

The grounds which I destine to improve in the style of the English gardens are in a form very difficult to be managed. They comprise the northern quadrant of a mountain for about 2/3rds of its height then spread for the upper third over its whole crown. They contain about three hundred acres, washed at the foot for about a mile, by a river of the size of the Schuylkill. The hill is generally too steep for direct ascent, but we make level walks successively along it's side, which in it's upper part encircle the hill & intersect these again by others of easy ascent in various parts. They are chiefly still in their native woods, which are majestic, and very generally a close undergrowth, which I have not suffered to be touched, knowing how much easier it is to cut away than to fill up. The upper third is chiefly open, but to the South is covered with a dense thicket of Scotch broom (*Spartium scoparium Lin.*) which being favorably spread before the sun will admit of advantageous arrangement for winter enjoyment. You are sensible that this disposition of the ground takes from me the first beauty in gardening, the variety of hill & dale, & leaves me as an awkward substitute a few hanging hollows & ridges, this subject is so unique and at the same time refractory, that to make a disposition analogous to its character would require much more of the genius of the landscape painter & gardener than I pretend to. I had once hoped to get Parkins to go and give me some outlines, but I was disappointed. Certainly I could never with your health to be such as to render traveling necessary; but should a journey at any time promise improvement to it, there is no one on which you would be received with more pleasure than at Monticello. Should I be there you will have an opportunity of indulging on a new field some of the taste which has made the Woodlands the only rival which I have kown in America to what may be seen in England.

Thither without doubt we are to go for models in this art. Their sunless climate has permitted them to adopt what is certainly a beauty of the very first order in landscape. Their canvas is of open ground, variegated with clumps of trees distributed with taste. They need no more of wood than will serve to embrace a lawn or a glade. But under the beaming, constant and almost vertical sun of Virginia, shade is our Elysium. In the absence of this no beauty of the eye can be enjoyed. This organ must yield its gratification to that of the other senses; without the hope of any equivalent to the beauty relinquished. The only substitute I have been able to imagine is this. Let your ground be covered with trees of the loftiest stature. Trim up their bodies as high as the constitution & form of the tree will bear, but so as that their tops shall unite & yield dense shade. A wood, so open below, will have nearly the appearance of open grounds. Then when in the open ground you would plant a clump of trees, place a thicket of shrubs presenting a hemisphere the crown of which shall distinctly show itself under the branches of the trees. This may be effected by a due selection & arrangement of the shrubs, & will I think offer a group not much inferior to that of trees. The thickets may be

varied too by making some of them of evergreens altogether, our red cedar made to grow in a bush, evergreen privet, pyrocanthus, Kalmia, Scotch broom. Holly would be elegant but it does not grow in my part of the country.

Of prospect I have a rich profusion and offering itself at every point of the compass. Mountains distant & near, smooth & shaggy, single & in ridges, a little river hiding itself among the hills so as to shew in lagoons only, cultivated grounds under the eye and two small villages. To prevent a satiety of this is the principal difficulty. It may be successively offered, & in different portions through vistas, or which will be better, between thickets so disposed as to serve as vistas, with the advantage of shifting the scenes as you advance on your way.

You will be sensible by this time of the truth of my information that my views are turned so steadfastly homeward that the subject runs away with me whenever I get on it. I sat down to thank you for kindnesses received, & to bespeak permission to ask further contributions from your collection & I have written you a treatise on gardening generally, in which are lessons would come with more justice from you to me.

THOMAS JEFFERSON to WILLIAM
HAMILTON, July 1806

GERTRUDE JEKYLL
(1843–1932)

Miss Jekyll, known to her collaborator Sir Edwin Lutyens as 'Bumps', whose benign influence is as strong today as it was within her own lifetime.

Nothing can be more absolutely unscientific than my ways, according to the usual sense of the word. I wish to gain a knowledge of all garden flowers, but only to see which can be used in a beautiful and picturesque way, and which had better be rejected or left alone. In gardening I try to paint living pictures with living flowers, paying attention to throwing them into groups both for form and colour, and so on. I am perpetually at amicable war with the gardener for over-trimness. His grand idea is that edges must be trimmed, and all walks brushed every Saturday, while I hold the heresy of not minding a little moss on a path, and of rather preferring a few scattered cluster rose-petals lying on its browngreen velvet. I wish I could show you some of my garden pictures that seem fairly successful: – The Primrose Garden, lately replanted and improved as to the lines of its boundaries. I grow mostly the large yellow and white bunch primroses; and the Primrose Garden in its season is a river of gold and silver flowing through a copse of silver-stemmed young birch trees for a hundred yards or more. Another of this year's pictures that pleased me, was a large isolated group of white foxgloves with bracken about their base, backed by a dusky wood of Scotch firs.

Letter from MISS JEKYLL to
E.V.B. [1885]

She is described alternately as 'gentle' and 'fierce'. She could be either. She had little patience with indifference or stupidity, and could settle both with quiet, but devastating remarks. She loved a jaunt or a 'treat' as children would say, and one of her passions was for playing the pianola. She was deeply, but unfussily, religious. She could say 'Forgive us our Christmases as we forgive them that Christmas against us', being supremely irritated by the sending of numerous cards to people 'for whom she felt no affection and hardly knew' and vice versa. She had a keen sense of fun and delight in adventure with children, understanding their love of magic and make-believe.

If all this is linked together there emerges a composite picture which has been clearly caught by William Nicholson. She sits in her chair, a stout, round figure, dressed in her usual style of voluminous blue serge: 'I remember her in her eighties, a dumpy figure in a heavy gardener's apron, her vitality shining from a face half concealed by two pairs of spectacles and a battered and yellowed straw hat'. Lady Emily Lutyens says: 'There was only one kind of dress she could really wear, and it was often largely concealed by an apron and finished off by her solid gardening boots. She had beautiful hands and a delicious chuckling laugh.' Mr Oliver Hill remembers her as 'lumpy, physically, but light and witty in conversation – she was delicious'. Mrs Barnes-Brand describes her as 'having great poise together with a wonderful sense of humour. Miss Jekyll was tremendously human and most helpful if she thought you were really interested.' And in spite of all the hard work accomplished and her respect for the good use of time she still 'gave a feeling of repose'. Mr Falkner goes on: 'Someone somewhere has talked of a "little old lady". G. J. was not little bodily or in any other way. She must have been, when I first knew her, some five feet ten and weighed ten or twelve stone; with rather a deep voice but not at all masculine, without the slightest gush, capable of considerable tenderness, always putting people at their ease or keeping them there, always thinking, contriving, giving or storing information . . .'

The no-nonsense side of her character could and did give way to the artist, and the poetry in her writing breaks through the hard core of facts and plain statements of actual experience.

'While May is still young, cowslips are in beauty on the chalk lands . . .'

'There comes a day towards the end of March when there is but little wind, and that is from the west . . .'

'How endlessly beautiful is woodland in winter. Today there is a thin mist; just enough to make a background of tender blue mystery . . .'
All this William Nicholson has brought into his portrait. But, unfortunately, there cannot be seen in the picture a piece of string hanging from the back of the chair. It must be there, I think, but would hardly be a necessary component of the painting. On the other hand, it would give an important clue to one side of her character. 'I hope', said an old friend of Miss Jekyll's, 'that you have mentioned her cats'. Lady Emily wrote: 'Bumps has about six cats, three quite kittens, and they romped about the room', and it was Lady Emily who told me that there was always a long piece of string hanging down from the back of Miss Jekyll's chair. At first, the point of this string was not clear until it was found to have a cork at the end of it which, of course, proved to be a perpetual attraction to whichever cats were present with the family.

BETTY MASSINGHAM, *Miss Jekyll.*
Portrait of a Great Gardener [1973]

WILLIAM KENT
(1684–1748)

The father of the landscape style, who had his admirers.

At that moment appeared Kent, painter enough to taste the charms of landscape, bold and opinionative enough to dare and to dictate, and born with a genius to strike out a great system from the twilight of imperfect essays. He leaped the fence, and saw that all nature was a garden. He felt the delicious contrast of hill and valley changing imperceptibly into each other, tasted the beauty of the gentle swell, or concave scoop, and remarked how loose groves crowned an easy eminence with happy ornament, and while they called in the distant view between their graceful stems, removed and extended the perspective by delusive comparison.

Thus the pencil of his imagination bestowed all the arts of landscape on the scenes he handled. The great principles on which he worked were perspective, and light and shade. Groups of trees broke too uniform or too extensive a lawn; evergreens and woods were opposed to the glare of the champain, and where the view was less fortunate, or so much exposed as to be beheld at once, he blotted out some parts by thick shades, to divide it into variety, or to make the richest scene more enchanting by reserving it to a farther advance of the spectator's step. Thus selecting favourite objects, and veiling deformities by screens of plantation, sometimes allowing the rudest waste to add its foil to the richest theatre, he realized the compositions of the greatest masters in painting. Where objects were wanting to animate his horizon, his taste as an architect could bestow immediate termination. His buildings, his seats, his temples, were more the works of his pencil than of his compasses. We owe the restoration of Greece and the diffusion of architecture to his skill in landscape.

But of all the beauties he added to the face of this beautiful country, none surpassed his management of water. Adieu to canals, circular basons, and cascades tumbling down marble steps, that last absurd magnificence of Italian and French villas. The forced elevation of cataracts was no more. The gentle stream was taught to serpentize seemingly at its pleasure, and where discounted by different levels, its course appeared to be concealed by thickets properly interspersed, and glittered again at a distance where it might be supposed naturally to arrive. Its borders were smoothed, but preserved their waving irregularity. A few trees scattered here and there on its edges sprinkled the tame bank that accompanied its maeanders, and when it disappeared among the hills, shades descending from the heights leaned towards its progress, and framed the distant point of light under which it was lost, as it turned aside to either hand of the blue horizon.

Thus dealing in none but the colours of nature, and catching its most favourable features, men saw a new creation opening before their eyes. The living landscape was chastened or polished, not transformed. Freedom was given to the forms of trees; they extended their branches unrestricted, and where any eminent oak, or master beech had escaped maiming and survived the forest, bush and bramble was removed, and all its honours were restored to distinguish and shade the plain. Where the united plumage of an ancient wood extended wide its undulating canopy, and stood venerable in its darkness, Kent thinned the foremost ranks, and left but so many detached and scattered trees, as softened the approach of gloom and blended a chequered light with the thus lengthened shadows of the remaining columns.

HORACE WALPOLE, *The History of the Modern Taste in Gardening* [1771–80]

And detractors.

Clipt hedges, avenues, regular platforms, strait canals have been for some time very properly exploded. There is not a citizen who does not take more pains to torture his acre and half into irregularities, than he formerly would have employed to make it as formal as his cravat. Kent, the friend of nature, was the Calvin of this reformation, but like the other champion of truth, after having routed tinsel and trumpery, with the true zeal of a founder of a sect he pushed his discipline to the deformity of holiness: not content with banishing symmetry and regularity, he imitated nature even in her blemishes, and planted dead trees and mole-hills, in opposition to parterres and quincunxes. *The World*, No. 6 [1753]

Saint-Simon provides this memorable glimpse of the creator of the gardens of Versailles for Louis XIV.

ANDRÉ LE NÔTRE (1613–1700)

Le Nôtre died at about this time. He had lived in perfect health for eighty-eight years and retained his faculties, excellent taste, and capability until the last. He was celebrated for designing the fine gardens that adorn all France and have so lowered the reputation of Italian gardens (which are really nothing in comparison) that the most famous landscape architects of Italy now come to France to study and admire. Le Nôtre was honest, honourable, and plain-spoken; everybody loved and respected him, for he never stepped out of his place nor forgot it and was always perfectly disinterested, working for private patrons as for the King himself, and with the same care and industry. His only thought was to aid nature and reveal true beauty at as low a cost as possible. There was an artlessness about him, a simple-hearted candour that was perfectly delightful. On one occasion, when the Pope had obtained the King's permission to borrow him for a few months, Le Nôtre entered his room, and instead of falling to his knees, ran towards him, and putting his arms round his neck kissed him on both cheeks, exclaiming, 'Ah! Holy Father, how well you look! How rejoiced I am to see you in good health!' The Pope, Clement X, Alfieri, laughed heartily. He thoroughly enjoyed this informal kind of greeting and treated Le Nôtre with much kindness. . . .

A month or so before he died, the King, who enjoyed seeing and talking to him, again took him into the gardens and because of his great age had him put into a chair, which a footman wheeled beside his own. Thereupon Le Nôtre exclaimed, 'Alas! my poor father, had he but been alive to see this poor gardener, his own son, riding in a chair beside the greatest king on earth, his happiness would have been complete.'

From *Saint-Simon at Versailles*, trans. Lucy Norton [1700]

JOHN CLAUDIUS LOUDON
(1783–1843)

A monument to industry in the Victorian sense, this account by his wife gives some insight into how he managed to write some 60 million words on gardening. After his right arm was amputated she became his amanuensis.

His love of order was also very great. The books in the library, and manuscripts in his study, were so arranged that he could at any time put his hand upon any book or paper that he might want, even in the dark. He instilled this system of order into the minds of his clerks too; for, when any new one came, his invariable instructions were – 'Put every thing away before you leave at night, as if you never intended to return.'

He was also a man of great punctuality as to time, money matters, and in every other respect. When any of his clerks happened to be behind time in the morning, he would take no notice for a few times; but, if it were often repeated, he would say very quietly but sarcastically – 'Oh, if 9 o'clock is too early for you, you had better come at 11 or 12; but let there just be a fixed hour, that I may depend upon you.'

Mr Loudon was a man of great fortitude and unwearied industry. The morning that Doctors Thompson and Lauder called upon him for the purpose of amputating his right arm, they met him in the garden, and asked if he had fully made up his mind to undergo the operation. 'Oh, yes, certainly,' he said; 'it was for that purpose I sent for you;' and added very coolly, 'but you had better step in, and just have a little lunch first before you begin.' After lunch he walked up stairs quite composedly, talking to the doctors on general subjects. When all the ligatures were tied, and every thing complete, he was about to step down stairs, as a matter of course, to go on with his business; and the doctors had great difficulty to prevail upon him to go to bed.

As a man of industry, he was not surpassed by any one. Deducting for the time he has been poorly, he has, during three fourths of his literary career, dictated about five and a half printed octavo pages of matter every day on an average. He has been frequently known to dictate to two amanuenses at the same time. He often used to work until 11 and 12 o'clock at night, and sometimes all night. It may not be amiss to mention here, as illustrative of his love of labour, that, whilst his man-servant was dressing him for church on the day of his marriage, he was actually dictating to his amanuensis the whole time.

JANE LOUDON, *An Account of the Life and Writings of John Claudius Loudon* [1845]

RUSSELL PAGE
(1906–85)

In his classic garden autobiography he tells us how it all began.

It must have been my father who told me of a certain elderly lady devoted to flowers who lived in a Victorian Gothic house almost in the shadows of the three great towers of Lincoln Minster. One day I knocked on her door. She opened it herself and stood there, tall and gaunt, with wild grey hair and the relics of great good looks, dressed in the fashion of thirty years before. 'Please be careful where you walk,' said the lady – a necessary warning as half the coloured encaustic tiles flooring the dark hallway had been taken up and one had to play hop-scotch to avoid a chequer board of Asiatic primula seedlings which grew in the spaces left by the missing tiles. The drawing-room was gardened in another way; ivy had been brought in through holes in the wall to garland windows, walls and ceiling with green. This lady had lived in India where, over many years, she had made lively precise water-colour drawings of flowers, musical instruments, jewels and household objects which filled the whole pile of albums. Outside, in an old sycamore tree, a rickety bamboo ladder led up to a platform among the branches which she called her 'machan' though the neighbour's cat was the only tiger she could stalk. There was a rock garden too, contrived as a home for frogs, lizards and grass snakes. Finding it colourless in the winter, she had imposed on it colonies of brightly coloured toad-stools which she told me she made herself from the lids of boot-polish tins and old tooth brushes. I was always welcome. There were no set meal-times; 'A little food every two hours is better,' she would say, bringing me a plate of pineapple, or custard, or a sandwich.

RUSSELL PAGE, *The Education of a Gardener* [1962]

Designer of that mega-conservatory the Crystal Palace and another Victorian workaholic.

SIR JOSEPH PAXTON (1803–65)

I left London by the Comet coach for Chesterfield, arrived at Chatsworth at half past four o'clock in the morning of the ninth of May, 1826. As no person was to be seen at that early hour, I got over the greenhouse gate by the old covered way, explored the pleasure grounds, and looked round the outside of the house. I then went down to the kitchen gardens, scaled the outside wall, and saw the whole of the place, set the men to work there at six o'clock, then returned to Chatsworth, and got Thomas Weldon to play me the waterworks, and afterwards went to breakfast with poor dear Mrs Gregory and her niece: the latter fell in love with me, and I with her, and thus completed my first morning's work at Chatsworth before nine o'clock.

SIR JOSEPH PAXTON, *Diary*, 9 May 1826

Along with Horace Walpole a master of self-publicity in the promotion of his own garden.

ALEXANDER POPE (1688–1744)

I write an hour or two every morning, then ride out a hunting upon the Downes, eat heartily, talk tender sentiments with Lord B. or draw Plans for Houses and Gardens, open Avenues, cut Glades, open Firrs, contrive waterworks, all very fine and beautiful in our own imagination.

ALEXANDER POPE [1718]

As an arbiter of taste, his swingeing pen lampooned the formal style in his description of the Duke of Chandos' garden at Canons under the guise of 'Timon's Villa'.

At Timon's Villa let us pass a day,
Where all cry out, 'What sums are thrown away!'
So proud, so grand, of that stupendous air,
Soft and Agreeable come never there.
Greatness, with Timon, dwells in such a draught
As brings all Brobdignag before your thought.

To compass this, his building is a Town,
His pond an Ocean, his parterre a Down:
Who but must laugh, the Master when he sees?
A puny insect, shiv'ring at a breeze.
Lo! what huge heaps of littleness around!
The whole, a labour'd Quarry above ground.
Two Cupids squirt before; a Lake behind
Improves the keenness of the Northern wind.

His Gardens next your admiration call,
On ev'ry side you look, behold the Wall!
No pleasing Intricacies intervene,
No artful wildness to perplex the scene;
Grove nods at grove, each Alley has a brother,
And half the platform just reflects the other.
The suff'ring eye inverted Nature sees,
Trees cut to Statues, Statues thick as trees,
With here a Fountain, never to be play'd,
And there a Summer-house, that knows no shade.
Here Amphitrite sails thro' myrtle bow'rs;
There Gladiators fight, or die, in flow'rs;
Un-water'd see the drooping sea-horse mourn,
And swallows roost in Nilus' dusty Urn.

*And tossed bouquets to Richard Boyle, Earl Burlington, to whose garden
at Chiswick (see pp. 300–1) both he and Kent had contributed.*

To build, to plant, whatever you intend,
To rear the Column, or the Arch to bend,
To swell the Terras, or to sink the Grot;
In all, let Nature never be forgot.
But treat the Goddess like a modest fair,
Nor over-dress, nor leave her wholly bare;
Let not each beauty ev'ry where be spy'd,
Where half the skill is decently to hide.
He gains all points, who pleasingly confounds,
Surprizes, varies, and conceals the Bounds.
  Consult the Genius of the Place in all;
That tells the Waters or to rise, or fall,
Or helps th'ambitious Hill the heav'ns to scale,
Or scoops in circling theatres the Vale;
Calls in the Country, catches op'ning glades,
Joins willing woods, and varies shades from shades;
Now breaks, or now directs, th'intending Lines,
Paints as you plant, and as you work, designs.
  Still follow Sense, of ev'ry Art the Soul,
Parts answ'ring parts shall slide into a whole,
Spontaneous beauties all around advance,
Start ev'n from Difficulty, strike from Chance;

Nature shall join you; Time shall make it grow
A Work to wonder at – perhaps a STOW.

ALEXANDER POPE, *Epistle IV. To
Richard Boyle, Earl of Burlington*
[1731]

HUMPHRY REPTON
(1752–1818)

*The 'inheritor' of the mantle of 'Capability' Brown, he attracted almost
as much odium as praise. His famous Red Books resembled children's
pop-up books with flaps which lifted revealing before and after. They
remain as seductive today as they did then.*

She [Fanny] must try to find amusement in what was passing at the upper end
of the table, and in observing Mr Rushworth, who was now making his
appearance at Mansfield, for the first time since the Crawfords' arrival. He
had been visiting a friend in a neighbouring county, and that friend having
recently had his grounds laid out by an improver, Mr Rushworth was
returned with his head full of the subject, and very eager to be improving his
own place in the same way; and though not saying much to the purpose,
could talk of nothing else . . .

'I wish you could see Compton,' said he, 'it is the most complete thing! I
never saw a place so altered in my life. I told Smith I did not know where I
was. The approach *now* is one of the finest things in the country. You see the
house in the most surprising manner. I declare when I got back to Sotherton
yesterday, it looked like a prison – quite a dismal old prison.'

'Oh! for shame!' cried Mrs Norris. 'A prison, indeed! Sotherton Court is
the noblest old place in the world.'

'It wants improvement, ma'am, beyond any thing. I never saw a place that
wanted so much improvement in my life; and it is so forlorn, that I do not
know what can be done with it.'

'No wonder that Mr Rushworth should think so at present,' said Mrs
Grant to Mrs Norris, with a smile, 'but depend upon it, Sotherton will have
every improvement in time which his heart can desire.'

'I must try to do something with it,' said Mr Rushworth, 'but I do not
know what. I hope I shall have some good friend to help me.'

'Your best friend upon such an occasion,' said Miss Bertram, calmly,
'would be Mr Repton, I imagine.'

'That is what I was thinking of. As he has done so well by Smith, I think I
had better have him at once. His terms are five guineas a day.'

JANE AUSTEN, *Mansfield Park* [1814]

He was, of course, anathema to the pioneers of Picturesque:

> See yon fantastic band,
> With charts, pedometers, and rules in hand,
> Advance triumphant, and alike lay waste
> The forms of nature, and the works of taste!
> T'improve, adorn, and polish, they profess;
> But shave the goddess, whom they come to dress;
> Level each broken bank and shaggy mound,
> And fashion all to one unvaried round;

Feather thatched Summerhouse

One even round, that ever gently flows,
Nor forms abrupt, nor broken colours knows;
But, wrapt all o'er in everlasting green,
Makes one dull, vapid, smooth, and tranquil scene . . .

Hence, hence! thou haggard fiend, however call'd,
Thin, meagre genius of the bare and bald;
Thy spade and mattock here at length lay down,
And follow to the tomb thy fav'rite Brown:
Thy fav'rite Brown, whose innovating hand
First dealt thy curses o'er this fertile land;
First taught the walk in formal spires to move,
And from their haunts the secret Dryads drove;
With clumps bespotted o'er the mountain's side,
And bade the stream 'twixt banks close shaven glide;
Banish'd the thickets of high-bow'ring wood,
Which hung, reflected, o'er the glassy flood;
Where screen'd and shelter'd from the heats of day,
Oft on the moss-grown stone repos'd I lay,
And tranquil view'd the limpid stream below,
Brown with o'erhanging shade, in circling eddies flow . . .

Oft when I've seen some lonely mansion stand,
Fresh from th'improver's desolating hand,
'Midst shaven lawns, that far around it creep
In one eternal undulating sweep;
And scatter'd clumps, that nod at one another,
Each stiffly waving to its formal brother;
Tir'd with th'extensive scene, so dull and bare,
To Heav'n devoutly I've address'd my pray'r, –
Again the moss-grown terraces to raise,
And spread the labyrinth's perplexing maze;
Replace in even lines the ductile yew,
And plant again the ancient avenue.
Some features then, at least, we should obtain,
To mark this flat, insipid, waving plain;
Some vary'd tints and forms would intervene,
To break this uniform, eternal green.

RICHARD PAYNE KNIGHT, *The
Landscape. A Didactic Poem* [1794]

*And he was superbly caricatured by Thomas Love Peacock in the guise of
Marmaduke Milestone.*

'I perceive,' said Mr Milestone, after they had walked a few paces, 'these
grounds have never been touched by the finger of taste.'

'The place is quite a wilderness,' said Squire Headlong: 'for, during the
latter part of my father's life, while I was *finishing* my *education*, he troubled
himself about nothing but the cellar, and suffered every thing else to go to
rack and ruin. A mere wilderness, as you see, even now in December; but in

summer, a complete nursery of briers, a forest of thistles, a plantation of nettles, without any live stock, but goats, that have eaten up all the bark of the trees. Here you see is a pedestal of a statue, with only half a leg and four toes remaining: there were many here once. When I was a boy, I used to sit every day on the shoulders of Hercules: what became of *him* I have never been able to ascertain. Neptune has been lying these three years in the dust-hole; Atlas had his head knocked off to make him prop up a shed; and only the day before yesterday we fished Bacchus out of the horse-pond.'

'My dear sir,' said Mr Milestone, 'accord me your permission to wave the wand of enchantment over your grounds. The rocks shall be blown up, the trees shall be cut down, the wilderness and all its goats shall vanish like mist. Pagodas and Chinese bridges, gravel walks and shrubberies, bowling-greens, canals, and clumps of larch, shall rise upon its ruins. One age, Sir, has brought to light the treasures of ancient learning: a second has penetrated into the depths of metaphysics: a third has brought to perfection the science of astronomy; but it was reserved for the exclusive genius of the present times, to invent the noble art of picturesque gardening, which has given, as it were, a new tint to the complexion of nature, and a new outline to the physiognomy of the universe!'

'Give me leave,' said Sir Patrick O'Prism, 'to take an exception to that same. Your system of levelling, and trimming, and clipping, and docking, and clumping, and polishing, and cropping, and shaving, destroys all the beautiful intricacies of natural luxuriance, and all the graduated harmonies of light and shade, melting into one another, as you see them on that rock over yonder. I never saw one of your improved places, as you call them, and which are nothing but big bowling-greens, like sheets of green paper, with a parcel of round clumps scattered over them like so many spots of ink, flicked at random out of a pen, and a solitary animal here and there looking as if it were lost, that I did not think it was for all the world like Hounslow Heath, thinly sprinkled over with bushes and highwaymen.'

'Sir,' said Mr Milestone, 'you will have the goodness to make a distinction between the picturesque and the beautiful.'

'Will I?' said Sir Patrick: 'och! but I won't. For what is beautiful? That which pleases the eye. And what pleases the eye? Tints variously broken and blended. Now tints variously broken and blended, constitute the picturesque.'

'Allow me,' said Mr Gall. 'I distinguish the picturesque and the beautiful, and I add to them, in the laying out of grounds, a third and distinct character, which I call *unexpectedness*.'

'Pray, Sir,' said Mr Milestone, 'by what name do you distinguish this character, when a person walks round the grounds for the second time?'

Mr Gall bit his lips, and inwardly vowed to revenge himself on Milestone, by cutting up his next publication.

A long controversy now ensued concerning the picturesque and the beautiful, highly edifying to Squire Headlong.

The three philosophers stopped, as they would round a projecting point of rock, to contemplate a little boat which was gliding over the tranquil surface of the lake below . . .

Mr Milestone had produced his portfolio for the edification and amusement of Miss Tenorina, Miss Graziosa, and Squire Headlong, to whom he

was pointing out the various beauties of his plan for Lord Littlebrain's park.

MR MILESTONE.   This, you perceive, is the natural state of one part of the grounds. Here is a wood, never yet touched by the finger of taste; thick, intricate, and gloomy. Here is a little stream, dashing from stone to stone, and overshadowed with these untrimmed boughs.

MISS TENORINA.   The sweet romantic spot! how beautifully the birds must sing there on a summer evening!

MISS GRAZIOSA.   Dear sister! how can you endure the horrid thicket?

MR MILESTONE.   You are right, Miss Graziosa: your taste is correct – perfectly *en règle*. Now, here is the same place corrected – trimmed – polished-decorated-adorned. Here sweeps a plantation, in that beautiful regular curve: there winds a gravel walk: here are parts of the old wood, left in these majestic circular clumps, disposed at equal distances with wonderful symmetry: there are some single shrubs scattered in elegant profusion: here a Portugal laurel, there a juniper: here a lauristinus, there a spruce fir; here a larch, there a lilac; here a rhododendron, there an arbutus. The stream, you see, is become a canal: the banks are perfectly smooth and green, sloping to the water's edge: and there is Lord Littlebrain, rowing in an elegant boat.

SQUIRE HEADLONG.   Magical, faith!

MR MILESTONE.   Here is another part of the grounds in its natural state. Here is a large rock, with the mountain-ash rooted in its fissures, overgrown, as you see, with ivy and moss, and from this part of it bursts a little fountain, that runs bubbling down its ragged sides.

MISS TENORINA.   O how beautiful! How I should love the melody of that miniature cascade!

MR MILESTONE.   Beautiful, Miss Tenorina! Hideous. Base, common, and popular. Such a thing as you may see anywhere, in wild and mountainous districts. Now observe the metamorphosis. Here is the same rock, cut into the shape of a giant. In one hand he holds a horn, through which that little fountain is thrown to a prodigious elevation. In the other is a ponderous stone, so exactly balanced as to be apparently ready to fall on the head of any person who may happen to be beneath; and there is Lord Littlebrain walking under it.

SQUIRE HEADLONG.   Miraculous, by Mahomet!

THOMAS LOVE PEACOCK, *Headlong Hall* [1816]

Poor Repton, already five years after his death his reputation had sunk, as this account of his proposals for Magdalen College Meadow in 1801 reveals.

Mr Repton a landscape gardener and Mr Nash a well-known professional architect, severally produced volumes of designs for the disfigurement of Magdalen College and the disposal of its pleasure grounds, touched, it is true, with the artist's magic pencil and secured in cases of red morocco and gold, yet by their preposterous absurdity, not to enlarge on their ruinous splendour, consigned to an oblivion from which I shall not risk their escape, by bestowing on them any further comments.

J. C. BUCKLER [1832]

The painter and dessinateur des jardins du roi *was the creator of many gardens in the anglo-chinois style. The Scottish garden designer, Thomas Blaikie, had no estimation of his talents.*

Dimanche 14 went to St Germains to deside a plantation for a vue from the Gardens of the Prince de Bauvaus at Lavalle a House he has between St Germains and Maison; those Gardens are Layd out under the Derections of Mr Robert one of the first Landskape painters in France yet however fine his ideas is upon canvas yet upon the ground they are without judgement as it is not astonishing he knows nothing of the effects of trees nor there color after a feu years' growth; his walks are much in the same confused crooked way and although all has been planted methodically according to the rules of painting yet the whole is real confusion; this prooves that a great painter may know how to take a vue to the best advantage when done but the despossing of those plantations requires judgement and experience . . .

> THOMAS BLAIKIE, *Diary of a Scotch Gardener*, 14 November 1779

HUBERT ROBERT
(1733–1808)

The 'Father of the English Flower Garden', yes, but I find it difficult to warm to him.

'Writing about *that* man . . . that vicious man! How horrible!'

> View of a 'well-known lady gardener' as quoted by MEA ALLAN, *William Robinson* [1982]

WILLIAM
ROBINSON
(1838–1935)

Your french boots have come & I send them up today – marking the parcel *Boots* outside for fear your people in your possible absence might think they were Flowers Perishable and put them in water – though they would stand it better than some of their kind – Don't be frightened at their new pale complexion – a few greasings and wettings will cure that.

I hope they will be right though I see the heels are a good 1/8th″ higher than you ordered – The pattern shoe & a box of grease are enclosed with them.

> GERTRUDE JEKYLL to WILLIAM ROBINSON, 5 February 1883

With her husband, Harold Nicolson, the creator of Sissinghurst and author of the poem, 'The Garden'.

May I assure the gentleman who writes to me (quite often) from a Priory in Sussex that I am not the armchair, library-fireside gardener he evidently suspects, 'never having performed any single act of gardening' myself, and that for the last forty years of my life I have broken my back, my finger-nails, and sometimes my heart, in the practical pursuit of my favourite occupation?

> VITA SACKVILLE-WEST

VICTORIA (VITA)
SACKVILLE-WEST
(1892–1962)

Vita only likes flowers which are brown and difficult to grow.

> HAROLD NICOLSON
> Both quoted in ANNE SCOTT-JAMES, *Sissinghurst. The Making of a Garden* [1974]

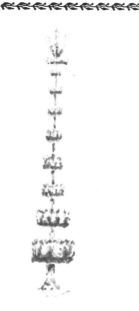

James Lees-Milne gives a wonderful impression of this formidable gardening couple in full flight on a tour of country houses in 1947.

Wednesday, 6th August

At 8.30 walking to buy a newspaper I met Vita who said she had just sent a telegram to Ben whose birthday it is today. I said, 'Oh, and not to me? for it is mine too.' So she bought me some lavender-water as a present. A very full day. We drove to Avebury and diverged to see the isolated gate-piers in the field at Hampstead Marshall, for they move me strangely. Then to see Inkpen Rectory. The gardener let us in for the owner was away. H. and V. were delighted with the little formal Le Nôtre layout and H. made drawings of it in his pocket-book. We drove up to Littlecote and the gardener said Sir E. Wills was away, so we walked round his house. Large; I did not like the orangery additions to the main front. The place was purring with gardeners. Long herbaceous borders, vast lawns admirably kept, but very much the rich man's garden, tastelessly laid out. I liked the bit where the Kennet tributary flows through a narrow lawny enclave . . .

Friday, 8th August

Harold worked till eleven when we left. We agreed that Eddy had been the perfect host. Drove to Ven and straight up the drive to the house in Vita's usual abrupt fashion that upsets Harold and now alarms me. There was a woman' at the door whom I asked if Sir Hubert Medlycott were about. I thought she was the housekeeper. She took me all round the garden to look for him and failing to find him disclosed that she was the tenant. So I explained who we were and asked if we might see the garden by ourselves. She readily consented and showed us inside the house as well. Then we drove to Montacute where we lunched and walked round the garden, V and H telling me what flowers to plant in the forecourt borders. They were not as enthusiastic over the interior as I had hoped . . .

Saturday, 9th August

This morning brought the first signs of autumn. Montacute was silvery with faint dew in the early light. H. and V. called at 9.45 and walked round the outside. They were much moved by the silent beauty of the house. We drove straight to Stoke-sub-Ham and looked at the Little Priory. To my surprise they thought this might prove a worthy property. The little 'great hall' can undoubtedly be made very attractive. Then to Barrington Court which they also found beautiful; and were struck by the Lyles' modern buildings and layout. The gardens have got back to their pre-war standard, the borders ablaze, and only six gardeners. The Lyles, who were away, are living in the red brick wing, the Court proper being empty. At one o'c we reached Knightstones, one mile south of Ottery St Mary, belonging to Colonel Reggie Cooper, a funny old thing who was at school with Harold, is round as humpty-dumpty, and wears an eyeglass. He bought this house just before the war. It is a plain, granity, Cornish-looking house with carved 'Jacobean' barge-boards, c 1820. He has made a pretty little garden with fountains, and has sumptuous farm buildings for his Guernsey cows . . .

Sunday, 10th August

Today gloriously sunny and hot. The Nicolsons do not really care for classical buildings, only liking the Gothic or Elizabethan. Harold is wonderfully untidy. Dust, ash all over his hat and clothes. Vita wears one terra cotta dress, very shiny and long in the skirt, and brown espadrilles, yet is always distinguished and 'grande dame' . . .

Thursday, 14th August

We set off for Hayles Abbey and Harold was appalled by the condition of this property. Then to Stanway where Vita demanded to see the house. We walked straight through the house to the garden beyond. Stanton we saw and Chipping Campden where we had the nastiest of all luncheons at the smart hotel. It being one of the hottest days we were given hot soup from a tin, stringy steaks, uncooked vegetables, trifle. Of all this V. and I hardly ate anything, neither of us indeed having eaten much at Gloucester, not being inclined to face the sausages. At 2.30 we arrived at Hidcote. To our dismay we saw the table laid for four. Lawrie Johnston had expected us and said rather tartly that he had provided a succulent meal. This blow was almost more than we could bear. Vita was given innumerable cuttings, Lawrie J having relented. Garden pronounced lovely: We arrived at Charlecote at four. I warned the Ns that Brian Fairfax-Lucy was a dress reformer. Behold, he appeared in a pair of tight little white shorts, white sandshoes, a white satin shirt open at the neck, and a blue ribbon tied in a bow at his navel. The Ns decided that of all the people we had so far met the Lucys were the nicest. They considered the gardens here a disgrace.

Friday, 15th August

So hot under the eaves that I slept badly. Vita was asked for her autograph on leaving the hotel. We drove to Packwood. The weather overcast and almost drizzling. On arrival the sun came out and the day turned into the hottest of all. The Ns rather liked this place and its contents and admired the scrupulous way it is kept up. They liked Joshua Rowley but thought he looked unhealthy. They shook hands and talked to Weaver the gardener, who said he was a wireless fan of Harold's. V. and I scolded Harold afterwards for not relishing this reference. They greatly admired the way Weaver arranged the flowers and decided that, so long as we could afford the bedding out and had so good a gardener, we should leave the garden as it is. We lunched at Banbury and spent the last money from the pool. Looked at Boarstall Tower and Long Crendon. At Slough I was dropped, and we said goodbye. They were sweet and kind in saying I had been a good guide. I kissed Vita on the cheek. I have grown to love her. She is an adorable woman. I have enjoyed this tour immensely.

JAMES LEES-MILNE, *Caves of Ice*
[1983]

Osbert Sitwell's affectionate if slightly waspish delineation of his father, the creator of the gardens at Renishaw and author of On the Making of Gardens.

SIR GEORGE
RERESBY SITWELL
(1860–1943)

In the happy days of the far-off first decade of the nineteen hundreds, about the time that Princess Ena became engaged to King Alphonso, that Melba was first singing in *Madame Butterfly*, that Miss Lily Elsie was appearing in *The Merry Widow*, in short, in the golden days of good King Edward, a visitor in the spring and autumn to any of the great Italian or remarkable

Sicilian gardens, especially those that were more remote, might have chanced to see a tall, distinguished-looking Englishman with a high-bridged nose, and with fair, fine hair and a slightly darker golden moustache, flourished upwards a little in the manner of the Kaiser, seated on a bench, regarding his surroundings with analytic attention. Probably he would be sitting on an air-cushion, and would be wearing a grey suit and a wide, grey hat, while beside him – for he was careful to sit in the shade – was a sun-umbrella lined with green. Not far off, within the carrying of a voice, from the thick blackness of an ilex grove would peer a ponderous figure, watchful, but with an eye for those who passed as well as for the safety of the square, varnished wicker box in his care; which each day contained a cold chicken. As he stood there he had something of an air of a night watch on a ship, and his appearance, though his skin was bronzed, or indeed copper-coloured, was as northern and national as that of the gentleman on the bench. He, meanwhile had taken an envelope out of his pocket and was scratching on it with the stub-end of a pencil, angry or meditative remarks; crossly, how a gardener had removed the patina of lichen from a stone moulding since last he was here, or reflectively, comparing the merits where an effect of mystery was desired of broad shaded ilex with thin spired cypress, or of the various hues, textures, and sounds of varying kinds and speeds of falling water, and the sense of coolness and peace these induced . . .

The visitors might perhaps enquire – as often they did when they got back to the hotel – who the English gentleman might be, and the nautical figure hovering so heavily in the background – and the answer would be, Sir George Reresby Sitwell and his servant, Henry Moat. For, in those years, my father was busy collecting material for the book he planned.

Osbert Sitwell in his introduction to
SIR GEORGE SITWELL, *On the Making of Gardens* [1949 ed.]

JONATHAN SWIFT
(1667–1745)

The Dean introduced to Ireland the precursor of the English landscape style as propagated by his friend, Pope.

The Dean [Swift] had a mind to surprise the Doctor [Sheridan] on his next visit, with some improvements made at his own expense. Accordingly he had a canal cut of some extent, and at the end of it, by transplanting some young trees, formed an arbour, which he called *Stella's bower*, and surrounded some acres of land about it with a dry-stone wall (for the country afforded no lime), the materials of which were taken from the ground, which was very stony. The Dean had given strict charge to all about him to keep this secret, in order to surprise the Doctor on his arrival; but he had in the meantime received intelligence of all that was going forward. On his coming to Quilca, the Dean took an early opportunity of walking with him carelessly toward this new scene. The Doctor seemed not to take the least notice of any alteration, and, with a most inflexible countenance, continued to talk of indifferent matters. 'Confound your stupidity,' said Swift in a rage, 'why, you blockhead, don't you see the great improvements I have been making here?' – 'Improvements Mr Dean; why, I see a long bog-hole out of which I suppose you have cut the turf; you have removed some of the young trees, I think, to a worse situation; as to taking the stones from the surface of the ground, I allow that is a useful work, as the grass will grow the better for it;

and placing them about the field in that form, will make it more easy to carry them off.' – 'Plague on your Irish taste,' says Swift; 'this is just what I ought to have expected from you; but neither you nor your forefathers ever made such an improvement; nor will you be able, while you like, to do anything like it.'

The Doctor was resolved to retaliate on the Dean the first opportunity. It happened when he was down there on one of his vacations, that the Dean was absent for a few days on a visit elsewhere. He took this opportunity of employing a great number of hands to make an island in the middle of the lake, where the water was twenty feet deep; an arduous work in appearance, but not hard to be executed in a place abounding with large stones upon the surface of the ground, and where long heath grew everywhere in great plenty; for by placing quantities of those stones in large bundles of heath, the space was soon filled up, and a large island formed. To cover this, a sufficient quantity of earth and green sods were brought, and several well-grown osiers, and other aquatics, were removed to it. The Doctor's secret was better kept than Swift's; who, on his return walked toward the lake, and, seeing the new island, cried out in astonishment, 'Heigh how the water of the lake is sunk in this short time to discover that island of which there was no trace before' – 'Greatly sunk indeed,' observed the Doctor with a sneer, 'if it covers the tops of those osiers.' Swift then saw he had been fairly taken in, and, acknowledged the Doctor had got the better of him, both in his stratagem, and the beauty of his improvement.

> SIR WALTER SCOTT, *Memoirs of*
> *Jonathan Swift, D.D.* [1814]

His advocacy of the landscape style was vigorous as we catch in this satire dedicated to Lady Acheson.

How proudly he talks
Of zigzacks and walks;
And all the day raves
Of cradles and caves;
And boasts of his feats,
His grottos and seats;
Shews all his gew-gaws,
And gapes for applause?
A fine occupation
For one of his station!
A hole where a rabbit
Would scorn to inhabit,
Dug out in an hour
He calls it a bow'r.

> JONATHAN SWIFT, *My Lady's*
> *Lamentation and Complaint against*
> *the Dean* [1728]

JOHN
TRADESCANT THE
ELDER (c. 1570–1638)
AND YOUNGER
(1608–62)

Both gardeners, through their travels in Europe, Russia and the New World they gave us many of our most familiar garden plants. The Elder's Russian diary shows that the spirit of the plant hunters was as alive in the England of James I as it was under Victoria.

I have also seene shrubs of divers kinds.

As Ribes, or as we call them currants, whit, red and black, far greatter than ever I have seene in this cuntrie.

Also roses, single, in a great abundance, in my estemation four or five acars together; they be single, and muche like our sinoment (cinnamon) rose; and who have the sence of smelling, say they be marvelus sweete. I hop they will bothe growe and beare heere, for amongst many that I brought hom withe the roses upon them, yet sume may grow.

For p(l)ants helebros albus enoug to load a shipe, which the Ruses call camaritza.

Also angellica grea(t) stor(e), and lisimachia, penttufylion maior, geranium flore scrulie, saxifrag, sorrell half the heyght of a man.

Also rosasollis I found theare.

3 or 4 sorts of whorts, red ons, and two sorts of blewe ons, and also on sort of plant, bearing his frut like hedge-mercury, which made a very fine showe, having 3 leaves on the tope of every stake, having in every leafe a berry about the bignes of a hawe, all the three berryes growing close together, of a finner bright red than a hawe, whiche I took up many roots, yet am afraid that non held, bécuse at our being on ground we staved most of oure frese watter, and so wear faint to watter withe salt watter, but was made beleeve it was freshe, whiche that plant having but a long whit thin root, littill biger than a small couch gras; and the boys in the ship, befor I pe(r)seved it, eat of the berries . . . JOHN TRADESCANT, *A Viag of Ambuscad . . .* [1618]

They lie buried next to Lambeth Palace where the epitaph celebrates their famous 'Ark' or cabinet of curiosities, now in the Ashmolean Museum, Oxford, as well as their gardening prowess.

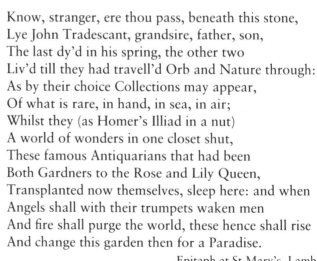

Know, stranger, ere thou pass, beneath this stone,
Lye John Tradescant, grandsire, father, son,
The last dy'd in his spring, the other two
Liv'd till they had travell'd Orb and Nature through:
As by their choice Collections may appear,
Of what is rare, in hand, in sea, in air;
Whilst they (as Homer's Illiad in a nut)
A world of wonders in one closet shut,
These famous Antiquarians that had been
Both Gardners to the Rose and Lily Queen,
Transplanted now themselves, sleep here: and when
Angels shall with their trumpets waken men
And fire shall purge the world, these hence shall rise
And change this garden then for a Paradise.

Epitaph at St Mary's, Lambeth

William and his wife, Mary II, were both passionate gardeners, introducing the formal Dutch style with its special articulation of space and use of clipped evergreens and canals. As a style it was anathema to Alexander Pope and Horace Walpole.

It is since the Revolution that our English gentlemen, began so universally, to adorn their gardens with those plants, we call ever greens, which leads me to a particular observation that may not be improper in this place; King William and Queen Mary introduced each of them two customs, which by the people's imitating them became the two idols of the town, and indeed of the whole kingdom . . .

The king on his part introduc'd (1) the love of gardening; and (2) of painting: In the first his majesty was particularly delighted with the decoration of ever greens, as the greatest addition to the beauty of a garden, preserving the figure of the place, even in the roughest part of an inclement and tempestuous winter.

Sir Stephen Fox's gardens at Istleworth, and Sir William temple's at Eastshene, mentioned above, were the only two gardens where they had entirely persued this method at that time, and of Sir Stephen's garden, this was to be said, that almost all his fine ever-greens were raised in the places where they stood; Sir Stephen taking as much delight to see them rise gradually, and form them into what they were to be, as to buy them of the nursery-gardeners, finish'd to his hand; besides that by this method of his greens, the finest in England, cost him nothing but the labour of his servants, and about ten years patience; which if they were to have been purchased, would not have cost so little as ten thousand pounds, especially at that time: It was here that King William was so pleased that according to his majesty's usual expression, when he lik'd a place very well, he stood, and looking round him from the head of one of the canals, Well says his majesty, I cou'd dwell here five days; every thing was so exquisitely contriv'd, finish'd and well kept, that the king, who was allow'd to be the best judge of such things then living in the world, did not so much as once say, this or that thing cou'd have been better.

With the particular judgment of the king, all the gentlemen in England began to fall in; and in a few years fine gardens, and fine houses began to grow up in every corner; the king began with the gardens at Hampton-Court and Kensington, and the gentlemen follow'd every where, with such a gust that the alteration is indeed wonderful thro' the whole kingdom; but no where more than in the two counties of Middlesex and Surrey, as they border on the river Thames; the beauty and expence of which are only to be wonder'd at, not describ'd; they may indeed be guess'd at, by what is seen in one or two such as these nam'd: But I think to enter into a particular of them would be an intollerable task, and tedious to the reader.

DANIEL DEFOE, *A Tour thro' the Whole Island of Great Britain* [1724]

KATHARINE
S. WHITE
(1892–1977)

A portrait by her husband of the author of the American garden classic Onward and Upward in the Garden *(1979). She gardened in Maine, New England.*

When Miss Gertrude Jekyll, the famous English woman who opened up a whole new vista of gardening for Victorian England, prepared herself to work in her gardens, she pulled on a pair of Army boots and tied on an apron fitted with great pockets for her tools. Unlike Miss Jekyll, my wife had no garden clothes and never dressed for gardening. When she paid a call on her perennial borders or her cutting bed or her rose garden, she was not dressed for the part – she was simply a spur-of-the-moment escapee from the house and, in the early years, from the job of editing manuscripts. Her Army boots were likely to be Ferragamo shoes, and she wore no apron. I seldom saw her *prepare* for gardening, she merely wandered out into the cold and the wet, into the sun and the warmth, wearing whatever she had put on that morning. Once she was drawn into the fray, once involved in transplanting or weeding or thinning or pulling deadheads, she forgot all else; her clothes had to take things as they came. I, who was the animal husbandryman on the place, in blue jeans and an old shirt, used to marvel at how unhesitatingly she would kneel in the dirt and begin grubbing about, garbed in a spotless cotton dress or a handsome tweed skirt and jacket. She simply refused to dress *down* to a garden: she moved in elegantly and walked among her flowers as she walked among her friends – nicely dressed, perfectly poised. If when she arrived back indoors the Ferragamos were encased in muck, she kicked them off. If the tweed suit was a mess, she sent it to the cleaner's.

The only moment in the year when she actually got herself up for gardening was on the day in fall that she had selected, in advance, for the laying out of the spring bulb garden – a crucial operation, carefully charted and full of witchcraft. The morning often turned out to be raw and overcast, with a searching wind off the water – an easterly that finds its way quickly to your bones. The bad weather did not deter Katharine: the hour had struck, the strategy of spring must be worked out according to plan. This particular bulb garden, with its many varieties of tulips, daffodils, narcissi, hyacinths, and other spring blooms, was a sort of double-duty affair. It must provide a bright mass of color in May, and it must also serve as a source of supply – flowers could be stolen from it for the building of experimental centerpieces.

Armed with a diagram and a clipboard, Katharine would get into a shabby old Brooks raincoat much too long for her, put on a little round wool hat, pull on a pair of overshoes, and proceed to the director's chair – a folding canvas thing – that had been placed for her at the edge of the plot. There she would sit, hour after hour, in the wind and the weather, while Henry Allen produced dozens of brown paper packages of new bulbs and a basketful of old ones, ready for the intricate interment. As the years went by and age overtook her, there was something comical yet touching in her bedraggled appearance on this awesome occasion – the small, hunched-over figure, her studied absorption in the implausible notion that there would be yet another spring, oblivious to the ending of her own days, which she knew perfectly well was near at hand, sitting there with her detailed chart under those dark skies in the dying October, calmly plotting the resurrection.

From E. B. White's introduction to
*Onward and Upward in the
Garden* [1979]

Manic gardener whose vast garden at Warley Place had 104 staff at its apogee. Eryngium giganticum, *the large pale sea holly, is known as Miss Willmott's ghost either in reference to her habit of scattering the seed in other people's gardens or, more likely, to her more than prickly character.*

ELLEN ANN WILLMOTT (1858–1934)

. . . as you know, my plants and my gardens come before anything in life for me, and all my time is given up to working in one garden or another, and when it is too dark to see the plants themselves I read or write about them.

ELLEN WILLMOTT to PROFESSOR
CHARLES SPRAGUE SARGENT [1906]

Henry Wise was the master of the baroque garden, designing Chatsworth, Longleat, Blenheim and Hampton Court besides running the Brompton Nursery on the site of the Victoria and Albert Museum. These lines are attributed to 'a labourer employed in Mr Wise's garden at Brompton'.

HENRY WISE (1653–1738)

If He who the first garden made
Had put in Wise to keep it,
Made Adam but a labourer there
And Eve to weed and sweep it;
Then men and plants had never died,
Nor the firstfruits been rotten;
Brompton had never then been known
Nor Eden e'er forgotten.

F. L. COLVILE, *The Worthies of
Warwickshire* [1829]

A Border of Beds

PART
IX

SOME

ENGLISH

GARDENS

Thomas Jefferson (1743–1826) was to be the third President of the United States and the creator of the garden at Monticello. His tour of English gardens in the 1780s is refreshingly acerbic.

CHESWICK. Belongs to D. of Devonshire. a garden about 6. acres; the Octagonal dome has an ill effect, both within & without; the garden shews still too much of art; an obelisk of very ill effect. another in the middle of a pond useless.

HAMPTON COURT. old fashioned. – clipt yews grown wild.

ESHER PLACE. the house in a bottom near the river. on the other side the ground rises pretty much. the road by which we come to the house forms a dividing line in the middle of the front. on the right are heights, rising one beyond & above another, with clumps of trees. on the farthest a temple. a hollow filled up with a clump of trees, the tallest in the bottom, so that the top is quite flat. on the left the ground descents. clumps of trees. the clumps on each hand balance finely. a most lovely mixture of concave & convex. the garden is about 45. a.s. besides the part which joins. belongs to Lady Francis Pelham.

CLAREMONT. L.ᵈ Clive's. nothing remarkeable.

PAYNSHILL. mr Hopkins. 323 acres. garden & park all in one. well described by Whateley. grotto said to have cost 7000.£. Whateley says one of the bridges is of stone. but both are now of wood. the lower 60.f.high. there is too much evergreen. the Dwelling house built by Hopkins. ill situated. he has not been there in 5. years. he lived there 4. years while building the present house. it is not finished. it's architecture is incorrect. a Doric temple beautiful.

STOWE. belongs to the M. of Buckingham, son of G. Grenville, & who takes it from L.d Temple. 15. men & 18. boys employed in keeping pleasure grounds. within the walk are considerable portions separated by inclosures & used for pasture. the Egyptian pyramid is almost entirely taken down by the late L.d Temple, to erect a building there, in commemoration of mr Pitt. but he died before beginning it and nothing is done to it yet. the grotto, and two rotundas are taken away. there are 4. levels of water, receiving it one from the other. the bason contains 7. a.s the lake below that 10. a.s Kent's building is called the temple of Venus. the inclosure is entirely by ha! ha! at each end of the front line there is a recess like the bastion of a fort. in one of these is the temple of Friendship. in the other the temple of Venus. they are seen the one from the other, the line of sight passing, not thro' the garden, but through the country parallel to the line of the garden. this has a good effect. in the approach to Stowe, you are brought a mile through a straight avenue, pointing to the Corinthian arch & to the house, till you get to the Arch. then you turn short to the right. the straight approach is very ill. the Corinthian arch has a very useless appearance, inasmuch as it has no pretension to any destination. instead of being an object from the house, it is an obstacle to a very pleasing distant prospect. the Graecian valley being clear of trees, while the hill on each side is covered with them, is much deepened to appearance.

LEASOWES. *in Shropshire.* – now the property of mr Horne by purchase. 150. a.s within the walk. the waters small. this is not even an ornamented farm. it is only a grazing farm with a path round it. here & there a seat of board, rarely any thing better. architecture has contributed nothing. the obelisk is of brick. Shenstone had but 300.£ a year, & ruined himself by what he did to this farm. it is said that he died of the heart-aches which his debts occasioned him. the part next the road is of red earth; that on the further part grey. the 1.st & 2.d cascades are beautiful. the landscape at No. 18. & prospect at 32. are fine, the walk through the wood is umbrageous & pleasing. the whole arch of prospect may be of 90.0 many of the inscriptions are lost.

THOMAS JEFFERSON, *Memorandums Made on a Tour to Some of the Gardens in England* [1786]

APPLETON HOUSE, YORKSHIRE

Andrew Marvell (1621–78) describes General Thomas, 3rd Lord Fairfax's garden at Nun Appleton, Yorkshire, constructed in the form of a fortress. For the poet, in the aftermath of the terrible Civil War, the garden becomes a metonym for England. At the time he wrote it he was tutor to the general's daughter.

> From that blest Bed the *Heroe* came,
> Whom *France* and *Poland* yet does fame
> Who, when retired here to Peace,
> His warlike Studies could not cease;
> But laid these Gardens out in sport
> In the just Figure of a Fort;
> And with five Bastions it did fence,
> As aiming one for ev'ry Sense.
>
> When in the *East* the Morning Ray
> Hangs out the Colours of the Day,
> The Bee through these known Allies hums,
> Beating the *Dian* with its *Drumms.*
> Then Flow'rs their drowsie Eylids raise,
> Their Silken Ensigns each displays,
> And dries its Pan yet dank with Dew,
> And fills its Flask with Odours new.
>
> These, as their *Governour* goes by,
> In fragrant Vollyes they let fly;
> And to salute their *Governess*

Again as great a charge they press:
None for the *Virgin Nymph*; for She
Seems with the Flow'rs a Flow'r to be.
And think so still! though not compare
With Breath so sweet, or Cheek so faire.

Well shot ye Firemen! Oh how sweet,
And round your equal Fires do meet;
Whose shrill report no Ear can tell,
But Ecchoes to the Eye and smell.
See how the Flow'rs as at *Parade*,
Under their *Colours* stand displaid:
Each *Regiment* in order grows,
That of the Tulip Pinke and Rose.

But when the vigilant *Patroul*
Of Stars walks round about the *Pole*,
Their Leaves, that to the stalks are curl'd,
Seem to their Staves the *Ensigns* furl'd.
Then in some Flow'rs beloved Hut
Each Bee as Sentinel is shut;
And sleeps so too: but, if once stir'd,
She runs you through, or askes *the Word*.

ANDREW MARVELL, *Upon Appleton
House* [early 1650s]

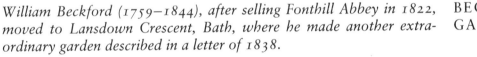

William Beckford (1759–1844), after selling Fonthill Abbey in 1822, moved to Lansdown Crescent, Bath, where he made another extraordinary garden described in a letter of 1838.

BECKFORD'S GARDEN IN BATH

We were now on the brow of the hill, and soon felt the influence of the genial breezes from the Bristol Channel. We quitted the open Down, and passing under a low doorway entered a lovely shrubbery. The walk (composed of small fossils) winds between graceful trees, and is skirted by odoriferous flowers, which we are astonished to find growing in such luxuriance at an elevation of nearly a thousand feet above the vale below. In many places the trees meet, and form a green arcade over your head, whilst patches of mignonette, giant plants of heliotrope, and clusters of geranium perfume the air.

We next enter a beautiful kitchen garden, and are presented with a broad and noble straight walk fully ten feet in width and nearly four hundred feet long, between beds of flowers, and on either side beyond fruit trees and vegetables. The garden terminates with a picturesque building, pierced by a lofty archway, through which the walk passes. This garden is about eighty feet wide and about twelve feet below the level of the Down, being formed in an old quarry, besides which a lofty wall on either side shelters it. One cannot describe one's sensations of comfort at finding so delicious a spot in so unexpected a place. I said to the gardener, 'I understood Mr Beckford had planted everything on the Down but you surely found those apple trees here. They are fifty years old.' 'We found nothing here but an old quarry and a few

nettles. Those apple trees were great trees when we moved them, and moving them stopped their bearing. They blossom in the spring and look pretty, and that is all master cares about.' We left this charming enclosure, passing under the archway before mentioned. And here I must pause a moment and admire the happy idea of placing this pretty building at the end of this cultivated spot. It closes the kitchen garden, and as its front is similar on either side, it harmonizes with the regular garden we have left, as well as with the wilder spot which we next approach. This building forms a complete termination to one of that succession of lovely scenes with which we are presented on our walk to the Tower. Each scene is totally distinct in character from the others, and yet with matchless taste they are united by some harmonious link, as in the present case.

Having then passed through the archway of this building, we observed before us a grotto, into which we entered. On the right is a pond of gold and silver fish which are fed every morning by the hands of the gifted possessor of this charming place. On the opposite side thirty or forty birds assemble at the same time to hail the appearance of St Anthony's devotee, and chirrup a song of gratitude for their morning meal. The grotto is formed under a road, and is so ingeniously contrived that hundreds have walked over it without ever dreaming of the subterranean passage beneath. The grotto-like arch winds underground for perhaps sixty or seventy feet. When coming to its termination we are presented with a flight of rustic steps, which leads us again directly on to the Down. Looking back you cannot but admire the natural appearance of this work of art. The ground over the grotto is covered with tangled shrubs and brambles. There is nothing formed, nothing apparently artificial, and a young ash springs as if accidentally from between the stones.

We pursued our way to the Tower by a path of a quarter of a mile on the Down, along a walk parallel to the wall of the public road, gently curved to take off the appearance of formality, yet so slightly that you can go on in a straight line. On our right hand venerable bushes of lavender, great plants of rosemary, and large rose trees perfume the air, all growing as if indigenous to the smooth turf. In one place clusters of rare and deeply crimsoned snapdragons, in another patches of aromatic thyme and wild strawberries keep up the charm of the place. As we draw nearer to the Tower the ground is laid out in a wilder and more picturesque manner, the walks are more serpentine. We turned a corner, and Mr Beckford stood before us, attended by an aged servant, whose hairs have whitened in his employment, and whose skill has laid out these grounds in this beautiful manner. Mr Beckford welcomed me in the kindest way, and immediately began pointing out the various curious plants and shrubs. How on this happy spot specimens of the productions of every country in the world unite! Shrubs and trees, whose natural climates are as opposite as the Antipodes, here flourish in the most astonishing manner. We were shown a rose tree brought from Pekin and a fir tree brought from the highest part of the Himalaya Mountains; many have been brought to this country, but Mr Beckford's is the only one that has survived. Here are pine trees of every species and variety – a tree that once vegetated at Larissa, in Greece, Italian pines, Siberian pines, Scotch firs, a lovely specimen of Irish yew, and other trees which it is impossible to describe. My astonishment was great at witnessing the size of the trees and I could scarcely believe my ears when told that the whole of this wood had been raised on the bare Down within the last thirteen years. The ground is broken and diversified in the most agreeable manner: here a flight of easy and water worn steps leads to an eminence, whence you have a view of the building and an old ruin overgrown with shrubs, which looks as if it had seen five hundred summers, but in reality no older than the rest of this creation. On ascending the easy though ruined steps of this building, passing under an archway, the view of the Tower burst upon us, and a long, straight walk led us directly to the entrance. From this point the view is most inspiring. On your right is a continuation of the shrubberies I spoke of, at the end of which is a lovely pine, most beautiful in form and colour, which by hiding some of the lower buildings thus makes a picture of the whole. The effect of the building is grand and stately beyond description. The long line of flat distance and the flatness of the Down here come in contact with the perpendicular lines of the Tower and lower buildings, producing that strikingly peculiar combination which never fails to produce a grand effect. This is the real secret of Claude's seaports. His stately buildings, moles and tall towers form a right angle with the straight horizon; thus the whole is magnificent. Nothing of the sort could be produced in the interior of a country but in a situation like the present. Who but a man of extraordinary genius would have thought of rearing in the desert such a structure as this, or creating such an oasis? The colouring of the building reminded me of Malta or Sicily, a rich mellow hue prevails; the ornaments of the Tower are so clean, so distinct, such terseness. The windows, small and few compared with modern buildings, give it the appearance of those early Florentine edifices reared when security and defence were as much an object as beauty. From every part of the ground the pile looks grand, the lines producing the most beautiful effect. The windows have iron gratings, which give it an Oriental character. We entered, and immediately ascended the Tower. A circular staircase was round the wall. The proportion of the interior is beautiful; you see from the bottom to the top. From the apparent size of the three or four loopholes seen from the outside I imagined it would be dark and gloomy from within, but I was agreeably surprised to find form, and banisters bronze. On reaching the top you find a square of plate glass, the floor covered with red cloth and crimson window curtains. The effect of distance seen through these apertures unobstructed by framework, contrasted with the bronze balustrade without and crimson curtains within, is truly enchanting.

CHARLOTTE LANSDOWN to her father,
21 August 1838

Philip Stanhope, Earl of Chesterfield (1633–1713), laid out his spectacular gardens in the 1680s. They appear to have been by George London and William Talman but their chief spectacle was the work of the hydraulics engineer, Mr Grillet.

BRETBY, DERBYSHIRE

But that which is most admired – and justly so to be – by all persons and excite their curiosity to come and see is the Gardens and Waterworks; out of the billiard roome the first was with gravell walks and a large fountaine in the middle with flower pots and greens set round the brimm of the fountaines that are paved with stone; you see but one garden at a tyme: the pipes in the fountaines play very finely, some of a great height, some flushes the water

about, then you come to a descent of severall steps which discovers another fine garden with fountaines playing through pipes, besett on the bancks with all sort of greens and flower trees dwarfes honeysuckles in a round tuft growing uppright and all sorts of flower trees and greens finely cutt and exactly kept; in one garden there are 3 fountaines wherein stands great statues, each side on their pedistalls is a Dial, one for the sun, the other a Clock which by the water worke is moved and strikes the hours and chimes the quarters, and when they please play Liliboloaro on the Chymes – all this I heard when I was there – on one side of this garden is a half compass with a breast wall on which are high iron pallisadoes divided with severall pillars, stone with images on their tops; about 2 yards distance this opens to view the parke and a sort of cannall or pond which is in it of a good bigness; beyond this garden is a row of orange and lemon trees set in the ground, of a man's height and pretty big, full of flowers and some large fruit almost ripe; this has a penthouse over it which is cover'd up very close in the winter; this leads to a great wilderness and just by it is another square with a fountaine whose brim is deck'd with flower potts full of flowers and all sorts of greens, on either side is 2 or 3 rows of orange and lemon trees in boxes one below another in growth.

Just against this is a wall cover'd over with lawrell finely cutt and also in the middle is an arch, and on either side stone staires ascends it which terminate in a sort of half pace all cover'd over with lawrell, and this enters a doore into another garden through a little garden house; this also has a fine fountaine like the others only as most off the others was green walks this was gravell, so was the garden on the right side of the house; the front garden which has the largest fountaine has also a fine green house and very fine flowers, and the beds and borders are cut in severall formes, the greens are very fine and the hedges cut in severall formes; there was one tree much unlike the cyprus green but the branches were more spread and of a little yellower green, the barke of the limbs yellow, it was the Cedar of Lebonus; where was also fine strip'd stocks double like a rose; there was a large Ewe tree in the middle of one garden cut in forms, fine firrs and cyprus and filleroy (phillyrea) of which some was striped like silver white others yellow like gold which gave them their different names, and fine gilded and striped hollys.

There was one green in a pott call'd St John the Baptists herb, it was full of many leaves and the coullour not much unlike the green they call Solomons Seale but longer and bigger leaves, its an annual plant; here just by the wilderness is the Tulip tree which runns up of a great height and the flower is on the top it flowers in August; there is a great avery of birds which stands like a sumer house open, there is also many close averys of birds and severall green shady walks and close arbours, there are very fine wood bines grows like tufts all in flower red and white; there is some of the fountaines that have figures in them that throws up water a greate height, a cascade of water.

Then I returned into the hall and so into a coole roome in which was a fountaine, where I dranke a glass of wine, and so proceeded . . .

CELIA FIENNES, 1698; in *The Journeys of Celia Fiennes*, ed. Christopher Morris [1947]

George London's final garden, undertaken for James Brydges, Earl of Carnarvon and later Duke of Chandos (1673–1744), was the last of the great baroque formal gardens. Alexander Pope mocked them in his satire under the guise of Timon's villa (see pp. 275–6) although, of course, he denied it.

There is a large Terras Walk, from whence you descend to the *Parterre*; this *Parterre* hath a row of gilded *Vases* on Pedestals, on each side down to the great *Cannal*, and in the middle, fronting the Canal, is a Gladiator, gilded also; and through the whole *Parterre*, Abundance of Statues, as big as the Life regularly disposed.

The Canal runs a great Way, and indeed one would wonder to see such a vast Quantity of Water in a Country, where are neither Rivers nor Springs. But they tell me, that the Duke hath his Water in Pipes from the Mountains of *Stanmore* about Two Miles off. The Gardens are very large and well disposed; but the greatest Pleasure of all is, that the Divisions of the whole being only made by Ballustrades of Iron, and not by Walls; you see the whole at once, be you in what Part of the Garden or *Parterre* you will. In his large Kitchen Garden, there are Beehives of Glass very curious.

J. MACKY, *A Journey through England* [1722]

William Cavendish, 1st Duke of Devonshire (1640–1707), employed George London and Henry Wise in the 1680s and 1690s to lay out a garden on a vast scale to match the new house by William Talman. The Great Parterre alone was 437 feet long and 227 feet wide. Visitors were duly impressed.

We go from Chesterffield to the Duke of Devonshires house and ascend a high hill at least two or three miles long . . . before the gate there is a large Parke and severall fine Gardens one without another with gravell walkes and squairs of grass with stone statues in them and in the middle of each Garden is a large fountaine full of images Sea Gods and Dolphins and Sea Horses which are full of pipes which spout out water in the bason and spouts all about the gardens; 3 Gardens just round the house; out of two of the Gardens you ascend by severall stepps into other Gardens which some have gravell walks and square like the other with Statues and Images in the bason, there is one bason in the middle of one Garden thats very large and by sluces besides the Images severall pipes plays out the water, about 30 large and small pipes altogether, some flush it up that it frothes like snow; there is one Garden full of stone and brass statues; so the Gardens lyes one above another which makes the prospect very fine; above these gardens is an ascent of 5 or 6 stepps up to green walk and groves of firrs, and a wilderness and close arbours and shady walks, on each end of one walke stands two piramidies full of pipes spouting water that runns down one of them, runns on brass hollow work which looks like rocks and hollow stones; the other is all flatts stands one above another like salvers so the water rebounds one from another, 5 or 6 one above the other; there is another green walke and about the middle of it by the Grove stands a fine Willow tree, the leaves barke and all looks very naturall, the roote is full of rubbish or great stones to appearance, and all on a sudden by turning a sluce it raines from each leafe

and from the branches like a shower, it being made of brass and pipes to each leafe but in appearance is exactly like any Willow; beyond this is a bason in which are the branches of two Hartichocks Leaves which weeps at the end of each leafe into the bason which is placed at the foote of lead steps 30 in number, the lowest step is very deep and between every 4 stepps is a half pace all made of lead and are broad on each side; on a little banck stands blew balls 10 on a side, and between each ball are 4 pipes which by a sluce spouts out water across the stepps to each other like an arbour or arch; while you are thus amused suddenly there runs down a torrent of water out of 2 pitchers in the hands of two large Nimphs cut in stone that lyes in the upper step, which makes a pleaseing prospect, this is designed to be enlarged and steps made up to the top of the hill which is a vast ascent, but from the top of it now they are supply'd with water for all their pipes so it will be easier to have such a fall of water even from the top which will add to the Curiositye.

CELIA FIENNES, 1697; in *The Journeys of Celia Fiennes*, ed. Christopher Morris [1947]

Twenty years later they were still improving the vistas!

Under this Front [of Chatsworth] lye the Gardens exquisitely fine, and, to make a clear Vista or Prospect beyond into the flat Country, towards *Hardwick*, another Seat of the same owner, the Duke, to whom what others thought impossible, was not only made practicable, but easy, removed, and perfectly carried away a great Mountain that stood in the way, and which interrupted the Prospect.

This was so entirely gone, that, having taken a strict View of the Gardens at my first being there, and retaining an Idea of them in my Mind, I was perfectly confounded at coming there a second time, and not knowing what had been done; for I had lost the Hill, and found a new Country in view, which *Chatsworth* it self had never seen before.

DANIEL DEFOE, *A Tour thro' the Whole Island of Great Britain* [1724–6 and 1742]

CHISWICK HOUSE, MIDDLESEX

One of the most celebrated gardens of its day, designed by Charles Bridgeman and William Kent for Richard Boyle, Earl of Burlington (1695–1753), it was hailed by Pope (see pp. 276–7) as the harbinger of the new landscape style.

But I must not pass over so slightly the noble Seat of the Right Honourable the Earl of *Burlington*; which was a plain, useful House, with a Number of good Offices about it: but as a Part of the old House was destroyed some Years ago, by Fire, his Lordship erected a most beautiful Villa, near to the old House; which for Elegance of Taste, surpasses every thing of its kind in *England*, if not in *Europe*. The Court in Front of the House is of a proportionable Size to the Building, which is gravelled, and kept always very neat. On each Side are Yew Hedges, in Panels, with *Termini*, placed at proper Distance; in Front of which are planted two rows of Cedars of *Libanus*, which at present have a fine Effect to the Eye, at a small Distance from the House; for the dark Shade of these solemn ever-green Trees occasions a fine Contraste with the elegant white Building which appears between them . . .

The Gardens are also laid out in an elegant Taste. When you descend from the House, you enter on a Lawn of Grass, planted with Clumps of ever-green Trees, between which are two Rows of large Stone Vases. At the Ends next the House are two fine Wolves in Stone, cut by Mr. *Sceidmaker* the famous Statuary: and at the farther End are two large Lions; and to terminate this View are three fine antique Statues, which were dug up in *Adrian's* Garden at *Rome*, with Stone Seats between each; and on the Back of the Statues is a close Plantation of Ever-greens, which terminates the Prospect.

On the Right-hand, as you go from the House, you look thro' an open Grove of Forest-trees, to the Orangery; which is separated from the Lawn by a Faussee, to secure the Orange-trees from being injured by Persons who are admitted to walk in the Garden; so that they are seen as perfectly, and when the Orange-trees are in Flower, the Scent is diffused over the whole Lawn to the House, as if the Trees were placed on the Lawn.

On the Left-hand you have an easy Slope of Grass down to the Serpentine River, on the Side of which are Clumps of Ever-greens, which make agreeable Breaks to the Eye, between which the Water is seen; and at the farther End is a Peep into an Inclosure, where are an Obelisk and a *Roman* Temple, with Grass Slopes, and a circular Piece of Water in the Middle.

From this Lawn you are led to the Wilderness, through which are three strait Avenues, terminated by three different Buildings; and within the Quarters are Serpentine Walks, thro' which you may walk near a Mile in constant Shade.

On each Side the Serpentine River is a Grass Walk, which follow the Turns of the River; and on the Right-hand of the River is a Building, which is the exact Model of the Portico of *Covent Garden* Church; and on the Left is a Wilderness, which is laid out in regular Walks, with clipp'd Hedges on each Side, which is too mean for the other Parts of the Garden; and it is much to be wondered his Lordship should suffer them to remain in the present Form.

Over the River, in the middle Part, is a *Palladian* Bridge of Wood, which his Lordship crosses in his Coach to come round to the House: for there is a Coach Road thro' the Garden, by which his Lordship passes when he comes from *London*, so that the Earl seldom goes thro' the Town of *Chiswick* to his House.

At the end of the River, next the Road, is a fine Cascade lately erected, which by an Engine to raise the Water, his Lordship proposed to have a constant Fall into the River; but the Engine failing, it is but seldom the Cascade can play, and then but for a short time.

Next the Road his Lordship has raised a Terrace, (with the Earth which came out of the River) from whence you have a Prospect of the adjacent Country; and when the Tide is up, you see the Water of the *Thames*, with the Boats and Barges passing, which greatly enlivens the Prospect. In a Word, there is more Variety in this Garden, than can be found in any other of the same Size in *England*, or perhaps in *Europe* . . .

DANIEL DEFOE, *A Tour thro' the Whole Island of Great Britain* [1724–6 and 1742]

EATON HALL,
CHESHIRE

The gardens at Eaton Hall were laid out in the grand manner by William Andrews Nesfield in the 1850s. Loelia Ponsonby, who became the third wife of the notorious 'Bendor', Duke of Westminster in 1930 catches how the Grosvenor riches maintained horticultural splendour right up to 1939.

Barnes, the gardener, was the fourth member of the team. A gruff old Caledonian, he seemed able to grow any flower he chose at whatever season he chose, and his management of the hothouses almost amounted to genius. Some of the houses were utilitarian and were used for forcing vegetables, early strawberries, melons, peaches, nectarines and flowers for the house; others were purely ornamental and one went and walked through them as one would stroll round a garden. The most sensational was enormously long, with very old camellia trees, thirty feet high, trained up the back wall. There were lilacs in pots, azaleas, scented varieties of rhododendron, mimosa, bougainvillaea and a mass of other flowers, the whole making a vista of extraordinary beauty . . .

There was also an orchid house under the management of its own expert. Before we were married I had asked Bendor if he had orchids at Eaton and he had said that he had never gone in for them but that they must be interesting to grow and I had thought no more about it. When we got back from our honeymoon there was a glass-house full of orchids in bloom and an expert in a white coat with test tubes and cultures, busy breeding new crosses. The whole business of orchid breeding seemed very mysterious. Growers guarded their own secrets and it appeared that you could only find the right culture by a process of trial and error. There were a lot of failures, but every now and then the jelly-like substance in the tubes got covered with a green moss composed of hundreds of tiny plants which in due course were transplanted and grown up until they flowered, when it would be seen whether any of them were worth keeping. Our expert lived in hopes of producing a marvellous new cross that would be worth hundreds of pounds and we sympathized with him when he came and complained that his most precious bloom, a pure white virgin veiled in white cellophane to keep away pollen-carrying insects, had been picked by Lord Carnarvon and presented to a girl friend.

All this, of course, went on in and around the kitchen garden. The ornamental gardens began with a balustraded terrace in front of the East windows. The ground fell away sharply and a formal French garden with pleached limes and stone steps at intervals led down to a lake. There was an island in the lake and Benny settled some hardy Himalayan monkeys on it. With their long arms stretched above their heads they looked as tall as *yeti* and we could easily see them from across the water. They would perform for our benefit like trapeze artists, flying through the air from tree to tree, now and again dropping plumb from a tree-top, but always managing to catch a branch just before they hit the ground. They were very ferocious-looking with long yellow teeth which they were known to sink into the hand of the keeper who used to row over to the island with their food. The year the lake froze there was a good deal of alarm among the crowd on the ice when the monkeys came slithering among them, especially as, being beginners, they naturally wanted to hold the hands of the more experienced skaters.

LOELIA, DUCHESS OF
WESTMINSTER, *Grace and Favour*
[1961]

A garden in the French taste planted by the poet Edmund Waller (1606–87) and re-worked by his grandson (1715–39) and John Aislabie (1670–1742), creator of Studley Royal.

HALL BARN, BEACONSFIELD, BUCKINGHAM-SHIRE

Now to give you an account of what we have seen. Fryday morning when we left Beceonsfeild, we went half a mile out of our way to see Hall Barn, Mr Wallers house, a London Box if I may so call a house of 7 windows every way. He was gone hunting, so we did not go into the house which promised nothing extraordinary, but we spent a full hour and half in viewing the gardens, which you will think are fine when I tell you they put us in mind of those at Versailles. He has 80 Acres in garden & wood, but the last is so managed, as justly to be counted part of the former, for from the parterre you have terraces and gravel'd walks that lead up to and quite thro the wood, in which, several lesser ones cross the principal one of different breadths, but all well gravel'd and for the most part green sodded on the sides. The wood consists of tall beach trees, & thick underwood at least 30 foot high. The narrow winding walks and paths cut in it are innumerable. A woman in full health cannot walk them all, for which reason my wife was carry'd in a windsor chair, like those at Versailles, by which means she lost nothing worth seeing. The walks are terminated by Ha-hah's, over which you see a fine country, and variety of prospects, every time you come to the extremity of the close winding walks that shut out the sun.

Versailles has indeed the advantage in fountains, for there is not one in all this garden, but there are two very noble peices of water full of fish, and handsomely planted & teraced on the sides. In one part of the wood, and in a deep bottom is a place to which one descends with horrour, for it seems the residence of some draggon, but there shines a gleam of light thro the high wood that surrounds & shades it, which recovers the spirits, and makes you sensible a draggon would seek some place still more retired. This place may be call'd the temple of Pan or Silvanus, consisting of several apartments, arches, Corridores &c composed of high thriving Ews, cut very artfully. In the Center of the Inner Circle or Court if I may call it so, stands the figure of a guilt Satyr on a stone pedestal with his finger in his mouth, as if he would have you tread softly, least you should interrupt a bewtifull Hermophrodite near at hand contemplating a flower. I pass over the bowling green & large plantations about the house which are but young, but I must not forget a bench or seat of the famous Edmund Waller's the Poet, which is so reverenced, that old as it is it is never to be removed, but constantly repaired like Sir Francis Drakes ship. The present Waller is his Grand son . . . There is a great deal more still to be done, which will cost a prodigious sum . . .

LORD PERCEVAL, 1ST EARL OF EGMONT [1683–1748], Letter of 9 August 1724

The gardens, laid out for Henry VIII in the 1530s, remained virtually unchanged throughout the sixteenth century.

HAMPTON COURT, MIDDLESEX

On descent and exit from the church the gardener presented himself, and after we had offered a gratuity to our first guide, the gardener conducted us into the royal pleasaunce.

By the entrance I noticed numerous patches where square cavities had

been scooped, as for paving stones; some of these were filled with red brick-dust, some with white sand, and some with green lawn, very much resembling a chess-board. The hedges and surrounds were of hawthorn, bush firs, ivy, roses, juniper, holly, English or common elm, box and other shrubs, very gay and attractive.

There were all manner of shapes, men and women, half men and half horse, sirens, serving-maids with baskets, French lilies and delicate crenellations all round made from the dry twigs bound together and the aforesaid evergreen quick-set shrubs, or entirely of rosemary, all true to the life, and so cleverly and amusingly interwoven, mingled and grown together, trimmed and arranged picture-wise that their equal would be difficult to find.

And just as there is a park on the one hand, so opposite this in the middle of the other side there is a marble fountain, so that time shall not drag in such a place; for should one miss one's way, not only are taste, vision and smell delighted, but the gladsome birdsongs and plashing fountains please the ear, indeed it is like an earthly paradise.

THOMAS PLATTER, *Travels in England* [1599]

HIDCOTE MANOR GARDEN, GLOUCESTERSHIRE

Lawrence Johnston (1871–1948), a bachelor francophile American, created one of the cult gardens of our age. One of the few references to it before it entered the public domain after the owner's death, occurs in James Lees-Milne's diaries in 1943.

Tuesday, 6th July

Papa drove me to Hidcote to tea with Laurie Johnston who took us round his famous garden. No reference was made by him to the National Trust. The garden is not only beautiful but remarkable in that it is full of surprises. You are constantly led from one scene to another, into long vistas and little enclosures, which seem infinite. Moreover the total area of this garden does not cover many acres. Surely the twentieth century has produced some remarkable gardens on a small scale. This one is also full of rare plants brought from the most outlandish places in India and Asia. When my father and Laurie Johnston were absorbed in talk I was tremendously impressed by their profound knowledge of a subject which is closed to me. It was like hearing two people speaking fluently a language of which I am totally ignorant.

JAMES LEES-MILNE, *Ancestral Voices* [1975]

KENILWORTH CASTLE, WARWICKSHIRE

The earliest great Elizabethan garden laid out for Robert Dudley, Earl of Leicester (1532?–88) between 1563 and 1575 and the setting for the 'Princely Pleasures' with which he entertained the Queen in the summer of 1575.

Untoo thiz, hiz honorz exquisit appointment of a beautiful Garden, an aker or more of quantitee that lyeth on the north thear. Wherain hard all along the Castl wall iz reared a pleazaunt Terres of a ten foot hy and a twelve brode: eeven under foot and fresh of fyne grass: as iz allso the syde thearof toward the gardein, in which by sundry equall distauncez: with obelisks, sphearz, and white bearz all of stone upon theyr curioouz basez, by goodly sheaw wear set: too theez, too fine arberz redolent by sweet trees and floourz, at each end one. The garden plot under that, with fayr alleyz green by grass, eeven voided from the borderz a both sydez, and sum (for chaunge) with sand, not light or to soft, or soilly by dust, but smooth and fyrm, pleasaunt too walk on, az a sea shore when the water iz availd: then, mooch gracified by du proporcion of foour eeven quarterz: in the midst of each, upon a base a too foot square and hy, seemly borderd of it self, a square pilaster rizing pyramidally of a fyfteen foot hy: Simmetrically peerced throgh from a foot beneath, untill a too foot from the top: whereupon, for a Capitell, an Orb of a ten inches thik: every of theez (with hiz base) from the groound too the top of one hole pees, heawen oout of hard Porphiry, and with great art and heed (thinks me) thyther conveyd and thear erected. Whear further allso by great cast and cost the sweetnes of savoour on all sidez, made so respiraunt from the redolent plants and fragrant earbs and floourz, in foorm, coller and quantitee so delicioously variaunt: and frute Trees bedecked with their Applz, Peares and rype Cherryez.

And untoo theez in the midst, against the Terres: a square Cage, sump-tuoous and beautifull, joyned hard too the North-wall (that a that syde gards the gardein, az the gardein the Castl) of a rare foorm and excellency wazs reyzed: in heyth a twenty foot, thyrty long, and a foourteen brode. From the ground strong and close, reared breast hy, whearat a Soyl of a fayr moolding waz coouched all aboout: From that upward, foour great wyndoz a froont, and too at each eend, every one a five foot wide, az many mo eeven aboove them: divided on all parts by a Transum and Architrave so lykewize raunging aboout the Cage. Each wyndo arched in the top and parted from oother, in eeven distauns by flat fayr bolteld Columns, all in foorm and beauty lyke, that supported a cumly Cornish coouched all along upon the hole square. Which, with a wyre net, finely knit, of mashez six square, an inch wyde (az it wear for a flat roof) and likewise the space of every wyndo: with great cunning and cumlynes, eeven and tight waz all over strained. Under the Cornish again, every part beautified with great Diamonds, Emerauds, Rubyes and Saphyres: poynted, tabld, rok and roound: garnisht with theyr gold, by skyllfull hed and hand, and by toyl and pensyl, so lyvely exprest, az it moought bee great marveyl, and pleazure too consider hoow neer excellensy of art coold approch untoo perfection of nature . . .

In the center (az it wear) of this goodly Gardein, was theer placed, a very fayr Foountain, cast intoo an eight square, reared a four foot hy: from the midst whereof a Colum up set in shape of too *Athlants* joyned togeather a backhallf, the toon looking East, toother west: with theyr hands, uphollding a fayr foormed boll of a three foot over: from wheans sundry fine pipez, did lively distill continuall streamz intoo the receyt of the Foountayn: mayn-teyned styll too foot deep by the same fresh falling water: whearin pleazauntly playing too and fro and roound aboout: Carp, Tench, Bream, and for varietee, Pearch and Eel, fysh fayrlyking all and large. In the top, the ragged Staff, which, with the boll, the piller, and eight sydez beneath, wear all heawen oout of rich and hard white Marbl. A one syde, *Neptune* with hiz *Tridental Fuskin* triumphing in hiz Throne, trayled intoo the deep by hiz marine horsez. On an oother, *Thetis* in her chariot drawn by her dollphins. Thne *Triton* by hiz fyshez. Heer *Protheus* hearding hiz sea bulz. Thear *Doris* and her dooughterz solacyng a sea and sandz. The wavez soourging with froth and fome, entermengld in place, with whalez, whirlpoolz, Sturgeonz,

Tunneyz, Conchs and wealks: all engraven by exquisit devize and skyll, so az I may think this not mooch inferioour untoo *Phoebus* gatez, which (*Ovid* sayz) and peradventur a pattern to thiz, that *Vulcan* himself dyd cut: whearof such waz the excellency of art, that the woork in valu surmoounted the stuff, and yet wear the gatez all of clean massy sylver.

Heer wear things ye see, moought enflame ony mynde too long after looking: but whoo so waz foound so hot in desyre, with the wreast of a Cok waz sure of a coolar: water spurting upward with such vehemency, az they shoold by and by be moystned from top too to. The heez to sum laughing, but the sheez too more sport. Thiz sumtime waz occupied too very good pastime.

A Garden then so appointed, az whearin a loft upon sweet shadoed wallk of Terres, in heat of Soomer, too feel the pleazaunt whysking winde aboove, or delectabl coolnes of the foountain spring beneath: Too tast of delicious strawberiez, cherryez and oother frutez eevn from their stalks: Too smell such fragrancy of sweet odoourz breathing from the plants, earbs and floourz: Too heer such naturall meloodioous musik, and tunez of burds. To have in ey, for myrth sumtyme theez undersprynging streamz: then, the woods, the waters (for both pool and chase wear hard at hand in sight) the deer, the peepl (that oout of the East arber, in the base coourt, allso at hand in view) the frute trees, the plants, the earbs, the floourz, the chaunge in coolers, the Burds flyttering, the Foountain streaming, the Fysh swymming: all in such delectabl varietee, order and dignitee: whearby at one moment, in one place, at hand withou travell too have so full fruicion of so many Gods blessings, by entyer delight unto all sensez (if all can take) at ones: for *Etymon* of the woord woorthy too be calld Paradis: and though not so goodly az Paradis for want of the fayr ryvers, yet better a great deel by the lak of so unhappy a tree. Argument most certain of a right nobl minde, that in this sort coold have thus all contrived. ROBERT LANEHAM, *A Letter: Whearin part of the entertainment untoo the Queenz Majesty at Killingworth Caste, in Warwick Sheer in this Soomerz Progress, 1575, is signified . . .*

KEW GARDENS, RICHMOND, SURREY

Kew was developed under the aegis of Augusta, Princess of Wales by Sir William Chambers in the 1750s and '60s. Not everyone, however, was impressed.

There is little invention or Taste shown. Being on a flat, Lord Bute raised hillocs to diversify the ground, & carried Chambers the Architect thither, who built some temples, but they are all of wood and very small. Of his design was the round Temple in the middle, with a circular portico, called the Temple of Victory on the battle of Minden; another with a Doric portico; the Corinthian semicircular arcade, a little round temple in the recess on the left hand, the Roman ruin, the Aviary, & a Chinese building in the Menagerie. The bridge & the round Temple were each erected in a night's time to surprize the Princess. HORACE WALPOLE, *Journals* [1760]

The experiences of a twentieth-century visitor strike one as very different.

From the oval-shaped flower-bed there rose perhaps a hundred stalks spreading into heart-shaped or tongue-shaped leaves half way up and unfurling at the tip red *or* blue or yellow petals marked with spots of colour raised upon the surface; and from the red, blue, or yellow gloom of the throat emerged a straight bar, rough with gold dust, and slightly clubbed at the end. The petals were voluminous enough to be stirred by the summer breeze, and when they moved the red, blue, and yellow lights pass one over the other, staining an inch of the brown earth beneath with a spot of the most intricate colour. The light fell either upon the smooth grey back of a pebble, or the shell of a snail with its brown circular veins, or, falling into a raindrop, it expanded with such intensity of red, blue, and yellow the thin walls of water that one expected them to burst, and disappear. Instead the drop was left in a second silver grey once more, and the light now settled upon the flesh of a leaf, revealing the branching thread of fibre beneath the surface, and again it moved on and spread its illumination in the vast green spaces beneath the dome of the heart-shaped and tongue-shaped leaves. Then the breeze stirred rather more briskly overhead, and the colour was flashed into the air above, into the eyes of the men and the women who walk in Kew Gardens in July.   VIRGINIA WOOLF, *Kew Gardens* [1927]

Created by the poet William Shenstone (1714–63) as a ferme ornée *between 1745 and 1763, it was one of the most visited gardens of its day (see pp. 94–5). Visitors had to follow a set route.*

THE LEASOWES, SHROPSHIRE

The day was yet young; I therefore, in passing the small town of Hales-Owen, took a slight but necessary repast, and after travelling about half a mile along the road leading to the large and opulent town of Birmingham, a shady, pleasant lane on my right, led me into a steep gloomy glen, covered with trees, to a rude wall, where a small gate, over-arched with stones, proclaimed

The PRIORY WALK

The moment I entered this quiet and sequestered valley, the superlative genius of Shenstone stood confessed on every object, and struck me with silent admiration. – I turned to a bench under the wall, and sat so absorbed, with the charms, of a cascade, so powerfully conducted in the very image of nature herself, plunging down a bed of shelving rock, and huge massy stones, that, for a long while, my attention was lost to every thing else – I strove to find out where the hand of the designer had been, but could not: – surely nothing was ever held to the eye so incomparably well executed! . . .

Sudden transitions from one extreme to another, catch the attention, and always render them more agreeable. – A sprightly, busy, and domestic scene, would succeed the solitary; opening to a neat house on a rising lawn; from whence the path would keep along the edge of the perpendicular sided chasm, to a seat, where the eye would rest upon a profusion of variety – a cascade roaring within a deep rocky cavern – a bridge – the high road, winding up a hill – and a woody valley; – on the other hand, under a mountain of a dam, that would be closely bushed with the Weymouth pine

and pine-aster, the large wheel of a mill, perpetually driving its frothy current down a narrow channel, collecting, and forming with that from the chasm, the neck of a river, running under the bridge into a pool below. ·

The walk from hence would dip into the irriguous area in front, and wind within the plantation of pines, up to a full and delicious view of the cascade, I substituted instead of the pool, bursting from the junction of the before-mentioned streams, down a promiscuous shelve of rock, into the extremity of a teeming river, between the gloom of interwoven thicket and trees, feathering the climbing sides of the glen.

A step or two from hence, to a bridge crossing the narrow neck of a pool, would immediately change the scene from the rage and fury of cataract, to a calm, spacious, and seemingly unbounded sheet of water; when after passing the bridge, the path might direct over some hilly ground, through well-designed plantations, into the valley I am now going to conduct you.

From the seat I left you at, to give you some idea of the variety such an operation would add to the Leasowes; the path curls most agreeably round the margin of the pool, and enters the lovely, sister valley of the Priory; where, though the Naiades do not discover so many of their charms, through an artful trick of the designer, to surprize us, in a subsequent scene with them, in all their fascinating powers, you may possibly find yourself, in the contemplation of its chaste sylvan character, equally happy.

JOSEPH HEELY, *Letters on the Beauties of Hagley, Envil, and The Leasowes* [1777]

Not everyone, however, viewed the garden in the same state of euphoria.

It was ridiculous to see Naiads (water nymphs) invited, by inscriptions, to bathe their beauteous limbs in *crystal* pools, which stood before the eye, impregnated with all the filth, which generates from stagnation ... Mr Shenstone's great deficiency lay in not draining his grounds. If he had made his verdure richer, tho at the expence of his buildings, he had shewn a purer taste. But he chose rather to lay out his money on what made most shew, than on what would have been most becoming.

THE REVEREND WILLIAM GILPIN, *Observations on Several Parts of England . . .* [1772]

MOOR PARK, HERTFORDSHIRE

In spite of Sir William Temple's attribution of Moor Park to Lucy Harington, Countess of Bedford (1582–1627) it may have been laid out by William Herbert, 3rd Earl of Pembroke (1580–1630). Whoever did it, the garden was one of the earliest italianate ones in England.

The perfectest Figure of a Garden I ever saw, either at Home or Abroad, was that of *Moor-Park* in *Hertfordshire*, when I knew it about thirty Years ago. It was made by the Countess of Bedford, esteemed among the greatest Wits of her Time, and celebrated by Doctor *Donne*; and with very great care, excellent Contrivance, and much Cost; but greater Sums may be thrown away without Effect or Honour, if there want Sense in Proportion to Money, or if Nature be not followed; which I take to be the great Rule in this, and perhaps in every thing else, as far as the Conduct not only of our Lives, but our Governments. And whether the greatest of Mortal Men should attempt the forcing of Nature may best be judged, by observing how seldom God Almighty does it Himself, by so few, true, and undisputed Miracles, as we see or hear of in the World. For my own part, I know not three wiser Precepts for the Conduct either of Princess or Private Men, than

> *Servare Modum, Finemque tueri,*
> *Naturamque sequi.*

Because I take the Garden I have named to have been in all Kinds the most beautiful and perfect, at least in the Figure and Disposition, that I have ever seen, I will describe it for a Model to those that meet with such a Situation, and are above the Regards of common Expence. It lies on the Side of a Hill, (upon which the House stands) but not very steep. The Length of the House, where the best Rooms and of most Use or Pleasure are, lies upon the Breadth of the Garden, the Great Parlour opens into the Middle of a Terras Gravel-Walk that lies even with it, and which may be, as I remember, about three hundred Paces long, and broad in Proportion; the Border set with Standard Laurels, and at large Distances, which have the Beauty of Orange-Trees out of Flower and Fruit: From this Walk are Three Descents by many Stone Steps, in the Middle and at each End, into a very large Parterre. This is divided into Quarters by Gravel-Walks, and adorned with Two Fountains and Eight Statues in the several Quarters; at the End of the Terras-Walk are Two Summer-Houses, and the Sides of the Parterre are ranged with two large Cloisters, open to the Garden, upon Arches of Stone, and ending with two other Summer-Houses even with the Cloisters, which are paved with Stone, and designed for Walks of Shade, there being none other in the whole Parterre. Over these two Cloisters are two Terrasses covered with Lead, and fenced with Balusters; and the Passage into these Airy Walks is out of the two Summer-Houses, at the end of the first Terras-Walk. The Cloister facing the *South* is covered with Vines, and would have been proper for an Orange-House, and the other for Myrtles, or other more common Greens; and had, I doubt not been cast for that Purpose, if this Piece of Gardening had been then in as much Vogue as it is now.

From the Middle of the Parterre is a Descent by many Steps flying on each Side of a Grotto that lies between them (covered with Lead, and Flat) into the lower Garden, which is all Fruit-Trees ranged about the several Quarters of a Wilderness which is very Shady; the Walks here are all Green, the Grotto embellish'd with Figures of Shell-Rock-work, Fountains, and Water-works. If the Hill had not ended with the lower Garden, and the Wall were not bounded by a common Way that goes through the Park, they might have added a Third Quarter of all Greens; but this Want is supplied by a Garden on the other Side the House, which is all of that Sort, very Wild, Shady, and adorned with rough Rock-work and Fountains.

This was *Moor-Park*, when I was acquainted with it, and the sweetest Place, I think, that I have seen in my Life, either before or since, at Home or Abroad.

WILLIAM TEMPLE, *Upon the Gardens of Epicurus: or, Of Gardening, the Year 1685* [1692]

Although the gardens were begun by Henry VIII, they were mainly the work of John, Lord Lumley (1534?–1609) between 1579 and 1591 when the palace returned to the crown. In them we have found the

earliest attempt to create an italianate 'bosco' with a grotto and focal
points. Diana, of course, was the Virgin Queen.

. . . we returned to the palace, and were shown the queen's garden laid out as
follows:

At the entrance to the garden is a grove (lucus) called after Diana, the
goddess, from here we came to a rock out of which natural water springs into
a basin, and on this was portrayed with great art and life-like execution the
story of how the three goddesses took their bath naked and sprayed Acteon
with water, causing antlers to grow upon his head, and of how his own
hounds afterwards tore him to pieces. Further on we came to a small vaulted
temple, where was a fine marble table, and the following mottoes were
inscribed here thus – on the nearest wall:

> *Nil impudicum pudicitate Dea*
> *Nil turpe suadet sceleris vindicta*
> *Sed mala mens malus animus*

being in English 'The goddess of chastity gives no unchaste councils, she does
not council disgrace, but avenges it, they are the fruits of an evil mind and an
evil spirit'.

On the right is written up:

> *Impuri fontis,*
> *Inclari rivuli*
> *Ingrate mentis,*
> *Impuri oculi*

which is in English 'From an unclean fountain impure springs, from an
unpleasant mind a sight defiled'.

On the left is:

> *Aestuanti umbra,*
> *Languanti sedes*
> *Noli in umbra umbratilis esse*
> *Nec sint sedenti serpentis oculi*

which is in English: 'Shade for the heated, a seat for the weary, in the shade
thou shalt not become shady, nor sitting grow serpent-eyed'.

Then I beheld a pointed tower (*pyramidem*) spurting out water, and a rock
from which issued water.

We next entered an arbour or pavilion (*pavillon*) where the queen sits
during the chase in the park. Here she can see the game run past. Then
through a wood in the gardens, with fine straight long alleys (*allées*) through
it, fashioned in this wise:

In the very densest part of the wood about here a great many trees are
uprooted and cleared, within a breadth of some eighteen to twenty feet,
along a straight course, so that there is a vista from one end to the other. And
here and there they are partitioned off on either side with high boards, so
that the balls may be played in the shade of these same alleys very pleasantly,
as in an enclosed tennis court, and other amusing pastimes may also be
pursued, while the delicious song of the birds in the tall trees, densely planted
along the sides in ordered array afford one great delight.

From here we came to a maze or labyrinth surrounded by high shrubberies to prevent one passing over or through them. In the pleasure gardens are charming terraces and all kinds of animals – dogs, hares, all overgrown with plants, most artfully set out, so that from a distance, one would take them for real ones.

THOMAS PLATTER, *Travels in England* [1599]

Laid out by Charles Hamilton (1704–86) between 1738 and 1773, this astonishing landscape garden was dotted with set tableaux from a Roman mausoleum to a Turkish tent. It was also famous for its exotic planting of American trees. At the moment it is being restored.

PAINSHILL, SURREY

Painshill, where 390 acres are kept in the most elegant manner as they are laid out with the greatest taste. I must observe here that a stranger coming from towards Thorp to this improvement is prejudiced inconceivably against it from the dreary wild heath he must pass over called Cobham Heath, as barren and wild as a mountain. This with another called Winter Downs and Esher Heath is what I mentioned before as seen from part of Clermont. Before you reach Painshill you see a Belvidere in the Improvements, of a great height built like a gothic tower. But to attempt a just description of Mr Hamilton's I will follow my method of going through each place as the gardener brought me.

You enter at a disadvantageous part of the garden by a little old house. Nothing before you but a flat, fine-grassed sheepwalk, with clumps of Scots fir and laurel interspersed with flowering shrubs: these are surrounded with pitched network to prevent the sheep, which are here in abundance, from spoiling the plants. In this plain you wait some time till the footman who opened the gate to you has brought a gardener who conducts you about two hundred yards, when all at once a beautiful country bursts on your eye at one side, and at the other an hill wooded and interspersed with pretty pavilions, which from its distance you are surprised to hear is within the pales of the improvement. You then enter some wilderness work of flowering shrubs which leads to an orangery where are some exotic plants and abundance of oranges. Here the gardener asks each person's name and formally writes it down in a book, for what purpose I cannot say, except that his master may thence make an estimate of what the gardener receives for showing the improvements. You return to the gate you entered at by another serpentine walk. From hence you keep the top of a bold terrace where you have a pleasing view of Cobham, Lord Ligonier's and other objects. From the terrace you descent a steep slope and mount as steep an hill through a Beech grove at the top of which you enter a walk which is continued along the side of a hill where a fine vineyard is planted, large enough to produce twelve hogsheads a year. This walk is near a quarter of a mile, and leads you to a sort of amphitheatre formed by old firs etc.: in the centre a group representing the Rape of the Sabines as the gardener said, but I take it rather for the Rape of Helen by Theseus and Pirithous. Be it which you please, it is well executed and stands in an agreeable spot amongst curious hollies, arbutus, laurestina and other shrubs. When you stand at this group you have a view of a most elegant gothic temple at the end of the amphitheatre, formed almost as finely as the old gothic work, on slender pillars. Through it as a vista you command a charming lake of several acres which lies far under it in a valley,

and on a hill beyond it, beautifully clumped with old forest trees, an hermitage, a tower, a Doric temple and a Turkish tent contend which shall please the beholder most. From the side of this temple you wind through walks on the side of a steep little hill to a serpentine walk formed of the most rare and beautiful shrubs, English and exotic, amongst them several acacia as large as I ever saw, above ten inches in diameter several of them, like an old elm. From this walk, which, as there are every shade of green in it, has a charming effect, you cross a Chinese bridge, and a little farther another over an arm of the water I before mentioned. Hence you pursue your walk through several shrubs till you find yourself on the top of a rustic arch which separates two pieces of water which will when finished flow through it and form a beautiful cascade under a rockwork grotto.

The stone is fretted naturally by time and is disposed in scattered fragments round the arch so as to imitate a natural ruin, made as you may suppose by the impetuous torrent of the water. From this arch you pursue your walk by the water edge which covers many acres and, though all artificial, by its irregular shape has all the appearance of a natural lake. How it is supplied I shall come to by and by. Towards one end you turn to the left, and there a beautiful Grecian ruin, seemingly of a triumphal arch, attracts your notice: it is paved with mosaic tesselated work; in niches are several antiques brought by Mr Hamilton from Italy; in the wall some basso relievos and inscriptions, so that, contrary to most other imitations, the more you examine this the more you believe it real, and but that the honest gardener in broad English puts you in mind that you are in Britain you would swear you had got into Italy. I had not time to examine those pieces of antiquity as particularly as I could have wished, so shall pass on to another ruin of another kind. This is where the stream enters that supplies the piece of water. As it falls down a little bank on the side of a wood there are two old trees supposed to have been torn away with it and have fallen together like an arch, several stumps of oak, loose flags etc. lying in well regulated disorder all round. This has a very pretty effect joined with the awful appearance of the wood. Along the side of this wood the walk is continued under a very steep hill, much more so than I should have expected in this part of England, the forest trees seeming to grow with their roots each in the tops of another like a Wicklow Mountain. At about two hundred yards from the water you see the River Mole lying 13 feet beneath you, yet it is raised up by one of the most ingenious wheels I ever saw, and supplies all the water in the improvements. Mr Hamilton brought the invention from some waterwork abroad. You continue your walk under the hill, winding through several turns till you come to the top of a little eminence where you strike into a wood of different firs, acacia etc. and serpentizing through it arrive at an Hermitage formed to the front with the trunks of fir trees with their bark on, their branches making natural Gothic windows. The first room is furnished with a little straw couch, an old table and a few old chairs: in the back room are a parcel of odd old things, and from it you command a pretty view of the country. It is built on the side of a steep hill so has another cave under its back apartment which you come to after several windings. From this you pass through other walks in this wood which was one part of the desert heath I mentioned we passed over, but bears prodigious fine trees and the heath mixed with them looks rather pretty than otherwise. I must observe that all the walks I have described from the entrance into the vineyard are kept mowed and dressed in the nicest manner, though several miles long. From the wood you enter a walk which leads to the extremity and highest part of the improvements. On it is erected the Belvidere or Gothic castle: it is five storeys high from the ground, with a round staircase at one angle and about 15 feet in the clear. From the upper rooms you command a truly charming scene of this fine cultivated place on two sides, you see to Windsor Forest on another side, and the fourth looks to the heath we came over. It is inconceivable how beautiful Mr Hamilton's grounds appear, all spotted with pavilions, clumps of evergreens or forest trees, while the rough heath withoutside shows what Industry and the Power of Cultivation can do, as most of Mr Hamilton's was once as rough as it. From this you proceed on the hill I described as seen from the Gothic temple. Here you come in to a large lawn, being part of what I mentioned at the entrance, but every hundred yards the path leads you through clumps of shrubs, flowers etc. fenced from the sheep by the network which answers the end and is much cheaper than a sunk invisible fence which is often used. The first building you come to is a Grecian temple of the Doric order after the model of that to Concord and Victory at Stowe, only Doric as that is Corinthian, and with Pilasters at the side as that has a range of insulated pillars. Over the entrance on a pediment is a fine basso relievo of Silenus drunk, supported by fauns, on his ass. At each side the door in niches stand fine casts of Apollo of Belvidere, Venus de Medicis, Mercury and Venus Marina. The windows are all thrown to the back which, as it stands very high, has a charming prospect of the country and the lake and improvements. In this temple, which seems by the relievo to be designed for a banqueting house, are a collection of antique statues and busts: I observed one very fine statue of Bacchus. After a little wilderness work you come to the Turkish tent, placed in the finest point for prospect in the whole improvement. It fronts the rock work cascade, commands the Gothic temple, Chinese bridges, the Grecian ruin etc. all surrounding a vale with a fine piece of water: while I sat in it three or four companies of strangers to see the improvements passed by in the vale and adorned and enlivened the scene very much. Here Mr Hamilton is to build his house, which he wisely delayed doing till he had brought his improvements to perfection, as then he can have a better opportunity of judging where to place it. The tent is elegantly finished, the back is built and plastered, the top leaded and painted blue, joining a sailcloth marquee that covers all and is painted white with a blue finge drawn up before in festoons, like Darius's Tent. From this you pass through many clumps of forest trees, acacia etc. and large lawns between them filled with sheep till you arrive at the gate where you entered, tired I'll answer for it with the length, as delighted with the variety and beauty of a walk which for its extent has few equals.

SIR JOHN PARNELL, *An account of the many fine seats of nobles I have seen* . . . [1763]

POPE'S VILLA,
TWICKENHAM,
MIDDLESEX

*A veritable shrine, Pope laid out this forerunner of the landscape style
from 1719 till his death in 1744. Through his writings he made it a cult in
his own lifetime.*

We set out early in the Morning, and made choice of the Road along the
South Banks of the *Thames*, which leads to *Richmond*, where we proposed
to bait; but arriving there before Noon, we found Time enough upon our
Hands to ride up as far as *Twit'nam* and return to Dinner. You will instantly
guess our Intention was to visit the Residence of the late Mr *Pope*: This
indeed was our Design; and as we approach'd it, I could not help being
agitated, with a kind of glowing Ardour, flutt'ring at my Heart . . .

Mr *Pope's* House stands in the South-west End of the Village; the Area of
the Ground is a gentle Declivity most agreeably sloping to the *Thames*,
which here exactly answers *Denham's* inimitable Description of it.

> 'Tho' deep yet clear, tho' gentle yet not dull;
> 'Strong without Rage, without o'erflowing full.'

Between the River and the House ascends a Parterre or Piece of Grass, near
Square . . .

The Sides of the Court, or Parterre, are bounded by deep Thickets of
Trees, Hedges, and various Evergreens and Shrubs, ascending in a wild, but
delightful Slope, beginning with these of the humblest Growth, and gradually rising, end with lofty Elms and other Forest Trees. This Grass plot is
join'd to the Garden by a subterraneous Passage, or Cavern; which entering
the House below the Middle of the Front, and passing cross under the high
Road, opens into a Wilderness Part of the Garden. Over the Front Entrance
into this Grotto lies a balustraded Platform, and serves the Building both as a
Vestible and Portico; for a Balcony projecting from the middle Window of
the second Story, and supported by Pillars resting upon the Platform, makes
so much of it resemble a Portico; but the Platform extending without these
Pillars, becomes more a Vestible: Add to this, the Window opening into the
Balcony being crowned with a Pediment, gives the several Parts an Air of one
Figure, or whole, and adds an inexpressible Grace to the Front.

Mr *Pope*, you may observe, in a Letter to Mr *Blount*, says that in forming
the subterraneous Way and Grotto, he there found a Spring of the clearest
Water, which fell in a perpetual Rill that eccho'd thro' the Cavern Day and
Night: The Discovery of this rilling Fountain was a fortunate Accident to Mr
Pope, whose Taste was so admirably suited to give a Thing of that kind the
happiest turn of poetical Improvement; as you will presently see. The Grotto
is an irregular Vault and Passage, open at both Extremities, and further
illuminated by two Windows to the Front: In passing it along, we are
presented with many Openings and Cells, which owe their Forms to a
Diversity of Pillars and Jambs, ranged after no set Order or Rule, but aptly
favouring the particular Designs of the Place: They seem as roughly hew'd
out of Rocks and Beds of mineral Strata, discovering in the Fissures and
angular Breaches, Variety of Flints, Spar, Ores, Shells, &c. among which the
Stream issuing from the Spring of Water is distributed to a Diversity of
Purposes: Here it gurgles in a gushing Rill thro' fractur'd Ores and Flints;
there it drips from depending Moss and Shells; here again, washing Beds of
Sand and Pebbles, it rolls in Silver Streamlets; and there it rushes out in Jets

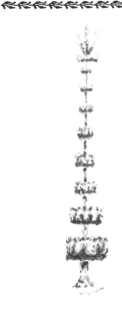

and Fountains; while the Caverns of the Grot incessantly echo with a soothing Murmur of aquatick Sounds. To multiply this Diversity, and still more increase the Delight, Mr *Pope's* poetick Genius has introduced a kind of Machinery, which performs the same Part in the Grotto that supernal Powers and incorporeal Beings act in the heroick Species of Poetry: This is effected by disposing Plates of Looking glass in the obscure Parts of the Roof and Sides of the Cave, where a sufficient Force of Light is wanting to discover the Deception, while the other Parts, the Rills, Fountains, Flints, Pebbles, &c. being duly illuminated, are so reflected by the various profited Mirrors, as, without exposing the Cause, every Object is multiplied, and its Position represented in a surprizing Diversity. Cast your Eyes upward, and you half shudder to see Cataracts of Water precipitating over your Head, from impending Stones and Rocks, while saliant Spouts rise in rapid Streams at your Feet: Around, you are equally surprized with flowing Rivulets and rolling Waters, that rush over airey Precipices, and break amongst Heaps of ideal Flints and Spar. Thus, by a fine Taste and happy Management of Nature, you are presented with an undistinguishable Mixture of Realities and Imagery. In passing out of the Grotto we enter into a Wilderness, and have a view directly before us a Rotundo, or kind of Temple, entirely compos'd of Shells, and consisting wholly of a Cupola, or Dome, supported upon rustick Columns, so as to leave it open every Way to the surrounding Garden. From the Grotto to the Temple we ascend along a Walk in the natural Taste, being rather strew'd than pav'd with Flints and Pebbles, inclos'd with Thickets, and over-arch'd with wild and interwoven Branches of Trees[.]From the Temple, this sylvan Arcade, together with the Passage of the Grotto, make a sort of continued Tube, thro' which a small Expanse of the *Thames* is beheld as in a Perspective, making a beautiful remote Appearance; where Vessels that pass up and down the River, suddenly glance on the eye, and again vanish from it in a Moment. Before I lose Sight of the Grotto, I must not omit taking Notice of an Inscription from *Horace*, placed over the Entrance from the Garden.

> *— Secretum iter, et fallentis semita vitae.*

An *English* Translation of this, equally poetical, elegant, and concise, I think is hardly possible: By attempting it, I have greatly fallen short in the last respect,

> A hid Recess, where Life's revolving Day,
> In sweet Delusion gently steals away.

I would next give you some particular Idea of the Garden, but am afraid I shall fail most of all in this Part of my Attempt: for that free natural Taste, and unaffected Simplicity, which presides every where in the Plan, wanders so much from all common Forms and stated Fashions, that a Wood or a Forest doth not deviate much more from Rule: It is not here,

> That — Grove nods at Grove, each Alley has a Brother,
>   And half the Platform just reflects the other,
> But — Pleasing Intricacies intervene,
>   And artful Wildness to perplex the Scene.

Near the Bounds of the Garden, the Trees unite themselves more closely together, and cover the Hedges with a thick Shade, which prevents all prying from without, and preserves the Privacy of the interior Parts. These Wilderness-Groves are either Quincunces, or cut thro' by many narrow serpentine Walks; and as we recede from the Boundary and approach towards the Center, the Scene opens and becomes less entangled; the Alleys widen, the Walks grow broader, and either terminate in small green Plots of the finest Turf, or lead to the Shell Temple. The Middle of the Garden approaches nearest to a Lawn or open Green, but is delightfully diversified with Banks and Hillocks; which are entirely cover'd with Thickets of Lawrel, Bay, Holly, and many other Evergreens and Shrubs, rising one above another in beautiful Slopes and Inter-mixtures, where Nature freely lays forth the Branches, and disports uncontroul'd; except what may be entirely prun'd away for more Decency and Convenience to the surrounding Grass-plots, for no Shear-work or Tonsure is to be found in all the Scene. Towards the South side of the Garden is a Plantation of Vines curiously disposed and dress'd; it adjoins the Wilderness, and is in the same Taste, but opener to the Sun, and with more numberous interveening Paths. Among the Hillocks on the upper Part of the open Area, rises a Mount much higher than the rest, and is composed of more rude and indigested Materials; it is covered with Bushes and Trees of a wilder Growth, and more confused order, rising as it were out of Clefts of Rocks, and Heaps of rugged and mossy Stones; among which a narrow intricate Path leads in an irregular Spiral to the Top; where is placed a Forest Seat or Chair, that may hold three or four Persons at once, overshaded with the Branches of a spreading Tree. From this Seat we face the Temple, and overlook the various Distribution of the Thickets, Grass plots, Alleys, Banks, &c. Near this Mount lies the broadest Walk of the Garden, leading from the Center to the uppermost Verge; where, upon the gentle Eminence of a green Bank, stands an Obelisk, erected by Mr *Pope* to the Memory of his Mother: It is a plain Stone Pillar resting upon a Pedestal: and the Plynth of the Pillar bears this Inscription on its four Sides, beginning with that which faces the Walk.

AH EDITHA!

MATRUM OPTIMA.

MULIERUM AMANTISSIMA.

VALE.

As this Obelisk terminates the longest Prospect of Mr *Pope's* Garden, it shall also put a Period to my Description; which is not of a Place that bears the high Air of State and Grandeur, and surprizes you with the vastness of Expence and Magnificence; but an elegant Retreat of a Poet strongly inspired with the Love of Nature and Retirement; and shews you, with respect to these Works, what was the Taste of the finest Genius that this or any other Age has produced.

ANON., *An Epistolary Description of the Late Mr Pope's House and Gardens at Twickenham* [1747]

Alas, it did not survive untouched for long.

Aug. 23 1781.

Sir William Stanhope was persuaded . . . to *improve* Pope's garden . . . The poet had valued himself on the disposition of it, and with reason. Though containing but five square acres, enclosed by three lanes, he had managed it with such art and deception, that it seemed a wood, and its boundaries were nowhere discoverable. It is true, it was closely planted and consequently damp. Refined taste went to work: the vocal groves were thinned, modish shrubs replaced them, and light and three lanes broke in; and if the Muses wanted to tie up their garters, there is not a nook to do it without being seen . . . I remember a story of old Thomas, Earl of Pembroke: he one day took it into his grave head to give eyeballs with charcoal to all his statues at Wilton, and then called his wife and daughters to see how much livelier the gods, goddesses, and emperors were grown!

HORACE WALPOLE, Letter of
23 August 1781

The gardens were laid out for George II's Queen, Caroline, by Charles Bridgeman with contributions by William Kent in the 1720s and '30s.

RICHMOND, SURREY

Richmond Gardens contain 537 Acres; they are laid-out in a most rural taste, widely different from those open Gardens at Kensington. There is a large Cover within the Gardens for Game. That part toward Kew is held by Lease. The Cave, seated by a piece of water, is thatched; the Door-way to it is in the old Gothic Taste, so are the Windows – they are glazed in the old way. Within 'tis a rough-cast Cieling. Here is a Collection of Books in Divinity, History, Poetry all bound-in or covered with Vellum. The six waxwork figures, all *actually* cloathed, are Merlin, the Boy his amanuensis, Queen Elizabeth, young, and her Nurse, an Amazonian Lady, and a Prophetess; the latter is ill-performed. Merlin's face is admirable, the lively attention of the Boy is surprising . . . the main exception to this Place is that they call it a Cave, for 'tis above ground. Call it then a Cottage or Cell. The Hermitage you descend-to by winding Walks through Woods; on the opposite bounds of the Grass-Area before it are large Stones cast to make the situation more natural; for the front of the Hermitage consists of large Stones thoroughly rustic and unadorned. Within are five Marble Busts; that in the principal Place is Robert Boyle; the others are Wollaston, Dr Clarke, Locke and Sir Isaac Newton. The Terrace towards the Thames commands a long Reach of that and a View of Sion House and Brentford.

JOHN LOVEDAY, *Diary* [1736]

William Kent's greatest creation from the 1720s still happily with us.

ROUSHAM HOUSE, OXFORDSHIRE

I lay one night at Rousham, which is the prettiest place for water-falls, jetts, ponds inclosed with beautiful scenes of green and hanging wood that ever I saw.

ALEXANDER POPE to MARTHA
BLOUNT [1728]

SEZINCOTE,
GLOUCESTERSHIRE

Humphry Repton had a hand in designing this tribute to British rule in India for Charles Cockerell in the Regency period to which the late Poet Laureate responded in customary style.

Down the Drive
Under the early yellow leaves of oaks,
One Lodge is Tudor, one in Indian style.
The bridge, the waterfall, the Temple Pool –
And there they burst on us, the onion domes,
Chajjahs and chattris made of amber stone:
'Home of the Oaks', exotic Sezincote!
Stately and strange it stood, the Nabob's house,
Looking from Gloucestershire to Oxfordshire:
And, by supremest landscape-gardener's art,
The lake below the eastward slope of grass
Was made to seem a mighty river-reach
Curving along to Chipping Norton's hills.

JOHN BETJEMAN, *Summoned by Bells* [1960]

HAGLEY HALL,
WORCESTERSHIRE

The garden was laid out by George, 1st Lord Lyttelton (1700–3) as an early response to the landscape style promoted by Pope, who was his friend. The ruined castle, designed by Sanderson Miller, is still there today. Here is how one eighteenth-century visitor saw it.

THE RUIN

Upon the first glimpse of this becoming object, which adds so much dignity to the scene, one cannot resist an involuntary pause – struck with its character, the mind naturally falls into reflections, while curiosity is on the wing, to be acquainted with its history; and I make no doubt that an antiquarian like my friend, would sigh to know in what aera it was founded, and by whom: – what sieges it had sustained; – what blood had been spilt upon its walls: – and would lament that hostile discord, or the iron hand of all-mouldering time, should so rapaciously destroy it.

Believe me, the appearance of this antique pile has the power of stamping these impressions on the mind, so masterly is it executed to deceive; for in reality, it is nothing but a deception, designed, and raised here, by the late noble possessor; and though on the nearest approach, it maintains the face of having been, some centuries ago, strong and formidable, it is a modern structure, intended, not meerly as an object only, to give a livelier conse-quence to the landscape, but for use; being a lodge for the keeper of the park.

This gothic ruin is very judiciously situated on the boldest eminence in the whole domain; and commands a most unbounded prospect: particularly so, form a neatly fitted-up room in the tower, which intentionally is left in a perfect state. And to keep the whole design in its purity – to wipe away any suspicion of its being any otherwise than a real ruin, the large and massy stones, which have seemingly tumbled from the tottering and ruinous walls, are suffered to lie about the different parts of the building, in the utmost confusion. This greatly preserves its intention, and confirms the common

opinion of every stranger, of its early date; while, to throw a deeper solemnity over it, and make it carry a stronger face of antiquity, ivy is encouraged to climb about the walls, and turrets; and it now so closely embraces those parts with its gloomy arms, that it is impossible to look upon it without a suggestion, of its being as ancient as it really appears.

Yet, perhaps, were I disposed to imitate those critics who love to cavil, and never allow any thing they look upon to have the least merit, I might be tempted to say, it would have shewn itself more in character, had its dimensions not been quite so much confined; and that if some detached remains had been visible in proper places, it possibly might have had a superior effect; – admitting it defective in this respect, there is, in my opinion, building sufficient for the place, and for the intention, as it certainly conveys every idea required.

The ground about this eligible ruin, without exception, surpasses any other in the whole park: to its loftiness is added, the most agreeable variety; and when you gain the summit, the amazing profusion of prospect over an unlimited and beautiful country, will hold you in astonishment and delight. Nor will your attention be less engaged with what immediately rises before you; this is a noble and spacious lawn, extending itself from the base of the tower in easy inequalities, matted in particular spots with patches of fern, and surrounded by wood and grove finely hanging on its precipite sides, in all the simplicity of natural freedom.

> JOSEPH HEELY, *Letters on the Beauties of Hagley, Envil and The Leasowes* [1777]

Not everyone, however, admired it.

The plan of Hagley, (if there be any plan) is so confused, that it is impossible to describe it. There is no coherency of parts. One scene is tacked on to another; and any one might be removed without the least injury to the rest.

> THE REVEREND WILLIAM GILPIN, *Observations on Several Parts of England . . .* [1772]

Harold Nicolson and Vita Sackville-West acquired the ruins of a Tudor castle in 1930 and turned it into one of the horticultural shrines of the century. It is surprising how little Harold Nicolson wrote about it . . .

SISSINGHURST CASTLE, KENT

DIARY   *2nd November, 1932*
Plant the five acacias round the Sissinghurst Crescent. Plant out Buddleia at the end of the moat. Plant the two *Souvenir du Docteur Jamain*. Plant the poplars down to the lake. A good day's work. Also do Peace Conference. Weight 11st. 4lbs.

DIARY   *27th September, 1933*
Work hard at *Curzon* chapter v all day. Write close on 5,000 words. Also dictate a huge long letter to Peter Quennell telling him what to look up for me at the Hendon newspaper museum. Measure the central path in the kitchen garden and Gwen helps me. Finally Vita refuses to abide by our decision or to remove the miserable little trees which stand in the way of my design. The romantic temperament as usual obstructing the classic.

H.N TO V.S.-W.   *8th June, 1937*
                                                    4 King's Bench Walk, E.C.4

. . . Sissinghurst looked more lovely or been more appreciated. I must say, Farley has made the place look like a gentleman's garden, and you with your extraordinary taste have made it look like nobody's garden but your own. I think the secret of your gardening is simply that you have the courage to abolish ugly or unsuccessful flowers. Except for those beastly red-hot pokers which you have a weakness for, there is not an ugly flower in the whole place. Then I think, si j'ose m'exprimer ainsi that the design is really rather good. I mean we have got what we wanted to get – a perfect proportion between the classic and the romantic, between the element of expectation and the element of surprise. Thus the main axes are terminated in a way to satisfy expectation, yet they are in themselves so tricky that they also cause surprise. But the point of the garden will not be apparent until the hedges have grown up, especially (most important of all) the holly hedge in the flower garden. But it is lovely, lovely, lovely – and you must be pleased with your work.

HAROLD NICOLSON *The Diaries and Letters of Harold Nicolson*, Volume I

STOWE, BUCKINGHAM-SHIRE

The most celebrated and most visited of all English eighteenth-century gardens which were planted and developed over a century by four successive owners: Sir Richard Temple (1634–97); Viscount Cobham (1675–1749); Richard Grenville, Earl Temple (1711–79) and George Grenville, 1st Marquis of Buckingham (1753–1813). To it contributed a whole succession of famous garden designers: Charles Bridgeman, Sir John Vanbrugh, William Kent and 'Capability' Brown.

Brackley.   14 Aug: 1724 Friday night
                              7 a clock.

DEAR DANIEL,

Yesterday we saw Lord Cobham's house, which within these five years, has gained the reputation of being the finest seat in England . . . The gardens by reason of the good contrivance of the walks, seem to be three times as large as they are. They contain but 28 acres, yet took us up two hours. It is entirely new, and tho' begun but eleven years ago, is now almost finished. From the lower end you ascend a multitude of steps (but at several distances) to the parterre, and from thence several more to the house, which, standing high, commands a fine prospect. One way they can see 26 miles. It is impossible to give you an exact Idea of this garden, but we shall shortly have a graving of it. It consists of a great number of walks, terminated by summer houses, and heathen Temples of different structure, and adorned with statues cast from the Anticks. Here you see the Temple of Apollo, there a Triumphal Arch. The garden of Venus is delightful; you see her standing in her Temple, at the head of a noble bason of water, and opposite to her an Amphitheater, with statues of God's and Goddesses; this bason is sorounded with walks and groves, and overlook'd from a considerable height by a tall Column of a Composite order on which stands a statue of Pr: George in his Robes. At the end of the gravel walk leading from the house, are two heathen Temples with a circle of water, 2 acres and a quarter large. In the midst whereof is a Gulio or pyramid, at least 50 foot high, from the top of which it

is designed that water shall fall, being by pipes convey'd thro' the heart of it. Half way up this walk is another fine bason, with pyramid in it 30 foot high, and nearer the house you meet a fountain that plays 40 foot. The cross walks end in vistas, arches and statues, and the private ones cut thro' groves are delightful. You think twenty times you have no more to see, and of a sudden find yourself in some new garden or walk, as finish'd and adorn'd as that you left. Nothing is more irregular in the whole, nothing more regular in the parts, which totally differ the one from the other. This shows my Lord's good tast, and his fondness to the place appears by the great expense he has been at. We all know how chargeable it is to make a garden with tast; to make one of a sudden more so; but to erect so many Summer houses, Temples, Pillars, Pyramids, and Statues, most of fine hewn stone, the rest of guilded lead, would drain the richest purse, and I doubt not but much of his wife's great fortune has been sunk in it. The Pyramid at the end of one of the walks is a copy in mignature of the most famous one in Egypt, and the only thing of the kind, I think, in England. Bridgman laid out the ground and plan'd the whole, which cannot fail of recommending him to business. What adds to the bewty of this garden is, that it is not bounded by walls, but by a Ha-hah, which leaves you the sight of a bewtifull woody country, and makes you ignorant how far the high planted walks extend.

Letter of Lord Percival to his brother-in-law, Dering, 14 August 1724

Twenty years later the 'queen of the blue-stockings' came:

The first of August we went to Stowe, which is beyond description; it gives the best idea of Paradise that can be: even Milton's images and descriptions fall short of it; and indeed a Paradise it must be to every mind in a state of tolerable innocence. Without the soul's sunshine every object is dark; but a contented mind, in so sweet a situation must feel the most 'sober certainty of waking bliss'. The buildings are indeed, in themselves, disagreeably crowded, but being dedicated to patriots, heroes, law-givers, and poets, and men of ingenuity and invention, they receive a dignity from the persons to whom they are consecrated. Others, that are sacred to imaginary powers, raise a pleasing enthusiasm in the mind.

What different ideas arise in a walk in Kensington gardens, or the Mall, where almost every other face wears impertinence! the greater part of them unknown, and those with whom we are acquainted, only discover to us that they are idle, foolish, vain and proud. At Stowe you walk amidst heroes and deities, powers and persons whom we have been taught to honour; who have embellished the world with arts, or instructed it in science; defended their country and improved it.

The temples that pleased me most, for the design to which they were consecrated, were those to Ancient Virtue, to Friendship, to the Worthies, and to Liberty. MRS ELIZABETH MONTAGU [1744]

Inheriting a famous garden had its complications even in the eighteenth century. In 1749 Stowe was inherited by Lord Cobham's nephew, Richard, later Earl Temple. As this letter reveals, his wife had run into mother-in-law problems: 'Brown' was the future 'Capability', then only head gardener.

Saturday

My dearest,

I went to Court yesterday and was very well receiv'd by the King. He asked if the Gardens at Stow were big enough or whether all the estate was to be put into gardens, but mighty good humour'd, laugh'd a good deal and I believe meant a little sneer at the last owner of them. I went to my Lady Cobham yesterday and she began in a violent manner about the Sheep being put into the garden. I told her they look'd mighty pretty and that everybody said it wou'd make the turf much firmer, but if they did harm they would be taken out I suppos'd, but that I really never disputed any thing with you for I thought you knew much better than I, and she said she shou'd scold you well when she saw you. I knew what I was to meet with for she told Brown she had cry'd all night and never slept a wink about it and raved (and tore) and said if my Lord Cobham cou'd know how Stow was used how vext he would be, and he said Lady Temple and Lady Hester were in an uproar about it too. They were both by when she begun with me but they button'd up their mouths and said not one word. Now one shou'd imagine they might try'd to stop her instead of setting her to work, considering you are a party concern'd. I wish you wou'd ask Brown what she said to him for I have not seen him, but she has begun with Farrand in hopes . . . It happened at a bad time for me for I was very ill and low spirited yesterday and she worried me almost to death. I fancy you will be tired enough with her and the less we see her and have to do with her the better.

ANNE GRENVILLE TO RICHARD
GRENVILLE, undated but 1750

But fashions change and twenty years later it received the censure of John Wesley:

The buildings called Temples are most miserable, many of them both without and within. Sir John Vanbrugh's is an ugly, clumsy lump, hardly fit for a gentleman's stable. The temples of Venus and Bacchus, though large, having nothing elegant in the structure, and the painting in the former, representing a lewd story, are neither well designed nor executed . . .

It is a childish affectation to call things here by Greek or Latin names, as Styx, and the Elysian Fields. It was ominous for my Lord to entertain himself and his noble company in a grotto on the bank of the Styx; that is on the brink of hell. The river on which it stands is a black, filthy puddle, exactly resembling a common sewer.   JOHN WESLEY, *Journal* [1779]

STUDLEY ROYAL,
YORKSHIRE

John Aislabie's (1670–1742) famous garden begun in 1720 became a Mecca for landowners anxious to learn how to improve their estates.

Spent 6 hours in riding over Mr Aislabie's park at Studley. The natural beauties of this place are superior to anything of the kind I ever saw, and improved with great taste both by the late and present owner. The extent of the whole is 710 acres, of which about 150 are reckoned into the garden, and the river Scheld, which runs through the ground, covers (as they told us) 23 of them. It is impossible from a single survey, however well conducted, to conceive oneself or give a stranger an adequate idea of Studley. Imagine rocks covered with wood, sometimes perpendicularly steep and craggy, at others descending in slopes to beautiful lawns and parterres, water thrown into 20 different shapes – a canal, a basin, a lake, a purling stream, now gliding gently through the plain, now foaming and tumbling in a cascade down 8 or 10 steps. In one place it is finely turned through the middle arch of a rough stone bridge. The buildings are elegant and well suited to the ground they stand upon. The temple of Venus is at the head of a canal in the midst of a thick wood; that of Hercules on another spot not less delightful. A Gothic tower overlooks the park and gardens from the summit of a rock. Mr Aislabie designs to erect a Chinese house of a pyramidical form, with a gallery encircling every story, upon the point of a ridge which encloses on each hand a valley finely wooded and washed by a rivulet. One side is formed into a number of small terraces interspersed with rocks, which makes a Chinese landscape. You have besides several agreeable views of Ripon, the adjacent country, and Fountains Abbey; and what seems almost peculiar to Studley is that the same object, taken at a different point of view, is surprisingly diversified and has all the grace of novelty.

The ruins of the Abbey lie just without the enclosure of the park. They are in the possession of a Roman Catholic gentleman, who has refused very large offers from the late Mr Aislabie. They would indeed have been a noble addition to the beauties of this place . . .

PHILIP YORKE, 2ND EARL OF
HARDWICK, *A Journal of What I
Observed Most Remarkable in a Tour
into the North* [1744]

Inevitably, it was to be censured by that apostle of the Picturesque, William Gilpin.

What a lovely scene might a person of pure taste have made at Studley, with one tenth of the expence, which hath been laid out in deforming it . . . On the whole it is hard to say, whether nature has done more to embellish the scenes of Studley or art to deform them.

THE REVEREND WILLIAM GILPIN,
Tour of The Lakes [1786]

THEOBALDS, HERTFORDSHIRE

William Cecil, Lord Burghley (1520–98), planted the most famous private garden in Elizabethan England at Theobalds, Hertfordshire. His gardener was John Gerard, the famous herbalist.

In the gallery was painted the genealogy of the Kings of England; from this place one goes into the garden, encompassed with a ditch full of water, large enough for one to have the pleasure of going in a boat, and rowing between the shrubs; here are great variety of trees and plants; labyrinths made with a great deal of labour; a jet d'eau, with its bason of white marble; and columns and pyramids of wood and other materials up and down the garden: After seeing these, we were led by the gardiner into the summer-house, in the lower part of which, built semi-circularly, are the twelve Roman emperors in white marble, and a table of touchstone; the upper part of it is set round with cisterns of lead, into which the water is conveyed through pipes, so that fish may be kept in them, and in summer time they are very convenient for

bathing; in another room for entertainment very near this, and joined to it by a little bridge, was an oval table of red marble.

PAUL HENTZNER, *A Journey into England in the year 1598*

There is a fountain in the centre of the garden: the water spouts out from a number of concealed pipes and sprays unwary passers-by. Quite a large obelisk of alabaster surmounted by a figure of Christ stands in the garden; nearby is an alabaster sundial, and the royal arms of England are displayed here surrounded by the Garter in gold. On the way up to the house there is a fountain: a little ship of the type they use in the Netherlands is floating on the water, complete with cannons, flags, and sails . . .

In the garden you see lilies and other flowers growing among the shrubs: the garden also contains some alabaster busts of the Caesars. An outstanding feature is a delightful and most beautifully made ornamental pool (at present dry, but previously supplied with water from 2 miles away): it is approached by 24 steps leading up to it. The water was brought up to this height by lead pipes and it flowed into the pool through the mouths of two serpents. In two of the corners of this pool you can see two wooden water-mills built on a rock, just as if they were on the shores of a river. The roof itself is painted in tempera with appropriate episodes from history, and is very finely vaulted. A space beside the pool houses white marble statues of the 12 Roman Emperors.

BARON WALDSTEIN, *Journal* [1600]

WILTON HOUSE, WILTSHIRE

The most glorious of the pre-Civil War gardens laid out by the Huguenot Isaac de Cavs for Philip Herbert, 4th Earl of Pembroke (1584–1650). In the eighteenth century it was destroyed to create the landscape park with its famous Palladian bridge.

Then I march'd doune through the fayre Great Hall, and stately 4. square built Court, beautify'd about, with the Kings and his oune Armes, by the archt Cellers into the Garden, and there with the fat Dutch Keeper thereof, a rare Artist, that way march'd doune into the middst of it, in a curous broad Alley of 500. Foot long, to a fayre House of Freestone built at the further end of the sayd walke, and Garden, below all Archt, with seats, and pav'd with Freestone; the Roofe flatt, and leaded with Freestone Battlements and Water-Pooles; The Statues of Venus, Luna, and 2. more, are cut in white Marble on the Frontispiece; Close to this Banquetting House, is that rare Water-worke now making, and continuing by this outlandish Engineer, for the singing, and Chirping of Birdes, and other strange rarities, only by that Element, the finishing which rare peece of Skill, with satisfaction to the inegnious Artist will cost (they say) a great Summe of Money.

From this House of Pleasure, on either side the whole breadth of this Garden, is rang'd double rankes of pleasant greene walkes, one above another, and sett along with Pots for Flowers of the best kind.

Next to the House are 4. great Squares, 2. on either side of the sayd long Walke, in the middst of which are 4. fine square Fountaines, with 4. white Alabaster Statues, neatly, and artificially cut: In one is Venus, with her sonne Cupid in her Armes; in another Diana, with her bathing sheet; in a third is Susanna pulling a thorne out of her Foote; and in the 4th. Cleopatra with the

Serpent: And next beyond is 2. wildernesses on each side one, in one whereof in the middst of it is the Statue of Flora; in the middst of the other the Statue of Bacchus, both artificially cutt. Next we pass'd on a faire Woodden Bridge, ouer a pleasant little Riuer, which runs quite through the middst of this precious Garden, to Salisbury; And on either side of the faire Walke, beyond the Bridge, are two great foure square Pooles, with stately high Rockes in the middst of them, and golden Crownes on the tops, and 4. lower Rockes about them, which by turning of Cockes that are close by, the water flyes spouting out, at the top of the Rockes; turning, and whirling the Crownes, and fall powring into the Rockes; and the 4. former little Pooles, we last left on the other side of this Riuer, next the Mansion, sends forth water in that manner with the turning of Cockes, washing and dashing the Eyes and Thighs of faire Venus and Diana.

Next beyond in the middst of the Alley vpon a Marble Piller stands the Statue of a Romane Gladiator all in brasse most artificially done, and set forth, in his earnest and true martiall Posture of Combatting, with his brandishing Sword in one hand, and impenetrable Target in the other. And next on either side a gaping Lion, neere to that pleasant chirping Banquetting House, that before I was att, and heere was the Period of my delightfull Garden Journey.

LIEUTENANT HAMMOND, *A Relation of a Short Survey of the Western Counties* [1635]

The garden of Richard Pococke, Bishop of Meath (1704–65), must have been a readers' paradise.

WIMBORNE ST GILES, DORSET

The Gardens are very beautifully laid out, in a serpentine river, pieces of water, Lawns, & c: & very gracefully adorn'd with wood. One first comes to an Island in which there is a Castle, then near the water is a Gateway with a tower on each side, & passing between two waters, there is a fine Cascade from the one to the other, a thatch'd house, a round pavilion on a Mount, Shake Spears house, in which is a small statue of him & his works in a Glass case; & in all the houses & seats are books in hanging Glass cases. There is a pavilion between the waters, and both a Chinese and stone-bridge over them. I saw here a sea duck which lays in rabbits burrows, from which they are call'd Burrow ducks, & are something like the shell drake. There is a most beautifull Grotto finished by Mr Castles of Marybone; – It consists of a winding walk and an antiroom. These are mostly made of Rockspar & c: adorn'd with Moss: In the inner room is a great profusion of most beautiful shells, petrifications and fine polished pebbles, and there is a chimney to it which is shut up with doors covered with shells in such a manner as that it does not appear. The Park also is very delightful . . .

RICHARD POCOCKE, *Travels Through England* [1750–7]

The famous ferme ornée *created by Philip Southcote from 1735. He writes that he began his garden so 'I could see what was doing in the grounds, and by the walk could have a pleasing access to either of them where I might be wanted'. The difference from farming today could hardly be more striking.*

WOBURN FARM, SURREY

You enter Wooborne Farm at an octagon Porter's Lodge built of brick whitened, with rustic coigns, so contrived as to afford a pretty side to ornament the improvement and to be of use as a dwelling for the Porter. From hence is a road prettily planted with double rows of trees to the house which lies in the middle of the farm and has little prospect but what the beauties of its own surrounding improvements afford; yet such charms they had to my eye I thought I should like to dwell constantly there as well as in a house which commanded a most extensive view, but how soon they might tire the constant beholder I will not determine. You leave the road on the right and, turning through a little hatch on the left hand, walk by the side of a fine meadow which is separated from you by low green pales within which are clumps of flowering shrubs, flowers &c. In the field are some beautiful spotted cows, beyond it you see clumps of old elms and beyond them some weeping Willows surrounding a neat spire. Through the walk I mentioned you pass on till you come opposite the house, where are three or four vases and a Colossian head. From this to the house is a canal too narrow to be handsome which divides the field you walk in from another full of sheep. You pass over the canal by a little Chinese bridge and continue through the walk of flowering shrubs to a little pavilion which fronts a walk between fine elms separated from the field last mentioned by an invisible fence and by the same from a fine field of corn on the other side. The walk of flowering shrubs is continued from the pavilion all round this corn field, but the gardener conducts you through the elm one which leads to one of the most pleasing objects I ever saw in an improvement: this is an old ruin or rather new-contrived so artificially that it has all the appearance of an ancient abbey. It fronts the side of the house and is what appears like a spire on first entering at the Lodge. The inside inspires all that awe so natural to ruined grandeur, when one conceives it might have been the mansion of greatness or wisdom now reduced to dust. The walls are all overgrown with ivy which hangs in festoons and branches from the top of the one entire spire. One thing I wished away which was a cypress that grew formally up against the wall like a clipped yew. From hence you pass through fine old forest trees scattered irregularly, and amidst them some plots of flowers, to an octagon building which has a charming prospect of the celebrated bridge at Walton, Chertsey Mead, the Thames and Lord Portmore's improvements. From hence you walk along a fine terrace on the brow of a sloping hill to the meadow where the flatness of that part through which the Thames runs contrasts the height you are on to a very good effect. Below you, in a large meadow spotted with fine oak and ash in clumps, many fine marked cows and bullocks graze, which vary the scene, and the top of the hill has all sort of Scots and spruce firs, laurel and other different greens and flowering shrubs. The first building you come to on the terrace is a seat under a pediment supported by four Doric columns; here there is a fine view of the bridge &c. before mentioned and beside this Cowpers Hill, St Annes Hill &c. After this you pass by a gothic seat in a recess, and continuing your walk down the brow come to a menagerie with a fine gothic front: it has a portico which makes a pretty seat, as the entrance is backwards. From this building to the end of the improvement are several enclosed squares of about ten yards each made with packthread sally like the bails of a chicken coop, covered with nets, where formerly were pheasants; but now ducks and turkeys supply their place. This

Heather thatched Summerhouse

sally enclosure seems particularly adapted to water-fowl, and for their convenience a canal runs all along the walk to a pavilion at the far end which is at one extremity of the farm. From hence you cross the field where the bullocks were to the Octagon Pavilion I mentioned at the end of the terrace. From this you are conducted by a row of old elm to a chinese bridge at the end of which is a little Rustic Cell with mosaic pavement. The path then leads you by the side of several fields of beans, barley &c. with little other prospect than what the harvest affords, as the ground is very flat, till you come to another extremity joining Lord Portmore's. Here is a gothic hut, thatched: this was one of the first building Mr Southcote had before he ornamented his land so highly as it now is. You now keep to the right, which makes the fourth side, and, passing along some barley and oat fields (which were in high beauty when I was there, all filled with reapers, binders &c) and some pasture-ground on a fine mowed walk, you come to the gate where you entered. I must observe that from the Hermitage to this is by no means so beautiful as from the Lodge to the Hermitage, so that I think it would be better if a stranger returned instead of going by the Ruin and other beauties of that side of the farm. Mr Southcote has vast merit in this improvement, as it was one of the first places in England where useful fields were ornamented with a walk all round them in the Manner he has done; and omne tulit punctum, qui miscuit utile dulci. The farm is separated from Chertsey Meadow by the River Bone, a small sluggish stream. The number of weeping willows here have a charming effect, and all together it is a delightful place and highly worth seeing, as it is ornamented rather with taste than great expence, and consequently of use to more who see it than the very costly improvements in several places. SIR JOHN PARNELL, *An account of the many fine seats of nobles I have seen . . .* [1763]

The gardens were made between 1701 and 1740 by Henry Grey, 1st Duke of Kent (1671–1748), and were noted for their splendid water effects. Between 1758 and 1760 they were improved by 'Capability' Brown for the Duke's daughter.

WREST PARK, BEDFORDSHIRE

The Gardens were fine and very ugly in the old-fashioned manner with high hedges and canals, at the End of the principal one of which is a frightful Temple designed by Mr Archer the Groomporter. Mr Brown has much corrected this garden and built a hermitage and cold bath in a bold good taste. In two quarters of the wood, the Duke erected in his lifetime two monuments to the memory of himself and his first Duchess.

HORACE WALPOLE [1771]

PART
X

SOME

FOREIGN
GARDENS

One of the Seven Wonders of the Ancient World and traditionally THE HANGING
constructed by Nebuchadnezzar II (605–562 BC). Those with even a GARDENS OF
modest roof garden will be comforted to learn of its distinguished BABYLON
ancestry.

. . . the account of the pensile or hanging gardens of Babylon, if made by
Semiramis, the third or fourth from Nimrod, is of no slender antiquity;
which being not framed upon ordinary level of ground, but raised upon
pillars, admitting under-passages, we cannot accept as the first Babylonian
gardens, – but a more eminent progress and advancement in that art than
any that went before it; somewhat answering or hinting the old opinion
concerning Paradise itself, with many conceptions elevated above the plane
of the earth.

Nebuchodonosor (whom some will have to be the famous Syrian king of
Diodorus) beutifully repaired that city, and so magnificently built his
hanging gardens, that from succeeding writers he had the honour of the first.
From whence over-looking Babylon, and all the region about it, he found no
circumscription to the eye of his ambition; till over-delighted with the
bravery of this Paradise, in his melancholy metamorphosis he found the folly
of that delight, and a proper punishment in the contrary habitation – in wild
plantations and wanderings of the fields.

The Persian gallants, who destroyed this monarchy, maintained their
botanical bravery. Unto whom we owe the very name of Paradise, wherewith we meet not in Scripture before the time of Solomon, and conceived
originally Persian. The word for that disputed garden expressing, in the
Hebrew, no more than a field enclosed, which from the same root is content
to derive a garden and a buckler.

Cyrus the Elder, brought up in woods and mountains, when time and
power enabled, pursued the dictate of his education, and brought the
treasures of the field into rule and circumscription. So nobly beautifying the
hanging gardens of Babylon, that he was also thought to be the author
thereof.

SIR THOMAS BROWNE, *The Garden of
Cyrus* [1658]

One of the most famous of all eighteenth-century French gardens it ERMENONVILLE
included in its vast terrain a canal, a water mill, windmills, low bridges, a
brewery and a Gothic tower. Part of it evoked Dutch and Italian
landscapes while on the Île des Peupliers there was Rousseau's tomb.
Thomas Blaikie was more appreciative of this garden than usual.

April 19.

Left Manicamp to return to Paris went and lodged at Compiegne and next morning sett out to go to Ermenonville having heard much of this place and being done as they told me by the same Architect that had laid out the Gardens at Guiscard; continued the Paris Road until I passed Verberie took a cross the country to the left passed by a ferme called La Boissierre from thence came across the fields, in some places no road, to Frenoy and from thence to Baron and form thence came to the Abbaye di Chaallis; this is an exceeding fine building; from thence they showed me the road to Ermenonville descended at a Publick house upon the right hand in entering the village where I ordered diner and inquired to whom I should aply to see the garden; they told me there was an Anglais that showed them so we went and found him who dined with me and after we went to see the grounds; they are in some place beautifull though more in a Romantick than an Elegante stile; there is plenty of wood and water; the house stands surrounded with the ancient fosse which is agreeably united with the rest of the Landscape; towards the South there is a noble cascade which falls from a fine Lake fronting the house formes a rever which serpents to the left hand forms another cascade falling into the fosse which surrounds the house; betwixt those two cascades passes the road to the Village which renders the scene more lively; at the extremity of this Landscape upon the hill to the right hand stands a temple surrounded by the forest; the other side of the house the Landscape is level but more extensive; here we have a fine veu of the river which runs serpentin along the vally surrounded by the rising ground and wood; in each side in the midle of this plaine stands a tower dedecated to the Belle Gabrielle Henry 4 Mistress; near the house is some fine tall Lombardy poplars, the height of those trees makes the Landscape seem more extensive; from the house we went towards the south Side to the great cascade which formes a Groto in which they have placed some old armour to make the thing seem more romantick; from this we come to the borders of the great Lake which is a beautifull peece of water; at the further end stands an Island planted with poplars where is buried the famouss J. J. Rousseau which Lately died here for whom John Bailly seems to have had a great veneration; next day went and saw the desert which is well named, this is a Mountainious heath full of large stons and rocks upon which they have sowen Bordaux and Scotch pins which thrives amazingly; the entry to this desert from the forest is through a sort of house made of roots &c called the Maison de Charbonnier; from different places of this desert there is some vues and almost at every rock or stone both here and through the wood there is poems or inscriptions not only in French but some in English Italian and Latin; however there is some of them not well adapted to the places where they are.

THOMAS BLAIKIE, *Diary of a Scotch Gardener*, 19 April 1779

THE VILLA D'ESTE, TIVOLI

These gardens were laid out in the 1560s for Ippolito d'Este, Cardinal of Ferrara on a steep western slope at Tivoli. They were famous throughout Europe for their architecture and spectacular water effects. But their impact on the pen as against the hoe was only to come with their decay.

'Of course you saw the Villa d'Este Gardens,'
Writes one of my Italianistic friends.
Of course; of course; I saw them in October,
Spired with pinaceous ornamental gloom
Of that arboreal elegy the cypress.

These fountains, too, 'like ghosts of cypresses'; –
(The phrase occurred to me whilst I was leaning
On an old balustrade; imbibing sunset;
Wrapped in my verse vocation) – how they linked me
With Byron, Landor, Liszt and Robert Browning.

Their Browning jogged my elbow; bade me hob nob
With some forgotten painter of dim frescoes
That haunt the Villa's intramural twilight.
(While roaming in the Villa d'Este Gardens
I felt like that . . . and fumbled for my notebook)

SIEGFRIED SASSOON, *Satirical
Poems* [1976]

A FRENCH GARDEN

*Here two middle-aged clerks, who have inherited a fortune, having gone
thorugh a series of disasters, alight upon gardening. The period is the
1840s.*

Fortunately, in their library, they came across Boitard's work, entitled *The
Garden Architect.*

Gardens are divided by the author into an infinity of styles. There is, first
of all, the melancholy and romantic style, which is distinguished by
Everlasting-flowers, ruins, tombs, and 'a votive tablet to the Virgin, marking
the spot where a nobleman fell under the blade of an assassin'. The sublime
and awesome style is composed with hanging rocks, shattered trees, and
burnt-out huts; the exotic style is achieved by planting Peruvian Lilies 'to
bring back memories to a settler abroad, or to a traveller'. The solemn style
should offer a temple of philosophy, as at Ermenonville. The majestic style is
characterized by obelisks and triumphal arches; the mysterious style, by
moss and grottoes; the thoughtful style, by a lake. There is even the fantastic
style, which was seen at its best in a garden in Wüttemburg – there, you
would discover in turn a wild boar, a hermit, several sepulchres and a boat
which would glide away from the bank of its own accord, to carry you to a
boudoir where you were drenched by fountain-jets when you reclined on the
sofa.

Bouvard and Pécuchet were bewildered and dazzled by this vista of
marvels. They felt that the fantastic style was really the prerogative of
princes. The temple of philosophy would be in the way. The votive tablet to
the Madonna would be meaningless, considering the lack of assassins, and it
was just hard luck on expatriates and travellers, since American plants were
far too expensive. But rocks were a possibility, like shattered trees,
Everlasting-flowers and moss – and so, with mounting enthusiasm, after
many preliminary schemes, with only one man to help them, and for a very

modest outlay, they built themselves a domain which was quite different from anything else in the Department.

The hedgerow was opened here and there to lead into the coppice, which was filled with serpentine paths to make a labyrinth. They had hoped to make an archway in the wall of the fruit garden, through which the perspective would be revealed. As the coping-stones wouldn't stay in place, this had resulted in an enormous breach, with ruins on the ground.

They had sacrificed the asparagus in order to build an Etruscan tomb – that is to say, a quadrilateral in black plaster, six feet tall, and looking like a dog-kennel. Four spruce trees at the corners stood guard over this monument. They intended to top it with an urn, and to embellish it with an inscription.

In the other part of the vegetable garden, a sort of Rialto spanned an ornamental pond, having a shell-work of mussels, encrusted with barnacles. The ground just drank up the water – but no matter. A layer of puddled clay would form at the bottom, and then the water would hold.

The garden shed had been transformed into a rustic cottage, by the use of panes of tinted glass.

At the top of the little vineyard, six squared-up tree trunks supported a sort of bonnet in tinplate, with upturned corners, and this represented a Chinese pagoda.

They had gone down to the banks of the river Orne to pick out block of granite; they had broken them up, numbered them, and brought them back themselves in a cart, and had then stuck the fragments together with cement, heaping them up one on top of another; and so in the middle of the lawn a rock reared up, looking like a gigantic potato.

There was still something needed to round off this creation. They felled the tallest tree in the hedgerow (it was three-quarters dead in any case), and laid it out down the length of the garden, so that one might think it had been washed up by a torrent, or thrown over by lightning.

With this labour complete, Bouvard, who was on the doorstep, shouted out:

'Over here! You can see it better!

'See it better!' floated back in the air.

Pércuchet replied:

'I'm coming'

– 'Coming'

'Hey, an echo'

'Echo'

Until then, the lime tree had prevented it, and the echo was now encouraged by the pagoda, standing opposite the barn, whose gable stood up over the hedge.

To try out the echo, they amused themselves by shouting funny phrases; Bouvard bawled out obscenities.

GUSTAVE FLAUBERT, *Bouvard et Pécuchet* [1881]

My favourite Italian garden laid out for the Cardinal Gambara in 1573 as an allegory of the progress of civilization from the Golden Age. St Charles Borromeo ticked the Cardinal off telling him his money would have been better spent on a nunnery.

THE VILLA LANTE, BAGNAIA

The Duke of Lante's garden is of another character, a place not of grandeur or tragedy but of enchanting loveliness, a paradise of gleaming water, gay flowers and golden light. The long, straight, dusty road from Viterbo leads at length by a bridge across a deep ravine to a gap in the town walls of Bagnaia, 'twixt Gothic castle and Baroque church, then turning at a right angle in the piazza one sees in front the great Renaissance gateway which opens into the garden. But it is better, if permission may be obtained, to enter the park, and striking upward by green lawns and ilex groves to follow from its source the tiny streamlet upon which pool, cascade, and water-temple are threaded like pearls upon a string. Dropping from a ferny grotto between two pillared *loggias*, this rivulet rises again in an elaborate fountain surrounded by mossy benches set in the alcoves of a low box hedge. Four giant plane trees lift a canopy against the sun, and tall stone columns rising from a balustraded wall warn off the intruding woodland. Thence, running under-ground, it emerges unexpectedly in the centre of a broad flights of steps between the claws of a gigantic crab – Cardinal Gambara's cognizance – and races down a long scalloped trough, rippling and writhing like a huge snake over the carved shells which bar its passage. From this it drops over the edge of a small basin between two colossal river-gods into a pool below. The fall to the next level gives us a half-recessed *temple d'eau*, with innumerable jets and runlets pouring from basin to basin; and here, flanked by stately plane trees and by the two pavilions which make up the casino, is a grass-plot commanding the loveliest view of the garden. Before us lies a square enclosure jutting out into the vale below, with high green hedges, sweet *broderies* of box bordered by flowers, and in the midst a broad water-garden leading by balustraded crossways to an island fountain which rises like a mount to four great figures of sombre-tinted stone. Water gushes from the points of the star which the naked athletes uplift, from the mouths of the lions by their side, from the masks on the balustrade, from the tiny galleys in which vagrant cupids are afloat upon the pools. It is a colour harmony of cool refreshing green and brighter flowers, of darkest bronze, blue pools and golden light. Much there is of mystery in the garden, of subtle magic, of strange, elusive charm which must be felt but cannot wholly be understood. Much, no doubt, depends upon the setting, upon the ancient ilexes and wild mountain flank, the mighty hedge of green at the further end with its great pillared gateway and the dark walls and orange-lichened roofs of the houses and tower irregularly grouped behind it; upon the quiet background, the opal hues of green, violent, and grey in the softly modelled plain, and shadowy outlines of the distant hills. But the soul of the garden is in the blue pools which, by some strange wizardy of the artist, to stair and terrace and window throw back the undimmed azure of the Italian sky.

SIR GEORGE SITWELL, *On the Making of Gardens* [1909]

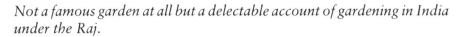

LUCKNOW, INDIA *Not a famous garden at all but a delectable account of gardening in India under the Raj.*

OCTOBER. At this time of year my verandah serves me for a drawing room. Between each pillar it is enclosed with bamboo trellis, called *jaffri* work. This answers the twofold purposes of tempering the outside glare to the room within, and of supporting the creepers, which are now rapidly running up and clothing it from the beds below. Inside, against the wall of the house, stand flowerpots on stages, wherein flourish palms and ferns, and my English seedlings, coming on fast. But it is a case of Darwinian survival. Most of the seeds sent out to me weeks ago, in tins, arrived mildewy and spoilt . . .

The verandah is full of life – captive and free. In a cage ringdoves coo a soft drone to the hoarse and discordant quartette of parrots, perched on iron rings hanging from the roof – green, scarlet and plum, dabs of brilliant colour against the prevailing greenery.

Captive, behind trellis-work at the end of the verandah, stalk the dignified white paddy birds, 'blind idiots', the Tamils call them. Happily they are also practically dumb . . .

In the corner of the compound, near the vegetable beds, is the well – the heart, the life-source of my garden. Morning and evening the great cream-coloured humped bullock labour up and down an inclined plane, drawing up the water in a kind of square bag made of the skins of one of their deceased relatives, and hanging on an iron ring, and which the gardener upsets unto the main runnel. Grouped around the well, to imbibe every particle of moisture, grow the broad-leaved plantains – bananas we call them in Covent Garden and on the coster barrows – mysterious, with clusters of spiky fruit, which make such excellent fritters.

Feathering round the well, too, waves the bamboo – the wonderful bamboo – which flowers but once in thirty years, when it has flowered, dies, attracting to its funeral feast all the fowls of the air, a babel of revellers, showering about them, as they perch, the ripened grain, on rodents and on monkeys, and, in wild jungle parts, even on the wild boar and the deer.

Where there is perpetual slop, from the emptying of the bullockskin, I have planted a pearl of great price – a watercress bed. With much care I can keep it going all the cold weather. How, out here, one prizes the common things of everyday 'home' life.

My geranium plants in pots, which Ida kindly summered for me in the hills, have returned to me after an adventurous journey by train, bullock-cart, and coolie-head, over plain and river and mountain safe and sound, but much overgrown. There have been the cuttings to take, and to set out in new rich earth, and the old straggling plants to cut back. They have done well, but they cannot stand a hot weather in the plains. The single and double scarlet, the pink salmony-white, and the ivy-leaved, have done best . . .

The *Hibiscus mutabilis*, twenty feet high, has covered itself all over with large pink-and-white blooms, exactly like paper flowers! The *Bauhinia accuminata* is graceful, with its pendulous branches of pointed divided leaves, with their large loose panicles of whitish and pale pink. The *Buddleias*, with their orange bells, are rampant. So are the *Lantanas*. About the stone pillars and jaffri work of the verandah are clambering the *bela bel*

Jasmine; the white-flowered *Bona Nox*, or 'Evening Glory' *Ipomea*; the *Ipomea grandiflora*, and the *Passiflora coerulea*, the handsome blue passion flower; the scarlet cypress vine (*Quamoclit*); the star *Ipomea (coccinea)*, a blaze of scarlet; the lilac Railway creeper *(Pulchella)*, and the blue-and-white *Limbata*.

The bougainvilleas we have always with us in flower. Some eight feet high, thriving in the very eye of the sun, this shrub forms an effective, if rather vulgar, mass of colour, maroony purple, against the dark green of the orange trees. I have three kinds, the *B. splendens*, the very handsome *B. spectabilis*, and the *B. glabra*, magenta and pale pink . . .

DECEMBER. The *malli* is, of course, the gardener . . . As will have been perceived, I keep both a *malli* and a garden. In India the two are not inseparable. A custom pertains in villadom in England of two or three little gardens depending upon the ministrations of one jobbing gardener. In India some people – generally the thriftless, unprincipled junior of either service – keep only a *malli*. Nevertheless, strange as it may appear, to them also comes the diurnal *dali*. This is a wicker tray, covered with vegetables of the season, and presided over by a stiff and garish bouquet devoid of greenery, which a muscular mahogany figure, dexterously draped about the loins and legs with a dirty *dhoti*, presents each morning with many signs of abject servitude. One's garden supplies others besides one's self, and one's neighbours appease the *malli* class by paying the wages of one.

We galloped past remains of these pre-Mutiny bungalows, mere fragments of crumbling walls devastated by smell and fire and time. It was very sad. As at dusk we rode homewards through our well gardened cantonments, I could not help thinking of the lives of the Sahib folk who had made and lived in these ruined gardens . . . I imagine them sitting in the evening on their *chabutras* in their gardens, the women doing Berlin-wool work or crochet, and talking most microscopic gossip; while the men smoked Indian cheroots, and drank bottled beer from England, or brandy and water. Indian breweries, soda-water, and ice machines were unknown; new books and magazines came only once a month, and even the Queen did not exist. Then fell the thunderbolt out of the blue. Their gardens knew them no more. Where are they all, the men who made the India we inherit, the white women, the whiter children? Some are dragging out days of livery old age at Cheltenham, or in the Asia Minor of South Kensington, their names well-nigh forgotten by this generation. Some lie in the crowded old cemetery across the river, some in scattered forgotten graves – some few, who knows where?

Yesterday the Captain Sahib was on a board to award prizes to the gunners' gardens at the Fish Market Fort. The men are given seeds and encouraged to grow vegetables and flowers, as the life of a garrison gunner in an Indian fort is a very dull one . . .

The quarters of the European garrison are inside the enclosure, but detached. As one stood adjudicating on the respective merits of cabbages and cauliflowers, what a sharp contrast was the scene outside – the elephants stalking down to the river to bathe, the camels swinging past into the city, and, overhead, against the clear blue sky, the massive pointed archway of the Turkish Gateway, with its ornamentations of acanthus leaves in stucco.

JANUARY. In the garden I have been very busy sowing fresh seeds in the hot bed. There has been a great deal to do pricking out annuals into the little beds that edge the verandah wall; and I have had all the roses and fruit trees opened out and mulched.

Be it well understood that when I speak of doing a thing in the garden myself, it merely means I sit, or stand, and see it done. In this land no one does any gardening personally, but the supervision of the ignorant, untrust-worthy, uninterested *malli* is far more trouble.

MARCH. Last night we were at an outdoor evening party at the Very Great Sahib's. He boasts one of the very few real lawns in the place. It cometh up like a flower each autumn, by dint of much toil on the part of the patient *bhisti*. But in April the hot wind passeth over it, and it is gone! The party may have been said to have been given in honour of the lawn, for it was prettily lit up, native fashion, with hundreds of little coloured lamps. We had the cavalry band, and a nigger entertainment by British soldiers.

MAY. The hot wind has withered up my poor roses, and it has been quite a business cutting off the dead heads . . . Ida has carried off my geraniums to the hills. Would I had gone with them!

Quite an occupation for me in the very early morning lately, on returning from my ride, has been the standing over the *malli* and seeing him take the cuttings of the poinsettias, *tabernae montana tecomas*, hibiscus, and layer the bougainvilleas.

JUNE. I rise, about 4.30 am., don a white cotton riding habit, and sip my tea in the verandah, a long-handled palm-leaf waved over me . . . This is the only hour of the twentyfour at which I can enjoy my garden. Yet the flowers and creepers are beautiful. Anything more lovely, for instance, than the tone of the colour of the sky-blue *ipomea*, the *coerulla*, a blue convolvulus, eight feet high, cannot well be imagined . . .

But the hour is so short. Up comes the sun – a fiery ball in the east – and with it, the hot winds . . .

Another night of horror, but joy has come in the morning! For the Captain Sahib has got his leave, and we are off to the hills! . . .

Ida has found a house for us. 'You will miss your garden', quoth she, as she introduced us to the little chalet, perched on the steep hillside, a tiny terrace cut out in front, wide enough to turn a *jampan* in.

But what care I? The world spread out before us, fold upon fold of montain, green and beautiful, is one wide garden.

ANON., *My Garden in the City of Gardens* [1905]

LUXEMBOURG
GARDENS, PARIS

The Luxembourg palace and gardens were the creation of Marie de'Medici and designed to recall the Boboli gardens of her childhood. The most famous feature was the huge box-embroidered parterre laid out by Jacques Boyceau de la Barauderie (d.c. 1633) which Evelyn describes.

I went [on 1st April 1644] more exactly to see the roomes of that incomparable Palace of Luxemburge in the Fauxbourgs St Germains, built by Mary de Medices and I thinke one of the most noble, entire and finish'd Pile[s] that is standing in any Citty of the World, taking it with the Garden and all its accomplishments . . . The Gardens containe neere an English mile in Com-

passe, enclos'd with a stately wall, & in good ayre, which renders it certainly one of the sweetest places imaginable; The Parterr is indeede of box; but so rarely designed, and accurately kept cut; that the [e]mbrodery makes a stupendious effect, to the Lodgings which front it; 'tis divided into 4 Squares, & as many circular knots; having in the Center a noble Basin of Marble neere 30 foot diameter (as I remember) in which a Triton of brasse holds a Dolphin that casts a girandola of water neere 30 foote high which plays perpetualy, & the water is excellent, being convey'd from Arceuil, whence it is derived by an Aquaeduct of stone built after the old Roman magnificence. About this ample Parterr, the spacious Walkes & all included, runs a bordure of free-stone adorn'd with Pedistalls for Potts & Statues; and part of it neere the Stepps of the Terrace, with a raile & baluster of pure white marble: The Walkes are exactly faire, long & variously descending, & so justly planted with limes, Elmes & other Trees, that nothing can be more delicious & surprizing, especially that of the hornebeame hedge, which being high & stately, butts full upon the fountaine: Towards the farther end is an excavation intended for a Vast Piscina, but never finish'd; & neere it is an enclosure for a Garden of simples, rarely entertained, & here the Duke keepes Tortoises in great number who use the pole of Water at one side of the Garden: here is also a Conservatory for Snow: At the upper part (towards the Palace) is a grove of tall Elmes cutt into a Star, every ray being a Walke whose center is a large fountaine.

JOHN EVELYN, Diary, 1 April 1644

Pliny the Younger's (AD c. 62–112) favourite villa was in Tuscany. The descriptions of its delights were to inspire the great gardens of the Renaissance.

PLINY'S TUSCAN GARDEN

My villa is so advantageiously situated, that it commands a full view of all the country round; yet you approach it by so insensible a rise that you find yourself upon an eminence, without perceiving you ascended. Behind, but at a great distance, stand the Apennine Mountains. In the calmest days we are refreshed by the winds that blow from thence, but so spent, as it were, by the long tract of land they travel over, that they are entirely divested of all their strength and violence before they reach us. The exposition of the principal front of the house is full south, and seems to invite the afternoon sun in summer (but somewhat earlier in winter) into a spacious and well-proportioned portico, consisting of several members, particularly a porch built in the ancient manner. In the front of the portico is a sort of terrace, embellished with various figures and bounded with a box-hedge, from whence you descend by an easy slope, adorned with the representation of divers animals in box, answering alternately to each other, into a lawn overspread with the soft – I had almost said the liquid – Acanthus: this is surrounded by a walk enclosed with tonsile evergreens, shaped into a variety of forms. Beyond it is the Gestatio, laid out in the form of a circus, ornamented in the middle with box cut in numberless different figures, together with a plantation of shrubs, prevented by the shears from shooting up too high; the whole is fenced in by a wall covered by box, rising by different ranges to the top. On the outside of the wall lies a meadow that owes as many beauties to nature, as all I have been describing *within* does to

art; at the end of which are several other meadows and fields interspersed with thickets. At the extremity of this portico stands a grand dining-room which opens upon one end of the terrace; as from the windows there is a very extensive prospect over the meadows up into the country, from whence you also have a view of the terrace and such parts of the house which project forward, together with the woods enclosing the adjacent hippodrome. Opposite almost to the centre of the portico stands a square edifice, which encompasses a small area, shaded by four plane-trees, in the midst of which a fountain rises, from whence the water, running over the edges of a marble basin, gently refreshes the surrounding plane-trees and the verdure underneath them . . . In the front of these agreeable buildings lies a very spacious hippodrome, entirely open in the middle, by which means the eye, upon your first entrance, takes in its whole extent at one glance. It is encompassed on every side with plane-trees covered with ivy, so that while their heads flourish with their own foliage, their bodies enjoy a borrowed verdure; and thus, the ivy twining round the trunk and branches, spreads from tree to tree, and connects them together.

Between each plane-tree are planted box-trees, and behind these, bay-trees, which blend their shade with that of the planes. This plantation, forming a straight boundary on both sides of the hippodrome, bends at the farther end into a semicircle, which being set round and sheltered with cypress-trees, varies the prospect, and casts a deeper gloom; while the inward circular walks (for there are several) enjoying an open exposure, are perfumed with roses, and correct, by a very pleasing contrast, the coolness of the shade with the warmth of the sun. Having passed through these several winding alleys, you enter a straight walk, which breaks out into a variety of others, divided by box-hedges. In one place you have a little meadow, in another the box is cut into a thousand different forms; sometimes into letters expressing the name of the master; sometimes that of the artificer; whilst here and there little obelisks rise, intermixed alternately with fruit-trees: when, on a sudden, in the midst of this elegant regularity, you are surprised with an imitation of the negligent beauties of rural nature: in the centre of which lies a spot surrounded with a knot of dwarf plane-trees.

Beyond these is a walk planted with the smooth and twining Acanthus, where the trees are also cut into a variety of names and shapes. At the upper end is an alcove of white marble, shaded with vines, supported by four small Carystian pillars. From this bench, the water gushing through several little pipes, as if it were pressed out by the weight of the persons who repose themselves upon it, falls into a stone cistern underneath, from whence it is received into a fine polished marble basin, so artfully contrived that it is always full without ever overflowing.

When I sup here, this basin serves for a table, the larger sort of dishes being placed round the margin, while the smaller ones swim about in the form of little vessels and water-fowl. Corresponding to this, is a fountain which is incessantly emptying and filling; for the water, which it throws up a great height, falling back into it, is, by means of two openings, returned as fast as it is received. Fronting the alcove (and which reflects as great an ornament to it, as it borrows from it) stands a summer-house of exquisite marble, the doors whereof project and open into a green enclosure; as from its upper and lower window the eye is presented with a variety of different verdures. Next to this is a little private recess (which, though it seems distinct, may be laid into the same room) furnished with a couch; and notwithstanding it has windows on every side, yet it enjoys a very agreeable gloominess, by means of a spreading vine which climbs to the top and entirely overshades it. Here you may recline and fancy yourself in a wood; with this difference only – that you are not exposed to the weather. In this place a fountain also rises and instantly disappears: in different quarters are disposed marble seats, which serve, no less than the summer-house, as to so many reliefs after one is wearied with walking. Near each seat is a little fountain; and, throughout the whole hippodrome, several small rills run murmuring along, wheresoever the hand of art thought proper to conduct them; watering here and there different spots of verdure, and in their progress refreshing the whole.

> PLINY THE YOUNGER translated by
> William Melmouth, *Letter to
> Appollinaris*

Today only the giant Appenino sculpted by Giovanni da Bologna and the chapel survive to evoke the greatest of the Medici gardens outside Florence. It was created for Duke Francesco in the 1570s and its extraordinary quality is well caught in the naive wondering pen of the Elizabethan traveller, Fynes Moryson, in 1594.

PRATALINO, near
FLORENCE

Early in the morning we went out by the plaine lying on the west side, & came to Pratoline, the Dukes famous garden, seven miles from the City, the conduits whereof for water if a man well consider, he may justly say of the gardens of Italy, as Mounster saith of the Towns of Valesia, that their water costs them more then their wine. This garden is divided into two inclosures, compassed with stone wals. In the upper inclosure is a statua of a Giant, with a curled beard, like a Monster, some forty sixe els high, whose great belly will receive many men at once, and by the same are the Images of many Nimphes, all which cast out water abundantly. Neere the same are many pleasant fish-ponds, and there is a Cave under the earth leading three miles to the Fountaine of water, from whence by many pipes the waters are brought to serve the workes of these Gardens. There is a Fountaine which hath the name of a Laberinth close by it. And a Fountaine of Jupiter & Iris distilling water; the Fountaine of the Beare; the Fountaine of Aesculapius; and the Fountaine of Bersia. I call these by the name of Fountaines, vulgarly called Fontana, which are buildings of stone, adorned with many carved Images distilling water, and such are placed in most parts of Italy in the market-places, open and uncovered: but in this and like Gardens, these Fountaines are wrought within little houses, which house is vulgarly called grotta, that is, Cave (or Den), yet are they not.

It remaines I should speak of the lower Garden, which is much more beautiful then the upper: for at the first entrance, there is a Pallace of little compasse, but stately building, being of a round forme, the midst whereof containeth the great chamber, larger then the other rooms, which round about the same are little, but beautiful, and richly furnished for private retreit. From under all the staires of the Pallace, and the pavements round about, with the turning of a cocke, spoutes of water rise up in great force. For in respect of the heat of the Country, they take great pleasure to wet the passengers in this sort. Under the Pallace there is a Cave, vulgarly called la

grotta Maggiore, (which and like Conduits made as is abovesaid, I will hereafter call fountaines, because they are so vulgarly called). In the said Cave, a head of marble distilleth water; and two trees by the turning of a cocke shed waters abundantly, and a little globe is turned about by Cupid, where the Images of Duckes dabble in the water, then looke round about them; and in the middest of a marble table is an instrument, which with great art and force driveth water into any furthest part of the Cave. So many and so divers are the castings of the water, as the most wary man cannot escape wetting, where they make sport to betray all lookers on in that kind. Neere this, and under the Pallace is a Bath, the wals whereof shine with glistering stones, and therein is a table of Alablaster. Neere this is a cave strongly built, yet by Art so made, as you would feare to enter it, lest great stones should fall upon you head: and here by the turning of a ripe, certaine images of Nimphes are carried by the water out of the Cave, and in againe, as if they had life, no water being seens: and in this cave seeming ruinous, are the most curious Images of many beasts that ever I did see. In the next fountaine, with the turning of a Cocke, the unseene waters cause a noise like thunder, and presently a great shower of raine fals. But among all the Caves or Fountaines under the Pallace, one is most faire and large, at the one end whereof, upon the turning of a cocke, by the same motion of water unseene, the Image of Fame doth loudly sound a Trumpet, while the image of a Clowne putteth a dish into the water, and taking up water, presents it to the Image of a Tyger, which drinketh the same up, and then moves his head, and lookes round about with his eyes, which is as often done as they please, who have the skill to order the Cocke. At the other end of that Cave, is the Image of Syrinx with her fingers halfe turned into reedes; and right against that, is the Image of Pan sitting upon a stoole, with a wreathed pipe in his hand, and Syrinx beckening to Pan, to play upon the pipe, Pan puts away his stoole with one hand, then standing on foot, plaies upon his pipe, and this done, lookes upon his mistresse, as if he desired thanks or a kisse for his paines: and then takes his stoole againe, and sits downe with a sad countenance. I know not that any place in the World affoords such rare sights in this kind; but lest I should be tedious, it shall suffice onely to name the other Images and Caves. As you goe downe from the Pallace, you shall first see the Cave of Aeolus, another of Parnassus, where, with the turning of a cocke, a paire of Organs doth make sweet musicke; and there is a head which together with the eyes is moved to and fro by the unseene water, and there is a pleasant shade with many statuaes (or Images) curiously carved, and there the Duke doth many times eat. The third fountaine is called Il villano, that is, the Clowne. The fourth La pescaria, that is, the Fish-pond, where a Ducke of India having foure wings did swimme in the water. The fifth Lauandara, the Laundresse, where the statua of a woman with the turning of a Cocke, beats a bucke, turning the clothes up and downe with her hand and the batttledor, wherewith shee beateth them in the water. The sixth vulgarly Caccioli, containess vessels to keepe the water cold. The Seventh Del Rosso. The eight Grotta Copito, and in this Cave on all sides are marble chaires, whereupon passengers willingly sit after their walking: but assoone as they lightly presse some of the seats, a paile of water fals upon his head that sits upon it; besides the pavement is of marble, and therein many stones are so placed, as lightly touched with a man's foot, they cast up water into his very face and eies. There be also well wrought Images, of a Serpent biting the finger of a Man, and of a Toade creeping to and fro, and of a Dragons head bowing downe to drinke water, which presently it vomits up againe. The ninth Il satiro, the Satire. The tenth La mascara, a woman with a vizard. To conclude, there is a large cage of birds, made of wier, and open to the aire, in which are birds of all kindes and many Countries, not onely singing to delight the eare, but of most pleasant and divers colours to delight the eye.

FYNES MORYSON, *An Itinerary* [1617]

These, of course, were celebrated in the seventeenth century and few impressions of their glory are better than John Evelyn's while making what was to become the Grand Tour during the Civil War.

ROMAN GARDENS

17th November 1644

The 17 I walked to Villa Burghesi, which is an house and ample Garden on Mons Pincius, yet somewhat without the Citty-Wales; circumscrib'd by another wall full of small turrets and banqueting houses, which makes it appear at a distance like a little Towne, within it tis an Elysium of delight; having in the center of it a very noble Palace (but the enterance of the Garden, presents us with a very glorios fabrick, or rather dore-Case adorned with divers excellent marble statues): This Garden abounded with all sorts of the most delicious fruit, and Exotique simples: Fountaines of sundry inventions. Groves, & small Rivulets of Water: There is also adjoynning to it a Vivarium for Estriges, Peacoks, Swanns, Cranes, &c: and divers strange Beasts, Deare & hares: The Grotto is very rare, and represents among other devices artificial raines & sundry shapes of Vessells, Flowers &c: which is effected by [changing] the heads of the Fountaines: The Groves are of Cypresse and Lawrell, Pine, Myrtil, Olive &c: The 4 Sphinxes are very Antique and worthy observation: To this is a Volary full of curious birds:

28th November

On the 28 I went to se[e] the Garden and house of the Aldobrandini, but now Cardinal Burghezes . . .

In the Garden are a world of fine fountaines, the wales all covered with Citron trees which being rarely spread invest the stone worke intirely; and towards the streete at a back gate the port is so handsomly cloath'd with Ivy, as much pleas'd me . . .

29th November

I went farther up the hill, to the Popes Palace at Monte Cavallo, where I now saw the Garden more exactly, and found it to be one of the most magnificent & Pleasant in Rome: I am told the Gardner is annually alow'd 2000 scudi for the keeping it: Here I observ'd the glorious hedges of myrtle above a mans height; others of Laurell, Oranges, nay of Ivy, & Juniper: The Close walkes and Rustic Grotto, and [another] admirable Crypta whereof the Lavor or Basin is of one vast intire Porphyrie, the fairest that ever I beheld, antique: Below this falls a plentiful Cascade of Water; the stepps of the Grott being all of rich Mosaique, as is also the roofe: Here are hydraulic Organs; a Fish-pond in an ample Bath: From hence we went to tast some rare Greco, and so home.

3rd May 1645

The next day after dinner, Mr *Henshaw* & I went againe to see the *Villa Borghesi* . . . This Garden about a Mile without the Cittie, being rather a Park or Paradise contrivd & planted with Walkes & shades of *Myrtils, Cypresse* & other trees & groves, adornd with aboundance of Fountains, statues & Bassrelievos: Here they had hung large Netts to Catch Wood-Cocks: there were fine glades, & several pretty murmuring rivulets trickling downe the declining Walkes: There was also a Vivarie where among other exotic foules there was an Ostridge, besids a most capacious Aviarie & in another inclosd part, an heard of Deere.

5th May

The 5 we tooke Coach and went 15 miles out of the Cittie to *Frascati* formerly *Tusculanum*, a villa of Card: *Aldobrandini*; built for a Country house but for its elegance, situation & accommodation of plentifull water, Groves, Ascents & prospect, surpassing in my opinion the most delicious places that my eyes ever beheld: Just behind the Palace (which is of excellent Architecture) and is in the center of the Inclosure, rises an high hill or mountaine all over clad with tall wood, and so form'd by nature, as if it had ben cut out by Art, from the summit whereof falls a horrid Cascade seeming rather a greate River than a streame, precipitating into a large Theater of Water representing a[n] exact & perfect Raine-bow when the sun shines out: Under this is made an artific[i]all Grott, where in are curious rocks, hydraulic Organs & all sorts of singing birds moving, & chirping by force of the water, with severall other pageants and surprizing inventions: In the center of one of these roomes rises a coper ball that continually daunces about 3 foote above the pavement by virtue of a Wind conveyed seacretly to a hole beneath it, with many other devices to wett the unwary spectators, so as one can hardly [step] without wetting to the skin: In one of these Theatres of Water, is an *Atlas* spouting up the streame to an incredible height, & another monster which makes a terrible roaring with an horn; but above all the representation of a storme is most naturall, with such fury of raine, wind and thunder as one would imagine ones selfe in some extreame Tempest: To this is a Garden of incomparable walkes & shady groves, aboundance of rare Fruit, Orangs, Lemons, &c; and the goodly prospect of Rome above all description, so as I do not wonder that *Cicero* & others have celebrated this place with such encomiums.

7th May

Ariv'd at *Tivoli* we went first to see the Palace 'Estè erected on a plaine, but where was formerly an hill: The Palace is very ample & stately: In the Garden at the right hand are plac'd 16 vast Conchas of marble jetting out Waters: in the midst of these stands a *Janus* quadrifrons that cast forth 4 girandolas, calld from the resemblance the *fontana di Speccho*; neere this a Place for Tilting: before the Ascent of the Palace is that incomparable fountain of *Leda*, & not far from that 4 sweete & delicious Gardens; descending thence two pyramids of Water, & in a Grove of trees neere it, the Fountaines of *Tethys, Esculapius, Arethusa, Pandora, Pomona* & *Flora*, then the pransing *Pegasus, Bacchus*, The Grott of *Venus*, the two Colosses of *Melicerta* & *Sybilla Tibertina*, all of exquisite Marble, Coper & other suitable adornments, The *Cupids* especialy are most rare, pouring out Water

& the Urnes on which are plac'd the 10 Nymphs: The Grotts are richly pav'd with *pietra Commessa*, Shells, Corall &c: Towards *Roma Triumphans*, leades a long spacious Walk, full of Fountaines, under which is historiz'd the who[le] *Ovidian* Metamorphosis in *mezzo Relievo* rarely sculptur'd, at the end of this, next the wall the Cittie of *Rome*, as it was in its beauty, all built of small models, representing that Citie with its Amphitheatres, Naumachia, Thermae, Temples, Arches, Aquaeducts, streetes & other magnificences, with a little streame runing through it for the River Tybur, gushing out of the Urne next the statue of that River: In another Garden a noble Aviarie, the birds artificial, & singing, til the presence of an Owle appeares, on which the[y] suddainly chang their notes, to the admiration of the Spectators: Neere this is the Fountaine of Dragons belching large streams of water, with horrid noises: In another Grotto calld the *Grotta di Natura* is an hydraulic Organ, below this divers stews and fish-ponds, in one of which is the Statue of *Neptune* in his Chariot, on a sea-horse, in another a *Triton*, & lastly a Garden of simples.   JOHN EVELYN, *Diary* [1644/45]

SPANISH GARDENS

Elizabeth, Lady Holland's (1770–1845) journal of her visit to Spain from 1802 to 1805 includes two splendid accounts of the royal palace gardens. The first is of those of the Alcazar in Seville, unchanged since laid out by the Emperor Charles V early in the sixteenth century. Her comments in favour of the old formal style anticipate by almost a decade Humphry Repton's revival of it.

Don Francisco conducted us to the gardens of the Alcazar, where he had previously given orders that the waterworks should be played. The gardens are preserved in the Moorish style; one part is precisely as at the Conquest, clipped hedges of myrtle and devices cut upon them. Another part was laid out by Don Pedro; rows of myrtle warriors, giants, and ladies with wooden heads and arms, carrying in their hands swords, clubs, musical instruments, &c. Farther on is the garden of Charles V, with a pavilion for refreshments, a delicious spot. The whole garden is full of *jets d'eau*, cascades, fountains, and water tricks and devices. I was to the full as much pleased with these hanging gardens as Charles or any child could be. The English taste for simplicity and nature, which places a house in the midst of a grazing field where the sheep din *ba ba* all day long, has, by offending me so much, perhaps driven me into the opposite extreme, and made me prefer to the *nature* of a grass field and round clump the *built* gardens of two centuries back.

(*Journal*, 26th May 1803)

This preference is elaborated upon in her account of the gardens of Arunjvez remodelled by Philip V in the French style.

The gardens are just praised; the shade is so thick from the lofty trees weighed down by luxuriant foliage, that one may defy the rays of a Spanish sun even at midday. In the garden we were shown a small hunting villa built by Charles V, now falling into decay; in front of it are three venerable trees (either elms or oaks), which according to oral tradition are said to have been planted by the Emperor Francis I during his captivity, and Philip II. Two are

flourishing, but one, which I hope may be that planted by Philip II, is in a piteous condition, and may be accepted as but too just an emblem of the state into which the monarchy has fallen in consequence of his pernicious political doctrines. In the evening the fountains played in another garden called *del Principe*: the King and the Princess of the Asturias were present. His amusement consists chiefly in running as fast as possible from one fountain to another, and in seeding the unwary spectator wetted with the spray or by the secret pipes.

(*Journal*, June 13th 1803)

The gardens are reckoned among the finest in Europe; they are in the old French style of high clipped hedges, *salons de verdure*, alleys, &c. Tho' that is the style I prefer far beyond any other, yet these gardens are *sombre*, and only striking from the number of their fountains, which stand unrivalled. We obtained permission from the *Intendente* to have the fountains play for us, a request usually complied with upon paying two ounces of gold. I was surprised at seeing channels to convey watger to the roots of the trees, the same as is used at Aranjuez and at Madrid. There there is no moisture or coolness, but here the neighbourhood of the mountains cause frequent storms of thunder and rain. Besides the great garden, we saw the private ones of the King and Queen; in one we were shown the hedge behind which the K. conceals himself to shoot at sparrows.

(*Journal*, June 17th 1903)

VERSAILLES

Although without doubt the most famous palace garden ever created, it has attracted a regular flow of bad press down the centuries. Few areas of land have undergone so many spectacular transformations and yet the spirit of Louis XIV and the genius of their creator, André Le Nôtre, remain untouched and still reign supreme.

The gardens, which are astonishingly magnificent, but discouraging to use, are in equally bad taste. One cannot reach the freshness of the shade without passing through a torrid zone, at the end of which one has no choice but to climb and then descend a small hill, and here the gardens end. The stone path burns one's feet, but without it, one sinks into the sand and into the blackest dirt. The violence done to nature everywhere disgusts; the abundant waters, forced up and collected again, are green, thick, muddy; they shed an unhealthy and perceptible humidity, a small which is even worse. The whole effect, which one must yet treat with respect, is incomparable, but it is something to admire, and to shun.   DUC DE SAINT-SIMON (1675–1755) *Memoires* translated by Lucy Norton

English visitors particularly relished running the gardens down. By the middle of the eighteenth century, with the radical decline of the French economy, they began to assume the melancholy, abandoned air captured in the canvases of Hubert Robert.

We went net day to Versailles, agreeable to the plan of the Marquis de Tarafiné who accompanied us in order to show us the apartments and everything that was curious. He informed us of the immense sums Louis XIV had expended to raise that palace and convert the gardens into the form we saw them; the difficulty he had of bringing water thither, contrary to the course of nature, for the use of the basins and the *jets-d'eau*. In a word, that from a poor contemptible village whose name was scarce known even at Paris, he had rendered it one of the most magnificent places in all Europe. It is true that we found the building very sumptuous, the gallery extremely elegant and the painting of the ceiling particularly fine; but that in general the furniture was very ancient, and there was neither that neatness, nor what the French themselves call that *air-riant*, which is so striking in the apartments of all our elegant edifices in England. As to the gardens, they were doubtless extremely well laid out; but the walks were insupportably dusty, for want of gravel. Many of the statues were mutilated, and most of the waterworks were in a state of inactivity by reason of the pipes being out of repair. Upon the whole, it conveyed to us at once an idea of Louis XIV's ambition, the sentiments of glory wherewith he animated the whole kingdom, and the present degeneracy of the French nation.

JOHN CLELAND, Memoirs of Maria Brown [1766]

A just pre-French Revolutionary English visitor describes Marie Antoinette's garden in the Anglo-Chinois style with its proliferation of incident much of which we can still see today.

To Trianon, to view the Queen's *Jardin Anglois* . . . It contains about 100 acres, disposed in the taste of what we read of in books of Chinese gardening, whence it is supposed the English style was taken. There is more of Sir William Chambers here than of Mr Brown – more effort than nature – and more expence than taste. It is not easy to conceive any thing that art can introduce in a garden that is not here; woods, rocks, lawns, lakes, rivers, islands, cascades, grottos, walks, temples and even villages. There are parts of the design very pretty, and well executed. The only fault is too much crouding; which has led to another, that of cutting the lawn by too many gravel walks, an error to be seen in almost every garden I have met with in France. But the glory of *La Petite Trianon* is the exotic trees and shrubs. The world has been successfully rifled to decorate it. Here are curious and beautiful ones to please the eye of ignorance; and to exercise the memory of science. Of the buildings, the temple of love is truly elegant.

ARTHUR YOUNG, Travels during the Years 1787, 1788 and 1789

Shelley looks at the gardens with the eyes of the Romantic Movement.

We saw the palace and gardens of Versailles and le Grand et Petit Trianon. They surpass Fountainebleau. The gardens are full of statues, vases, fountains and colonnades. In all that essentially belongs to a garden they are extraordinarily deficient. The orangery is a stupid piece of expense. There was one orange-tree not apparently so old, sown in 1442. We saw also the gardens and the theatre at the Petit Trianon. The gardens are in the English taste and extremely pretty.

PERCY BYSSHE SHELLEY, Journal,
3 September 1816

PART
XI

EVENTS
AND
ENCOUNTERS

One of Alice's more unnerving encounters. Tiger lilies were brought to the West from Canton in 1804.

ALICE AND
THE TIGER LILY

This time she came upon a large flower-bed, with a border of daisies, and a willow-tree growing in the middle.

'O Tiger-lily,' said Alice, addressing herself to one that was waving gracefully about in the wind, 'I *wish* you could talk!'

'We *can* talk,' said the Tiger-lily: 'when there's anybody worth talking to.'

Alice was so astonished that she couldn't speak for a minute: it quite seemed to take her breath away. At length, as the Tiger-lily only went on waving about, she spoke again, in a timid voice – almost in a whisper. 'And can *all* the flowers talk?'

'As well as *you* can,' said the Tiger-lily. 'And a great deal louder.'

'It isn't manners for us to begin, you know,' said the Rose, 'and I really was wondering when you'd speak! Said I to myself, "Her face has got *some* sense in it, though it's not a clever one!" Still, you're the right colour, and that goes a long way.'

'I don't care about the colour,' the Tiger-lily remarked. 'If only her petals curled up a little more, she'd be all right.'

Alice didn't like being criticized, so she began asking questions: 'Aren't you sometimes frightened at being planted out here, with nobody to take care of you?'

'There's the tree in the middle,' said the Rose. 'What else is it good for?'

'But what could it do, if any danger came?' Alice asked.

'It could bark,' said the Rose.

'It says "Bough-wough!"' cried a Daisy: 'that's why its branches are called boughs!'

'Didn't you know *that*?' cried another Daisy, and here they all began shouting together, till the air seemed quite full of little shrill voices. 'Silence, every one of you!' cried the Tiger-lily, waving itself passionately from side to side, and trembling with excitement. 'They know I can't get at them!' it panted, bending its quivering head towards Alice, 'or they wouldn't dare to do it!'

'Never mind!' Alice said in a soothing tone, and stooping down to the daisies, who were beginning again, she whispered, 'If you don't hold your tongues, I'll pick you!'

There was silence in a moment, and several of the pink daisies turned white.

'That's right!' said the Tiger-lily. 'The daisies are worst of all. When one speaks, they all begin together, and it's enough to make one wither to hear the way they go on!'

LEWIS CARROLL, *Through the Looking Glass* [1872]

CHELSEA FLOWER SHOW

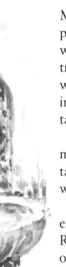

Christabel, Lady Aberconway remained remarkable to the end. She had married into gardening, her husband being President of the Royal Horticultural Society, and as a consequence gives us this delicious account of a tour by King George V.

My husband, being President of the Royal Horticultural Society, had the privilege of taking the King and Queen round the Chelsea Flower Show. I was told that I would walk in front with the King, and that at all costs I must try to prevent him from marching forward too quickly, while my husband would follow with Queen Mary, whose progress, because of her intense interest in all she saw, was always slow. I foresaw that it wouldn't be an easy task.

Ten minutes before King George and Queen Mary were due to arrive, a message came from Buckingham Palace: 'The King is in a bad temper: please take him round the shortest way.' Since then I have tried in vain to discover who sent that message, which drained my courage.

King George and Queen Mary arrived and we set forth. The King and I exchanged a few dreary remarks about the weather. Then I spoke of the Royal Hospital at Chelsea and of Nell Gwynn. The King brightened: it was obvious that he was not interested in flowers, so I thought that ancestors and history were a possibility. We were getting on quite well, discussing, if I remember rightly, the Duke of Clarence and the butt of Malmsey wine, and were getting on to wine in general, when four or five photographers jumped out, knelt down, and photographed the King. He stopped dead. 'This is intolerable, intolerable,' he said. 'They've taken quite enough photographs of me today; these journalists – these journalists – I'm going back to the Palace.'

I suppose I should have murmured about the disappointment of everyone present; instead I risked all, which some might call 'a gaffe', by saying: 'Sir, who has encouraged journalists more than yourself: have you not ennobled Northcliffe, Rothermere, Beaverbrook?'

It was touch and go. I was given 'an old-fashioned look', and then in a low voice he said: 'Well, well, yes, yes, let's go on.'

CHRISTABEL ABERCONWAY, *A Wiser Woman?* [1966]

IN THE CONSERVATORY

Disraeli in an early novel uses the conservatory for precisely the kind of encounter it alone could make plausible.

'These orange groves remind me of Palermo', said Ferdinand.

'Ah!' said Miss Temple. 'I have never been in the sweet south!'

'You seem to me a person born to live in a Sicilian palace', said Ferdinand, 'to wander in perfumed groves, and to glance in a moonlight, warmer than this sun.'

'I see you pay compliments', said Miss Temple, looking at him archly, and meeting a glance serious and soft.

'Believe me, not to you.'

'What do you think of this flower?' said Miss Temple, turning away rather quickly and pointing to a strange plant.

'It is the most singular thing in the world: but if it be tended by any other person than myself it withers. Is it not droll?'

'I think not,' said Ferdinand.

'I excuse you for your incredulity; no one does believe it; no one can; and yet it is quite true. Our gardener gave it up in despair. I wonder what it can be.'

'I think it must be some enchanted prince,' said Ferdinand.

'If I thought so, how I should long for a wand to emancipate him!' said Miss Temple.

'Oh! I don't know,' said Ferdinand, 'I suppose because I believe you are sufficiently enchanting without one.'

'I am bound to consider that most excellent logic,' said Miss Temple.

'Do you admire my fountain and my birds?' she continued, after a short pause. 'After Armine, Ducie appears a little tawdry toy.'

'Ducie is Paradise,' said Ferdinand. 'I should like to pass my life in this conservatory.'

'As an enchanted prince, I suppose?' said Miss Temple.

'Exactly', said Captain Armine; 'I would willingly this instant became a flower, if I were sure that Miss Temple would cherish my existence.'

'Cut off your tendrils and drown you with a watering-pot', said Miss Temple; 'you really are a very Sicilian in your conversation, Captain Armine.'

'Come', said Mr Temple, who now joined them, 'if you really should like to take a stroll round the grounds, I will order the keeper to meet us at the cottage.'

BENJAMIN DISRAELI, Henrietta Temple [1837]

ENTERTAINMENTS

The royal progresses of Elizabeth I and her successors, James I and Anne of Denmark, were the occasion of most delightful garden entertainments. At Lord Burghley's great house, Theobalds, in 1591, the Virgin Queen encountered a gardener who describes a knot garden being made in her honour at Pymms, Burghley's son Sir Robert Cecil's house.

Most fortunate and fair queen, on whose heart Wisdom hath laid her crown, and in whose hands Justice hath left her balance, vouchsafe to hear a country controversy, for that there is as great equity in defending of poor men's onions as of rich men's lands.

At Pymms, some four miles hence, the youngest son of this honourable old man (whom God bless with as many years and virtues as there be of him conceived hopes and wishes!) devised a plot for a garden, as methought, and in a place unfit for pleasure, being overgrown with thistles and turned up with moles, and besides so far from the house that, in my country capacity, a pound had been meeter than a paradise. What his meaning was I durst not inquire for *sunt animis celestibus irae*; but what my labours were I dare boast of.

The moles destroyed and the plot levelled, I cast it into four quarters. In the first I framed a maze, not of hyssop and thyme, but that which maketh time itself wither with wondering; all the Virtues, all the Graces, all the Muses winding and wreathing about your majesty, each contending to be chief, all contented to be cherished: all this not of potherbs, but flowers, and of flowers fairest and sweetest; for in so heavenly a maze, which astonished all earthly thought's promise, the Virtues were done in roses, flowers fit for the twelve Virtues, who have in themselves, as we gardeners have observed, above an hundred; the Grace[s] of pansies partly-coloured, but in one stalk, never asunder, yet diversely beautified; the Muses of nine several flowers, being of sundry natures, yet all sweet, all sovereign.

These mingled in a maze, and brought into such shapes as poets and painters use to shadow, made mine eyes dazzle with the shadow, and all my thoughts amazed to behold the bodies. Then was I commanded to place an arbour all of eglantine, in which my master's conceit outstriped my cunning: 'Eglantine,' quoth he, 'I most honour, and it hath been told me that the deeper it is rooted in the ground, the sweeter it smelleth in the flower, making it ever so green that the sun of Spain at the hottest cannot parch it.'

GEORGE PEELE [1591]

In September of the same year Elizabeth was entertained by the Earl of Hertford at Elvetham with the grandest of all the garden entertainments which stretched over four days. We must picture the following one taking place in a knot garden planted beneath the Queen's rooms.

THE FOURTH DAIES ENTERTAINMENT

On Thursday morning, her Majestie was no sooner readie, and at her Gallerie window looking into the Garden, but there began three Cornets to play certaine fantastike dances, at the measure whereof the Fayery Quene came into the garden, dauncing with her maides about her. Shee brought with her a garland, made in fourme of an imperiall crowne; within the sight of her Majestie shee fixed upon [sic] a silvered staffe, and sticking the staffe into the ground, spake as followeth:

> *The Speech of the Fairy Quene to her Majestie.*
> I that abide in places under-ground,
> Aureola, the Quene of Fairy land,
> That every night in rings of painted flowers
> Turne round, and carrell out Elisaes name:
> Hearing, that Nereus and the Sylvane gods
> Have lately welcomde your Imperiall Grace,
> Oapend the earth with this enchanting wand,
> To doe my duety to your Majestie,
> And humbly to salute you with this chaplet,
> Given me by Auberon, the Fairy King.
> Bright shining Phoebe, that in humaine shape,
> Hid'st Heaven's perfection, vouchsafe t'accept it:
> And I Aureola, belov'd in heaven,
> (For amorous starrs fall nightly in my lap)
> Will cause that Heavens enlarge thy goulden dayes,
> And cut them short, that envy at thy praise.

After this speech, the Fairy Quene and her maides daunced about the Garden, singing a Song of Sixe parts, with the musicke of an exquisite consort; wherein was the lute, bandora, base-violl, citterne, treble-violl, and flute. And this was the Fairies Song:

> Elisa is the fairest Quene,
> That ever trod upon this greene.
> Elisaes eyes are blessed starres,
> Inducing peace, subduing warres.
> Elisaes hand is christal bright,
> Her wordes are balme, her lookes are light.
> Elisaes brest is that faire hill,
> Where Vertue dwels, and sacred skill,
> O blessed bee each day and houre,
> Where sweet Elisa builds her bowre.

This spectacle and musicke so delighted Her Majesty, that shee commaunded to heare it sung and danced three times over, and called for divers Lords and Ladies to behold it: and then dismist the Actors with thankes, and with a gracious larges, which of her exceeding goodnesse she bestowed upon them.

The Honorable Entertainement given to the Queene's Majestie in Progresse, at Elvetham in Hampshire, by the Right Hon'ble the Earle of Hertford [1591]

On May Day 1604 Sir William Cornwallis gave this entertainment for the new King and Queen, James I and Anne of Denmark, at his house on Highgate Hill. We must imagine a knot garden with a mount on which sat three singers in the guise of Aurora, Zephyrus and Flora seated around an actor attired as May.

The king, and queene being entred in at the gate where MERCURY *with a second speech, received them, walking before them.*

MER. Retyre, you household-gods, and leaue these excelent creatures to be entertayned by a more eminent deitie. Hayle King, and Queene of the Islands, call'd truely fortunate, and by you made so . . .

This place, whereon you are now aduanced (by the mightie power of *Poetrie*, and the helpe of a faith, that can remoue mountaynes) is the *Arcadian* hill CYLLENE, the place, where my selfe was both begot, and borne; and of which I am frequently call'd CYLLENIVS: Under yound' purslane tree stood sometime my cradle. Where, now, behold my mother MAIA, sitting in the pride of her plentie, gladding the aire with her breath, and cheering the spring with her smiles. At her feet, the blushing AVRORA, who, with her rosie hand, casteth her honie dewes on those sweeter herbs, accompanied with that gentle winde, FAVONIVS, whose subtile spirit, in the breathing forth, FLORA makes into flowers, and sticks them in the grasse, as if shee contended to haue the imbroyderie of the earth, richer then the cope of the skie. Here, for her moneth, the yeerely delicate *May* keepes state; and from this *Mount*, takes pleasure to display these valleys, yond' lesser hills, those statelier edifices, and towers, that seeme enamour'd so farre off, and are rear'd on end, to behold her, as if their vtmost object were her beauties. Hither the *Dryads* of the valley, and *Nymphs* of the great riuer come euery morning, to taste of her fauors; and depart away with laps fill'd with her bounties. But, see! vpon your approch their pleasures are instantly remitted. The birds are hush'd, ZEPHYRE is still, the MORNE forbeares her office, FLORA is dumbe, and herselfe amazed, to behold two such maruailes, that doe more adorne place, then shee can time; Pardon, your Majestie, the fault, for it is that hath caus'd it; and till they can collect their spirits, thinke silence and wonder the best adoration.

Here, AVRORA, ZEPHYRVS, *and* FLORA, *began this song in three parts.*

SONG

See, see, ô see, who here is come a Maying!
The master of the Ocean;
And his beautious ORIAN:
Whe left we off our playing?
To gaze, to gaze,
On them, that gods no lesse then amaze.
Vp *Nightingale*, and sing
Jug, jug, jug, jug, &c.
Raise *Larke* they note, and wing,
All birds their musique bring,
Sweet *Robin*, *Linet*, *Thrush*,
Record, from euery bush,
The welcome of the King;
And Queene:
Whose like wer neuer seene,
For good for faire.
Nor can be; though fresh *May*,
Should euery day
Inuite a seuerall paire,
No, though shee should inuite a seuerall paire.

BEN JONSON, *A Private Entertainment
of the King and Queene . . .* [1604]

In 1613 Lord Knollys welcomed the pleasure-loving Anne of Denmark en route to Bath at his house at Caversham. As at Theobalds in 1591 a gardener appeared.

. . . and so soon as her Majesty with her train were all entered into the lower garden, a Gardener, with his man and boy, issued out of an arbour to give her Highness entertainment. The Gardener was suited in gray with a jerkin double jagged all about the wings and skirts; he had a pair of great slops with a cod-piece, and buttoned gamachios all of the same stuff: on his head he had a straw hat, piebaldly drest with flowers, and in his hand a silvered spade. His man was also suited in gray with a great buttoned flap on his jerkin, having large wings and skirts, with a pair of great slops and gamachios of the same; on his head he had a strawn hat, and in his hand a silvered mattox. The Gardener's boy was in a pretty suit of flowery stuff, with a silvered rake in his hand. When they approached near the Queen, they all vailed bonnet; and lowting low, the Gardener began after his antic fashion this speech.

GARD. Most magnificent and peerless deity, lo I, the surveyor of Lady Flora's works, welcome your grace with fragrant phrases into her bowers, beseeching your greatness to bear with the late wooden entertainment of the wood-men; for woods are more full of weeds than wits, but gardens are weeded, and gardeners witty, as may appear by me. I have flowers for all fancies. Thyme for truth, rosemary for remembrance, roses for love, heart-sease for joy, and thousands more, which all harmoniously rejoice at your presence; but myself, with these my Paradisians here, will make you such music as the wild woodists shall be ashamed to hear the report of it. Come, Sirs, prune your pipes, and tune your strings, and agree together like birds of a feather.

A song of a treble and bass, sung by the Gardener's boy and man, to music of instruments, that was ready to second them in the arbour.

1.

Welcome to this flowery place,
Fair Goddess and sole Queen of grace:
All eyes triumph in your sight,
Which through all this empty space
Casts such glorious beams of light.

2.

Paradise were meeter far
To entertain so bright a star:
But why errs my folly so?
Paradise is where you are:
Heav'n above, and heav'n below.

3.

Could our powers and wishes meet,
How well would they your graces greet!
Yet accept of our desire:
Roses, of all flowers most sweet,
Spring out of the silly brier.

THOMAS CAMPION, *A Relation of the Late Royall Entertainment Given By . . . The Lord Knowles at Cavsome House neere Redding . . .* [1613]

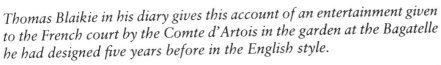

Thomas Blaikie in his diary gives this account of an entertainment given to the French court by the Comte d'Artois in the garden at the Bagatelle he had designed five years before in the English style.

. . . the 20th May the count gave a great fete at Bagatelle to the King and Queen and the court which was at this time at La Muette; here was the Superbe Band of Musick placed upon a scaffold on the thicket of trees which as the company walked round to see the Gardins played which with the echo of the trees made an enchanting affects and in differant parts of the wood was Booths made of the Branches of trees in which there was actors who acted differant pieces agreeable to the scene; on the further side towards Longchamp there was erected a Pyramide by which was a Marble tomb; this

part of the wood being neuly taken in to the grounds there remained the wall of the bois de Boulogne and to rendre this scene More agreeable Mr Belanger had an invention which made a Singulare effect by undermining the wall on the outside and placing people with ropes to pull the wall down at a word; at this pyramide there was an acteur who acted the part of a Majician who asked there Majestys how they liked the Gardins and what a beautifull vue there was towards the plaine if that wall did not obstruct it, but that there Majestys need only give the word that he with his inchanting wand would make that wall dissapear; the queen not knowing told him with a Laugh 'Very well I should wisht to see it disappear' and in the instant the signal was given and above 200 yards oposite where the company stood fell flat to the ground which surprised them all. This fete terminated with a ball in the Pavillion at which they all danced except the King who amuzed in playing at Billiards at half a crown a game; at this rate he could never ruin his fortune; the whole terminated by illuminations all round the Gardin. This day the King came from Lamuette to Bagatelle afoot; this fete was conducted with great Order and decorum with mirth; this was the first day that Bagatelle begane to make its apearance; this day I was presented to the King & Queen as Inspecteur of the counts Gardins who complimented me upon what I had already done.

THOMAS BLAIKIE, *Diary of a Scotch Gardener*, 20 May 1780

George III's Queen, Charlotte, was a great giver of fêtes particularly at her house at Frogmore. In July 1800 one of her daughters was responsible for the organization. Britain was at war against Napoleon at the time.

On the fourteenth of the following month the Queen gave an entertainment of a new character in Frogmore Gardens, the management of which was entirely under the direction of the Princess Elizabeth. About two o'clock the royal family repaired from Windsor Lodge in their carriages to the house, consisting of their majesties, the five princesses; the Prince of Wales, the Duke and Duchess of York, the Dukes of Clarence and Cumberland, and the Prince and Princess of Orange; after whom came the company who were invited to dinner. The royal party dined in the temporary room; and for the accommodation of the nobility, three tents adjoining to this apartment were pitched in a direct line so that their majesties had a complete view of the whole assembly. The dinner, consisting of every delicacy of the season, was served up in great style; and during the repast the band of the Stafford militia played several martial airs. As soon as dinner was over, the Princess Elizabeth conducted her royal parents and the visitors to the grotto, where some of the principal, vocal performers entertained them with glees and songs. The company then proceeded across the lawn to another part of the gardens, where a group, in the character of gypsies, made their appearance; and on the approach of their majesties, Mrs Mills, who personated the queen of the vagrant tribe, advanced from behind a thicket, leading an ass bearing two children, and sang a gypsey song; after which she delivered her poetical destinies of good fortune to the several members of the royal family. The King and the royal dukes took great notice of the two children placed on the ass, and His Majesty desired that they might be led round for the Queen to see them, as they belonged to two of the soldiers wives. Mrs Mills and her gypsey throng, having concluded their part with a dance, retreated into the thicket; after which the princess led the way to a space of ground near what is called the Hermit's Cell, where a stage was erected, on which one Du Crow, termed the Flemish Hercules, exhibited his wonderful performances on the slack wire, and afterwards his extraordinary powers of strength, such as balancing on his chin three large coach-wheels, also a ladder, to which were affixed two chairs with two children on them; and bearing at the same time on his hands and feet a table in the form of a pyramid, with eight persons on its surface.

When these exploits were over, the company walked towards the canal, where a large boat, having the royal standard flying, was placed on the stocks, to represent the Royal Sovereign ready for launching. Here Mrs Mills appeared in the dress of a sailor, while Mr Fawcett, in that of the St James's association, delivered a loyal address. On the return of their majesties to the lawn in front of the grotto, six Hungarian hussars performed the peculiar dances of their country; after which, Fawcett entertained the company with a humorous song, on the conclusion of which the company repaired to the Princess Elizabeth's Thatched Barn. In this beautiful arbour, which was fitted up for a ball-room, seats were erected for the' accommodation of six hundred of the nobility, who were invited by tickets from Her Majesty, none others being admitted. The entrance consisted of arched colonnades of crystal lamps; the room was decorated with flowers, and lighted up with chandeliers in the form of a bee-hive, the upper part suspended by a tassel resembling ears of corn. The ball lasted till twelve o'clock, when their majesties returned to Windsor; and the rest of the company, after partaking of a cold collation, soon followed. JOHN WATKINS, *Memoirs of Her Most Excellent Majesty Sophia-Charlotte, Queen of Great Britain* [1819]

Katherine Mansfield opens a bitter-sweet short story thus.

GARDEN PARTY

And after all the weather was ideal. They could not have had a more perfect day for a garden-party if they had ordered it. Windless, warm, the sky without a cloud. Only the blue was veiled with a haze of light gold, as it is sometimes in early summer. The gardener had been up since dawn, mowing the lawns and sweeping them, until the grass and the dark flat rosettes where the daisy plants had been seemed to shine. As for the roses, you could not help feeling they understood that roses are the only flowers that impress people at garden-parties; the only flowers that everybody is certain of knowing. Hundreds, yes, literally hundreds, had come out in a single night; the green bushes bowed down as though they had been visited by archangels. KATHERINE MANSFIELD, *The Garden Party and Other Short Stories* [1922]

Just over a decade later 'Chips' Channon records a very different kind of garden party staged as part of the notorious 1936 Olympics in Berlin.

The Goering Party
I don't know how to describe this dazzling crowded function. We drove to the Ministerium in the centre of Berlin, and found its great gardens lit up and

700 or 800 guests gaping at the display and the splendour. Goering, wreathed in smiles and orders and decorations received us gaily, his wife at his side. When he spied Honor he was especially genial; a table was reserved for us, with the Brunswick clan, Ernest August, in a green uniform, and the daughter Princess Frederika, typically royal of another age with a marabou boa, and the Hamilton boys. Towards the end of dinner a corps de ballet danced in the moonlight: it was the loveliest coup-d'œil imaginable, and there were murmurs of delighted surprise from all the guests who agreed that Goering had indeed eclipsed Ribbentrop, which indeed we had been told had been his ambition. The end of the garden was in darkness, and suddenly, with no warning, it was flood-lit and a procession of white horses, donkeys and peasants, appeared from nowhere, and we were led into an especially built Luna Park. It was fantastic, roundabouts, cafés with beer and champagne, peasants dancing and 'schuhplattling' vast women carrying pretzels and beer, a ship, a beerhouse, crowds of gay, laughing people, animals, a mixture of Luna Park and White Horse Inn, Old Heidelberg and the Trianon . . . Reinhardt could not have done it better. The music roared, the astonished guests wandered about. 'There has never been anything like this since the days of Louis Quatorze,' someone remarked, 'Not since Nero', I retorted, but actually it was more like the Fêtes of Claudius, but with the cruelty left out . . . SIR HENRY CHANNON, *Diaries*
15 August 1936

GARDEN VISITING   *Although foreign visitors described our gardens in the Tudor and Stuart periods it was only in the eighteenth century that serious garden visiting became the norm. Here a steward reports to his master such a visit. The garden was Lord Fortescue's at Castle Hill, South Moulton, Devon.*

On Monday Mr George Grenville, a young gentleman, made the tour of Your Lordship's grounds. Mr Grenville left Oxford about a fortnight ago and I had the pleasure to hear by him that Mr Hughie was then very well. In the afternoon His Excellency the French Ambassador accompanied by Lord Pembroke on the same day in another part my Lord Folkestone's eldest son John with another young gentleman. Mr Grenville came early in the morning from Barnstaple and I had the honour to attend him before His Excellency arrived. As the morning was far advanced before we left Castle Hill, he was pleased to accept a cup of chocolate and proceeded on his return to Bath from whence he came on purpose. Mr Grenville observing to me he should be in Oxford again very soon. I was happy in the opportunity to presenting my duty to Mr Hughie. This young gentleman has a little impediment in his actions which must be lamented, his conceptions being very prompt and clear. I take the liberty to make this remark as Your Lordship will probably know him bide. Mr Grenville and his companion express great pleasure in the diversity and softness of the scenery and the attention paid to the lesser instances as well as the capital improvements and appropriateness of the whole to the genius of the country. The shortness of time was greatly complained of, they seemed very unwilling to leave so engaging a place. It so far exceeded expectations so greatly predisposed in its favour by descriptions, but the appointment would not permit a longer stay. Mr Grenville told me Lord Lyttleton was then in the West and he ap-

prehended at Lord Edgcombe. Perhaps His Lordship may make Castle Hill in way to take a cursory view of Your Lordship's improvements. My Lord Pembroke observed to me that he was here about three years ago and His Lordship recollects every place at that time and spoke much in commendation of the late additions. The happy choice of the situation of the Temple, the style of the building and the surrounding views, to which he remarked the new water were a great embellishment and much admired. A long stand was made upon the platform at the Temple and the Castle and both His Excellency and His Lordship were minute in their observations on the separate scenes and the easy disposition of the whole so suitable to the face of the country. The late rains have thrown a fine lively verdure on the fields which particularly struck His Excellency. He seemed to enjoy the beauties of the place with that practical spirit which distinguishes the peculiar but natural taste of the English Gardens abundantly more than I expected the imagery of Versailles would permit of. His Excellency was pleased to honour me with a corner in his carriage, which gave me an opportunity of hearing the remarks which were made on the occasion of explaining Your Lordship's intentions. Some bunches of Your Lordship's grapes and a little present of fine melons were received with great pleasure and I was repeatedly charged with confidence to Your Lordship. I hope Your Lordship will please not to disapprove the attention to which I thought it my duty to pay such visitors of Your Lordship's justly admired grounds. I have the honour to be Your Lordship's most dutiful servant. Mr Hilliard, the steward to Matthew,
2nd Lord Fortescue, 19 July 1771

More than a century later Gertrude Jekyll was quite capable of giving a visitor to her garden his come uppance.

I had been saying how necessary good and deep cultivation was, especially in so very poor and shallow a soil as mine. Passing up through the copse where there were some tall stems of *Lilium giganteum* bearing the great upturned pods of seed, my visitor stopped and said, 'I don't believe a word about your poor soil – look at the growth of that Lily. Nothing could make that great stem ten feet high in a poor soil, and there it is just stuck into the wood!' I said nothing, knowing that presently I could show a better answer than I could frame in words. A little farther up in the copse we came upon an excavation about twelve feet across and four deep, and by its side a formidable mound of sand, when my friend said, 'Why are you making all this mess in your pretty woods? . . . and what on earth are you going to do with that great heap of sand? Why, there must be a dozen loads of it.' That was my moment of secret triumph, but I hope I bore it meekly as I answered, 'I only wanted to plant a few more of those big Lilies, and you see in my soil they would not have a chance unless the ground was thoroughly prepared: look at the edge of the scarp and see how the solid yellow sand comes to within four inches of the top; so I have a big wide hole dug; and look, there is the donkey-cart coming with the first load of Dahlia-tops and soft plants that have been for the summer in the south border.' GERTRUDE JEKYLL, *Wood and Garden* [1899]

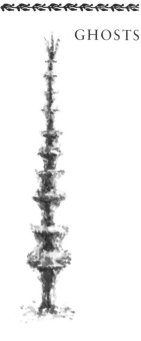

GHOSTS *Surely the most famous of all garden encounters, Miss Moberly and Miss Jourdain's vision of the court of Marie Antoinette. Although debunked on publication it nonetheless retained its hold on the public imagination for half a century.*

MISS JOURDAIN'S ACCOUNT OF HER FIRST VISIT TO THE PETIT TRIANON IN 1901
AUGUST, 1901

. . . After spending some time in the Palace, we went down by the terrace and struck to the right to find the Petit Trianon. We walked for some distance down a wooded alley, and then came upon the buildings of the Grand Trianon, before which we did not delay. We went on in the direction of the Petit Trianon, but just before reaching what we knew afterwards to be the main entrance I saw a gate leading to a path cut deep below the level of the ground above, and as the way was open and had the look of an entrance that was used, I said, 'Shall we try this path? it must lead to the house,' and we followed it. To our right we saw some farm-buildings looking empty and deserted; implements (among others a plough) were lying about; we looked in, but saw no one. The impression was saddening, but it was not until we reached the crest of the rising ground where there was a garden that I began to feel as if we had lost our way, and as if something were wrong. There were two men there in official dress (greenish in colour), with something in their hands; it might have been a staff. A wheelbarrow and some other gardening tools were near them. They told us, in answer to my enquiry to go straight on. I remember repeating my question, because they answered in a seemingly casual and mechanical way, but only got the same answer in the same manner. As we were standing there I saw to the right of us a detached solidly built cottage, with stone steps at the door. A woman and a girl were standing at the doorway, and I particularly noticed their unusual dress; both wore white kerchiefs tucked into the bodice, and the girls' dress, though she looked thirteen or fourteen only, was down to her ankles. The woman was passing a jug to the girl, who wore a close white cap.

Following the directions of the two men we walked on: but the path pointed out to us seemed to lead away from where we imagined the Petit Trianon to be; and there was a feeling of depression and loneliness about the place. I began to feel as if I were walking in my sleep; the heavy dreaminess was oppressive. At last we came upon a path crossing ours, and saw in front of us a building consisting of some columns roofed in, and set back in the trees. Seated on the steps was a man with a heavy black cloak round his shoulders, and wearing a slouch hat. At that moment the eerie feeling which had begun in the garden culminated in a definite impression of something uncanny and fear-inspiring. The man slowly turned his face which was marked by smallpox: his complexion was very dark. The expression was very evil and yet unseeing, and though I did not feel that he was looking particularly at us, I felt a repugnance to going past him. But I did not wish to show the feeling, which I thought was meaningless, and we talked about the best way to turn, and decided to go to the right.

Suddenly we heard a man running behind us: he shouted, 'Mesdames, mesdames,' and when I turned he said in an accent that seemed to me

unusual that our way lay in another direction. 'Il ne faut' (pronounced *fout*) 'pas passer par lá.' He then made a gesture, adding, 'par ici . . . cherchez la maison.' Though we were surprised to be addressed, we were glad of the direction, and I thanked him. The man ran off with a curious smile on his face: the running ceased as abruptly as it had begun, not far from where we stood. I remember that the man was young-looking, with a florid complexion and rather long dark hair. I do not remember the dress, except that the material was dark and heavy, and that the man wore buckled shoes.

We walked on, crossing a small bridge that went across a green bank, high on our right hand and shelving down below us to a very small overshadowed pool of water glimmering some way off. A tiny stream descended from above us, so small as to seem to lose itself before reaching the little pool. We then followed a narrow path till almost immediately we came upon the English garden front of the Petit Trianon. The place was deserted; but as we approached the terrace I remember drawing my skirt away with a feeling as though someone was near and I had to make room, and then wondering why I did it. While we were on the terrace a boy came out of the door of a second building which opened on it, and I still have the sound in my ears of his slamming it behind him. He directed us to go round to the other entrance, and, seeing us hesitate, with the peculiar smile of suppressed mockery offered to show us the way. We passed through the French garden, part of which was walled in by trees. The feeling of dreariness was very strong there, and continued till we actually reached the front entrance to the Petit Trianon and looked round the rooms in the wake of a French wedding-party. Afterwards we drove back to the Rue des Rèservoirs.

An Adventure [1911]

Gardens and gardening figure little in the novels of Dickens. One, however, forms the setting for this famous encounter. MR PICKWICK

'I have forgotten my flowers,' said the spinster aunt.

'Water them now,' said Mr Tupman, in accents of persuasion.

'You will take cold in the evening sir,' urged the spinster aunt, affectionately.

'No, no,' said Mr Tupman, rising; 'it will do me good. Let me accompany you.'

The lady paused to adjust the sling in which the left arm of the youth was placed, and taking his right arm led him to the garden.

There was a bower at the further end, with honeysuckle jessamine, and creeping plants – one of those sweet retreats which humane men erect for the accommodation of spiders.

The spinster aunt took up a large watering-pot which lay in one corner, and was about to leave the arbour. Mr Tupman detained her, and drew her to a seat beside him.

'Miss Wardle!' said he.

The spinster aunt trembled, till some pebbles which had accidentally found their way into the large watering-pot shook like an infant's rattle.

'Miss Wardle,' said Mr Tupman, 'you are an angel.'

'Mr Tupman!' exclaimed Rachael, blushing as red as the watering-pot itself.

'Nay,' said the eloquent Pickwickian – 'I know it but too well.'

'All woman are angels, they say,' murmured the lady, playfully.

'Then what can *you* be; or to what, without presumption, can I compare you?' replied Mr Tupman. 'Where was the woman ever seen, who resembled you? Where else could I hope to find so rare a combination of excellence and beauty? Where else could I seek to – Oh!' Here Mr Tupman paused, and pressed the hand which clasped the handle of the happy watering-pot.

CHARLES DICKENS, *Pickwick Papers* [1836]

THE GARDEN AS SILENT ACTOR

Enid Bagnold's The Chalk Garden *is the only play I know where the garden runs as a metaphorical counterpoint to the characters. The play focuses on the relationship between an elderly society hostess, Mrs St Maugham, and her mysterious new companion, Miss Madrigal. Edith Evans as Mrs St Maugham had the memorable opening-line, heard off-stage, 'Are my teeth on the table?'*

Place: A room in one of those Manor Houses which border a Village Green in Sussex. The soil is lime and chalk. The village is by the sea . . .
Beyond the open french window a bosky, be-lillied garden runs slightly uphill. A June gale blows. The room has a look of vigour and culture. The furniture is partly inherited, partly bought in MRS ST MAUGHAM'S *young days. It is probably Regency but the owner of this house does not tie herself to anything. She has lived through many moods, and is a jackdaw for the Curious and Strange. The only object necessarily described is her worktable backstage, running the length of the windows. It is a rough table, rather high and long. Under it lie in disorder baskets, garden trugs, a saw, two long-handled grass-cutters, a tin of Abol, a sack of John Innes potting soil, a log basket full of raffia, and rubber clogs, etc. On top of the table are strewn scissors, string, gardening books, flower catalogues, gardening gloves, a small watering can for vases in the room, a trowel, etc.*

The NURSE *rushes in.*

NURSE: The madonna lilies have blown over!

MRS ST MAUGHAM: Oh – great heavens – this mule of a garden! – *Maitland!* . . . He was to order the bamboos and he forgot them! . . . Are they all down?

NURSE (*with triumph*): All. And not for want of warnings!
(*Exits.*)

MRS ST MAUGHAM: Oh my lilies! My lilies! One waits a year for them! . . .
Exits fast into the garden.
Enter MAITLAND (*the butler*).

MAITLAND: What was that I heard?

LAUREL (Mrs St Maugham's granddaughter): The calm of Grandloo.

MAITLAND: But what's happened?

MADRIGAL: There's been an accident in the garden.

MAITLAND (*to* LAUREL, *denouncingly, he starts for garden*): Fire!

LAUREL (*stopping him*): Wind. You didn't stake the lilies!

MAITLAND (*frantic, rushing to the window to look out*): Oh are they

down? The nurse told me and I forgot! How the old bastard will be crowing!

MADRIGAL (*primly*): Stake in May.

MAITLAND (*turning on her fiercely*): They weren't full grown in May!

MADRIGAL: They should have been.

MAITLAND (*more fiercely*): Is that a criticism?

MADRIGAL: So you are the gardener here as well?

MAITLAND: I'm everything! I'm the kingpin and the pivot and the manservant and the maidservant and the go-between (*turning on* LAUREL) and the fire-extinguisher!

The garden imagery is splendidly developed at the close of the act.

Enter MADRIGAL *from the garden (on a high wave of indignation . . .).*

MADRIGAL (*menacing – accusing – pulling on a glove*): Mrs St Maugham – there must be some *mistake*! *This* is a chalk garden! *Who has* tried to grow rhododendrons in a *chalk garden*?

MRS ST MAUGHAM (*taken aback*): Rhododendrons? We put them in last autumn. But they're unhappy?

MADRIGAL (*magnificent; stern*): They are *dying*. They are in pure lime. Not so much as a little leaf-mould! There is no evidence of palliation! (*Passes on across room.*)

MRS ST MAUGHAM: Wait . . . wait! . . . Where are you going?

MADRIGAL (*over her shoulder – going*): They could have had compost! But the compost-heap is stone-cold! Nothing in the world has been done for them.

A gay scream is heard from the garden.

OLIVIA: (*Laurel's mother*) (*to* MADRIGAL): Is that Laurel? She's screaming. What's the matter?

MADRIGAL (*withering*): There is nothing the matter! She is dancing round the bonfire with the manservant.

MRS ST MAUGHAM: I should have told you – *this* is Miss Madrigal. Not so fast! I want to ask you . . . the bergamot . . . and the gunnera . . .

MADRIGAL (*over shoulder, on way out*): . . . won't thrive on chalk.

MRS ST MAUGHAM: There's an east slope I can grow nothing on.

MADRIGAL (*same*): . . . the soil can't give what it has not got.

Reaches door.

OLIVIA: *Don't go!* The wind blows from the sea here and growing things need protection!

MADRIGAL (*suddenly halted by the look in* OLIVIA's *face*): . . . and the lilies have rust . . . there is blackspot on the roses . . . and the child is screaming in the garden . . .

MRS ST MAUGHAM: The *roses*! What would you have done for them! Pinkbell ordered . . . and I sprayed them! –

MADRIGAL (*turning, magnificent, contemptuous, a few steps towards* MRS ST MAUGHAM): With *what*, I wonder! You had better have prayed for them!

ENID BAGNOLD, *The Chalk Garden*,
Act I [1956]

IN THE SUMMER HOUSE

A romantic encounter in a summer house in Ruritania between the hero, an English gentleman Rudolf Rassendyl, and the Princess Flavia. Hollywood made more than one version of this.

'What's the letter?'

I opened it and read it loud:

> *'If the King desires to know what it deeply concerns the King to know, let him do as this letter bids him. At the end of the New Avenue there stands a house in large grounds. The house has a portico, with a statue of a nymph on it. A wall encloses the garden: there is a gate in the wall at the back. At twelve o'clock to-night, if the King enters alone by that gate, turns to the right, and walks twenty yards, he will find a summer-house, approached by a flight of six steps. If he mounts and enters, he will find someone who will tell him what touches most dearly his life and his throne. This is written by a faithful friend.'*

I sprang to my feet. Sapt laid down his pipe.

'I shall go, Sapt.'

'No, I shall go,' said he.

'You may go as far as the gate.'

'I shall go to the summer-house.'

'I'm hanged if you shall!'

'I either go to the summer-house or back to England,' said I . . . 'Sapt, we must play high; we must force the game.'

'So be it,' he said, with a sigh . . .

We arrived outside the gate. Sapt held out his hand.

'I shall wait here,' he said. 'If I hear a shot, I'll –'

'Stay where you are; it's the King's only chance. You mustn't come to grief too.'

'You're right, lad. Good luck!'

I pressed the little gate. It yielded, and I found myself in a wild sort of shrubbery. There was a grass-grown path and, turning to the right as I had been bidden, I followed it cautiously. My lantern was closed, the revolver was in my hand. I heard not a sound. Presently a large dark object loomed out of the gloom ahead of me. It was the summer-house. Reaching the steps, I mounted them and found myself confronted by a weak, rickety wooden door, which hung upon the latch. I pushed it open and walked in. A woman flew to me and seized my hand.

'Shut the door,' she whispered.

I obeyed, and turned the light of my lantern on her. She was in evening dress, arrayed very sumptuously, and her dark striking beauty was marvellously displayed in the glare of the bull's-eye. The summer-house was a bare little room, furnished only with a couple of chairs and a small iron table, such as one sees in a tea-garden or an open-air café.

'Don't talk,' she said. 'We've not time. Listen. I know you, Mr Rassendyl. I wrote that letter at the duke's orders.'

ANTHONY HOPE, *The Prisoner of Zenda* [1894]

Tennyson's Maud *is almost too well known to include, with its evocation of the lover and the garden at night, but it is needed for Joyce Grenfell's wonderful riposte.*

I

Come into the garden, Maud,
   For the black bat, night, has flown,
Come into the garden, Maud,
   I am here at the gate alone;
And the woodbine spices are wafted abroad,
   And the musk of the rose is blown.

II

For a breeze of morning moves,
   And the planet of Love is on high,
Beginning to faint in the light that she loves,
   On a bed of daffodil sky,
To faint in the light of the sun she loves,
   To faint in his light, and to die.

III

All night have the roses heard
   The flute, violin, bassoon;
All night has the casement jessamine stirr'd
   To the dancers dancing in tune;
Till a silence fell with a waking bird,
   And a hush with the setting moon.

IV

I said to the lily, 'There is but one
   With whom she has heart to be gay.
When will the dancers leave her alone?
   She is weary of dance and play.'
Now half to the setting moon are gone,
   And half to the rising day;
Low on the sand and loud on the stone
   The last wheel echoes away.

V

I said to the rose, 'The brief night goes
   In babble and revel and wine.
O young lord-lover, what sighs are those,
   For one that will never be thine?
But mine, but mine,' so I sware to the rose,
   'For ever and ever, mine.'

VI

And the soul of the rose went into my blood,
   As the music clash'd in the hall;
And long by the garden lake I stood,
   For I heard your rivulet fall
From the lake to the meadow and on to the wood,
   Our wood, that is dearer than all;

VII

From the meadow your walks have left so sweet
   That whenever a March-wind sighs
He sets the jewel-print of your feet
   In violets blue as your eyes,
To the woody hollows in which we meet
   And the valleys of Paradise.

VIII

The slender acacia would not shake
   One long milk-bloom on the tree;
The white lake-blossom fell into the lake
   As the pimpernel dozed on the lea;
But the rose was awake all night for your sake,
   Knowing your promise to me;
The lilies and roses were all awake,
   They sigh'd for the dawn and thee.

IX

Queen rose of the rosebed garden of girls,
   Come hither, the dances are done,
In gloss of satin and glimmer of pearls,
   Queen lily and rose in one;
Shine out, little head, sunning over with curls,
   To the flowers, and be their sun.

X

There has fallen a splendid tear
   From the passion-flower at the gate.
She is coming, my dove, my dear;
   She is coming, my life, my fate:
The red rose cries, 'She is near, she is near';
   And the white rose weeps, 'She is late';
The larkspur listens, 'I hear, I hear';
   And the lily whispers, 'I wait'.

XI

She is coming, my own, my sweet;
   Were it ever so airy a tread,

My heart would hear her and beat,
    Were it earth in an earthy bed;
My dust would hear her and beat,
    Had I lain for a century dead;
Would start and tremble under her feet,
    And blossom in purple and red.

                ALFRED, LORD TENNYSON [1855]

Maud won't come into the garden
Maud is compelled to state.
Though you stand for hours in among the flowers
Down by the garden gate.
Maud won't come into the garden,
Sing to her as you may.
Maud says she begs your pardon
But she wasn't born yesterday.

But Maud's not coming into the garden
Thanking you just the same.
Though she looks so pure, you may be quite sure
Maud's on to your little game.
Maud knows she's being dampening,
And how damp you already must be,
So Maudie is now decamping
To her lovely hot water b.

Frankly, Maud wouldn't dream of coming into the garden,
Let that be understood,
When the nights are warm, Maud knows the form,
Maud has read 'Little Red Riding Hood'.
Maud did not need much warning,
She watched you with those pink gins,
So she bids you a kind 'Good Morning'
And advises you two aspirins.

You couldn't really seriously think that Maud was going to be such a sucker
                     as to come into the garden,

Flowers set her teeth on edge
And she's much too old for the strangle hold
In a prickly privet hedge.
Pray stand till your arteries harden
It won't do the slightest good,
Maud is not coming into the garden
And you're mad to have thought she would!

                JOYCE GRENFELL

THE CURTAIN
FALLS

I end not with laughter but tears. Early in Chekov's The Cherry Orchard *the landowner learns that he must sell the orchard.*

LOPAHIN (*a businessman*) . . . You know, of course, that your cherry orchard is going to be sold to pay your debts. The auction is to take place on the twenty-second of August, but there's no need for you to worry. You can sleep in peace, my dear; there's a way out. This is my plan, please listen carefully. Your estate is only twenty miles from town, and the railway line is not far away. Now, if your cherry orchard and the land along the river are divided into plots and leased out for summer residences, you'll have a yearly income of at least twenty-five thousand roubles.

GAYEV [*the owner's brother-in-law*]. But what nonsense!

LIUBOV ANDRYEEVNA [*the owner*]. I don't quite understand you, Yermolai Aleksyeevich.

LOPAHIN. You'll charge the tenants at least twenty-five roubles a year for a plot of one acre, and if you advertise now, I'm prepared to stake any amount you like that you won't have a spot of land unoccupied by the autumn: it will be snatched up. In fact, I really feel I must congratulate you, you're saved after all! It's a marvellous situation and the river's deep enough for bathing. But, of course, the place will have to be cleaned up, put in order. For instance, all the old outbuildings will have to be pulled down, as well as this house which is no good to anybody. The old cherry orchard should be cut down, too.

LIUBOV ANDRYEEVNA. Cut down? My dear man, forgive me, you don't seem to understand. If there's one thing interesting, one thing really outstanding in the whole county, it's our cherry orchard.

LOPAHIN. The only outstanding thing about this orchard is that it's very large. It only produces a crop every other year, and then there's nobody to buy it.

GAYEV. This orchard is actually mentioned in the Encyclopaedia.

LOPAHIN [*glancing at his watch*]. If you can't think clearly about it, or come to a decision, the cherry orchard and the whole estate as well will be sold by auction. You must decide! There's no other way out, I assure you. There's no other way.

FEERS [*the octogenarian servant*]. In the old days, forty or fifty years ago, the cherries were dried, preserved, marinaded, made into jam, and sometimes . . .

GAYEV. Be quiet, Feers.

FEERS. And sometimes, whole cartloads of dried cherries were sent to Moscow and Kharkov. The money they fetched! And the dried cherries in those days were soft, juicy, sweet, tasty . . . They knew how to do it then . . . they had a recipe . . .

LIUBOV ANDRYEEVNA. And where is that recipe now?

FEERS. Forgotten. No one can remember it.

Act I

In the last scene Liubov Andryeevna and Gayev are left alone in the emptied house to exchange a final word only interrupted by the cries of voices off. They leave and all that we hear is the old manservant mumbling away as the curtain slowly descends while an axe strikes a blow at a cherry tree and metaphorically at the human heart.

[LIUBOV ANDRYEEVNA *and* GAYEV *are left alone. They seem to have been waiting for this moment, and now they embrace each other and sob quietly, with restraint, so as not to be heard.*]

GAYEV [*with despair in his voice*]. Sister, my sister . . .

LIUBOV ANDRYEEVNA. Oh my darling, my precious, my beautiful orchard! My life, my youth, my happiness . . . good-bye! . . . Good-bye!

ANIA'S VOICE [*gaily*]. Mamma! . . .

TROFIMOV'S VOICE [*gaily and excitedly*]. Ah-oo! . . .

LIUBOV ANDRYEEVNA. For the last time — to look at these walls, these windows . . . Mother used to love walking up and down this room . . .

GAYEV. Sister, my sister! . . .

ANIA'S VOICE. Mamma!

TROFIMOV'S VOICE. Ah-oo!

LIUBOV ANDRYEEVNA. We're coming . . . [*Both go out.*]

[*The stage is empty. The sound of doors being locked is heard, then of carriages driving off. It grows quiet. The stillness is broken by the dull thuds of an axe on a tree. They sound forlorn and sad.*

There is a sound of footsteps and from the door on the right FEERS *appears. He is dressed, as usual, in a coat and white waistcoat, and is wearing slippers. He looks ill.*]

FEERS [*walks up to the middle door and tries the handle*]. Locked. They've gone . . . [*Sits down on a sofa.*] They forgot about me. Never mind . . . I'll sit here for a bit. I don't suppose Leonid Andryeevich put on his fur coat, I expect he's gone in his light one . . . [*Sighs, preoccupied.*] I didn't see to it . . . These youngsters! . . . [*Mutters something unintelligible.*] My life's gone as if I'd never lived . . . [*Lies down.*] I'll lie down a bit. You haven't got any strength left, nothing's left, nothing . . . Oh, you . . . you're daft! . . . [*Lies motionless.*]

[*A distant sound is heard, coming as if out of the sky, like the sound of a string snapping, slowly and sadly dying away. Silence ensues, broken only by the sound of an axe striking a tree in the orchard far away.*]

CURTAIN

ANTON CHEKOV, *The Cherry Orchard*, Act III, trans. Elisaveta Fen

Epilogue

Before you put this little book away,
Please promise me that you will never say:
'You should have seen my garden yesterday.'

REGINALD ARKELL, *Green Fingers*
[1934]

ACKNOWLEDGEMENTS

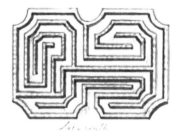

We are grateful to the undermentioned for kindly granting permission to reproduce material in this volume.

Christabel, Lady Aberconway, *A Wiser Woman*, Hutchinson, 1966. Reprinted by permission of Hutchinson as one of the Random Century Group.

Reginald Arkell, 'I made a fire', 'Green Fly', 'Mr Gardener', 'Added to which', 'What is a Garden', 'Epilogue' from *Green Fingers, A Present for Good Gardeners*, Herbert Jenkins, 1934. Reprinted by permission of Herbert Jenkins, one of the publishers in the Random Century Group. 'Mr Pinnegar' from *Old Herbaceous*, Michael Joseph, 1950. Reprinted by permission of Michael Joseph Ltd.

Enid Bagnold, 'The Chalk Garden' (1956) from *Four Plays*, Heinemann, 1970. Reprinted by permission of William Heinemann Ltd.

N. W. Barritt, 'Shaw's Pippin'. First published in *The Countryman* Magazine, 1973. Reprinted by permission.

Cecil Beaton, *Ashcombe, The Story of a Fifteen-year-Lease*, Batsford, 1949. Reprinted by permission of Batsford Ltd; *The Restless Years: Diaries 1953–63*, 1976, Weidenfeld and Nicolson. Reprinted by permission of George Weidenfeld and Nicolson Ltd.

John Betjeman, *Summoned by Bells*, John Murray, 1960.

Ruth Bidgood, 'Mole-trap'. First published in *The Countryman* Magazine, Winter 1968. Reprinted by permission.

Laurence Binyon, from *The Burning of the Leaves and other Poems*, Macmillan, 1944. Reprinted by permission of Mrs Nicolete Gray and The Society of Authors on behalf of the Laurence Binyon Estate.

Michael Bird, 'The Devil among the Lettuces', *The Countryman* Magazine, Winter 1958. Reprinted by permission.

Maureen and Bridget Boland, *Old Wives' Lore for Gardeners*, The Bodley Head, 1977. Reprinted by permission of The Bodley Head.

E. A. Bowles, *My Garden in Autumn and Winter*, Nelson, 1915; *My Garden in Summer*, Nelson, 1914. Reprinted by permission of Thomas Nelson and Sons Ltd.

Alan Brownjohn, 'In a Convent Garden', from *Collected Poems 1952–88*. Hutchinson, 1988. Reprinted by permission of Hutchinson.

Gerald Bullett, from *Collected Poems*, Dent, 1959. Reprinted by permission of Mrs Rosemary Seymour.

John Carey, 'The Pleasures of Vegetable Gardening', *The Sunday Times*, 24 February 1980. Reprinted by permission of the author.

Sir Henry Channon, *Chips: The Diaries of Sir Henry Channon*, edited by Robert Rhodes James, Weidenfeld and Nicolson, 1967. Reprinted by permission of George Weidenfeld and Nicolson Ltd.

J. Cheng, *The Craft of Gardens*, translated by Alison Hardie, Yale University Press, 1981.

Richard Church, 'Twelve Noon' from *Collected Poems*, Dent, 1919. Reprinted by permission of the Estate of Richard Church.

Nigel Colborn, 'Take me to your Hostas', *Hortus*, Spring, 1989. Reprinted by permission.

C. Day Lewis, 'Snowfall on a College Garden' from *Collected Poems*, edited by Ian Parsons, Jonathan Cape, date. Reprinted by permission of Jonathan Cape.

Walter de la Mare, 'The Sunken Garden' from *Collected Poems*, Faber and Faber 1969. Reprinted by permission of the Literary Trustees of Walter de la Mare and The Society of Authors as their representative.

Alan Dixon 'The Sunflower Compared', from *New Poems 1973–4*, A PEN Anthology, Hutchinson, 1974. Reprinted by permission of the author.

Michael Dower, first published in *The Countryman*, Summer 1974. Reprinted by permission.

Freda Downie, 'Her Garden' from *A Stranger Here*, Secker and Warburg, 1977. Reprinted by permission of Martin Secker and Warburg Ltd.

Georges Duhamel, *In Sight of the Promised Land*, translated by Béatrice de Holthoir, Dent, 1935. Reprinted by permission of J. M. Dent and Sons Ltd.

Eugenie Fraser, *The House by the Dvina*, first published by Mainstream Publishing (Edinburgh), 1984. Reprinted by permission.

Robert Frost, 'The Rose Family' from *The Poetry of Robert Frost* edited by Edward Connery Lathem, Jonathan Cape, 1971. Reprinted by permission of the Executors of the Estate of Robert Frost, and Jonathan Cape.

Phoebe Hesketh, 'Death of a gardener', from *New and Collected Poems: Netting the Sun*, Enitharmon Press, 1989. Reprinted by permission of the author.

Hermahn Hesse, from *Hours in the Garden and other Poems*, and 'Page from a Journal' translated by Rika Lesser, Jonathan Cape, 1980.

Ted Hughes, 'Big Poppy' from *Flowers and Insects*, Faber and Faber, 1986. Reprinted by permission of Faber and Faber Ltd.

Edward James, *Swans Reflecting Elephants: My Early Years*, edited by George Melly, Weidenfeld and Nicolson, 1982. Reprinted by permission of George Weidenfeld and Nicolson Ltd.

Barbara Jones, *Follies and Grottoes*, Constable, 1953. Reprinted by permission of Constable.

Frank Kingdon-Ward, *The Romance of Gardening*, Jonathan Cape, 1935. Reprinted by permission of Jonathan Cape.

Miles Kington, 'Avec le part-time gardener', *Punch*, August 1981.

Susanne Knowles, 'Notes on the Globe Artichoke' from *The Sea Bell and Other Poems*, Dent, 1974. Reprinted by permission of the author.

Elizabeth Lawrence, *A Southern Garden, A Handbook for the Middle South*, University of North Carolina Press, 1942. Reprinted by permission of the University of North Carolina Press.

Laurie Lee, 'Apples' from *My Many-coated Man*, André Deutsch, 1955. Reprinted by permission of André Deutsch Ltd.

James Lees-Milne, *Ancestral Voices*, 1975; *Caves of Ice*, 1983, Chatto and Windus. Reprinted by permission of the author and Chatto and Windus.

Audrey le Lièvre, *Miss Willmott of Warley Place, Her Life and Gardens*, Faber and Faber, 1980. Reprinted by permission.

Lesley Lewis, *The Private Life of a Country House*, David and Charles, 1980. Reprinted by permission of David and Charles, Newton Abbot, Devon, England.

Robert Lowell, 'The Public Garden' from *For the Union Dead*, Faber and Faber, 1974. Reprinted by permission of Faber and Faber Ltd.

Percy Lubbock, *Earlham*, Jonathan Cape, 1922. Reprinted by permission of Jonathan Cape.

Betty Massingham, *Miss Jekyll, Portrait of a Great Gardener*, Country Life Ltd, 1966.

Henry Mitchell, *The Essential Earthman*, Indiana University Press, 1981. Reprinted by permission of the Indiana University Press.

Nancy Mitford, *The Pursuit of Love*, Hamish Hamilton, 1945. Reprinted by permission of the Peters Fraser and Dunlop Group Ltd.

John Mortimer, *A Voyage round my Father*, Methuen, 1971.

Beverley Nichols, *Down the Garden Path*, 1932. *Merry Hall*, 1951. *Garden Open Today*, 1963, Jonathan Cape.

Harold Nicolson, *Diaries and Letters 1930–39*, Collins, 1966. Reprinted by permission of Collins.

Russell Page, *The Education of a Gardener*, Collins, 1962. Reprinted by permission of Collins.

Eleanor Pérenyi, *Green Thoughts: A Writer in the Garden*, Allen Lane, 1982. Reprinted by permission of Penguin Books Ltd; copyright © Eleanor Pérenyi; 1981.

Mrs Peters and Penelope Masters, 'The Flower Show'. First published in *The Countryman Gardening Book*, compiled by D. Macer-Wright, 1973. Reprinted by permission.

Eden Phillpotts, *My Garden*, Country Life, 1906.

Sylvia Plath, 'The Manor Garden' from *Collected Poems*, edited by Ted Hughes, Faber and Faber, 1985. Reprinted by permission of Faber and Faber Ltd.

Thomas Platter, *Travels in England*, translated by Clare Williams, Jonathan Cape, 1951. Reprinted by permission of Jonathan Cape.

James Pope-Hennessy, *Queen Mary*, George Allen and Unwin, 1959.

Beatrix Potter, *The Tale of Peter Rabbit*, Frederick Warne, 1902. Reprinted by permission of Frederick Warne and Co.

I. A. Richards, 'Winter-flowering prunus' from *New and Selected Poems*, Carcanet, 1978. Reprinted by permission of the Literary Estate of I. A. and D. E. Richards.

Cecil Roberts, *Gone Rustic*, Hodder and Stoughton, 1934. Reprinted by permission of The Society of Authors as the literary representative of the Estate of Cecil Roberts.

Eleanour Sinclair Rohde, *The Scented Garden*, Medici Society 1931.

A. L. Rowse, 'Jeremiah, the Tabby Cat, Stalks in the Sunlit Garden' from *Collected Poems*, Blackwood, 1981. Reprinted by permission of the author.

V. Sackville-West, *The Garden*, 1946; *In Your Garden Again*, 1951; 'Lobelia' from *More for Your Garden*, 1955, Michael Joseph. Copyright Vita Sackville-West, reprinted by permission of Curtis Brown Ltd.

Siegfried Sassoon, 'The Villa d'Este' from *Collected Poems 1908–56*, Faber and Faber, 1971.

Simon Schama, *The Embarrassment of Riches*, Collins, 1987. Reprinted by permission of HarperCollins.

W. C. Sellar and R. J. Yeatman, *Garden Rubbish*, Methuen, 1936.

Sir George Sitwell, *On the Making of Gardens*, The Dropmore Press, 1909 (1949 edition). Reprinted by permission.

Sir Osbert Sitwell, 'Mr Nutch' from *Collected Poems and Satires*, Duckworth, 1931; Introduction to *The Making of Gardens*, The Dropmore Press, 1909 (1949 edition). Reprinted by permission of David Higham Associates.

Flora Thompson, *Lark Rise to Candleford*, Oxford University Press, 1939. Reprinted by permission of Oxford University Press.

W. J. Turner 'Magic' from *Selected Poems 1919–36*, Oxford University Press, 1939.

Denton Welch, 'The Judas Tree' from *Brave and Cruel*, Hamish Hamilton.

Loelia, Duchess of Westminster, *Grace and Favour*, Weidenfeld and Nicolson, 1961. Reprinted by permission of George Weidenfeld and Nicolson Ltd.

Katherine S. White, *Onward and Upward in the Garden*, with an introduction by E. B. White, Farrar, Straus and Giroux, 1979. Copyright © 1979 by Katherine S. White. Introduction copyright © 1979 by E. B. White. Reprinted by permission of Farrar, Straus and Giroux inc.

Henry Williamson, *Goodbye West Country*, The Bodley Head, 1937. Reprinted by permission of the Bodley Head and the estate of the late Henry Williamson.

Colin Wilson, from *A Book of Gardens* edited by James Turner, Cassell, 1963. Reprinted by permission of the author.

Virginia Woolf, from *Kew Gardens*, The Hogarth Press, 1927. Reprinted by permission of the Estate of Virginia Woolf and The Hogarth Press.

Louisa Yeomans King, *Chronicles of the Garden*, Scribner's, 1925. Reprinted by permission of Charles Scribner's Sons, an imprint of Macmillan Publishing Company. Copyright 1925 Charles Scribner's Sons.

Every reasonable effort has been made to contact copyright holders and secure permission. In the instances where this has not proved possible, we offer our apologies to all concerned.

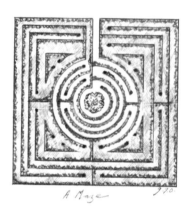

A Maze   970.

INDEX OF AUTHORS CITED

GENERAL INDEX